Experience of Mediated Learning

An Impact of Feuerstein's Theory in Education and Psychology

ADVANCES IN LEARNING AND INSTRUCTION SERIES

Series Editors:
Andreas Demetriou, Erik DeCorte, Stella Vosniadou and Heinz Mandl

PUBLISHED

VAN SOMEREN, REIMANN, BOSHUIZEN & DE JONG
Learning with Multiple Representations

DILLENBOURG
Collaborative Learning: Cognitive and Computational Approaches

SCHNOTZ, VOSNIADOU & CARRETERO
New Perspectives on Conceptual Change

BLISS, SÄLJÖ & LIGHT
Learning Sites: Social and Technological Resources for Learning

KAYSER & VOSNIADOU
Modelling Changes in Understanding: Case Studies in Physical Reasoning

FORTHCOMING TITLES

COWIE, AALSVOORT & MERCER
Social Interaction in Learning and Instruction

ROUET, LEVONEN & BIARDEAU
Integrating Text and Graphics in Computer-Supported Learning Environments

GARRISON & ARCHER
A Transactional Perspective on Teaching and Learning

OTHER TITLES OF INTEREST

REIMANN & SPADA
Learning in Humans and Machines: Towards an Interdisciplinary Learning Science

Computer Assisted Learning: Proceedings of the CAL series of biennial Symposia 1989, 1991, 1993, 1995 and 1997 (five volumes).

RELATED JOURNALS – SAMPLE COPIES AVAILABLE ON REQUEST

Learning and Instruction
International Journal of Educational Research
Computers and Education
Computers and Human Behavior

Experience of Mediated Learning

An Impact of Feuerstein's Theory in Education and Psychology

edited by

Alex Kozulin
Yaacov Rand

2000

PERGAMON
An imprint of Elsevier Science
Amsterdam – Lausanne – New York – Oxford – Shannon – Singapore – Tokyo

MT

ELSEVIER SCIENCE Ltd
The Boulevard, Langford Lane
Kidlington, Oxford OX5 1GB, UK

First edition 2000

Library of Congress Cataloging in Publication Data
A catalog record from the Library of Congress has been applied for.

British Library Cataloguing in Publication Data
A catalogue record from the British Library has been applied for.

ISBN: 0 08 043647 1

∞ The paper used in this publication meets the requirements of ANSI/NISO Z39.48-1992 (Permanence of Paper).
Printed in The Netherlands.

6/9/05

Table of Contents

Acknowledgement

Producing this book would not have been possible without the support of the European Science Foundation, Strasbourg. The European Science Foundation is an association of 62 major national funding agencies devoted to basic scientific research in 21 countries. The ESF assists its Member Organisations in two main ways: by bringing scientists together in its Scientific Programmes, Networks and European Research Conferences, to work on topics of common interest; and through the joint study of issues of strategic importance in European science policy. The scientific work sponsored by the ESF includes basic research in the natural and technical sciences, the medical and biosciences, the humanities and social sciences. The ESF maintains close relations with other scientific institutions within and outside Europe. Through its activities, the ESF adds value by co-operation and co-ordination across national frontiers and endeavours, offers expert scientific advice on strategic issues, and provides the European forum for fundamental science. This book is one of the outcomes of the ESF Scientific Programme on "Learning in Humans and Machines".

Contributors

Stacey Baskind
York University
Department of Psychology
North York
Ontario
Canada

Jens F. Beckmann
Faculty of Life Sciences, Pharmacy and
    Psychology
University of Leipzig
Leipzig
Germany

Robert Burden
University of Exeter
School of Education
Exeter
UK

Ruth Burgess
Southwest Missouri University
Springfield
Missouri
USA

Arthur L. Costa
Institute for Intelligent Behavior
Cameron Park
California
USA

J. D. Das
University of Alberta
Developmental Disabilities Center
Edmonton
Alberta
Canada

Samantha Dworsky
York University
Department of Psychology
North York
Ontario
Canada

Louis H. Falik
Department of Counseling
San Francisco State University
San Francisco
California
USA

Rafi S. Feuerstein
International Center for the Enhancement of
    Learning Potential; Hadassah-WIZO-Canada
    Research Institute; The BENEHEV Institute
    for Dynamic Assessment
Jerusalem
Israel

Shmuel Feuerstein
Bar Ilan University
School of Education
Ramat Gan
Israel

Jürgen Guthke
Faculty of Life Sciences, Pharmacy and
    Psychology
University of Leipzig
Leipzig
Germany

Charles Hadji
Pierre Mendes-France University
Grenoble
France

Carl Haywood
Touro College
Graduate School of Education and Psychology
New York City
NY, USA

Janice Johnson
York University
Department of Psychology
North York
Ontario
Canada

Pnina S. Klein
Bar Ilan University
School of Education
Ramat Gan
Israel

Alex Kozulin
International Center for the Enhancement of
   Learning Potential
Jerusalem
Israel

Carol S. Lidz
Touro College
Graduate School of Education and Psychology
New York City
NY
USA

Timothy C. Papadopoulos
University of Cyprus
Cyprus

Rauno K. Parilla
Queen's University
Kingston
Ontario
Canada

Juan Pascual-Leone
York University
Department of Psychology
North York
Ontario
Canada

Yaacov Rand
Bar Ilan University and Touro College
Jerusalem
Israel

Rivka Reichenberg
Beit-Berl College of Education and
   Mofet Institute
Israel

Elizabeth Severtson
York University
Department of Psychology
North York
Ontario
Canada

Robert J. Sternberg
Department of Psychology
Yale University
New Haven
CT
USA

Abraham J. Tannenbaum
Colombia University
Teachers College
New York City
NY
USA

David Tzuriel
Bar Ilan University
School of Education
Ramat Gan
Israel

Preface

This volume focuses on the impact made by Reuven Feuerstein's theory on contemporary understanding of learning, instruction, and cognitive modifiability. One may distinguish five different aspects in Feuerstein's contribution to psychology and education.

The first is a belief system encompassing the notion of Structural Cognitive Modifiability. According to Feuerstein, human individuals are capable of altering their "natural" developmental course through radical restructuring of their cognitive system. Human beings are thus perceived as open systems whose future cannot be predicted on the basis of the set amount of biological, medical, or psychometric data. This belief is translated into a number of educational strategies regarding individuals who are facing genetic, developmental, or sociocultural challenges. It helps to broaden substantially educational and social horizons of children with Down Syndrome, brain impairment, non-organic learning problems, and children brought up in an adverse social environment.

The second aspect of Feuerstein's system is the concept of Mediated Learning Experience (MLE). The theory of MLE emerged from a series of studies that have been conducted by Feuerstein since the 1950s with culturally different, educationally deprived and learning disabled students. At the core of this theory lies a distinction between the experience of direct learning and the experience of mediated learning. MLE is defined as a quality of interaction between the learner and the world of stimuli he/she is coping with, when this interaction is mediated by an adult or a more competent or initiated individual who selects, emphasizes, changes, and interprets the stimuli for the learner. Feuerstein claims that an insufficient amount or an inadequate type of parental or school-based teaching is responsible for the reduced learning potential of some individuals. Depending on other conditions, these MLE-deprived students can be classified as underachievers, learning disabled, or even mentally retarded. The infusion of MLE into educational intervention is capable of reversing this state of affairs and significantly enhancing the individual's learning potential.

The third aspect is Feuerstein's concept of dynamic cognitive assessment, proposed as a radical alternative to standard IQ tests. From his work with educationally deprived and culturally different children and adolescents Feuerstein learned that the manifest level of their performance in IQ tests is often misleading. Consequently Feuerstein proposed assessing the individual's capacity to learn and to become modified, rather than to measure the "amount", i.e. the quantitative aspects, of intelligence. The Learning Potential Assessment Device (LPAD) invented and developed by him and his colleagues, is a dynamic assessment procedure in the course of which individuals not only solve cognitive tasks but also receive instruction based on the principles of MLE. As a result, the evaluation of learning potential is based on taking into account both the improvement of performance from pre- to post-test and the amount and nature of mediation required to attain such an improvement.

The fourth aspect is the cognitive intervention program called Instrumental Enrichment (IE) designed by Feuerstein and his colleagues as a tool for the remediation of the individual's deficient cognitive functions and the enhancement of learning potential. IE offers a paradigm of a cognitive education program that is directly aimed at improving the individual's ability to become a better learner. The major target of the IE intervention program are those cognitive prerequisites of effective learning, that, for whatever reason remained underdeveloped in a given individual. IE materials include 14 booklets of paper-and-pencil tasks in such domains as analytic perception, orientation in space and time, principles of comparison and classification, and so on. Teaching IE presupposes special didactics based on the principles of MLE which emphasize intentionality of teacher/student interaction, transcedence of the principles discovered in the course of study into other spheres of activity, mediation of meaning, and a number of other parameters characterizing MLE. The fifth area is the shaping of a modifying environment. Feuerstein suggested that the entire learning environment including its physical parameters, scheduling of activities, student grouping and so on should function as a source of modifiability. Feuerstein was amongst the first proponents of integration of children with Down Syndrome and other developmental and learning problems into regular educational frameworks.

In this volume we have grouped a number of studies that reflect the broader influence of Feuerstein's ideas on psychology and education. This influence transcends the boundaries of the Feuersteinian school and attests to the emergence of a whole range of new alternatives in the fields of cognitive assessment and intervention.

The first chapter written by Ruth Burgess provides us with the necessary background information on Feuerstein's life and career. She attempts to reconstruct the formative influences that helped to shape the human modifiability belief system. Among these influences was Feuerstein's early experience with the learning problems of children who survived the Holocaust, and his experience working with educationally deprived new immigrant children. Academically, Burgess mentions Feuerstein's studies in Geneva under Piaget and his apprenticeship with Andre Rey, a pioneer in the field of learning process assessment.

Charles Hadji places Feuerstein's contributions into wider scientific, pedagogical, and ethical perspectives. At the core of all three lies the question of human modifiability; whether human intelligence can be modified; how increased modifiability can be achieved; what kind of ethical questions should be answered by the educators in their pursuit of students' modifiability. In his analysis Feuerstein's theory is compared to other cognitive theories such as those of Jean Piaget and Lev Vygotsky. Feuerstein's active modification position is contrasted with that taken by followers of J. J. Rousseau who emphasize the positive natural character of human abilities and perceive education as fostering natural propensities.

Arthur Costa places Feuerstein's theory into the context of the need to create a new educational leadership. The concept of mediation plays an important role in redefining the teacher's role. The new educational leadership should be able to clarify the goals of education in each specific case. New leaders should introduce coaching to the teachers' room helping them to become an efficient educational team. Costa advocates the necessity of recognizing a broad range of teachers' responsibilities including that of instructional strategists, meaning makers and researchers who generate feedback information to guide and assess their own, as well as their students' progress toward materializing their goals.

Robert Burden suggests that Feuerstein's theory and applied systems may serve as a bridge between educational psychologists and school psychologists who need a conceptual framework that would guide their everyday activity. Feuerstein's approach may offer such a conceptual framework, because, on the one hand it is theory-based, but on the other it offers specific instruments and procedures for the assessment and enhancement of the students' learning potential. Burden also demonstrates that Feuerstein's ideas correspond to the current change of attitude on the part of the psychological and educational establishment that moves, though slowly, in the direction of more authentic, dynamic, and ecologically valid forms of assessment and evaluation.

Robert Sternberg acknowledges the pioneering role played by Feuerstein in questioning the wisdom of IQ measures and in offering an alternative approach to cognitive assessment. Sternberg provides a systematic critique of the attempts to equate human cognitive abilities with IQ scores. In doing this he touches upon one of the central themes of Feuerstein's critique of IQ — the harmful consequences of the interpretation of intelligence as a quantifiable "thing". Sternberg offers his Triarchical Theory of Intelligence as a possible framework for broadening our understanding of thinking. The discussion is extended to include the issue of mental retardation. It is argued that adaptation of an individual with lower IQ to his/her environment can be achieved by utilizing those of their abilities which are not necessarily reflected in the IQ scores. The inter-group differences in cognitive test scores are considered in the broader context of socio-cultural determinants affecting our thinking and learning practices.

Yaacov Rand and Abraham Tannenbaum suggest that a predominance of certain personality characteristics does not necessarily preclude their modifiability. By examining various typological systems the authors arrive at the Modes of Existence paradigm that includes such basic attitudes as "To Be", "To Have", and "To Do". In a related chapter of Rivca Reichenberg and Yaacov Rand the Modes of Existence paradigm is applied in analyzing the interaction between pre-service teachers and their training supervisors. The findings of this study suggest a significant relationship between the predominant Mode of Existence and various reflective teaching components.

Shmuel Feuerstein inquiries about the place of questioning in the mediated interactions between teachers and students. As an illustration he examines different modes of questioning used in Jewish studies and arrives at the conclusion that the development of higher forms of reasoning constitutes an important aspect of the students' study of ancient religious texts over and beyond their importance as a basis for Jewish Law.

Drawing both from the published sources and from personal communication with his father, Rafi S. Feuerstein presents an important background material for understanding of the development of Reuven Feuerstein's theory of structural cognitive modifiability and its applied systems.

Carol Lidz starts by relating her experiences as a doctoral student who was deeply dissatisfied with the existent assessment tools available to a school psychologist. Feuerstein's MLE theory and the dynamic cognitive assessment concept provided her with an alternative approach. Lidz shows how the concept of MLE can be operationalized with the help of a rating scale, and how this scale can be used by educators and psychologists interested in evaluating the quality of child-adult interations in the home and school environments. She also describes a new dynamic cognitive assessment tool for pre-school children that she constructed on the basis of Feuerstein's theory: "The Applications of Cognitive Functions Scale". The last application described by Lidz is a program for parental training aimed at turning parents into more sensitive mediators.

Juergen Guthke and Jens Beckmann put Feuerstein's concept of dynamic cognitive assessment in the context of the current debate between the proponents of so-called learning tests and the supporters of more traditional psychometric procedures. In particular, the critics of the dynamic approaches emphasize the lack of standardization and insufficient validation of the learning potential assessment procedures. The authors critically examine the issue of standardization and validation, and describe their own diagnostic programs that combine some features of the standard assessment with the principles of dynamic cognitive assessment. They also discuss whether the material to be used in the diagnostic programs should be curriculum-related or purely cognitive, and the nature of the learning activities incorporated into the assessment procedure.

Juan Pascual-Leone with his co-authors acknowledge Feuerstein's role in focusing the researchers' attention on the incompatibility of the standard IQ type of testing and the goal of culturally-fair assessment. One possible direction in developing such an assessment is to base it on the notion of mental attention or mental capacity. The authors offer both the conceptual model and empirical material to substantiate this claim. Two types of tasks typically used in assessment are discussed: misleading and facilitating. It is claimed that opposite models of the developmental process — linear growth versus discontinuous "stages" — depend on the types of tasks used. The "low-road" and "high-road" processing strategies are explored and it is shown how the "low-road" processing may hinder students' reasoning in the elementary math tasks. To prove that the tests of mental capacity are indeed culturally fair they were administered with the population of regular deaf students, gifted deaf students, and regular mainstream students. Deaf students demonstrated the same mental capacity as hearing students, but showed some executive-strategy deficiency that can be eliminated by practice.

David Tzuriel explores different criteria of parent–child interaction and the methods of their identification and registration. He also points to the necessity of developing a more precise methodology to study the relationships between parental mediation and the child's cognitive enhancement. Tzuriel asserts that MLE interactions, such as representing learning processes within the family, are more accurate in predicting the post-teaching scores of the dynamic assessment procedure rather than the pre-teaching scores. A number of dynamic assessment procedures are described including the Children's Analogical Thinking Modifiability Test (CATM) and the Children's Inferential Modifiability Test (CITM) developed by Tzuriel. The summary of relevant empirical studies includes the investigation of MLE in the families of different socio-economic levels and in the free-play versus structured activity contexts.

Pnina Klein developed an observational scale that helps to identify and record different parameters of parent–child interactions. The mediational quality of these interactions can be improved with the help of a special parental training program — Mediational Intervention for Sensitizing Caregivers (MISC). Klein reports a number of studies using MISC with families that include infants at risk (e.g. very low birth weight) or mothers at risk (single, teenage, drug dependent, etc.). Both the mothers' mediational style and the children's cognitive performance were registered. Results showed that the mothers' expanding and rewarding behaviours were most frequently related to children's cognitive performance. The most important results were obtained, however, during a follow-up study conducted three and six years after the intervention. The children in the experimental group outscored those of the control group in both language performance and verbal reasoning. While only a few mothers from the control group reported any changes, 75% of the mothers who participated in the MISC program found jobs outside the home and otherwise used the MISC experience to better organize their everyday activities. Klein concludes that the parental mediational style not only can be changed, but that the changes have a lasting character affecting the learning potential of both parents and children.

Alex Kozulin presents an analysis of Feuerstein's Instrumental Enrichment program applications conducted over the last decade in different countries and with different populations of students. Particular attention is paid to the issue of the relationships between the special needs of the given population and the mode of IE application. The results from the application of IE with learning disabled, normal underachieving, culturally different, and sensorially handicapped students are reported. Some new versions of the IE program, such as the Braille IE program for the blind, are discussed, as well as the conditions for the optimal application of the IE program with different types of learners.

J. P. Das and his co-authors outline a cognitive approach to reading that utilizes both Feuerstein's concept of mediation and Vygotsky's and Luria's notion of psychological activity. This approach focuses on four cognitive processes: Planning, Attention, Arousal, Simultaneous and Successive Processing (PASS). A number of studies that applied the PASS model to the analysis of reading are reviewed. On the basis of these studies a reading enhancement program was developed by J. P. Das and his colleagues. Similarly to Feuerstein's approach, this program attempts to improve students' reading through enhancing and improving their cognitive strategies. It contains both global non-reading tasks that require the application of simultaneous and successive strategies, and a more specific application of the same strategies to reading and spelling tasks. The program proved to be effective both for the remediation and for prevention of reading difficulties.

Carl Haywood proposes using the principles of mediated learning and the Instrumental Enrichment cognitive education program as components of therapeutic activities. One reason for introducing cognitive methods into the field of psychotherapy is that some interpersonal and inter-psychic problems encountered by people may be due to their failure in developing effective thinking models rather than classical psychopathology. Among the more important of cognitive exercises, Haywood mentions planning, identifying choice situations, making choices, considering alternative interpretations, classifying one's problems, situations, and activities, and evaluating the effectiveness of solutions and plans. The group that seems to benefit more from this type of intervention is disturbed, low functioning and delinquent adolescents.

Louis Falik demonstrates in his chapter how one can integrate the principles of mediated learning experience into a counseling process. The proposed model has two major dimensions: 1) Developmental phases or stages of the counseling process which represent temporal and experiential aspects of a counseling relationship, and 2) The functional components of the mediated learning experience that guide the general and specific treatment objectives of the encounter. The model also outlines two response modalities: a) The focus of the interaction on the content or process, and b) The formulation of the quality of the response.

A. K. & Y. R

PART 1

1

Reuven Feuerstein: Propelling Change, Promoting Continuity

Ruth Vassar Burgess

1 Introduction

The theory of Structural Cognitive Modifiability conceptualized by Professor Reuven Feuerstein emerges late in the twentieth century. The theory, as well as the applied products — the Instrumental Enrichment (IE) Program, the Learning Propensity Assessment Device (LPAD), and the concept of Mediated Learning Experiences are the most significant innovations in educational psychology of the twentieth century. Developed largely in response to perceived human needs and based on grounded research methods, the theory stands in opposition to both behaviorism and psychodynamic theories. Feuerstein's theory is a synthesis of Judaic thought, social psychology, developmental psychology and classical tenets first proposed by other seminal thinkers, such as the Socratics.

A few basic points need to be made at the onset. A single chapter only can provide an overview and touch on major periods of Feuerstein's life. As an interpretative biography, the approach uses descriptive narrative. The story introduces significant people, events and circumstances that pushed Feuerstein's paradigm forward. Through these interactions, the evolution of his intellectual struggles and their subsequent resolutions emerge. This is followed by a discussion of grounded research theory and its application to the formation of Feuerstein's theory. Feuerstein's legacies illustrate his multidimensional impact. The chapter concludes with a final summary portraying Feuerstein as a man quite extraordinary, who with enthusiasm and vigor propelled change, yet at the same time promoted continuity. As such, he helped to prepare us for the twenty-first century.[1]

[1]This chapter results from 23 years of study on the life and work of Prof. Reuven Feuerstein, including the past 12 years during which I have worked with him. Feuerstein, his family members and his staff were gracious to allow interviews during summer 1994 and spring 1996.

Sincere appreciation is extended to my husband, Stanley M. Burgess, Ph.D., Professor of Religious Studies, Southwest Missouri State University, who suggested that I study with Prof. Feuerstein nearly two decades ago. He provided scholarly insights beyond my psychological and educational background. By participating in the interviews and through editorial assistance, he has facilitated my search for the evolution of the Theory of Structural Cognitive Modifiability and my efforts to better understanding Reuven Feuerstein as a person.

2 Changing Contexts: the Quest for Order Amid Disorder
"Did I live in the climate and nature of Romania or was it in the dream of Zion?"

Reuven Feuerstein, the fifth of nine children of Aharon Feuerstein, was born in Botosani, Romania, August 21, 1921. More than half of Botosani's residents were Jews, with seventy-two synagogues. Aharon was *"shochet"* (ritual slaughterer) for the community, and was frequently sought after as a counselor or mediator. Every morning at 5 a.m. he taught his sons, giving them a love for books and learning, and sharing his dream of reestablishing a Jewish homeland in Eretz Israel. Reuven also learned hospitality from his parents — who opened their home to others — as well as a deep awareness of the need for facilitating maximal development in all humans. Above all, he was influenced by his mother's tear-stained prayer book.

Always a dreamer, Reuven became a storyteller by the age of five or six years. His dreams and stories usually revolved around the reestablishment of the Jewish homeland. At the age of eight, he was given responsibility to teach several children to read. Shortly thereafter, he was given the same charge for a forty-year-old illiterate man. Then he was asked to teach Hebrew to people who had committed themselves to go to Israel.

Reuven already was confronted with questions about learning by the age of eight. How can the learner be changed? How does one overcome learning deficiencies? What pedagogy is successful in given cases?

By the age of nine, Reuven was a member of the Bnei Akiva youth movement, a religious Zionist organization, for which he gathered money to be used in planting trees and in purchasing pieces of land in Israel. In the process, he learned to live in an imaginary world — outside of time and space, dreaming of the possibility of creating a society where justice, peace, and positive possibilities existed. His imagined reality became more vivid to him than the real world, which for Eastern European Jews had become one of misery and pain. As a result, he was better prepared to cope with what lay ahead.

Even before the Second World War, the Feuerstein family had been touched by the strong arm of Nazism. Reuven's older sister, Paula, was imprisoned for her activity in the communist party. Father Aharon wondered whether Paula might have remained more traditional had she not been away from home in order to study. His pain grew as his eldest son, Ya'cov, followed the lead of Paula. Meanwhile, Reuven, at the age of seventeen, decided to go to Bucharest to join an Hakhshara, a Zionist community preparing to become agriculturists in Eretz Israel.

At the Hakhshara, Reuven joined a group of highly intelligent young people, many of whom had been denied access to advanced studies in philosophy or medicine. They had abandoned higher education in order to become peasants in the land of their dreams. But life in this agrarian setting did not remain idyllic. The Zionist group became the focus of anti-Semitic activity. The Romanian police visited them frequently, terrorizing the group.

Meanwhile, Reuven joined Youth Aliyah, and was sent to organize religious youth for emigration to Palestine. On such a mission in Vatra-Dornei, he stayed in the home of the Rands. In the hollow heel of his right shoe, Reuven kept a list of the youth he enrolled. Through high placed connections, the Rands learned the police were aware of Reuven's subversive work and were trying to arrest him. Yaacov Rand, his future brother-in-law, helped Reuven escape.

Shortly thereafter, Reuven, along with hundreds of Jewish men, women and children, were arrested and taken to a labor camp along the Transylvanian border. Their job was to prepare the trail by which Jews from Romania would be transferred to the German death camps. While here Reuven, exhibiting unbounded optimism, organized a cultural education program for the children. He fashioned positivistic approaches for them and instilled in them a dream of someday going to Israel, thereby helping them transcend present miseries with a new sense of meaningful existence. For Reuven, the children became "roses growing in rocky soil."

Back in Bucharest, Reuven finished the course of study at Teachers' Seminary and attended Ionescu College. In addition, he worked with children from horrific backgrounds. He discovered that they could be taught to dance, to read and to write the basics. He gathered food, books, and musical recordings for the children, and facilitated their spiritual renewal. But once again in danger from the Romanian soldiers, Reuven's life was spared as he escaped from those sent to arrest him. Within a week he traveled from Bucharest to the port of the city of Constanza, where he boarded a refugee boat named Milka I, for the voyage to Istanbul. There he boarded a Turkish train to Beirut, and another train to Haifa. His dream of "Zion" had become a reality!

In reflecting on his years in Bucharest, Reuven recognizes that uncertainty affected both his philosophy and later his Theory of Structural Cognitive Modifiability. Uncertainty or disequilibrium leads one to plan, to anticipate, and to "create conditions of life which are adaptable in states of oppression".[2]

"Be strong. I need you."

Passover 1944 was meaningful on many levels. For Reuven, the angel of death had passed over, and he was directed by Youth Aliyah to join his brother, Shimshon, at a religious kibbutz in the Hebron Hills, Kefar Ezyon. Together with a talented group of colleagues, Reuven was asked to engage in long-range (five-year) planning for the community — this while repelling frequent Arab attacks on the kibbutz. For Reuven, this was a shock. Why waste their time planning, when they might not survive five years?

But Reuven came to learn that it was imperative in such times to engage in representational behavior, and to consider positive alternatives while systematically planning. Ironically, Kefar Ezyon was destroyed by the Arab Legion in 1948, with 350 of Reuven's friends and students massacred.

Reuven was sent by Youth Aliyah to the first teachers' training college (called Seminar) in Israel, located on Mt. Scopus in Jerusalem. Here Reuven quickly rejected

[2]Interviews with Reuven Feuerstein on 6/20/1994 and 6/24/1994; interview with Yaacov and Bella Rand on 6/1/1994; interview with Jacob Feuerstein on 7/8/1994.

the behaviorist model: "Already I was too sophisticated and had too many successful experiences as a mediator to accept such things. I knew humans were not simply registers of things … Certainly behaviorism did not provide long-term positive possibilities." Reuven believed that humans had the potential of inner modification, when nurtured by active, involved mediators who cared enough to transmit their heritage. He argued that humans were not static beings, but rather were dynamic in that they could reach towards unlimited positive (or negative) potentials.

During this time, Reuven joined his brother Shimshon, at Mikve Yisra'el, an agricultural community near Holon, outside Tel Aviv. Here he met youngsters from extermination camps, including "the children from Teheran". Most were from Poland who had seen their families massacred, and then had walked eastward through southern Russia and southward into Iran, where they had been quartered in tents outside of Tehran.

Aged beyond their years by holocaust horrors, these children affected Reuven deeply. He taught them during the day, and at night, when they were revisited by past terrors, he sat with them. He was convinced that, "Israel could not lose one more child".

Reuven recognized that the educational program had to be powerful. It was necessary to mediate a positive belief system, to help these children realize that they had a past rich with thoughtful traditions, and that they were a vital part of the dynamic present and future. They were taught to develop ownership of the land, its peoples, and their traditions. They learned that they must work for others in need. Reuven would look at them and plead, "Be strong. I need you".

And the children gained strength at Mikve Yisra'el. Artists from Jerusalem and Tel Aviv were brought for concerts, served as role models, and encouraged a sense of belonging. The children learned to sing, even with an orchestra, and to recite poetry.

On vacations and holidays, Reuven and many others traveled north to build houses at new settlement villages, first at Mechorah and later at Kefar Ya'betz. But his participation was cut short by his rapidly deteriorating health.

Faced with advanced tuberculosis, Reuven searched for inner strength to survive. When treatment at the sanitarium near Tel Aviv proved ineffective, the doctors recommended that a change of climate and temperature might be a treatment of last resort. Youth Aliyah decided to send Feuerstein to Davos, Switzerland to another sanitarium. "I decided that I must go to study and to work, not to be an invalid …. The power of the human belief is enormous. I wanted to live."[3]

> "I was constantly moving between philosophy, psychology, and Biblical sciences …. It took me years to put shutters on my eyes, to focus on one thing."

At Davos, Reuven Feuerstein immediately became involved with children coming, with tuberculosis, from Germany. Despite his physical weaknesses, Reuven

[3]Interviews with Reuven Feuerstein on 6/20/1994, 6/24/1994, and 6/25/1994, and taped response to inquiries 4/1996; interview with Yaacov and Bella Rand on 6/1/1994; interview with Shmuel Feuerstein on 6/8/1994; interview with Jacob Feuerstein on 7/8/1994.

gathered money and presented their case so that the Swiss authorities would allow them to enter their country. Although he could barely walk, and each breath he took was accompanied by stabbing pain, he forgot his illness and became very active. He lectured in several youth camps, as well as in Basle and Zurich, often bringing the young tubercular children with him. He also tried to find places for a few of the children from Mikve Yisra'el, who were hospitalized with tuberculosis.

In late 1949 Reuven became more actively involved with Jewish youth, and was named the delegate of the Jewish Agency to the youth movement in Switzerland. He started both summer and winter camps for them. He was also lecturing in a variety of settings. His future wife, Berta Guggenheim, took one of his courses.

Meanwhile, Reuven began to study with Karl Jaspers in Basle, and with Carl Jung in Zurich, who helped him focus on Psychology from among his many on-going intellectual pursuits. He learned that Jaspers had lost his chair of philosophy because of Heidegger's dislike for Jews, and of Jung's tendency towards anti-Semitism. Reuven did find common grounds between Jung and mystic experience. This lifted psychology above the level in which it was a mere reflection of our sexual needs, to a higher plane in which humans were transformed through universal archetypes. Reuven was also very attracted to botany, literature, poetry, art and Biblical studies at this time. He actually traveled to Bern to meet Professor Widmer, who was interested in him writing a dissertation on the prophet Amos. Reuven was especially interested in Amos' concern for the poor and their loss of the land.

Eventually, Reuven Feuerstein came to Geneva to study with Jean Piaget because of his decision to pursue cognitive psychology. Piaget's interest in human development, and, as a corollary, individual potential for growth in adaptive capacities interested him greatly. In addition, because of his study of Maimonides' writings, Reuven already understood that the cognitive process was extremely important in determining human behavior and destiny.

In Geneva, Feuerstein came to a better understanding of cognition and its basic processes. He became exposed to both scientific and clinical methods to investigate those processes. Piaget's scientific manner and modes of questioning provided a protocol for systematic inquiry that significantly impacted Feuerstein's later ability to assess cognition. In addition, Piaget provided Reuven with a research design model. This included collaborative inquiry in which the old master posed a question and then sent his students out to test the experimental hypothesis. Subsequently, they reported back to Piaget, who synthesized their findings. Piaget also introduced Feuerstein to the concept of "magical thinking", in contradistinction to analytic thought.

However, because Piaget was committed to a fixed succession of stages of development, he was not open to Reuven's concept of modifiability. Piaget insisted that children could not jump over these stages. In contrast, his student, Feuerstein, contended that the order and timing of cognitive development is set, not by maturation, but by mediated social experiences. He had learned from age eight onward that humans could be challenged, modified, and changed in critical areas of their cognitive functioning. So professor Piaget and student Feuerstein were at loggerheads over developmental theory.

Reuven's confidence in a dynamic model was only strengthened by his research studies in Morocco. Youth Aliyah was experiencing unusual difficulties integrating Moroccan Jewish children into Israeli life and culture. They turned to Reuven Feuerstein, asking him to examine whether Moroccan children could be educated and thereby qualify for immigration to Israel. Reuven understood the real question to be whether these children, who manifested such low levels of cognitive functioning, could be modified. So he traveled to Marseilles and other locations in the south of France where Jewish children from Morocco immigrated, and eventually to Morocco to study human modifiability in a more systematic manner.

In this enterprise, Reuven collaborated with the Genevan Professor André Rey. Rey, like Feuerstein, interpreted human cognitive development differently than Piaget. Feuerstein and Rey discovered that many of the referred Moroccan children, who would have been classified as mentally retarded by conventional psychometric measures, were suffering from overwhelming cultural deprivation. Many of the Jewish families experienced oppression and difficult living conditions when they moved into urban mellahs.

Feuerstein (1996) recalls that many of these children had virtually no access to the types of thinking necessary for them to respond even to the simplest tasks. They had no logical systematic way of understanding the world around them. Feuerstein concluded that children living as oppressed minorities, when they could not predict today or tomorrow, experienced trauma that affected their psyche and caused high anxiety. These factors led to low functioning.

Could the children learn these cognitive strategies? Reuven attempted to teach them in order to modify their cognitive behaviors. These mediated interventions showed positive results. Moreover, in the process of Feuerstein's investigation and systematic experimentation, his understanding of modifiability was becoming crystallized.

Meanwhile, Reuven was faced with a most awkward dilemma. Rey would work with him, but not if he continued with Piaget. Reuven was forced to tell the old Genevan master of his decision to work with Rey, whom Piaget had kept at a distance to maintain the upper hand at the University of Geneva. Only later did Piaget show any interest in the Moroccan project.

Since the late 1920s, Piaget knew of Vygotsky's research, and had received correspondence from him. However, Piaget chose not to share Vygotsky's work with his students. He remained committed to his epistemological mode of inquiry and theory building. Reuven Feuerstein independently began to develop his early concepts of Mediated Learning Experience before he was aware of several parallel conclusions of the Russian scholar.[4]

Feuerstein observed many children coming from cultures less technologically advanced (such as Yemen) but had maintained the transmission of heritage beliefs and practices were still cognitively modifiable. Having learned their own culture they were usually able to learn and integrate in different cultures. Children who were deprived of their cultural heritage, having come from what Feuerstein calls "exploded cultures", were less able to adapt and to acquire a different culture. They had weaker learning skills, being less able to self-modify. Often natural causes, human deprivation, war, and other socioeconomic infringements are examples leading to "exploded cultures" and lack of intergenerational continuity.

This awareness strengthened his belief that Youth Aliyah and the State of Israel must support and reinforce the respective cultures of immigrant groups, so that they could integrate successfully into their new society. It also led him to an awareness of the need for a mediator — whether a parent, grandparent, sibling, caretaker or teacher — who would shape the way the child perceives the world. Piaget's formula Stimuli–Organism–Response (S–O–R) that presumes that children learn simply through contact with stimuli, was being transformed by Feuerstein to S–H–O–H–R, with the insertion of an "H", standing for human intervention or mediation.

Based on experiences stretching back to childhood days in Botosani, Reuven recognized the strength of humans investing in a dynamic, intergenerational cultural model. As Feuerstein moved back to Israel, Youth Aliyah and other organizations provided the means whereby he applied these beliefs to curriculum, research and theory building. Subsequently, applications were made to many in need.[5]

> "Jerusalem is ours …. Our existence extends itself over time, and
> we are dwelling with the same level of intensity in the past as in
> the present as in the future." (Reuven Feuerstein after the Six Day
> War in 1967.)

In 1954 Reuven Feuerstein, who served as Director of Psychological Services for Youth Aliyah in Europe and North Africa, was called back to Israel by the Jewish Agency. The country was torn by serious internal strife and grave threats from surrounding Arab countries. The population of Israel had more than doubled since the state was founded in 1948. Israel was absorbing huge numbers of immigrants, many of them from remote and less technically advanced societies. This population explosion posed major educational problems.

Feuerstein's new role was to work with immigrant children and youngsters, facilitating their entry into Israel and adaptation to life there. He gathered like-minded colleagues, such as his brother-in-law, Yaacov Rand, and David Krasilowsky, head of a psychiatric hospital, to work with him in the new Child Guidance Clinic of Youth Aliyah in Jerusalem. Satellite clinical and research sites

[4]Kozulin, A. (Ed.). (1986), Lev Vygotsky, *Thought and Language*. Cambridge, MA, London: MIT Press; Presseisen, B. & Kozulin, A. (1994). Mediated Learning: The Contributions of Vygotsky and Feuerstein in Theory and Practice. In Ben-Hur, M. (Ed.), *On Feuerstein's Instrumental Enrichment: A Collection* (pp. 51–81), Palatine, IL: IRI/Skylight Publishing.
[5]Interviews with Reuven Feuerstein on 6/28/1994, and 7/6/1994, and taped response to inquiries 4/1996; interview with David Krasilowsky on 5/25/1994; interview with Shimon Tuchman on 5/30/1994; interview with Yaacov and Bella Rand on 6/1/1994; interview with Shmuel Feuerstein on 6/8/1994.

were located elsewhere in Israel. As Director of this Clinic, Reuven was also responsible for raising badly needed funding. Shimon Tuchman, who earlier collaborated with Feuerstein through Youth Aliyah in Europe and North Africa now served as treasurer for Youth Aliyah.

Reuven continued to serve the Jewish Agency for many years, and in turn his unique approaches were supported by Youth Aliyah, although not all within this organization or Israeli psychological circles accepted his educational philosophy and practices. As in Geneva, Reuven was in a continuous struggle for his ideas and his children, against bureaucratic inertia, educational inflexibility, and individuals who opposed him for other reasons.

Andre Rey visited Israel shortly after Feuerstein's return from Geneva and together they toured the country, giving conferences and lectures for six weeks. But Rey was already suffering from leukemia, and succumbed to this disease in 1964.

Feuerstein's work in Youth Aliyah and in Ministry of Education sites continued to expand. In 1957 a research unit was established, having developed out of the Jerusalem Child Guidance Clinic of Youth Aliyah. Financial underpinnings came from the Hadassah-WIZO Organization of Canada. The clinic's purpose has been to build on the fifteen years of Feuerstein's work with children from North Africa, Yemen, and other culturally different and socio-economically disadvantaged groups. Immediate attention was focused on educational, psychological, and mental hygiene problems among adolescents and their need for mediation.

The research unit began in a two-room apartment, with one research assistant, and a secretary provided by Youth Aliyah. In 1966, with the assistance of Professor Abe Tannenbaum of Columbia Teachers' College and Professor Martin Hamburger of New York University, who recognized the worldwide potential of Feuerstein's work, a research proposal was submitted to the Ford Foundation. These funds and additional funding from the United States National Institute of Child Health and Development assisted the Clinic and Research Institute to expand. In addition to action research studies, the Research Institute provided a forum for lectures, symposia, meetings with teachers and psychologists, and collaboration with scholars from abroad.

These were difficult years, because Israel was fighting for its very existence. Finally, in the Six Day War (1967) Arab forces were defeated in a brilliant battle led by the Israeli army, and the Old City of Jerusalem was liberated. The Feuersteins, together with most Israeli families, suffered personal losses, including the death of a member of their extended family. But in his typical survivalist mentality, Reuven only stiffened in resolve to preserve Israel and its children. Throughout the years leading up to this conflict and the War itself, his creativity and resilience seemed only to grow while others were stifled by circumstances.

During these years, Feuerstein's Theory of Structural Cognitive Modifiability continued to take shape, although it had not yet been named and its parameters, premises and goals were not yet fully articulated. Most significant was the emergence of his so-called "cognitive map" which he articulated in its seven dimensions by 1970. Clearly, this was not born overnight. The infrastructure of the cognitive map seems to have been in place from his years in Geneva. But it has grown steadily in content and specificity since that time, and that growth continues even to the present. His colleagues report that Reuven has experienced moments of special insight — sometimes in a lecture, or in a discussion, or in a time of focused thought.

From 1954 to 1970, Feuerstein developed the standard set of instruments of his now famous "Instrumental Enrichment Program" almost fully. By this time, the dimensions of Mediated Learning Experience had been articulated. In decades to come, however, he conceptualized additional instruments, now in various stages of development and testing. He contends that these instruments are evolving as more is learned from theory and from practical implementation.

The basic Learning Potential Assessment Device (LPAD) (now Learning Propensity Assessment Device) was already in place by 1969. Reuven credits Andre Rey for inspiring him in developing this revolutionary assessment approach.

The LPAD provides an alternative to conventional testing procedures. In 1981 Feuerstein proclaimed, "Adhering to a psychometric conception is an irrational endeavor." It is his belief that psychometric measures do not provide a framework for meaningful cognitive change. Furthermore, he insisted modifiability be included among assessment standards.

The LPAD was an attempt to relate assessment and educational concerns, both sharing underlying cognitive dysfunctions. While the goal is cognitive modifiability, this assessment provides a baseline of unassisted performance. Then, with the assistance of a mediator, and through precise cognitive probes, the learner displays types of representational behaviors, a type of induced modifiability. This is compatible to Vygotsky's position, who wrote of the distance between the baseline of unassisted performance and the level of assisted performance as the "zone of proximal development". Although Feuerstein acknowledges "zones of proximal and distal development", he asserts that assessments must include specific intervention suggestions for cognitive modifiability for the teacher or mediator.[6]

> "I formulated a need to look not for capacity, but for modifiability."

With general principles of his concept of Mediated Learning Experience, as well as with the IE and the LPAD programs, in place by 1970, Feuerstein entered a stage of system fine-tuning and definition, program expansion, and international acceptance and replication (1971–1985). Scholars and practitioners from around the world learned of his work, and requested clarification of his concepts, terminology and procedures. Many expressed interest in replicating his programs abroad.

In response, Mildred Hoffman joined the Research Institute staff in 1971. Her first task was to express Feuerstein's ideology in language comprehensible to

---

[6]Reuven Feuerstein taped response to inquiries 4/1996; interview with David Tzuriel on 5/15/1994; interview with David Krasilowsky on 5/25/1994; interview with Yaacov and Bella Rand on 6/1/1994; interview with Abe Tannenbaum on 6/5/1994; interview with Pnina Klein on 6/16/1994.

Western educators, especially those in the United States, Canada, and the United Kingdom. Shortly thereafter, she developed a teacher training model that was used successfully, first in Israel and eventually in 35 countries and in 53 languages throughout the world. Hoffman also served as a sounding board for Feuerstein, who assumed that whatever she did not understand in his theory and practices would be a problem for most other educators. In response, Reuven attempted to redefine and to otherwise clarify points of uncertainty. Similarly, he turned to Professors Abe Tannenbaum, Harry Passow, and Martin Hamburger for critique.

Mildred Hoffman endeavoured to maintain Feuerstein's system free from variation or dilution. She, like Reuven, had a deep and abiding love for children, and was successful among educators in Israel and abroad. Because she worked so closely with Reuven, it is impossible to determine precisely the extent of her influence on the training programs. There is no question that it was a significant impact, however.

When asked to specify those elements and techniques needed to produce dispositions for thinking, Feuerstein formulated two lists and specified elements of both the normal cognitive functions and deficient cognitive functions (cognitive dysfunctions). Each list was divided into three levels: the input, elaboration, and output levels. Feuerstein proposed that "inadequate mediated learning experiences leads to cognitive functions that are undeveloped, impaired, or inefficiently used". Similarly, Feuerstein delineated the parameters and criteria for his Theory of Structural Cognitive Modifiability (SCM), which he made public initially in a speech at Yale University (1980).

The purpose of mediation is to assist in the transition from exterior to interior locus of control, which Feuerstein labels "autoplasticity". An individual controlled by externals — the "alloplastic" — is more compliant, more dependent, and fragmented over time as reinforcers satiate or disappear. Alloplastic individuals tend to base their social behavior on present considerations, and live predominantly in a sensorial bound existence.

Autoplastic individuals, on the other hand, are able to make reasoned decisions, based upon time-honored systems of value. They are dynamic, changing organisms, and are self modifiable. Their behavior grows out of an interior locus of control, hence they are less affected by primary sensorial experience.

During this extremely productive period in his career, Feuerstein amazingly found time and energy to complete his doctorate in Developmental Psychology at the Sorbonne (1970). Reuven early resisted the idea of doctoral studies. But he was encouraged by friends, such as Professor Abe Tannenbaum, who convinced him of the long-term benefits of the doctorate.

Since 1970, Feuerstein has served as a Professor of Education at the Bar Ilan University's School of Education in Ramat Gan, Israel. From 1978 he holds the position of Adjunct Professor at Vanderbilt University's Peabody College of Education.

From his earliest years at Botosani when he learned that humans are made in the image of God with unlimited potential, Reuven has been guided by the "principle of the possible". This he applied to his own life, with astounding results as he has overcome seemingly impossible odds and obstacles. In turn, he applies his "principle of the possible" to others, including low-functioning children. This conviction led to his Theory of Structural Cognitive Modifiability, which revolutionized educational horizons and expectations.[7]

2.1 Aging, but still Sageing

In his mature years (1986–present), Reuven Feuerstein continues a breathtaking pace of activity, ever taking delight in the expansion of his educational programs and institutes, personally assuming responsibility for fundraising and public relations efforts, but still finding time for his first professional love — the at-risk children of the world. In 1986 Reuven complained, "They want me to focus just on my writings and not spend so much time on the children (at the Institute). What they do not understand is that the children are my life!"

The Professor who would not accept the notion of static intelligence has been equally unwilling to accept a static personal existence. Abe Tannenbaum points out that Reuven "has constantly moved in depth to a more detailed and complex understanding of human frailty or elements of human handicap". At the same time, Tannenbaum suggests, "He has this calling, almost a religious need, to imprint himself on history …. However, I think that there is a deeper motivation there … a profound religious conviction about the sanctity of the human being, and it doesn't matter who that human being is."

Even his times of weakness have been transformed somehow into new strengths. For example, immediately after he underwent by-pass heart surgery (1993) and while in Intensive Care, the Professor dictated to Rafi, his eldest son, some ideas about one of the IE instruments for the blind. Shortly thereafter, he supervised the move of his International Center for the Enhancement of Learning Potential from Karmon Street to the current facility on Narkis Street, overlooking the Knesset and the Israeli Museum.

He continues to be actively involved in writing projects, as well as in teaching and training large audiences of psychologists, teachers, parents, social workers, behavioral scientists, and decision makers from around the world. Chief among these training programs are the annual summer international workshops held since 1979 at the Shoresh Hotel, located west of Jerusalem. He persists in supporting research relating to the effects of Youth Aliyah's programs on Holocaust survivors. In addition, Feuerstein continues programs preparing individuals with Down Syndrome for Israeli military service as well as for paraprofessional work as caregivers for the handicapped and elderly. He has also been working on adaptations of the IE program for use in industrial settings in France and the USA. He has extended his dynamic assessment and intervention programs downward for

[7]Reuven Feuerstein taped response to inquiries 4/1996; interview with Noa Feuerstein on 7/5/1994; interview with Abe Tannenbaum on 6/5/1994; interview with Nilli Ben-Shachar on 6/7/1994.

pre-school children. One of his top priorities has been to help solve the problems of recent massive waves of Soviet and Ethiopian Jewish immigrants to Israel.

Now world famous, Feuerstein has been distinguished by a large number of honors. In 1986 he received commendation by the Detroit Public Schools. During 1990, he received city medals from Aix-les-Bains and Nevers, France. In 1991, he was appointed recipient of the Variety Clubs International Humanitarian Award and Chevalier dans l'Ordre des Palmes Academiques in France. In 1992, he was nominated Jerusalem's distinguished citizen and received the highly esteemed Israel Prize for his life-long contribution to society. Hundreds of theses, dissertations, scientific reports and articles in many languages have been written about his theory and methods. Recently, the British Broadcasting Company produced television programs about his activities, such as the Transformers series documentary, "Out of the Wilderness," and a course presentation for the Open University. He is featured in Gary Marcuse's video, "The Mind of a Child" (1995), which describes applications of his theory and practice with first nation children in Canada. His work has been widely acknowledged around the world in such magazines and newspapers as *Psychology Today*, *The New York Times*, *Le Monde* and *La Stampa*.[8]

3 Feuerstein and Post-Positivism

Feuerstein's work appears to be an enigma when viewed from the popular twentieth century positivist "Zeitgeist". Positivism doctrine advocates society can be analyzed in purely objective mechanistic terms and that social values and normative standards are mere epiphenomena. Studies attempted to objectify, label, and classify humans, which frequently brought static results. There was little talk of positive alternatives for those who were displaced, disabled, or disenfranchised by society. Feuerstein's theory of SCM provides a distinct alternative. A discussion of positive and post positivist approaches follows.

Methods of determining validity or truth vary depending on people, time, place and circumstance. Positivist research represents an attempt to objectify human behavior primarily through quantification of numeric data. Several tests purport to measure "cognitive capacity". In this approach, humans are classified or categorized with labels and compared to norms derived from stratified or random samples and analyzed as aggregate data. Frequently, this information is used for prediction, diagnostics, and educational placements. Positivistic assessments are used to support a "limiting model" that tends to measure static learning and past learning experiences. These measures enhance the probability that those "deprived

---

[8]Reuven Feuerstein taped response to inquiries 4/1996; interview with Rafi Feuerstein on 7/4/1994; interview with Abe Tannenbaum on 6/5/1994; interview with Moshe Egozi on 6/3/1994; interview with Pnina Klein on 6/16/1994; interview with Jacob Boussidan on 6/18/1994; interview with Eitan Vig on 6/18/1994; interview with Nilli Ben-Shachar on 6/7/1994.

of their heritage and cultural mediation" would be placed in segregated and less cognitive challenging settings. These tests reflect cultural tenets, provide biased results in multicultural settings, and give little assistance for intervention leading to either cognitive growth or scientific learning.

In contrast, post positivist research is grounded in "the assumption that features of the social environment are constructed as interpretations by individuals and these interpretations tend to be transitory and situational" (Gall, Borg & Gall, 1996). Post-positivist research is a type of qualitative research. "Qualitative research is multimethod in its focus, involving an interpretive, naturalistic approach to its subject matter. This means that qualitative researchers study things in their natural settings, attempting to make sense of, or to interpret, phenomena in terms of the meanings people bring to them" (Denzin & Lincoln, 1994).

In post-positivist research one develops knowledge by collecting data to intensively study people and then to subject this data to analytic induction. Over the years, Feuerstein collected data on how individuals learned and their propensity toward modifiability. Then, through processes of induction, he formed inferences, hypotheses, and principles. In this fashion, Feuerstein is closer to the post-positive than the positive approach.

Human needs impacted Feuerstein at every stage of life. He encountered endogenous factors such as heredity or genetic factors, organicity, and critical stage beliefs. Endo-exogenous conditions samples, such as differences in maturation levels, emotional balance of the child or parents, and varying types and degrees of environmental stimuli conditions, provided opportunities to investigate. Additional challenges were offered by samples illustrative of varying exogenous factors. These included differences in socioeconomic status, educational insufficiencies, and cultural differences. Feuerstein writes of these as "distal factors".

Feuerstein's authentic laboratories were naturalistic environments, such as homes, classrooms, clinics, and workplaces. Most certainly, the research division of the Hadassah-WIZO-Canada Institute, with a day school, provided a ready learning laboratory for Feuerstein and his associates. As time passed, Feuerstein's laboratories spread internationally as researchers, teachers, parents, and industry began applying his instruments and procedures and later, his theory of Structural Cognitive Modifiability.

A unique contribution to post-positivist approaches, is Feuerstein's dynamic interactional mediation assessment process. Whether used for assessment or in the classroom, mediated learning experiences are known as "proximal factors". He requires more than silent observation and the collection of work samples. In addition, he does not advocate a cold, detached laboratory approach. As a distinction, Feuerstein introduces a positive disequilibrium and then provides supportive mediation until insight and resolution are attained. An energetic delivery is used both in the assessment and learning phases of intervention. He is seeking a measure of cognitive modifiability, supported by dynamic mediated interactions. These practices are a distinct departure from positivist approaches.

Feuerstein insists that mediated assessments and interventions must be true to theoretical underpinnings, applied systematically in interventions, and eventually provide feedback to theory. Through years of scholarly practice in this line of scholarship, seemingly stable inductive understandings have been synthesized. The result was his formulation of the theory of Structural Cognitive Modifiability. Even today, Feuerstein and associates (1997) consider the theory as still in development. Feuerstein and Rand insist that "It is neither rarefied nor set in stone" (1994).

4 The Feuerstein Legacies

Feuerstein's legacies are numerous and varied, and will hopefully continue to unfold in the future. The first three of the following four legacies demonstrate the range of his contributions to science, philosophy, and theory applied. Finally, we will turn to the personal legacy of this remarkable man and his family, who shared their home with us. One meets few creative, intuitive geniuses in life. Professor Reuven Feuerstein is one in this select company.

4.1 Legacy of Theory Development

What compels a person to discount orthodox educational systems, and to seek positive, but heretofore unknown alternatives? Does a person set out to create seminal works, or is it that through pursuing an inquiring, scholarly path such products emerge? This is up for discussion. Some argue that it is the context and times in which one experiences life that molds the creative mind to produce novel and outstanding works. Others argue that at some point the creative genius reverses common intellectual passivity. The intellect becomes the instrument that acts upon conditions in life and through synergy creates new systems. Regardless of the validity of these differing arguments, Feuerstein produced a new paradigm out of the ashes of classic philosophers, fanned the new embers of dynamic interactions, and called for the recognition of the vital place of tradition and heritage logic in human development. This paradigm required humans to consider a new world-and-life-view with novel dimensions.

For most of the twentieth century, Feuerstein accepted and relished this challenge. First, reaching back into classical philosophy, he required the teacher mediator to become active, reasoned practitioners. These dynamic, mediated interactions required mediators to access multiple realms of representational thought and encourage applications to scientific, heritage, and experiential content. Furthermore, Feuerstein delineated "ways of seeing and of not seeing". He argued that possibilities and potentials existed beyond common psychometric measures. Humans were more than stimulus response beings who rely on others to mold and make their decisions. Feuerstein contends human limitations exist because of a lack of mediated learning experiences. Unmediated individuals have been denied access to the reasoned, survival skills preserved in their culture's ethnologic or tradition. Thus when individuals do not know how to problem solve or to gain access to privilege and goods within their culture, they are deprived of their culture.

This legacy expanded when Feuerstein conceptualized a cognitive framework and an interactive mediation system that enabled autoplastic development. This approach required temporal continuity and strengthened representational thought. Through the extrapolation of transcendent principles, the student emerges from "episodic grasps of reality" to seeing relationships, patterns, and systems.

Similar to Piaget's field research approach but focused on different intent, Feuerstein field-tested his hypotheses, mediated strategies, and materials with various populations. Feuerstein integrated and synthesized the findings. He studied responses through the cognitive framework and formulated additional hypotheses. Once again these were field-tested by teachers, researchers, and parents. When "child change" occurred, the types of interactions and behaviors were analyzed against his framework and theory. Eventually through the process of synergy, Reuven Feuerstein birthed and fashioned a new paradigm.

When asked about how he as a theorist explained the path leading to the development of the theory of Structural Cognitive Modifiability, Feuerstein (1996) offered a sequential developmental path. "Conceptualizations begin by recognizing the condition of human need in an authentic learning place. First, it is necessary to gather data in a systematic way. The next step is to invest cognitively by going beyond the details or elements that have been gathered, in other words, to assess the data from a higher representational level or through another component of the cognitive map. Then the investigator must find the common denominator to which the factor(s) in the sample show pattern similarity or seem related linearly. Which parts seem essential? Which elements seem redundant? Which aspects seem without meaning?" Feuerstein then analyzes the efforts through reductionism, a process of reducing complex data to simple terms. Finally, these steps lead to the emergence of a theory that links the various elements together.

After analysis of the findings from the field-tested practices, the theory and its components are conveyed to larger audiences with different interests. The theorist then assesses elements that achieve different levels of acceptance. From feedback derived from these larger audiences, Feuerstein reflects and once again tests against "reality" in the field. Data is gathered from samples and the theorist engages in inferences and hypothesis building.

The complexities of theory development are intricate, complex, and energy consuming. Reuven Feuerstein's legacy as a theory developer is extraordinary.

4.2 Centrality of the Child to the Whole Legacy

"The real battle was fought by me and my colleagues for the child, and in favor of the child … For many years my colleagues and I were considered as iconoclasts. We were fighting against some things considered valid. There were issues they believed in. Why not rely on the Intelligence Quotient? Why do I have to bring my doubts? If the reality does not correspond to the test, let it be. This reality is unfortunate. We can't help it."

"We have been confronted with problems and we have attempted to solve them.

By doing so we have built systems that have enabled us to go beyond (an) individual. We went to the issues related to the present problems." (Reuven Feuerstein taped response to inquiries 4/1996)

To Feuerstein, what is the meaning of an individual or a child? Particularly, why is his belief about the value of a child considered to be such a significant component of his legacy? To Feuerstein, it is only through the child that private and public heritage tradition or ethnologic can be transmitted into the future. The child is the prime culture bearer, the hope of all people who live or have lived in past times. Each child becomes a fresh opportunity to mold and to shape through mediated learning experiences, both knowledge and dispositions of the mind and spirit.

Playmates in Botosani, youngsters in the Transylvania work camps, and youth in Bucharest were valued because they held this promise. Subsequently, children from the prison camps, young immigrants from a plethora of countries, and young Moroccan children were worthy of investment, because they alone could carry forward a reasoned and principled tradition.

Then came the challenge of valuing the children labeled with pre-existing conditions. Until now, these hereditary and acquired conditions were associated with limited potentials and were treated by isolation in segregated classrooms and even by institutionalization. But Feuerstein demanded normalization of settings, and enriched curricula with skilled mediators. "Not one more child could be lost."

Feuerstein's recognition of the child's inherent worth, prompted societies to reevaluate the status of the child to the whole. Those societies who do not value the child as the prime culture bearer will not know the strength of interrelational bonds. They cannot continue to sustain transcendent human values because they do not comprehend the central role of the child as a transmitter of their culture, especially their ways of making meanings. The children, in turn, suffer from the absence of intergenerational mediated learning experiences. The centrality of the child to the whole legacy is about the survival of humankind.

4.3 Legacy of Products, Tools, and Process

In the twentieth century several notable theorists emerged to extend the parameters of thought. Most of these new constructs were developed in laboratories and became entities unto themselves. In other words, the theorists did not bridge the gap between theory and practice.

Feuerstein not only developed the theory of Structural Cognitive Modifiability, he conceptualized assessments, curricular applications, and an interactive pedagogy that served as companions to his theory of Structural Cognitive Modifiability. In essence, Feuerstein developed a system with dynamic components. This is quite an extraordinary legacy.

First, the LPAD has individual and group formats. Through videotaped mediated experiences, parents and teachers gain insights relating to the mode through which change occurs, information about the cognitive functions and dysfunctions, and learning suggestions for home and mediated classroom interventions.

The second product, the IE program is unique in many ways. IE teaches prerequisites for learning in a technical society. But the IE program also provides for transference of abstract principles of reasoning or behavior into school curricular areas and cross cultural applications. Feuerstein calls this aspect of the lesson "bridging." In the latter part of the twentieth century, other "thinking programs" have come on the market. None have reached the distinction of the IE program, however. Most of them are selections of materials that teach dispositions of thinking. Other "thinking methods" attempt to infuse "thinking" into the content area, but they miss Feuerstein's key interactive mediation strategies that provide the energy to change cognitive structures. Thus, Reuven Feuerstein's legacy through his integrated systems approach is a distinct and powerful achievement.

4.4 Legacy of the Person

Legacies and legends followed Reuven Feuerstein for most of the twentieth century. Legends and stories set a rich story grammar from his early days in Romania. Others were added through the years. Each story seems to have multiple meanings beyond the obvious storyline. Reuven is a master at storytelling. His face animates, his arms and hands make grand gestures, and voice timbre rises and falls. This gift he shares with his family and friends.

Another talent is his melodious, booming baritone voice. From singing extemporaneously with a touring Porgy and Bess drama group, serving as a cantor in the synagogue, or listening to Bach's Etudes, Feuerstein participates in the fullness of life, which he enjoys to the full.

Politically and spiritually, Feuerstein maintains his vision of a restored Zion, a time and place of peace, reasoning, and principled behavior. He is a patriot, who mourns that some may have lost either their vision or their commitment. Reuven reminds citizens in the worldwide community about the meaning of the city of peace, Jerusalem. It is more than coincidental that the final training of the trainers phase must be completed in this city.

The ultimate legacy Reuven and Berta Feuerstein leave are their four children and numerous grandchildren. As Rafi, the oldest son, said, "The theory was birthed in our bones. Even for a small trip from Jerusalem to Tel Aviv, both my mother and father continued to mediate the meanings of everything we saw." This continues with the grandchildren. The Feuersteins believe that the grandparents are vital culture bearers to successful intergenerational transmissions of ethnologic.

Feuerstein, having substantial cognitive power and a high energy level, rises early and begins his dictation while the city is wrapped in darkness. His office hours are full of energetic interactions, interrupted by frequent international calls. There are always children who are to be assessed or evaluated. Colleagues collaborate with him on projects. Dignitaries make appearances. Yet, everything stops if one of the children comes to his door in distress. Feuerstein walks over, bends over gently, looks the child directly in the eyes, and says, "Tell me, what are you thinking?"

The Feuersteins of Jerusalem continue to have an "Open Door" house, similar to the Aharon Feuersteins of Botosani. Instead of the physically and emotionally weary travelers and passers by of war-torn eastern Europe, now from around the world, families accompanied by children with problems, scholars, philanthropists, and curious citizens come, peer through their open door. Not surprisingly, a high percentage of these eventually will accept the theory of Structural Cognitive Modifiability and Feuerstein's applied practices.

5 Summary

Although geophysical, political, and societal conditions often changed, in each period of Reuven Feuerstein's life, he and his colleagues continued to meet human needs. While others retreated or were blocked by adversity, Feuerstein savored these opportunities, and far exceeded normal expectations.

Like philosophers of old, Feuerstein searches for the precipitating inquiry questions that will stimulate understanding of reasoned behavior. Through reflection and metacognition, the learner is led to understand the many facets of cognition. Through the processes encouraging insight and bridging, the student's learning potentials expand. Finally, from an ethical position, Feuerstein protests the absurdity of removing values from study.

With disintegrating social systems, Feuerstein again provides a positive alternative. Through the assistance of a mediator and intergenerational community, individuals are encouraged to set personal identity, relational and task oriented goals. The theory of Structural Cognitive Modifiability is about hope, dignity, and positive potentials even beyond present dreams. It is "The Principle of the Possible".

As with all humans, Feuerstein has been framed by his times. But he has never been content to be limited by time, place, or circumstance. Rather, with lofty vision, boundless vigor, creative thought, and abiding commitment to positive traditions Reuven Feuerstein continues to impact his world as few others of the twentieth century.

2

Science, Pedagogy and Ethics in Feuerstein's Theory and Applications*

Charles Hadji
Professor, Pierre Mendes-France University, Grenoble 2

In the world of education and training, the works of Reuven Feuerstein have filled certain people with enthusiasm and evoked great hope. These works raised the question as to the possibility of developing intelligence in all individuals, even those who appeared to be severely deprived or systematically underachieving. Each spectacular success, however, prompts further questions regarding the person's conditions, even his very essence. In fact these cases, while raising hope in some people, evoke skepticism in others; at times Feuerstein's work has been subject to fierce criticism. Attempts have been made to show that the results of the application of the cognitive remedial program (Instrumental Enrichment) were much less impressive than those promised by the promoters of the program and that the idea of cognitive educability was merely an illusion.

The question is how to offer an unprejudiced and objective appraisal of Feuerstein's contribution and of the precise effect of his work. How can one avoid using either excessive praise which would be little short of hagiography, or bitter criticism that would only be malicious? There seems to be one way and that is to check how Feuerstein's propositions are supported and clarified in our own research. This, of course, offers no guarantee of impartiality and/or objectiveness, as we both could have been victims of the same illusions and be equally far from truth and reality. It is for this reason that a presentation of possible convergence between our position and that of Feuerstein must include consideration of this relationship itself. Thus the possibility of presenting proof regarding Feuerstein's work will, consequently, include an investigation of the validity of our own analyses!

In actual fact, however, although this has not been sufficiently noted to date, Feuerstein's work was not conducted within only one domain, i.e. scientific research, where the truth can be established (as far as possible) through the construction of an adequate theoretical model and the obtaining of proof. Three different fields are involved in Feuerstein's work. The first is scientific, the second pedagogical, the third ethical. Feuerstein has proposed a theory of the development

*French original: *Reuven Feuerstein, Théoricien, Explorateur et Témoin de la Perfectibilité Humaine: Science, Pédagogie et Ethique*, Charles Hadji, Professeur, Université Pierre Mendes-France Grenoble 2.

and functioning of human cognition (the scientific aspect); practical instruments aimed at promoting development and learning through improved cognitive functioning (the pedagogical aspect), and finally, and perhaps most important of all, he prompted reflection regarding the legitimacy and the meaning of an educational action (the contribution to educational ethics), from which the other two aspects can be put into perspective and ultimately be appraised.

This is why these few pages aim at affirming that it would be a pure reductionism to question works belonging to one particular dimension, by using requirements which would only be relevant elsewhere: For instance to question Instrumental Enrichment (IE), as a pedagogical practice, for the sake of proving a scientific hypothesis on cognitive functioning. Additionally, if any stance were to be a major determinant in the comprehension of Feuerstein's work as a whole, overcoming the risk of reductionism which we denounced above, it would be an ethical stance because it unites all the three distinct dimensions. The first two models — the cognitive development model and the efficient pedagogical action model — take on a meaning within an ethical view of inter-human relations. We will, in fact, examine each of the three dimensions (scientific, pedagogical and ethical) in order to try and appraise Feuerstein's contribution.

1 Feuerstein, Theoretician of Human Perfectibility: the Validity of a Model of Cognitive Development

It is clear that Feuerstein is a theoretician and that theory is not the least interesting aspect of his work. One can place his contribution into the context of a grand debate between psychologists holding different views regarding the respective importance and role of learning vs. development. Discussing this question in a text written between 1933 and 1934, Vygotsky (1935) distinguishes three major groups of theories before going on to propose his own model. For the first group development precedes learning. The two processes are perceived as being independent with learning following the process of development and benefiting from it. Teaching can only follow the development without being able to influence it in any significant way. Vygotsky considered this to be Piaget's stance. In a second group of theories, learning coincides with development. It is development itself. The laws of development are the natural laws which cannot be changed by teaching. Both processes develop simultaneously. For each advance in one dimension, there is a corresponding advance in another. And finally in a third group, though the two processes are considered being independent, they are nevertheless mutually conditioned. There is an interaction between maturation and learning. Maturation leads the way facilitating learning, while learning stimulates and causes maturation to progress. In this way these theories endorse the role of learning throughout a child's development. One can go as far as to perceive all specific learning as empowered by general development. In any case it is thought that learning is never simply specific and is quasi-automatically reflected on other abilities. Vygotsky suggests a fourth path based on the critique of the notion of general mental capacity and the idea of a non-specific effect. To him learning activates development. Both processes are linked in an original manner from the earliest days of one's life.

There is also education at a pre-school age and here two decisive factors must be taken into consideration. Learning always occurs in relation to the child's developmental level. For each developmental level there is a corresponding level of "learning potential". Thus, two levels of development must, therefore be considered. Current development, which corresponds to a level of performance which the child is capable of reaching alone, and the potential development which is implied by the performance level attained with the help of adults. The distance between the two is defined as the zone of proximal development (Vygotsky, 1935). In this way teaching can precede development, or, in Vygotsky's terminology, it will activate or arouse it. Learning activates mental development by arousing the processes of change. School learning arouses internal processes of development but development is not an automatic product of learning. Vygotsky writes that we should imagine a dynamic relationship of inter-dependence between the two processes and from this viewpoint understand that certain learning (of basic subjects) have greater power to bring about developmental change, e.g. learning to write contributes more to the development than learning to type.

We cannot overlook the connection between these notions and those of Feuerstein regarding at least three points. Firstly, the possibility of activating the development process. The existence of a potential capacity for development overlooked in classical assessment tests and the conviction that if all learning does not necessarily have a general, non-specific developmental effect, certain prudently chosen activities can, nevertheless, have a strong effect and thus some tasks have a higher developmental value. The inadequacy of standard tests prompted Feuerstein to develop the Learning Potential Assessment Device (LPAD). We do not intend here to make Feuerstein a disciple of Vygotsky, but rather to show how his theoretical work deals with the same problems that were debated by Vygotsky and others in their era. Feuerstein's work can thus be located within this context of fundamental scientific research.

Is this work scientifically acceptable? This is the only question which should be asked at this point. It would not be serious to appraise its scientific validity by "measuring" the efficiency of an applied program based on the particular scientific theory. Of course, as Feuerstein himself affirms, IE is the "result of a theory". However the possible "verification" of the practical efficiency of a program does not contribute more to the scientific value of the theory, than the absence of practical efficiency to the refutation of it. As wisely pointed out by Buchel (1990, p. 83), insignificant practical results would certainly not signify that the program is inefficient, but rather that the intervention conducted within the given framework has led to given results. At best, only the efficiency of a program can be proved, not its inefficiency. And this would not prove the scientific value of the ideas which inspired the program. The fields of knowledge and action are different.

Under conditions such as these, what can be said of the scientific validity of the theories formulated by Feuerstein? The function of all theories is to account for reality by offering an adequate model. A theory offers the answer to a dual question — how is reality (the object of scientific research) structured? And how does it operate? So which reality are we referring to here? The Human Being as he/she develops and learns. This is what is discussed here. It is clear why from the outset we find ourselves at the heart of the development/learning debate. A basic anthropology should be constructed and the essence of Man should be accounted for. The 20th century anthropological debate evolved round the question of what should be the nature of Man for him to be able to develop and learn? Feuerstein answered that Man is a modifiable being endowed with the propensity to learn. Development and learning are facts. The scientific problem is to construct a model of Man which will incorporate these facts. The model should allow us to scientifically discuss modifiability, its scope and limits, as well as the scope of learning ability possessed by every individual. The first discussion should focus on the issue of the relationship between heredity and the environment. The second raises the question of intelligence. In these two debates, as far as we can tell (Hadji, 1992), Feuerstein's position is scientifically acceptable for us. He claims that plasticity is the primary characteristic of an underachieving individual, and he rejects reification of intelligence. Feuerstein's theory that presents cognitive modifiability as a "characteristic which is unique to Man" (Feuerstein, 1990, p. 121) and which concerns itself with the "structural nature of modifiability" — accounts particularly well for the essential adaptability of Man. In this way Feuerstein observes and describes the ability particular to Man to change the structures within which he "functions", i.e. to build up new abilities, especially cognitive ones. What is described here is the ability to change which is the root of both development and learning. It is that "ability of the individual to change" aiming towards "different modalities of functioning" (id., p. 123) which is the first of the anthropological universals. To a certain extent we return here to the problem encountered by Piaget, to whom variable structures are formed in the course of constant functioning. At the heart of development lie common functional mechanisms which are translated into constant movement, perpetual readjustment and balancing which "engender" successive mental structures. However, Feuerstein goes a step further or rather deeper, reaching for the root of development in speaking about "structural modifiability" which is a "fundamental process of change" that has a "self-perpetual nature". The change of which Man is capable does not consist simply of the content he attributes to thought, but also of instruments to act upon this content which is the cognitive structures. The change does not relate merely to performance but also (and particularly) to abilities which contain an essential cognitive dimension.

The fact that fundamental "automodifiability" (Feuerstein, 1990, p. 133) of Man (every human being is modifiable) is translated into changes which predominantly occur in the cognitive structures, does not mean that Man is reduced to his cognitive dimension. The cognitive factor cannot be separated from the emotional factor (Feuerstein, 1996, p. 23). The cognitive factor is merely an auxiliary of the affective factor in so much as it plays an essential role in the genesis of affective elements (Feuerstein, 1990, p. 122). The aim of IE is to reach the affective factor via the cognitive, for ultimately, as we ourselves have written (Hadji, 1994, p. 194) the affective is the driving force of change. IE aims at reaching the cognitive factor in order to create "the vigorous affective modalities which direct, orient and guide the behavior of individuals" (Feuerstein, 1990, p. 123). The aim is to create a "sensitivity" which allows for the use of all our life-experience in order to "undergo continual modification" (id., p. 124). Cognitive modifiability is just an aspect of a fundamental human modifiability in which affect constitutes the driving force. By the same token the "propensity to learn" is just a dynamic dimension of the "need to modify oneself" (ibid). We know that in need Piaget saw the source of all human action, whether physical or mental.

It is therefore precisely the "ability of the human being to undergo constant modification" (id., p. 151), which is expressed in the dual dimension of development and learning, that Feuerstein's theoretical analysis wishes to account for. It is in this dynamic perspective that he analyzes the mental act, as organized around seven parameters. What we call intelligence is perceived as propensity thus challenging naturalistic and substantialist conceptions. His theoretical vision of the human being, is therefore doubly coherent. The internal coherence relates to the model constructed around the essential ability of human beings to develop themselves. (This model includes the notions of modifiability, potential and propensity.) This "internal" coherence has a perfect correspondence to the "external" coherence in the framework of major contemporary debates on the relationships between development and learning and findings of cognitive anthropology. From this point of view Feuerstein is a theoretician of the human being and in this anthropological dimension the scientific value of his work, given the present state of knowledge, is beyond doubt.

2 Feuerstein as an Explorer of Human Perfectibility: the Productivity of a Model of Educational Action

Feuerstein is known mainly through his applied program of Instrumental Enrichment (IE). So should not his work be appraised primarily via this program? But how does one appraise a program? Based on which requirements and which criteria?

Pondering the true relationship of the educational act (Hadji, 1998), we proposed that a praxeological model of action should aim at efficiency whilst adhering to a philosophical model which ideally represents our goals, and being compatible to a scientific model, which, for our purposes here, represents the human being as he is. The praxeological model is an ideal representation of a dynamic process which, under certain conditions allows one to advance from the presently real to ideal state. We will also examine adherence of action to a philosophical ideal. Firstly, however, we will examine the problems of compatibility between the scientific aspect of action and its efficiency.

When Feuerstein insists that IE is theory-based, it is precisely the necessary compatibility between the praxeological discourse and the scientific discourse that he wishes to emphasize. In a sense the concrete device translates the theory. However, we must not fall into the trap here of the idea of a direct application of the theory in practice. Such an idea could make theory and practice the guardians and the witnesses of each other's validity. The scientificity of the theory would then be taken as a guarantee of the pertinence of practice and the ultimate efficiency of practice could be taken as a guarantee of the scientificity of the theory. But it is an illusion to believe in the possibility of education based on scientific theory. A science can never establish a practice and it is never possible to deduce a pedagogy from a science. As Avanzini (1985, p. 183) writes, a descending and deductivist vision (from science to practice) is wrong here. It is impossible to advance from a register of knowledge to a register of action without causing a rupture. Science can never say anything other than what already exists. The future goals and what should be done to achieve these goals is something which escapes science. This is why the efficiency (or inefficiency) of a model of action cannot serve for the inference of the validity (or invalidity) of a scientific model which ultimately "establishes" this action. One can be the source of the other, but this is neither a relationship of deduction, nor one of justification. The former (the model of action) should be compatible with the latter (the scientific model). From a scientific point of view, this is all we can demand of a model of action — that it not be in contradiction with scientific data. Action can be judicious — but it should not pretend to be scientific.

In fact, when Feuerstein affirms that the Instrumental Enrichment program "applies" a theory, he is referring to the theory of mediation (1990, p. 152), but this is already a pedagogical (rather than a scientific) theory. It focuses on the manner in which the human being is able to develop or to free his potential, as Carl Rogers would have said. How, then, can the non "deductive" link be established between the scientific theory of the human being as an essentially modifiable entity and the praxeological theory of mediation as a factor of development within which IE features as an aid program?

The first connection is undoubtedly the emergent awareness of the "practical" importance of the concept of "modifiability". If Man is modifiable then we can make every effort to save, accompany, free, arouse — if such should be the case — his ability to develop, which is the dynamic side of modifiability. We will see further on that an ethical demand will prompt us to conclude that this must be done. The concept of modifiability opens up a perspective of action. Feuerstein is very assertive on this point: "if you think that Man is modifiable ... then you will be researchers, creative people to find a prop" for that modifiability (1990, p. 165). We consider Feuerstein to be the prototype of these creative men: an explorer of modifiability, a seeker of susceptible conditions which will allow him the best course of action. It is in this sense that scientific theory can "establish" a practice — by firstly allowing one to think that this is possible, by somehow beckoning to it. However, in actual fact, the beckoning is entirely ethical.

Therefore the theory of modifiability is a natural invitation to seek modalities appropriate to promoting change, i.e. realizing the potential for development. The logical follow-up is to give thought to the conditions of development which begins with research into these factors. Nevertheless, this research is still scientific as it always describes and explains reality. On this point Feuerstein proposes a theory of factors of development which, remarkably, join up with Rousseau's theory of the three "masters". To Rousseau, education comes from Nature or Man or Things. The first is made up of the internal development of our faculties and our organs; the second is made up of the use we are taught to make of this development, and the third of what we acquire from our experience of things. One could term this maturation, social modeling and individual experience. Feuerstein also distinguishes three factors — organism with its hereditary features and maturation; direct experience of the world in the active interaction with the environment; and mediated experience or interaction through a mediator (1990, pp. 154 & 155). The third major factor will decisively orient the organism/ environment dialectic toward the action of "mediator" and provide an "orientation" which is fundamental to development and creates its essential "diversification". It is the quality and quantity of mediated experience that Feuerstein perceives as an explanatory factor of individual differences which manifest themselves in development and learning.

This is why the notion of mediation becomes pivotal in the analysis of educational facts. Feuerstein, himself, talks of a theory of mediation, i.e. mediating action. This is the point where we diverge from the truly scientific field and enter praxeology. Asking himself about the conditions of change, Feuerstein identifies three:

1. Understanding that Man is "modifiable" and becoming familiar with each individual's potential and abilities through a process of dynamic assessment (the precise objective of LPAD).
2. Causing subjects whose potential to develop is thus recognized, to benefit from explicit mediating intervention. In fact one can distinguish explicit mediating intervention in which a mediator intentionally places himself between the stimuli of the environment and the individual (this intention is the primary criterion of mediation), and implicit mediating interaction which corresponds to the creation of an environment which promotes mediation.
3. Shaping the environment in such a way that it becomes modifying in a sense that it creates an awareness toward modifiability and conditions necessary for change (id. p. 144).

So must the environment have specific conditions? And are they of the type that will render useless the actions of an explicit mediator? One could say that what is important is the quality of the interactions which have become possible thanks to the environment. But what is an interaction that provides a quality of experience? (A valid question, in fact, for both the environment and the individual mediator.)

Clearly it is impossible to determine scientifically what makes up the quality of mediation. A formal answer to this question would undoubtedly be that the quality of interaction is primarily determined by the presence of mediation. The notion of deprivation is also understood as an absence of mediation in this manner. The insufficiency of interaction is, in itself, a negative factor especially when affecting child-parents interactions at an early age. Unfavorable family integration or unfavorable integration in one's own culture lead to a deficit in mediated learning experience. In this respect we can talk of educationally weak environments which tend to be translated into individual cognitive deficiencies. And from this stems the idea that as insufficient exposure to mediating experience has engendered cultural deprivation (social aspect) and/or cognitive deficiency (individual aspect) which can be corrected by appropriate exposure — in quality and quantity — to mediated learning. In this way each individual's potential for development could be revived or restored. However, this revival, made plausible by the theory of development, can only be proved through experience. Educational action must organize itself in such a way as to show that it is possible to "revive intelligence" in a concrete way.

But to do this the participants in the educational process must be familiar with the nature of the quality interactions which they must establish. The formal answer, i.e. that an interaction should take place is the first step. However a content must be added to this formal definition. At first it can be understood that interaction has quality when it has a goal. What is the goal? To offer a structural change, increase the modifiability of the individual, contributing in this way to the emergence of a "creative being" (id. p. 131). In aspiring to adaptability, mediating action takes on the aim of saving and developing this ability. This is why, in a certain way, the ideal lies in reality. The aim of educational action is to make Man conform to his very essence. If Man is modifiable, everything which contributes to "maintaining" this modifiability can be perceived as positive. The ideal model of Man, as a goal of educational action, can only be the model of a Man who is ideally developed. In order to claim to making a contribution to the development of intelligence, it is necessary to first understand the logic of development.

But this is not enough. As we have just seen the scientific model of modifiable Man can contribute towards a definition of the goal of educational work, but it tells us nothing of the concrete nature of this work. A model of practical action must be elaborated, thereby giving a more precise content to the notion of "quality" of the interaction. Feuerstein proposes here an analysis of educational action, bringing to the fore three "partners" in interaction: Mediator, mediatee, material, much like the famous didactic triangle — teacher, pupil, knowledge (id. p. 130).

The *Mediatee* is not just a mere consumer of information or data. If the mediation is effective, he becomes a self-evolving actor. This is normal considering that the goal of mediation is to arouse the potential he possesses by virtue of his basic modifiability. This is why it is possible to imagine mediation without an external mediator (implicit mediation). It is this situation which promotes the individual's "automodifiability" (id. p. 133).

The *Material* is to the mediatee only one element of the situation and this is why he should not make a fetish of the object. Of course, to Feuerstein the IE program is important. But, he himself, affirms "that one can live without IE, in fact one can live well without it" (id. p. 136). There is no compulsory material. The content matter can be diversified, the language different (oral, gesticulatory, written). Language may even be absent. A series of wordless acts may suffice. And IE cannot be a desert island isolated from the other continents of meaning: knowledge or cultural elements. The mediator must bridge the material to the world of knowledge. So why must there be a "program"? And what exactly does it aim at? A program is needed to organize the environment.

IE represents an "effort to organize situations" to lend mediational value to the interaction. Stimuli to which the subject is exposed must be channeled and fixed within certain boundaries to prevent drowning in them. The mediator's primary task lies in making that effort to organize, to put it concretely, to construct the material, for if the "human environment" is the "mediator *par excellence*" (id. p. 143), the reality of mediation lies in the possibility of real interaction between the subject and the situation, which implies a certain number of conditions (Feuerstein's twelve criteria of MLE). At the very least it will be incumbent upon the mediator to arrange the surroundings and to explicitly include himself in the environment/individual interaction through the use of appropriate material, thereby turning implicit mediation into explicit mediation.

So, IE aims at enhancing thought activity and the formation of central cognitive skills through an appropriate system of exercises which are systematic, abstractive and correspond to generalized mental tools. It is therefore the systematicity and the orientation towards the essential and the generalizable which characterizes the material which Feuerstein, the explorer of modifiability, placed at the disposal of mediators.

The *Mediator* plays a major role in the interaction. It is he who orients the environment/individual dialectic and this is why social interaction plays a very important "formative" role, in human development. The mediator is animated by specific intentionality. This intentionality is the first criteria of mediation. We know that the goal of IE is to "rekindle" the person's modifiability. Because of this the dominant intention of the mediator is to equip the mediatee with the essential prerequisites for success in the learning tasks (id. p. 129). For this reason IE aims at cognitive functioning and concerns itself, above all, not with content, but with tools which will act upon the content.

Finally the mediator is characterized by his "active modifying attitude" (id. p. 140). He exerts pressure toward change. He does not content himself with the present state of the mediatee. He is demanding. His effective, emotional and cognitive commitment is manifested by the fact that he will not hesitate to impose meaning. Feuerstein writes: "There is no such thing as a good neutral education" (id. p. 163). This is not a eulogy to partiality, merely the opposition to the "passive accepting attitude" (id. p. 140). Mediation is the opposite to abandonment. Pressure is applied. Impositions are committed. However, imposing meanings within a context of mediation (i.e. of exchange and thought, metacognitive distancing) the mediator fosters the mediatee's need for meaning and provides him with the means to investigate and construct his own meanings.

So what is it, in actual fact, that makes the quality of an interaction? The answer could be given in terms of conditions of possibility. Firstly, to speak of quality of interaction is to avoid being imprisoned by the content. The material is less important than the intention served by it. Secondly, the quality of interaction attracts attention to the principal idea: that of organizing the conditions of possible modifiability (its ingredients, writes Feuerstein) in order to use them where modifiability is not (yet) evident. It is in this way that theoretical research (on the conditions of development) clarifies practical "research". One could quite reasonably assume that by organizing these conditions the development can be enhanced. A general condition is the existence of permanent change at the core of the mediator/material/mediatee triangle. It is in this way that we understand Feuerstein's claim that "the message of mediation will be considered to have been accomplished when a veritable closed circuit is established between the three partners" (id. p. 160). This change will modify the mediator as well as the mediatee. The material itself will then have to evolve so as not to fetter the functioning of the "circuit". And no material is, in itself, absolutely and definitely appropriate. Practical research will point to the appropriate material and it is here that science falls mute. Finding handy materials and a "bricolage" technique becomes a necessity, particularly in selecting exercises focused on mental tools. However, *a priori*, there is no certainty. One must imagine, seek, construct, try and explore. Feuerstein has acted exactly like an explorer. It could be said that, paradoxically, IE represents a weak point in the proposed model of educational action. However, as we have seen, Feuerstein himself helps us to understand why. Any program could never be anything but a temporary setback in the effort to organize the environment and lend it a mediating value. It is the effort to organize that is essential. The exploration of possible tools can never end and it is in reference to this effort that the work of Feuerstein, the explorer of modifiability, should be appraised, and not just within the context of the battery of IE tools in its set form.

These thoughts allow us to place the problem of the evaluation of IE's efficiency into perspective and to be concise on this point. We have explained elsewhere (Hadji, 1996) why IE was worthy of "smart" evaluation with an aim to understanding what happened when it is applied and not only "measuring" its efficiency. It seems obvious that a strictly experimental assessment is impossible here and a quasi-experimental assessment can only clear up uncertain causal imputations. On the other hand it is no longer possible to consider a method as an independent explanatory variable with which one could objectively appraise the effects. Moreover mediation should never be reduced to a fixed material where application, given time, would be mechanical and self-resembling. The mediator's action largely transcends the simple use of the material. This should not lead us to refusal to assess the program — which would be a dubious decision, but rather to refusal to be caught in the assessment trap — be it in the form of control or of settling of accounts which would be no more than the responsible administration of educational practices. We say "yes" to assessment, but on condition that our questions, area of observation and tools become significantly expanded by shifting the goal of assessment from that of recording the measurable effects of the "program", to exploring the process of application. The "program" thereby changes its status. From an accountable object it becomes an object which offers the opportunity to learn and understand. The concrete exploration of modifiability promoted by IE, in turn, definitely has an effect on the work of theoretical modeling which it made possible. The effort of acting upon Man allows one to be better acquainted with him. If knowledge clarifies action, action, in turn, becomes revealed as a producer of knowledge.

3 Feuerstein: the Value of an Ethical Attitude

We see finally that there is a central idea in Feuerstein's thought and actions — the idea of human perfectibility. Feuerstein does not use this term. We know that it was proposed by Rousseau to designate what he felt to be the distinctive feature of the human species: the faculty to perfect oneself, which, he writes, aided by circumstance, successively develops all others and dwells both within the species and within the individual. However, in Feuerstein's work everything points to the fact that he focuses on the ability of the human being to perfect oneself, that his effort of theoretical modeling shows that perfectibility is the very essence of the human being and that a model of educational action should be considered a goal. For, if Man is perfectible then perfectibility should be considered a central goal in all action concerning Man. Why should this be so? And this is where we approach a third dimension — the ethical one.

In fact, science can only describe Man as he is and pedagogy can only imagine and design the conditions which could allow it to achieve the best from what Man is. But as it is, the determination of the ultimate goal of educational action escapes both. If it appears "logical" to take Man himself, in his essence, as the goal of organized action enabling him to develop, other goals could also be envisaged. For example the development of communities with Man becoming no more than a means to perpetuate the group and losing his self-purpose. The choice of a goal which goes hand in hand with the specification of a model of the positive development of the human being raises philosophical considerations regarding what philosophers have called "supreme good", in other words worth. What is worth being promoted absolutely? Is it absolutely desirable? This is the question which is answered by the choice of a model of positive development. In order to design the necessary conditions, pedagogy must respond to this question; but the nature of the answer which will, in fact, lend a significance to the pedagogical action, does not really belong to pedagogy proper. The humanistic response is not the only foreseeable one but we would willingly say that, ethically speaking, it is the only possible one. And why?

Because the decision to make of Man an objective in itself, in our opinion, constitutes the *basic ethical decision*. Nothing compels one to decide. We could content ourselves with passively submitting to events, and slipping into a "passive accepting attitude". Here there is a first basic choice, not determined by any simply scientific or pragmatic reason. It is the choice to be an actor and not just a spectator. An agency of action, not just an object. Evidently, this is a choice which has been made by Feuerstein and this testifies to perfectibility.

This decision is an *ethical* one. What, therefore, is ethical? The search for principles which can guide action absolutely. The search for indisputable reasons to act. Etymologically, ethics signifies the science of morality, but in actual fact, morality is not a science and an ethical problem cannot receive a scientific answer. Should we pursue Good? On this point science is silent. Each one to his own, but in terms of what? In terms of what he feels is worthy of being desired and pursued — worthy of being an absolute objective in human action. Feuerstein's answer to this is clear. It can only be Man himself, in so much as he is capable of developing. As we ourselves have said, he who is worthy as a person never restricts himself to his present state (Hadji, 1992). Worth emerges from and in existence, however it goes beyond simple existence. Man is worthy because he has the potential to go beyond all existential form. He is only worthy because he is where ethical demands can be understood to develop and to surpass themselves.

An ethical decision is a *fundamental* one. Everything is connected from this point. We could very well decide not to serve Man but to destroy him. However to make the choice in favor of Man (a free choice, an essential choice, a choice which can always be remade), is to think that Man is worthy and to try to understand why. Basic positive orientation, translated by an attempt at scientific theorization to see if Man is what is expected of him or what we imagine him to be — dare we say — as we believe, perfectible. Capable of worse but also of better. And if the scientific model makes perfectibility both perceptible and intelligible, the choice of performing a goal-oriented action (a second choice compared to the choice of acting instead of submitting) which is no more compulsory than the former, becomes more coherent with it, strengthening it. It will help to find the necessary force to construct and set up a program of Instrumental Enrichment.

In this way the essential coherence of a life and of an act which take on an ethical sense can be seen from the free decision to serve Man. This places will in the foreground. Feuerstein's life itself testifies to the importance of will as a primary force and consequently a primary virtue of Man. The will to be a man, in other words an actor of, and within one's own life. The will to act in the service to mankind. The will to account for this human force which will appear in scientific works. The will to invent a program which will allow for the realization of this will in the form of pedagogical works.

To Feuerstein, "Man is the only being capable of deciding on the direction he is going to take in life" (1990, p. 151). This is the essential fact (as he writes, "reality") which illustrates both his life and his work. For, this ability to decide goes hand in hand with the ability to constantly modify oneself, manifested by the anthropological research conducted by the theoretician of human perfectibility. It will lend its direction and meaning to the model of educational action to be proposed by the explorer of this perfectibility who is the pedagogue who invented IE. In this way human perfectibility is finally translated by a double correlative potential to give a direction to one's life and to modify oneself constantly. However, without an "ethical willful act" (id.) this double potential will remain inoperative. Specifically, to Feuerstein, a scientist's work, just as that of a pedagogue, testifies to the efficiency of that establishing act. It is therefore, in reference to Feuerstein, who offers a testimony to the ethical demand for perfection, that we are able to appreciate Feuerstein as the theoretician of modifiability and Feuerstein as the explorer of that modifiability. Scientific and pedagogical works are pertinent in their own areas but it is ethical enlightenment which causes the truth to emerge from a work which is coherent with life, and vice versa.

3

Mediative Environments: Creating Conditions for Intellectual Growth

Arthur L. Costa

This article is dedicated to Reuven Feuerstein — my friend,
mentor and Teacher. You have enriched my life!

Many out-of-conscious factors influence teachers' thinking as they make daily decisions about curriculum and instruction. Their own culture, knowledge of content, their cognitive style, knowledge about their students, their professional values and beliefs about education influence their judgments about when to teach what to whom. Jack Frymier (1987), however, states: "In the main, the bureaucratic structure of the workplace is more influential in determining what professionals do rather than personal abilities, professional training or previous experience. Therefore, change efforts should focus on the structure of the workplace, not the teachers."

Frymier suggests that less obvious, but vastly more persuasive influences on teacher thought, are the norms, policies, and culture of the school setting in which teachers work. Hidden, but powerful cues emanate from the school environment. These subtle cues signal the institutional value system which governs the operation of the organization (Saphier & King, 1985).

Recent efforts to bring educational reform will prove futile unless the school environment signals the staff, the students, and the community that the development of the intellect and co-operative decision making are the school's basic values. While efforts to enhance the staff's instructional competencies, develop curriculum, revise instructional materials, and assessment procedures may be important components in the process of educational re-engineering, it is also crucial that the climate in which parents, teachers and students make their decisions be aligned with these goals of development of intellectual potential. Teachers will more likely teach for thinking, creativity and co-operation if they are in an intellectually stimulating, creative, and co-operative environment themselves.

1 Educational Stressors

Research by O. J. Harvey (1966) found that teaching is the second most stressful profession! Goodlad (1984), Rosenholtz (1989), Sarason (1991), Fullan (1992) and other authors have identified several sources of stress:

- Teachers often lack a sense of power and efficacy. They are often cast at the bottom of a hierarchy while the curricular, in-service, and evaluation decisions affecting them are handed down from "above".
- Teachers feel isolated. Ours is probably the only profession that performs our most beautiful and creative craft behind closed doors. Contributing to this situation is the inadequate amount and inflexibility of time for teachers to reflect and meet, plan, observe, and talk with each other.
- The complex, creative, intelligent act of teaching is often reduced to a recipe, a simplistic formula or a series of steps and competencies, the uniform performance of which naively connotes excellence and elegance in the art of teaching.
- The feedback of data about student achievement is for political, competitive, evaluative or coercive purposes. It neither involves nor instructs the school staff members in reflecting on, evaluating, and improving their curriculum and instructional decisions.
- Educational innovations are often viewed as mere "tinkerings" with the instructional program. They are so frequent and limited in impact that frustrated teachers sometimes feel, "this, too, shall pass". Instead of institutionalizing the change, deeply entrenched traditional practices and policies in the educational bureaucracy such as testing, reporting, securing parent understanding and support, teacher evaluation, scheduling, school organization, and discipline procedures are seldom revised to be in harmony with the overall innovation.

The effects of excessive stress on cognition, creativity and social interaction are well documented (MacLean, 1978). In such barren, intellectually "polluted" school climate conditions, some teachers understandably grow depressed. Teachers' vivid imagination, altruism, creativity and intellectual prowess, soon succumb to the humdrum daily routines of unruly students, irrelevant curriculum, impersonal surroundings and equally disinterested co-workers. In such an environment, the likelihood that teachers would value the development of students' intellect and imagination would be marginal.

2 Toward an Ecology of the Intellect

> The difference between a mechanistic and an ecological vision is striking. In an ecological view, people are intrinsically motivated, self-organization will occur spontaneously if the environment is conducive, emphasis on control is bad for structurally sound growth, the future is not an extrapolation of the present (Goerner, 1995, p. 30).

We know that adults continue to move through stages of cognitive, conceptual, and ego development (Hunt, 1978) and that the level of their development has a direct relationship to student behavior and student performance. Research shows that teachers with higher conceptual levels are more adaptive and flexible in their teaching style, and they have a greater ability to empathize, to symbolize human experience, and to act in accordance with a disciplined commitment to human values (McNerney & Carrier, 1981). These teachers choose new practices when classroom problems appear, vary their use of instructional strategies, elicit more conceptual responses from students, give more corrective and positive feedback to students, (Oja, 1980) and produce higher achieving students who are more co-operative and involved in their work.

Witherall and Erickson (1978) found that teachers at the highest levels of ego development demonstrated greater complexity and commitment to the individual student; greater generation and use of data in teaching; and greater understanding of practices related to rules, authority, and moral development than their counter-parts. Teachers at higher stages of intellectual functioning demonstrate more flexibility, toleration for stress, and adaptability. They take multiple perspectives, use a variety of coping behaviors, and draw from a broader repertoire of teaching models (Glickman, 1985). High-concept teachers are more effective with a wider range of students, including students from diverse cultural backgrounds.

Educational leaders, therefore, redefine their role as mediators of school and community-wide conditions for continual learning and intellectual development. A mediator is one who deliberately intervenes between the individual or group and the environment with the intention of creating conditions which will engage and promote intellectual growth (Feuerstein et al., 1997). They design strategies for achieving their vision of a learning organization; they generate data as a means of assessing progress toward that vision; they constantly monitor the intellectual ecology of the school community to determine its contribution to or hindrance of intellectual growth.

Systems analysts have a belief in "leverage points". These are places within a complex system where a small shift in one condition can produce big changes in the rest of the system. As mediators of the school's "intellectual ecology", the following seven strategies are offered as leverage points intended to enhance continual intellectual growth and sustained professional zest of the stakeholders in the educational enterprise. It is not intended to alleviate stress entirely. It is, however, intended to shift from *DI*stress to *EU*stress. (*EU* is taken from the word *euphoria*).

2.1 Goal Clarification

"If your vision statement sounds like motherhood, and apple pie and is somewhat embarrassing, you're on the right track. You bet the farm." (Peter Block, 1987).

Peter Senge (1990) states that leadership in a learning organization starts with the principle of "Creative Tension." He goes on to describe how creative tension emerges from seeing clearly where we want to be — the vision, and describing truthfully where we are now — our current reality. The gap between the two generates creative tension.

Creative Tension

Our Current Reality   ⟵————————⟶   Where We Want to Be

This principle of creative tension has long been recognized by leaders such as Martin Luther King Jr., when he proclaimed, "I have a dream ...". King believed:

> "Just as Socrates felt that it was necessary to create a tension in the mind, so that individuals could rise from the bondage of myths and half truths ... so must we create the kind of tension in society that will help men rise from the dark depths of prejudice and racism."

This tension, according to Senge, can be resolved by raising current reality toward the vision. Effective leaders, therefore, stimulate intellectual growth by causing creative organizational tension. Leaders create for themselves and facilitate staff, students' and the community's visions of what could be, images of desired states, valued aspirations, outcomes and scenarios of more appropriate futures.

Mission and vision statements, however, are not just idle exercises. They are employed continually as criteria for making decisions, developing policies, and allocating resources, hiring staff, designing curriculum, disciplining, and lesson planning. When our values are clear, the decisions we make are easy. What gives an organization integrity is how the staff members perceive the congruence between its policies, vision and mission with its daily practices.

2.2 Group Development

> Teamwork is the ability to work together toward a common vision. The ability to direct individual accomplishment toward organizational objectives. It is the fuel that allows common people to accomplish uncommon results. George Land and Beth Jarman. *Break-Point and Beyond: Mastering the Future Today.*

Humans, as social beings, mature intellectually in reciprocal relationships with others. Collaboratively, individuals generate and discuss ideas eliciting thinking that surpasses individual effort. Together and privately, they express different perspectives, agree and disagree, point out and resolve discrepancies, and weigh alternatives. Because people grow their intellect through this process, collegial interaction is a crucial factor in the intellectual ecology of the school. [Costa and O'Leary (1992), refer to this as Co-cognition — thinking together.]

Trust and Collegiality. The essence of building trust and collegiality is when people work together to better understand how to work together. People are more likely to engage and grow in higher-level, creative, and experimental thought when they are in a trusting, risk-taking, co-operative climate. The leader constantly monitors the school's ecology for signs of stress that might close down complex and creative thinking. Risk-taking requires a non-judgmental atmosphere where information can be shared without fear that it will be used to evaluate success or failure.

2.3 Coaching

"The current management culture, with its focus on controlling behavior, needs to be replaced by a management culture in which skillful coaching creates the climate, environment, and context that empowers employees and teams to generate results." Evered & Selman (1989).

Coaching is one of the most powerful means to overcome the extreme isolation and intellectual depression of teachers. Coaching produces intellectual growth for a variety of reasons:

Coaching enhances instructional thought. The act of teaching is, itself, an intellectual process. Jackson (1968) found that teachers make over 1300 decisions a day. The behaviors observed in the classroom are artifacts of decisions that teachers make before, during, and after instruction (Shavelson, 1976). The purpose of coaching, therefore, is not to install, modify or evaluate behaviors of teaching. The purpose is to enhance decision making, perception and the intellectual functions of teaching — to internalize the self-analysis thinking pattern that can develop from repetitive use of this (planning and reflective) cycle. Costa and Garmston (1994) cite the ultimate purpose of coaching is to modify teachers' capacities to modify themselves.

Humans who desire to continually improve their craft, seek, and profit from being coached. Skillful artists, athletes, musicians, dancers — like Greg Louganis, Mikhail Baryshnikov, Kristi Yamaguchi, Jackie Joyner-Kersey never lose their need for coaching. Likewise, in education, to continually perfect their craft, teachers profit from coaching as well.

To work effectively as a member of a team requires coaching. Welding together the individual efforts of team members into a well-organized and efficient unit requires the persistence and stamina of an expert coach.

An orchestra might serve as fitting metaphor because it engenders a desired vision of precision, harmony, working diligently together towards a common goal, and, ultimately, producing beautiful music. An orchestra is a collection of extremely talented musicians. Likewise, each member of a staff is an extremely talented professional. Each, in their own right, is an expert. (The Italian word for teacher is "maestro" which comes from the Latin, *magister* or master.)

In an orchestra, however, musicians play in the same key, and at the same tempo. They rehearse together and have a common vision of the entire score, each knowing well the part they play that contributes to the whole. While they do not all play the same music at the same time — there are rests, harmonies, and counterpoint — they support each other in a totally co-ordinated and concerted effort. In the same way, members of the school community support each other in working towards achieving the organization's vision. While teachers neither teach the same subjects at the same time, nor do they approach them in the same way, their cumulative effect, is beautiful, harmonious "music" in the mind and learning of the student.

This concerted effort, however, does not "just happen". It takes someone — a conductor — who "knows the score" to provide the synergy. It takes time, persistence, practice and *coaching* to develop a winning athletic team, a celebrated symphony orchestra, or a learning organization.

Few educational innovations achieve their full impact without a coaching component. Joyce and Showers (1988) found that efforts to bring about changes in classroom practice are fruitless unless the teacher is coached in the use of the innovation. They found that providing staff development at the theory level, in which inspirational speakers give speeches about ideals and abstractions, produces minimal application of that knowledge into classroom practice. With the addition of staff development opportunities in which teachers observe demonstrations of the innovations and even have time to practice and receive feedback about their skillfulness in using the innovation, the transference to classroom practice is still low. Not until the component of coaching was added that the innovation was internalized, valued, and transferred to classroom use.

Coaching enhances the intellectual capacities of teachers which, in turn, produces greater intellectual achievements in students.

> "Every function in ... cultural development appears twice: first, on the social level, and later on the individual level; first between people (inter-psychological), and then inside (intra-psychological). This applies equally to voluntary attention, to logical memory, and to the formation of concepts. *All the higher functions originate as actual relationships between individuals*." Lev Vygotsky (1978).

Vygotsky's statement gives us a strong theoretical support for coaching as a means of intellectual growth. It is through social interaction that new concepts and all intellectual behaviors are formed and grown.

Furthermore, research has shown that higher level intellectually functioning teachers produce higher level intellectually functioning students. Sprinthall and Theis-Sprinthall (1983) report compelling evidence that teachers who function at higher cognitive levels produce higher achievement in students. Characteristic of these teachers is their ability to empathize, to symbolize experience, and to act in accordance with a disciplined commitment to human values. They employ a greater range of instructional strategies, elicit more conceptual responses from students, and produce higher achieving students who are more co-operative and involved in their work. Glickman (1985) concluded that successful teachers are thoughtful teachers and they stimulate their students to be thoughtful as well.

2.4 Investing Leadership in All

It is only when we develop others that we permanently succeed ...
Harvey S. Firestone, Firestone Rubber Company.

A large and very successful department store in the Western United States transformed the work of "sales clerks" by changing their titles to "associates". Waiters on Amtrak's dining cars are called "service representatives" Customers in Target Discount stores are referred to as "guests". Giving more expansive titles alters the paradigm of the person's role. Intellectual shifts can result when the identities and roles of the participants in the educational process: students, teachers, administrators, and trustees are redefined.

As students' roles are redefined as *envisioners* of their own desired states, establishing goals, making plans, clarifying outcomes for themselves, they come to realize that they are in charge of developing their own strategies for achieving those goals and generating ways of assessing their own growth toward those ends. When they view their role as *knowledge producers* and *meaning makers* for themselves and others, they contribute to a co-operative environment in which others can grow toward their desired state.

Teachers re-conceptualize their role not only as *mediators* of students' learning, but also as *members of a collaborative team*, whose role it is to envision those desired states for themselves and their students and for the classroom climate which they both share. Teachers are *instructional strategists* designing ways to achieve those desired goals They view themselves as *knowledge managers*, *knowledge-producers* and *meaning makers*. As *researchers* they generate data as feedback to guide and assess their own, their students, and the classroom climate's progress toward these desired states. They realize their role as members of a profession both drawing from and contributing to the professional knowledge base of research, theory, and practice.

The role of the district trustees is that of *community educators* — keeping and protecting the value system of the district and monitoring their decisions to be consistent with the district's mission and vision.

2.5 Valuing Diversity

"It is acceptance and trust that make it possible for each bird to sing its own song — confident that it will be heard — even by those who sing with a different voice." Hateley, B. & Schnidt, W. (1995).

Human beings are made to be different. Diversity is the basis of biological survival. Each of us has a different genetic structure, unique facial features, a distinguishing thumb print, a distinctive signature, diverse backgrounds of knowledge, experience and culture, and a preferred way of gathering, processing and expressing information and knowledge. We even have a singular frequency in which we vibrate (Leonard, 1978). Leaders are sensitive to and capitalize on these differences to enhance intellectual growth.

Intellectually effective people seem able to "be at home" in multiple areas of functioning. They move flexibly from one style to another as the situation demands it. They have an uncanny ability to read contextual cues from the situation or the environment as to what is needed, then they draw forth from their vast repertoire those skills and capacities needed to function most effectively in any setting.

Organizational life might seem easier if all members of the learning community thought and acted in a similar fashion, and remained in their own departments and grade levels. Limitations of time, isolation, and our obsession with the archaic compartmentalization of the disciplines and grades is what keeps school staffs separated; thus teachers' intellectual growth is diminished. Leaders realize that humans grow intellectually through resolving differences, achieving consensus, and stretching to accommodate dissonance. They realize there is a greater possibility for making connections, stimulating creativity, and growing the capacity for complex problem solving when such differences are bridged. (In some businesses, this is referred to as "Skunkworks" — deliberately bringing together personnel from different departments, positions and grade levels to make connections and find new and divergent ways to solve problems.)

Interdependent learning communities are built not by obscuring diversity but by valuing the friction those differences bring and resolving those differences in an atmosphere of trust and reciprocity. Therefore, leaders mediate appreciation for this diversity by deliberately bringing together people of different political and religious persuasions, cultures, gender, cognitive styles, belief systems, modality preferences and intelligences. They structure groups composed of representatives from different schools, diverse departments, community groups and grade levels to envision, describe learning outcomes, plan curriculum and staff development activities and to allocate resources.

Leaders help staff, students, and parents become aware of, value, know how and when to draw upon and manage the multiplicity of their own and others' unique forms of intelligence; to know how and when to employ and evaluate the usefulness of each intelligence, how to respect other peoples' preferences for and level of intellectual development, and to illuminate a vision of an educational community where each member's range of multiple capacities would be maximally developed.

2.6 Curriculum Development

To change practice, change minds. Caine & Caine, 1997, p. 22.

Senge (1990) emphasizes a characteristic of the learning organization is that it challenges existing mental models. The leader, in an atmosphere of trust, challenges existing practices, assumptions, policies, and traditional ways of delivering curriculum. Intellectual growth is found in disequilibrium, not balance. It is out of chaos that order is built, that learning takes place, that new understandings are forged, that new connections are bridged and that organizations function more consistently with its mission, vision and goals.

We must finally admit that the process IS the content. The core of our curriculum must focus on such processes as thinking, learning to learn, knowledge production, metacognition, transference of knowledge, decision making, creativity, and group problem solving and knowing how to behave when correct answers are not readily apparent. These ARE the subject matters of instruction. Content, selectively abandoned and judiciously selected because of its fecund contributions to the thinking/learning process, becomes merely the vehicle to carry the processes of learning. The focus is on learning FROM the objectives instead of learning OF the objectives.

Since these process-oriented goals cannot be assessed using product-oriented assessment techniques, our existing evaluation paradigm must shift as well. Thus assessment of students' thinking will focus on students becoming more conscious, more reflective, more efficient, more flexible, and more transferable (Costa & Kallick, 1995; Costa & Liebmann, 1997).

The leader continually challenges the organization's mental models about what learning is of most worth as students face an uncertain, technological, and global future.

2.7 Continual Learning Through Experimentation and Action Research

Autopoesis: (Greek) Self-production. The characteristic of living systems to continuously renew themselves and to regulate this process in such a way that the integrity of their structure is maintained. It is a natural process which supports the quest for structure, process renewal and integrity. Margaret Wheatley (1992). *Science and the New Leadership*.

Experimentation implies that an atmosphere of choice, risk-taking and inquiry exists. Data are generated without fear that they will be used as a basis for evaluating success or failure. Creativity will more likely grow in a low-risk atmosphere. Frymier (1987) goes on to state:

> "The solution is to empower teachers, to help them develop an internalized locus of control. Teachers and principals, supervisors and superintendents, boards of education and state legislators all must appreciate the possibilities of school improvement efforts that marshal the motivations and unleash the talents of those who work directly with children day after day."

For too long the process of assessment has been external to teachers' goal setting, curriculum and instructional decision making. School effectiveness, student achievement and teachers' competence have often been determined by a narrow range of standardized student achievement test scores in a limited number of content areas: reading, mathematics, and language acquisition. Rank order test results have been published in newspapers. Awards of excellence have been granted to schools that show the highest gains in scores. Teachers have been given merit pay based on their students' performance on standardized tests.

In the process, teachers have become disenfranchised. Educators have had little say about what the test measured. In fact, what tests do measure is usually irrelevant to the curriculum, and the results of testing disclose little about the adequacy of the teachers' curriculum and instructional decisions. In many ways the desire for measurable outcomes has signaled teachers that they are "incompetent" to assess student achievement. They, in effect, were told they could not be trusted to collect evidence of students' growth, that the observations they made daily in the classroom was suspect and of little worth.

The accountability movement caused educators to search for "hard data" by which to assess their efforts. What teachers observed, by inference, therefore, was "soft data." The "hardest," most objective data available may be that collected by an *enlightened* teaching team which systematically, and collectively, gathers data over time in the real-life, day-to-day interactions and problem solving of the classroom. Conversely, the "softest," most suspect data may be that which is designed and collected by testing "experts" external to the school setting and ignorant of the school's mission, values, and goals, the community's culture and socio-economic, the classroom's mix of learning styles, teaching strategies, and group dynamics in which their tests are administered!

Leaders assist the teaching staff to design strategies for collecting data and to use the assessment data as feedback and guide to informed and reflective practice. Staff members will need help in learning how to design feedback spirals including multiple ways of gathering such data, establishing criteria for judgment, working together to develop their common understanding and reliability of observations and reporting of results.

Because learning to think, to co-operate, and to respect human uniqueness is best learned through imitation and emulation of significant others, leaders strive to model in their own behaviors those same qualities and behaviors that are desired in students and staff.

3 In Summary

Some people think that it is holding on that makes one strong. Sometimes it is letting go. Sylvia Robinson.

The development of thinking, individuality, and collegiality as goals of education is not just kid-stuff. Education will achieve an intellectual focus when the school becomes an intellectually stimulating environment — a home for the mind for all who dwell there; when all the school's inhabitants realize that freeing human intellectual potential is the goal of education; when they strive to get better at it themselves; and when they use their energies to enhance the intelligent behaviors of others. Educational leaders serve as an "environmental protection agency" — constantly monitoring the intellectual ecology of the school. Their chief purpose is to insure that thinking, creativity and collaboration will become neither endangered, nor worse, extinct.

4

Feuerstein's Unique Contribution to Educational and School Psychology

Robert Burden

1 Introduction

At the time of writing this paper I have been an applied educational psychologist for thirty-two years. After gaining my first degree in an excellent psychology department in the early 1960s, I entered the teaching profession with a sound knowledge of accepted theories of learning and a commitment to the scientific methods of logical positivism as the only way to achieve a true understanding of human behaviour. I spent the next three rewarding but frustrating years as a teacher of children with learning and behavioural difficulties during which time I found little in my psychological knowledge which could be used for the benefit of the children in my care. I subsequently trained as an educational psychologist at a highly reputable training establishment where I became an expert at the administration and interpretation of intelligence tests.

When I took up my first post as an educational psychologist with a local government department, I gradually began to realise that nothing in my academic background and training had prepared me to perform the role that was needed to foster the education of children with a widely diverse range of learning and behavioural difficulties. I felt that psychology had taken the wrong path but I didn't know why nor did I have any idea what to do instead.

In 1971 I was appointed to establish a new training course for educational psychologists at the University of Exeter. I was determined that this should provide a totally different form of training for educational psychologists than that which was commonly on offer in the United Kingdom at that time. I spent the next ten years examining different psychological theories and exploring different approaches to applying psychology in educational settings. I then discovered the two key texts of Feuerstein and his collaborators, *The Dynamic Assessment of Retarded Performers* (1979) and *Instrumental Enrichment* (1980), which inspired me to seek out the man himself. We subsequently became friends and my academic and professional life as a trainer of teachers and educational psychologists was changed forever. This paper is a homage to Feuerstein and his ideas with particular reference to his influence upon my chosen profession.

2 What is Educational Psychology?

In 1992 the International School Psychology Association (ISPA) was commissioned by UNESCO to provide a survey of trends and developments in educational psychology from an international perspective. The subsequent report of that survey (Burden, 1994) began by identifying a terminological confusion in the general understanding of what was meant by educational psychology. In the United States and many other parts of the world a clear distinction continues to be drawn between researchers and theoreticians with a psychological background working mainly in faculties of education in universities or teacher training colleges and those professionals employed by schools and school districts to apply psychological techniques in educational and family settings. The first group are generally referred to as educational psychologists, whilst the latter group tend to carry the title of school psychologist or some such similar title. Just to confuse matters, however, in the United Kingdom both groups are referred to as educational psychologists.

The problem with this state of affairs is that each of these groups lays claim to bringing psychological concepts, knowledge and skills to bear upon the problems faced by educators whilst at the same time rarely bothering to communicate with each other. Thus, at its worst, a situation developed by the late 20th century in which educational psychologists could be seen as producing erudite papers and research findings on such areas as teacher effectiveness, student learning, motivation and various aspects of self-perception, which rarely if ever become translated into professional practice. In comparison, school psychologists tended to function pragmatically, often employing time-honoured techniques such as intelligence tests without reference to recent theory or research. This gap between the two groups has been well-documented (Barden, 1983, 1986) but little concerted effort has been made to draw them together in any really meaningful manner.

3 Feuerstein's "Bridging" Role

It is the contention of this paper that one of the most abiding contributions of Reuven Feuerstein will be the bridge that his work offers to the two branches of educational psychology. Feuerstein does this by presenting us with an elegant theory of structural cognitive modifiability which has its roots in a belief system about human potential and cultural transmission and which provides practical guidance with regard to assessment practice and curriculum intervention. He has been unfairly judged by many critics who appear to be only conscious of one small section of his work without fully understanding the theoretical strengths of its foundations or the interactive nature of its subsystems. Figure 1 provides a simple visual metaphor to illustrate this point. Most school psychologists and classroom practitioners are unaware that Instrumental Enrichment and the LPAD merely represent the tip of an iceberg with their substantial theoretical substructure mainly existing unseen beneath the ocean's surface.

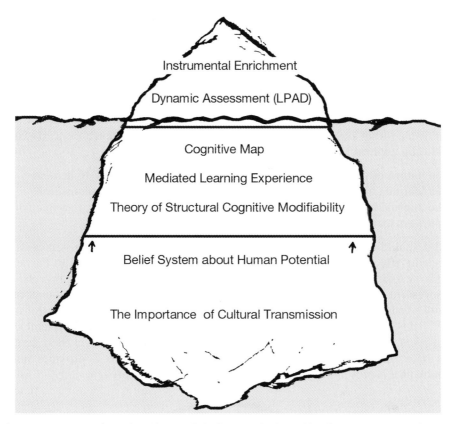

Figure 1: Feuerstein's theories and their practical applications represented as an iceberg.

4 The Need for a Conceptual Framework to Guide Action

School psychologists are generally employed to identify and advise on how best to meet the needs of children in schools demonstrating learning and behaviour difficulties. Historical influences upon the main ways in which they have tradition-ally come to perform these functions has led to an over-reliance upon formal psychometric testing, particularly in the employment of IQ tests as measures of learning potential (Kamin, 1974; Anderson, 1994). At the same time, an unques-tioning acceptance of behaviourist methods as the most favoured approach to dealing with problems of behaviour or learning has epitomised the form of practical advice offered by such specialists.

It is regrettable that in most parts of the world school psychologists have come to be seen as gatekeepers to special schools or to valuable but dwindling resources. In making decisions associated with this role, they are often seen to fall back on such outmoded practices as applying IQ-achievement test discrepancy scores without apparent awareness of their theoretical or political naïvety.

Academic educational psychology, on the other hand, has a tendency towards fragmentation, focusing its research efforts and theory building on one or another sub-area rather than developing broad-based pedagogical theories with well thought-through practical implications for classroom teachers or parents. One rare, thoughtful attempt to construct a theoretical framework with practical implications for teachers is offered by Tomlinson et al. (1992) who argue for a psychological perspective to education which is concerned with the nature of action and experience within and between individuals. They suggest that teachers need to have practically applicable understanding of

- the nature of intended learning outcomes they are attempting to achieve
- the learning activities and experiences that can lead to these acquisitions
- the internal and external influences on action which may affect these activities
- the ways learners vary as individuals and groups.

This should help to form a basis for identifying helpful teaching strategies for managing effective learning activity which is appropriately matched to particular pupils, teaching aims and contexts, and effectively assessed for progress and achievement. It also provides a set of criteria against which the interventions of school psychologists can be measured.

Williams and Burden (1997) provide a slightly different but complementary framework for structuring a psychological approach to education in their description of a social interactionist approach to learning. Figure 2 provides a diagrammatical representation of the key elements of this approach.

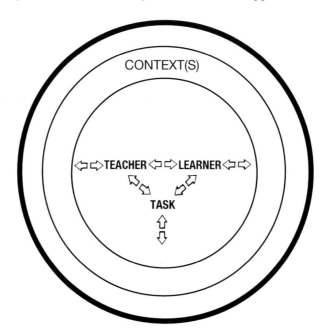

Figure 2: A social-interactionist model of the pedagogical process.

It can be seen that four elements acting in some form of dynamic equilibrium form the basis of social interactionist theory. Aspects of an ecosystemic approach are contained within the identifications of series of contexts in which education takes place — cultural, societal, regional, family, school and classroom based. This helps us to recognise that education is not merely something which occurs in schools and classrooms, but which has far wider implications. Teachers are the main directors of action within classrooms, a role which they undertake from a basis of beliefs and value systems about education and with varying degrees of expertise. They perform their pedagogical functions by setting learning activities which represent the school curriculum and which are centred around specific learning tasks, success at which is usually measured by means of normative tests. The key players in this educational game are the students or learners who bring to it their individual knowledge, skills and attitudes which are increasingly shaped by the schooling process. Williams and Burden suggest that unless all of these factors are taken into account, it will not be possible to fully understand why some students are more or less successful in school than are others, nor will it be possible to offer advice on how to improve the educational process for individuals or groups.

5 Confirmation of Feuerstein's Theories from other Psychologists and Educators

It is becoming increasingly clear that our understanding of such issues and the implications for educational action is considerably enhanced by drawing upon the work of Feuerstein and his colleagues. *The Dynamic Assessment of Retarded Performers* (1979) and *Instrumental Enrichment* (1980) together with subsequent papers and book chapters (Ben-Hur, 1994; Kozulin, 1997) provide us with a rich source of inputs into each of the above-mentioned areas and a theoretical structure which pulls them all together.

Firstly, Feuerstein's fundamental belief that any person of whatever age, however handicapped, can become a fully effective learner, is a precursor to the current movement towards the inclusion of all children with disabilities into mainstream schools. Without such a belief system on the part of teachers, any move towards inclusion is bound to fail, however . Not that this is enough in itself. Teachers also need the necessary understanding and skills to provide mediated learning experiences together with a curriculum which fosters such activities.

Feuerstein's emphasis upon the need to understand cultural differences and the way in which cultural deprivation acts as a process helps us to contextualise learning and also forces us to focus on the nature of the learning outcomes that we wish our students to attain. Implicit in all of Feuerstein's work are the twin aims of education — the transmission of culture from one generation to the next and the development of cognitive skills and strategies that will prepare young people to meet the demands of a world that is moving ever more rapidly through a process of discontinuous change. There are echoes also of the critical pedagogy of Paulo Freire which invites students to think critically about subject matter, doctrines, the learning process itself, and their society (Freire, 1970, 1973). For Freire, pedagogy must be participatory, critical, context-bound, democratic, dialogic, multicultural, research-oriented, activist and affective in the process of empowerment (Freire & Faundex, 1989). These are all sentiments with which Feuerstein would undoubtedly concur.

Thus we move to the central and possibly most important aspect of the theory of structural cognitive modifiability, the provision by parents and teachers of mediated learning experiences. It will come as no surprise to those who are committed to the notion of teacher-as-mediator that considerable and increasing independent research bears out most if not all of the elements of MLE. Work in the area of motivation in particular has borne out mediation theory as also has the work of the guru of educational change, Michael Fullan.

In his 1993 book, *Change Forces*, Fullan points out that "to restructure is not to reculture" (p. 49) by which he means that changing formal structures in schools is not the same as changing norms, habits, skills and beliefs. This he sees as the hardest core to crack in education. For Fullan the ultimate aim of education is to produce a learning society which will only emerge if there are teachers who combine continuous inner and outer learning. He goes on to suggest that (p. 136) "The abilities to think and present ideas on the one hand, and to work with others on the other hand are being recognised by education and business alike as central to the world's future. Permeating these twin purposes is a third purpose — the positive disposition to keep on learning in the face of constant change and societal complexity. Put another way, the ability to cope with change, learning as much as possible with each encounter is the generic capacity needed for the twenty-first century."

In reviewing recent literature on motivation, Williams and Burden (1997) identify a number of important variables. These include the perceived value of an activity to the individual concerned, neatly encapsulated by Male (1992) in the phrase "personal authenticity" of the task, and represented by Feuerstein as the investment of meaning. Also included is the importance of an appropriate level of challenge, described by Csikszentmihalyi and Csikszentmihalyi (1988) as "flow experience" within which all our minds and bodies are completely involved, our concentration is very deep, we know what we want to do and how well we are doing, we are not worried about failing and time passes very quickly. An operational definition of "flow experience" is a situation in which people perceive themselves as having a high level of skill and are posed with challenges that stretch these skills, two important aspects of MLE.

An aspect of learners' developing beliefs about themselves which has come to be seen as highly significant is a sense of agency. This incorporates the notions of *locus of causality* (de Charms, 1984) whereby choice, creativity and ownership of behaviour can be seen as lying within oneself or in the hands of others, *locus of control* (Wang, 1983) which relates to the control that people consider they possess with regard to the outcomes of their actions, and the ability to set and achieve personal goals. The concept of a "goal" is somewhat more complex than might appear on the surface, and it has become common practice amongst cognitive psychologists to distinguish between *performance* and *mastery* goals (Ames, 1992) or *performance* and *learning* goals (Dweck & Leggett, 1988). "Put simply, with performance goals an individual aims to look smart, whereas with learning goals the individual aims at becoming smarter" (Dweck, 1985, p. 291). A similar distinction is drawn here between ego and task involvement (Nicholls, 1979), where the former represents an involvement in learning tasks in order to do better than others whilst the latter represents involvement in learning tasks for their own sake. This latter form of activity is also referred to as intrinsic motivation. The links with MLE are again very clear.

Fullan (1993) has a number of points to make about education which mirror various aspects of MLE. He sees change as a lifelong challenge to be embraced. "Productive educational change, like productive life itself, really is a journey that doesn't end until we do ... (but) ... if people do not venture into uncertainty, no significant change can be made ... Problems are inevitable, but the good news is that you cannot learn or be successful without them." (p. 25) He goes on to suggest (p. 26) that "successful change management requires problem-finding techniques ... and regular review of problem-solving decisions". Problems, he emphasises, are our friends.

Fullan also takes up the issues of sharing and individuation (p. 34). "For complex change you need many people working insightfully on the solution and committing themselves to concentrated action together." However, (p. 35) "The freshest ideas often come from diversity and those marginal to the group. Keeping in touch with our inner voice, personal reflection, and the capacity to be alone are essential under conditions of constant change forces." All in all (p. 36) "Honoring opposites simultaneously — individualism and collegiality — is the critical message."

Feuerstein's *cognitive map* represents the other key element of his theory of structural cognitive modifiability. Although this has been criticised by some as being vague and ill-defined, it nevertheless provides a helpful working model for the analysis of tasks at a much deeper level than that proposed by behaviourism and for the diagnosis of individual cognitive differences that draws upon a superior information-processing approach to one dependent upon IQ measurement.

Williams and Burden (1997) present an overview of task analytic and task construction approaches in language teaching, many of which overlap to a considerable extent with the cognitive map. Prabhu (1987), for example, identifies five contributing factors to task difficulty — the amount and type of information provided, the amount of reasoning or cognitive operation needed, the precision needed, the learner's knowledge of the world and familiarisation with the purposes and constraints of the task, and the degree of abstractness of the concepts dealt with in the task. Such approaches to task analysis have become relatively common in the language teaching literature (e.g. see Nunan, 1989; Crookes & Gass, 1993), but few offer the breadth of scope provided by Feuerstein's cognitive map.

In particular, the notion of learning *phase* has provided school psychologists with the means to break away from the icy grip of IQ testing by drawing upon an information processing model from cognitive psychology. By focusing upon the efficiency/deficiency with which individuals approach cognitive tasks, it becomes possible to take a developmental perspective towards subsequent action in contrast to one which stops at providing global classifications of an inhibitory nature.

The construction of the Learning Potential Assessment Device and Instrumental Enrichment upon the foundations of the theory of structural cognitive modifiability is in itself a unique contribution to the school psychologist's repertoire. It has provided also a powerful impetus for change which is only just beginning to be recognised.

One of the complaints that is sometimes levelled against school psychologists is that they refuse to function from a values perspective, or rather that they refuse to acknowledge that all human action must inevitably reflect human values. Since most academic psychology remains firmly wedded to the positivist tradition with its emphasis upon the experimental method and the search for objectivity in making judgements, this is hardly surprising. A growing body of psychologists, however, having taken note of Thomas Kuhn's notion of paradigmic revolutions, have begun to argue persuasively for *interpretative* and *critical* paradigmic approaches to understanding human behaviour and helping it to change (Fox & Prilleltensky, 1997).

Since the critical paradigm in particular emphasises the importance of personal awareness of one's own values in carrying out research or acting professionally, it is entirely appropriate for the International School Psychology Association to have taken the advocacy of children's rights as its *raison d'être*, in keeping with the United Nations Convention on the Rights of the Child (John, 1994). However, as Burden (1997a) has pointed out, it is not enough to claim to work from a position which respects and works on behalf of the rights of children, whilst continuing to act in ways which appear to be objective but actually deny and abuse those rights. Nowhere is this more implicit than in the long-standing tradition of administering intelligence tests. Children are not usually asked whether they wish to be tested, nor are they given the option of refusing to do so; they are not asked whether they understand the purpose of the assessment, nor are they informed of that purpose; they are not allowed to ask questions or to deviate in their responses in any way which runs counter to the standardised procedures; they are not usually informed of the outcome of their endeavours nor how that outcome will be interpreted and used to determine some aspect of their future life careers.

The LPAD and subsequent forms of dynamic assessment (Lidz, 1987) make it possible for school psychologists to carry out assessments from a critical perspective whilst at the same time keeping the rights of the child as the central participant in the assessment process very much to the forefront. It is only recently, however, that school psychologists in the UK have begun to recognise the freedom from their psychometric chains that is afforded them by changing paradigms in this way (Cline, 1992; Gupta & Coxhead, 1988; Lauchlan & Elliott, 1998).

Instrumental Enrichment has received more than its fair share of criticisms despite a considerable amount of impressive evidence as to its efficacy (Burden,

1987; Savell et al., 1986). Much of this criticism has centred upon the content of the IE materials or the nature of the programme itself (Blagg, 1991), without taking into account the revolutionary messages which it contained about the purpose of education, the structure of an appropriate curriculum, the vital importance of the mediating function of teachers and, once again, the limitless possibilities for lifelong learning and development.

Whilst researchers continue to employ simplistic experimental methods in their attempts to evaluate the effectiveness of IE, such issues will continue to be overlooked. Blagg (1991) began to touch upon them in his Bridgwater study, but in his haste to manufacture his own Somerset materials, the true political significance of his findings was overlooked and ultimately buried.

Ironically, Blagg's Somerset Thinking Skills materials have served as the focus of a recent study which employed a more eco-systemic design in its attempt to evaluate one school's efforts to introduce thinking skills into its curriculum (Burden & Nichols, 2000). The design employed is known by the acronym of SPARE, referring to the suggestion that school psychologists should see themselves as "researchers in the real world", carrying with them a "spare wheel" model for evaluative research (Burden, 1997b).

The acronym SPARE in this instance indicates the need to fully describe the *Setting* into which the new curriculum materials are to be introduced, the *Plans* that have been made to ensure that the innovation works, the *Action* that actually occurs within the setting once the new scheme has started, the *Results* or *Reaction* of the system to the innovation, and *Evaluative* comments that can be made on the basis of the information gathered. This information may be of a quantitative nature or based on more qualitative interviews.

In this instance the pupils involved in the programme were asked to rate curriculum subjects in terms of their interest and usefulness and also to comment in an open-ended way on their reactions to thinking skills lessons. Thinking skills were not rated highly because they were not seen as "real work" which produced marks and were not taught in a didactic manner as in "proper" subjects like science and maths. The issues were complex and are discussed in depth elsewhere, but the main point to be made here is that thinking skills cannot be grafted onto a rejecting host culture which does not begin from the same value system, particularly when they are introduced by teachers who have not been taught to function as mediators.

The issue of whether thinking skills can or should be taught separately from other curriculum subjects is tackled in depth in a number of essays collected under the title of *Thinking Through the Curriculum* (Burden & Williams, 1998). Teacher trainers in several different curriculum areas make the case here for teaching their subject (science, mathematics, music, art etc.) in a way that fosters cognitive development whilst at the same time acknowledging their debt to Instrumental Enrichment and other cognitive programmes for helping to restructure their ideas. In the book's concluding section, however, a strong case is made for both independent and integrated cognitive approaches complementing each other within the same curriculum.

6 What are the Final Implications for Educational and School Psychology?

The case was made at the beginning of this paper for the formation of a bridge between educational and school psychology by means of Feuerstein's theoretical position and recommended practices. What has emerged as this exposition has unfolded is that this could be a very special bridge indeed.

Firstly, it would enable school psychologists to break out of their traditional, historically imposed constraints and face up to the demands of their beliefs and values. They would need to act with *intentionality* whilst making sure they establish *reciprocity* with their clients. They would need to invest their professional actions with true *meaning* and to ensure that the *transcendent* nature of those actions were emphasised.

Secondly, it would help school psychologists to identify within the enormous range of research and other studies in educational psychology that which was of particular value in fostering their endeavours to enhance the education of all children in a truly meaningful way. By drawing links between different aspects of MLE and research into motivation, self-concept, attributions and other similar areas, it should be possible to legitimise the former and provide direction for the latter.

Thirdly, it should provide a fresh impetus for different ways of approaching the assessment role with which school psychologists would seem to be forever saddled, whilst at the same time underpinning the development of a more consultative role with regard to the cognitive curriculum for both individuals and whole school systems.

Fourthly, such a bridge can function in both directions by fostering innovative research by educational psychologists in such areas as children's rights, dynamic assessment, curriculum development and the evaluation of change.

In some areas a great deal of this kind of work is already happening, but in a piecemeal fashion. In other areas the sleeping giant is only just beginning to stir. What is clear to this writer at least is that Feuerstein's contribution to this process will come to be seen as both unique and enormous.

5

Group and Individual Differences in Intelligence: What Can and Should We Do about Them?

Robert J. Sternberg

What makes a person intellectually gifted, or mentally retarded? Ethnic and racial groups differ in measured intelligence on conventional tests: Why? To what extent can these differences or any differences be attributed to heredity, and to what extent to environment? Most importantly, what can we do about these differences? These are the kinds of questions that Reuven Feuerstein has addressed throughout his career (e.g. Feuerstein, 1979, 1980), especially in the formation of his landmark *Learning Potential Assessment Device* and *Instrumental Enrichment* program, and they are the questions I will address in this chapter. I will talk first about individual differences in intelligence, then about what we can do to modify such differences, then about heritability of intelligence, then about group differences, and finally, draw some conclusions.

1 Extremes in Intelligence

1.1 Intellectual Giftedness

Although most people fall within the broad middle range of intellectual abilities, there are, of course, people at both the upper and the lower extremes. People at the upper extreme are referred to as intellectually gifted.

Psychologists differ in terms of how they define intellectual giftedness. Some use an exclusively IQ-based criterion. For example, many programs for the gifted screen largely on the basis of intelligence tests, taking children in perhaps the upper 1% (IQ of roughly 135 or above) or 2% (IQ of roughly 132 or above) for their programs. Other programs also supplement the assessment of IQ as the basis of giftedness with other criteria, such as school or career achievements or other measures of gifted performance.

Probably the most well-known studies of giftedness were conducted by Lewis Terman. Terman conducted a longitudinal study, which followed particular gifted individuals over the course of their life spans (Terman, 1925; Terman & Oden, 1959). The study has continued even after Terman's death. In his sample of the gifted, Terman included children from California under age 11 with IQs over 140, as well as children in the 11–14-year-age bracket with slightly lower IQs. The mean

IQ of the 643 subjects selected was 151; only 22 of these subjects had IQs lower than 140.

The accomplishments in later life of the selected group were extraordinary by any criterion. By 1959, there were 70 listings among the group in *American Men of Science* and three memberships in the highly prestigious National Academy of Sciences. In addition, 31 men were listed in *Who's Who in America*, and 10 appeared in the *Directory of American Scholars*. There were numerous highly successful businessmen as well as individuals who were successful in all of the professions.

The sex bias in these references is obvious. Most of the women became housewives, so it is impossible to make any meaningful comparison between the men (none of whom were reported to have become househusbands) and the women.

Many factors other than IQ could have contributed to the success of Terman's sample, among the most important of which is familial socioeconomic status and the final educational level achieved by these individuals. Thus, as with all correlational data, it would be difficult to assign a causal role to IQ in accounting for differences in the accomplishments of the successful individuals in the study.

The prognosis for describing people as gifted merely on the basis of IQ is probably not good. Subotnik et al. (1993) have analyzed data from follow-ups of students admitted to Hunter College Elementary School in New York, an elite public school for children with very high IQs. Although the students have done well economically, they have been notable as well for what appears to be a lack of major creative accomplishments. They are, for the most part, people who have adapted very well to the world, but not people who have shaped it.

Herrnstein and Murray (1994) have noted, correctly, that in our society, people at the top of the heap — lawyers, doctors, business executives, college professors — tend to have higher IQs than do those at the bottom of the heap — day laborers, house cleaners, street sweepers, and the like. Despite their knowing about the danger of confusing causation and correlation, they nevertheless do, suggesting that high IQ leads to success in these various occupations.

The dangers of confusing causation and correlation are easy enough to see. We know, for example, that most people in Nigeria are black, and that most people in Norway are white. It would be foolhardy to conclude, however, that living in Nigeria causes you to be black, or that living in Norway causes you to be white. So much for confusing correlation and causation: There is a correlation, but as always, there are at least three possible causal explanations. Suppose there is a correlation between two things, such as measured intelligence and job placement. But for generality, let us call them Factor X and Factor Y. It may be that Factor X causes Factor Y; it may be that Factor Y causes Factor X; or it may be that some higher order factor causes both of them.

Thus, the correlation between IQ and job placement could be due to three kinds of mechanisms. High intelligence may indeed cause better job placement, which is plausible. Or better job placement may cause high intelligence, which, it turns out, is true (Schooler, 1987): Being in a better job enables you to practice your intellectual skills, which in turn results in higher intelligence. Or it may be that both high IQ and good job placement are dependent on some other factor or factors. But what might such a factor or factors be?

Well, consider the situation in the United States, the situation that generated the many apparently impressive graphs in the Herrnstein–Murray book. Of course, the situation differs from one country to another, but is probably similar, to greater or lesser extent, in countries requiring test scores for admission to various institutions. In order to get into law school, you have to take the law boards (*LSAT*); to get into business school, you have to take the business boards (*GMAT*); to get into medical school, you have to take the medical boards (*MCAT*); to get into graduate school, you have to take the graduate boards (*GRE* or *MAT*). Well, you get the idea: Graduate education requires you to take a test, and admission to competitive programs requires high scores. Competitive colleges, of course, also require such tests, as do competitive private schools.

So what is the relation between these facts and the correlation between IQ and job placement? Plenty. Conventional tests of intelligence correlate as highly with these various boards as they do with each other, which is to say, that for all the differences in name, these tests measure practically identical skills. Using slightly different names and test content may be good business, but makes relatively little difference in terms of results. People who tend to do well on one of the tests tend to do well on all of them.

Suppose that someone, for one reason or another, does not test well. Maybe they are creatively smart but not analytically smart. Maybe they are practically smart — they have a lot of common sense — but it does not translate into abstract, academic skills. Maybe they are test anxious, as I used to be. Maybe they grew up in the U.S. speaking a language other than English, such as Spanish or French or Vietnamese, and have not learned English well. Maybe their native language was English, but their parents both had to work to make a living, and did not have time either to read to them or otherwise give them much verbal exposure in the household. Whatever the reason, they simply do not test well.

If they want to go to a competitive graduate school — the kind that provides a ticket up the occupational ladder — they are pretty much out of luck, because all of the schools, within a given subject but even across subjects, require basically the same test. So such a person will find him or herself systematically excluded from many different kinds of educational opportunities. Ultimately, on average, they are likely to drift down the occupational ladder. Compare this individual to another individual who does well on such tests. Maybe this individual is not really all that talented in a lot of ways, but taking tests is definitely one of the individual's talents. High test scores will be a definite plus in admission to the graduate program of the person's choice. The person may not be admitted to all the programs to which he or she applies, but the person is likely to get into at least some. Test scores become the ticket to occupational level.

As a result, it is scarcely surprising that those at the top of the occupational ladder have high test scores. They could not have gotten into the access routes to high-level occupations if they did not pull off high test scores. In effect, *we create the correlation between IQ and job level.*

It is important to realize that it was not always this way, nor is it quite this way in most of the world today. If you go back to the 1950s, you will find average *SAT* (*Scholastic Assessment Test*, used for college admissions in the U.S.) scores at Harvard University, a highly prestigious school, 100 points (one standard deviation) lower on each of the verbal and quantitative tests than these scores were a decade later. What happened? Did the population suddenly become much smarter? Obviously not. Rather, Harvard and many other colleges changed their criteria for admission, emphasizing test scores more and social class less. From this point of view, reliance on test scores gave individuals a better, not a worse chance of being admitted for their intellectual qualifications. In other countries, many other factors still influence who is given access to higher education, including social class or even just luck. For example, in the Netherlands, college admissions are determined by a lottery, a system that, rather than making use of limited information about abilities, makes use of no information at all.

Of course, if you go way back to the Middle Ages, if you were born a serf, it did not matter one whit what your IQ was: You died a serf. The smartest serf, according to any existing test, had less opportunity than the stupidest child of the nobility. And, in fact, inbreeding probably led to many stupid children of the nobility. By marrying among themselves, they created a situation in which people with the same deleterious recessive traits would interbreed, resulting in various deficits, including, often, intellectual ones.

All of this may seem abstract, but consider an analogy. Suppose that a society decided that it just does not care that much about test scores because when people take tests, their scores are just so variable. You can take the *SAT* one day and get 500 (the mean), and then take it again the next day and get, say, 570. So the society decides instead to go with something it can measure much more consistently — height. In other words, henceforth, admission to college and graduate school will be determined on the basis of height.

Now, to get into Harvard, maybe you have to be extremely tall. To get into Yale, maybe you only have to be a bit less tall, but good looking. And so on down we go, until we get to Podunk, a school for losers, which allows you to be short. Of course, to get into a competitive medical school or law school, you will need to be even taller. This may all sound totally ridiculous, but actually it is not. In fact, people at the top of the occupational ladder do tend to be taller than those at the bottom: We do count height, whether we admit it or not.

Anyway, 25 years after starting to use height as the main variable for making admissions decisions, you decide to compare the average IQs of people in different occupations, for example, lawyers, doctors, and chief executive officers of major companies, on the one hand, versus day laborers, cleaning people, and assembly-line workers on the other. What do you find? You find that the higher you are on the occupational ladder, the taller you are. Have you shown that height is somehow advantageous to good work in any of the higher level occupations? No. What you've shown is that you used height as a basis for deciding what jobs people will — and will not — be allowed to pursue.

Of course, I am not saying that IQ is unrelated to job success. It is related, although weakly. What I am saying is that we should not say, as do Herrnstein and Murray, that there is some invisible guiding hand — some force of nature — that is leading the cream to rise to the top and the dregs to fall to the bottom. Rather, we need to recognize that we will get as a society what we create. It was not nature that decided whom to value; it was society.

IQ matters, but not much. If you read Herrnstein and Murray (1994), you probably would not get to the appendices at the back of this book of more than 850 pages. And if you read the appendices, you probably would not get to Appendix 4. And if you read Appendix 4, you might not understand the complex statistics, which require advanced background in statistical methods to understand. But boiled down, the statistics say that despite all the impressive-looking graphs, IQ-based measures typically account for less than 10% of the variation in who is more and less successful according to societal standards. That means that IQ leaves more than 90% of the variation among individuals unexplained. Scarcely a basis for claiming that IQ is what really matters!

Today, many, if not most psychologists look to more than just IQ for the identification of the intellectually gifted. For example, Renzulli (1986) believes that high commitment to tasks (motivation) and creativity are important to giftedness, in addition to above-average although not necessarily outstanding intelligence. Notice that Renzulli argues only that intelligence needs to be above-average, not that it needs to be superb. Among those at the low end of the scale on tests, say, those with IQs of 50, you probably would not now or ever find many CEOs. But you will find many people who could succeed as CEOs if they are above the average in IQ. Renzulli's theory also points out that without motivation, intelligence is not worth a whole lot. There are any number of stories of failed IQ geniuses who just were not motivated to make much of their IQs. Indeed, excessive pushing of these children can result in their burning out before they even have an opportunity to use their intelligence in ways that are productive to society.

William James Siddis is a famous example of such an individual: An intellectually brilliant youngster, he was pushed beyond where he was comfortable going, eventually faded into obscurity, and ended his life very sadly. Such cases are not common, of course. But they do illustrate the need for motivation, and for people to be allowed to develop for themselves. We see in many societies how pushing children beyond what is good for them results in early burnout and underuse of their talents.

In addition to intelligence, creativity, and motivation, Feldhusen (1986) looks in the gifted for high self-concept, knowledge, and specialized talents. I would emphasize a sense of self-efficacy (Bandura, 1977) rather than self-concept. Self-efficacy refers to someone's sense that they can accomplish what they want to in life, whereas self-concept refers to a generalized positive view of oneself. In fact, many gifted people have somewhat negative self-concepts, especially in domains other than that of their giftedness, but occasionally even in that of their expertise. What they more seem to have in common is a sense that they can do what they need to do, whatever they may think of themselves.

I believe that our current views of giftedness in school are for the most part short-sighted, especially in their concentration on IQ. In fact, there are almost certainly many more gifted individuals than we realize, given our means of identification.

My own interest in broadening our means of identifying potential high performers came from an experience in my own career. Because of my wretched performance on IQ tests as a child, I became very interested in psychology. As a result, by the time I was in seventh grade, I decided I wanted to study intelligence. I did. I did a project on the development of mental tests, and constructed my own test. I also found in my hometown library the Stanford–Binet intelligence test, and decided to give it to some of my classmates.

The first classmate I gave it to was a girl in whom I was romantically interested. I figured I would break the ice by giving her the test. Not a good idea. The relationship not only terminated at that point, it also never got started at that point. So if you are romantically interested in someone, giving the person an IQ test is probably not a great idea.

The next person I gave the test to was also a mistake. It was a guy I had known from the Cub Scouts, but it turned out that this kid, whom I thought was a good friend, was in fact mentally ill. In technical terms, he was a tattle-tale. He told his mother I had given him the test. Apparently being a tattle-tale is inherited. She told the junior high school guidance counselor. Apparently it is also contagious. She told the head school psychologist. The whole affair came to an unpleasant conclusion when the psychologist took me out of social studies class and bawled me out for 50 minutes, ending with the statement that he would personally burn the book containing the test if I ever brought it into school again. Sometimes psychologists just do not recognize those who are doing something rather extraordinary. He did, I must confess, suggest that if I wanted to continue studying intelligence, I should limit my studies to rats. Perhaps he was suggesting himself as a first subject. Who knows?

By the time I got to Yale as a first-year student, I was eager to study intelligence and figure out why I was so stupid. By then, I was getting better grades because of my fourth-grade teacher having given me the confidence I needed, as well as the self-efficacy, to perform well. But because of the low test scores, it never occurred to me that my now high performance in school might be due to intelligence, since I knew I had a low IQ. I came to believe that I had discovered a secret to school success that very few children knew: To get good grades, you needed to go to sleep early. I still do.

There is a not-so-hidden point here, though. Once students get low scores on aptitude tests such as the *SAT* or the *ACT* (*American College Test*, also used for college admissions in the U.S.), they come to view themselves as dumb. Even if they achieve, they may view themselves as achieving in spite of their being dumb. Society may view them in the same way. They may come to be labeled over-achievers, people whose achievements exceed their grasp, and who ought to be pushed down to size.

Many societies do not value gifted performance. In Norway, they speak of the Law of Jante, according to which if someone's head sticks up over the heads of the rest, then the head needs to be cut off to get the person down to size. This same mentality is rather common in many parts of the world, and is not unknown in the U.S. Often, the person who is average in every respect is most valued. Many of us grew up in families or went to schools where nothing was valued more than one's not standing out from the crowd. Those who did, or do, are viewed as needing to be brought down to size.

By the time I was a first-year college student, I was eager to study psychology. Unfortunately, I got off to a bad start. I received a grade of "C" in the introductory-psychology course, scarcely an indication of a bright future in the field of psychology. I came to the conclusion that, for sure, the IQ tests were right, and I did not have the ability. My psychology professor apparently agreed with me, because he commented to me one day in handing back a test that there was a famous Sternberg in psychology (Saul), and it appeared that there was not about to be another.

I took the message to heart and decided to switch to another major. I chose mathematics because I thought it was useful. The choice turned out to be fortunate. After receiving a worse grade in the introductory course for mathematics majors than I had received in the introductory-psychology course, I decided to switch back to psychology. And I did well in the upper level courses.

I have now been a psychologist for 26 years, and one thing of which I am sure is that I have never — not even once — had to do in the profession what I needed to do to get an "A" in the introductory course, as well as some of the other courses. In particular, I have never had to memorize a book or a lecture. If I cannot remember something, I just look it up. The way we set things up, though, we reward with "A's" the students who are good memorizers, not just at the college level, but at many other levels as well. In our defense, many other countries are much worse.

The problem is that not just in psychology, but in other fields, the demands of the field bear little or no resemblance to the demands of the training that is needed in order to enter the field. For example, my son once said to me that he hated history and wished he never had to take another history course. I said to him that I, personally, had always found history interesting, and I wondered why he did not. His response was that he hated memorizing dates. Indeed, memorizing dates, battles, and historical documents constitutes the way many history courses are taught. But historians are not experts in their fields by virtue of being walking encyclopedias of dates or names of battles or historical documents.

If we go to the sciences, in general, we find the same thing. Often, what gets an "A" is memorizing a book or lectures. At times, students also need to solve problems at the backs of chapters and on tests. But scientists do not memorize formulas for a living, nor do they solve problems in the backs of textbooks. Rather, they need to generate problems for themselves. Indeed, to a large extent they are judged on the importance of the problems they decide to study.

I went to one of my son's English classes on Parents' Day, a day for parents to attend classes with their school-aged children. The children were studying *The Odyssey*. The whole class consisted of the teacher's saying a quote, and the students having to identify who said it, or what was happening at the time the quote was made. For students who love to memorize, it was a great class. But the students who excelled in that class were not, for sure, those who were showing the talents of either a writer or a literary critic. And those who did not do well may potentially have had the talent to be the next Shakespeare. Unlikely, perhaps, but the teacher would never know, given the way the class was taught.

The danger is that we miss many of the potentially most talented people in any field because they are not good memorizers. Some of the best potential psychologists, biologists, historians, or whatever, may get derailed because they think that they do not have the talent to pursue their interest. Their teachers may think the same. We need to teach in a way that recognizes the talents that are important to pursuing a career, not just to memorizing books.

We decided a few years ago to do a five-year study to check out my hypothesis about teaching, and fortunately, received funding from the U.S. Office of Educational Research and Improvement. The goal of the study was simple. It was to see whether students would perform better in the classroom if they were taught in a way that allowed them to make use of their natural patterns of abilities. Here is what we did (Sternberg, 1997; Sternberg & Clinkenbeard, 1995; Sternberg et al., 1996).

We sent a test based on the triarchic theory of intelligence to students all around the country. The test contained analytic, creative, and practical items, in the verbal, quantitative, figural, and essay domains. The idea was to look in a wide variety of ways for students' patterns of abilities. We did not want to limit ourselves to the analytical kinds of items found on IQ tests; nor did we want to limit ourselves just to, say, the verbal domain, or just to multiple-choice items. But testing the three aspects of my theory of intelligence in four different domains, we were greatly increasing the chances that, if a student had high intellectual abilities of some kind, we would be able to detect them. Some sample items from the test are shown in Table 1.

The students taking the test were high school students from all around the U.S.A. and from abroad who had been identified by their teachers or schools as potential candidates for the program. They were not necessarily identified as conventionally gifted. We then chose students for the program who met one of five types of criterion. Either they were very high in analytical abilities, very high in creative abilities, very high in practical abilities, high but not necessarily very high in all three kinds of abilities, or relatively low in all three kinds of abilities. This gave us five different ability groupings.

It is worth saying right out that the groups differed from each other not only in abilities, but in some other fairly obvious ways. For example, the high analytic group was most notable for its traditional composition in terms of the usual "gifted" students: It was mostly white, middle- to upper-middle class, and composed of students who had been identified as gifted in their schools many times in the past. The high-creative and high-practical groups, in contrast, were much more diverse, ethnically, racially, and with respect to socio-economic class. Many of the students in these groups had never been identified as gifted before, and they were

Table 1: Sample questions from the Sternberg triarchic abilities test

Analytical Multiple Choice (Verbal)	The *vip* was green, so I started to cross the street. *Vip* most likely means: A. car B. sign C. light D. tree
Creative Quantitative	There is a new mathematical operation called *graf*. It is defined as follows: $x\ graf\ y = x + y$, if $x < y$ but $x\ graf\ y = x - y$, if otherwise. How much is 4 *graf* 7? A. -3 B. 3 C. 11 D. -11
Practical Figural (Students are shown a map)	After attending a performance at the theater, you need to drive to House A. If you want to avoid the traffic jam at the intersection of Spruce Avenue and Willow Street and take the shortest alternative route, you will drive A. west on Maple Avenue to Route 326. B. west on Pine Street to Hickory Street. C. east on Maple Avenue to Oak Street. D. east on Pine Street to Oak Street.

generally not the highest achievers in their schools. The high balanced group (who did well on all the tests) again looked more like a typical gifted group, presumably because they were high in the more conventional analytical abilities. The low balanced group was diverse.

The students were brought to Yale to take a college-level course in introductory psychology. All students received the same basic introductory-psychology text (Sternberg, 1995), which is based on my triarchic theory of intelligence (Sternberg, 1985). Students all also received identical lectures in the mornings from a star teacher at Yale, who had won teaching awards.

The critical treatment distinguishing the groups occurred in the afternoon. There were four different types of afternoon instruction. One kind emphasized analytical thinking: comparing and contrasting, judging, evaluating, analyzing. A second kind of instruction emphasized creative thinking: discovering, inventing, imagining, supposing. A third kind of instruction emphasized practical thinking: using, utilizing, and applying. And the fourth kind of instruction — the so-called control group — emphasized memory, as do most introductory courses, in psychology or in other areas. Of course, these techniques are applicable not just to psychology, but to other fields as well. Table 2 shows examples of the kinds of questions teachers can ask in various fields if they want to teach analytically, creatively, and practically.

It is important to realize one thing about the instruction. Because we were doing an experiment, we assigned students to sections that emphasized only one of analytical, creative, or practical thinking, or memory. A good course, however, will be a combination of all of these different types of thinking. The reason is that you want to help students both to learn in ways that are comfortable to them, and to learn in ways that are not.

In my own theory, the gifted student is very different from the gifted student in a conventional sense. Gifted students or professionals are people who know what they do well. They figure out their strengths. They also know what they do not do well. They figure out their weaknesses. Most importantly, they are people who figure out how to capitalize or to make the most of their strengths, and to compensate for and to remediate their weaknesses. In other words, they are people who figure out what they do well, and make the most of it. They figure out what they do not do well, and find ways around these weaknesses, and ways to make themselves good enough at least to get by.

If you look at truly gifted individuals in the everyday world, you invariably find that they are not good at everything. Rather, they are really good at something, and sometimes, just one or two things. But they know what these things are, and make the most of them. Similarly, they know what they do not do well, and find ways around these things, or ways to get by.

For example, Gordon Bower, one of the great cognitive psychologists of our time, has succeeded in part because he has an uncanny ability to anticipate the field. He knows where things are going, and gets there just a little before the field. Successful entrepreneurs share this trait. Steve Jobs and Steve Wozniak created Apple Computer just before the microcomputer explosion. Bill Gates had himself entrenched in Microsoft just before the software explosion. None of these people were uniformly talented in everything, as later events showed. No one is. Rather, they figured out their strengths and made the most of them.

In our summer course, we evaluated all students for four kinds of achievements: memory, analytical, creative, and practical. Thus, students could not just show that they had memorized the book. They had to show different kinds of proficiencies. Teaching in analytical, creative, and practical ways is important, because it actually enhances learning of material rather than detracting from it. Everyone knows that memorizing a book results in very short-term learning. Most students forget the material as soon as they take the exam, or, unfortunately, sometimes before. By thinking about the material in different ways, students are forced to process it more deeply, and thus to learn it better. By thinking to learn, they learn to think.

When we looked at the results, they were strong and clear. Students who were placed in afternoon sections that matched their pattern of abilities performed better

Table 2: Triarchic theory applied to student instruction and assessment methods

	Analytical	**Creative**	**Practical**
Psychology	Compare Freud's theory of dreaming to Crick's.	Design an experiment to test a theory of dreaming.	What are the implications of Freud's theory of dreaming for your life?
Biology	Evaluate the validity of the bacterial theory of ulcers.	Design an experiment to test the bacterial theory of ulcers.	How would the bacterial theory of ulcers change conventional treatment regimens?
Literature	In what ways were Catherine Earnshaw and Daisy Miller similar?	Write an alternative ending to *Wuthering Heights* uniting Catherine and Heathcliff in life.	Why are lovers sometimes cruel to each other and what can we do about it?
History	How did events in post-World War I Germany lead to the rise of Nazism?	How might Truman have encouraged the surrender of Japan without A-bombing Hiroshima?	What lessons does Nazism hold for events in Bosnia today?
Mathematics	How is this mathematical proof flawed?	Prove … How might catastrophe theory be applied to psychology?	How is trigonometry applied to construction of bridges?
Art	Compare and contrast how Rembrandt and Van Gogh used light in …	Draw a beam of light.	How could we reproduce the lighting in this painting in the same actual room?

than did students who were placed in afternoon sections that mismatched. For example, if a creative student was given at least some chance to exercise his or her creative abilities in the course, the student's performance would be better than if not given such a chance. The same was true for analytical and practical students.

In a way, the results are not surprising. It makes sense that students would do better if allowed to show their strengths. But the way we teach in school, students rarely are given such a chance. We value the students with strong memory and perhaps analytical abilities, and practically write off those with strong creative and practical abilities. If we want to capitalize on the gifts of our students, at any level, we need to change and teach and assess students in ways that recognize their strengths, not just their weaknesses.

The study also revealed some other interesting findings. For example, although the high-analytical group was mostly white and middle- to upper-middle-class, the high-creative and high-practical groups were not. When you expand the range of abilities considered, the range of students identified as gifted increases as well. We also found from factor analysis that there was no general factor in the intelligence we used. In other words, when you expand the range of abilities, the so-called general factor of intelligence drops out. It is probably largely an artifact of using a narrow range of ability tests. Finally, we found that we could improve prediction of course grades by measuring creative and practical as well as analytical abilities. In other words, so long as teaching recognizes these abilities and achievement is assessed in terms of these abilities, they will be important for success.

It is interesting to consider some successful people with high IQs, because one soon realizes that their success is not necessarily due to their high IQs. Again, correlation can be confused with causation. Consider, as an example, Marilyn Vos Savant, who is listed in the *Guinness Book of World Records* as having the highest IQ of any living person on record. She has written a number of puzzle books that challenge people's mental abilities, and also has a column in *Parade*, a weekly magazine found in newspapers and of enormous circulation.

How one judges Savant's success depends, of course, on the criteria one uses. From the standpoint of major contributions to the world, she would probably rank very low among great thinkers. Her high IQ certainly has not put her in, or near, the class of the great world thinkers in literature, science, or the arts. Actually, if you read her column, you may well conclude that she is not a world-class psychologist either. But from another point of view, she has been enormously successful — in getting the column, in getting media attention, and in getting into a book of world records. From the standpoint of my own theory of intelligence, Savant is capitalizing on her practical rather than her academic or analytical abilities. A physicist or a mathematician might capitalize on great analytical abilities: Savant's columns do not. But she has the high practical abilities to use her IQ to get attention, and then to write her books and columns. And one could argue she deserves a lot of credit for that. After all, ultimately, that is what intelligence is about: finding one, strengths, and making the most of them. And she has.

Personally, I would give her a lot more credit than many failed writers, business people, artists, or whatever, who never could figure out what they really do well, or who figured it out but insisted on doing something else anyway. They are often unhappy, largely because they may or may not have figured out their strengths, but for sure, they did not make the most of them.

Success in any field requires one to distinguish, as do Csikszentmihalyi and Robinson (1986), between a domain of expertise and a field of expertise. The domain refers to the work itself, the field to the people who do the work. To do outstanding work in a domain is one thing; to be recognized by the field is another. Domain-expertise can be a reflection of some balance of analytical, creative, and practical strength, but recognition by a field as being gifted in that field almost always requires a substantial measure of practical intelligence. It also requires a good measure of luck.

We like to think that good work is enough, but sooner or later, we learn that it is not. Artists need to get their work displayed in galleries; authors need to get their work published. Multitudes of talented artists and authors never get to be known, whereas many with less talent become household names. Partly the well-known people were at the right place at the right time, partly they made the right connections, and partly they knew what the field wanted. Moreover, most fields are divided, so that success in one part of the field does not necessarily mean success in another.

Andrew Lloyd Webber is a good candidate for the wealthiest as well as the most well-known composer alive today. At one level, he has been enormously successful. In the world of "serious music," however — the world of concertos, sonatas, operas, and the like — Webber is not among the élite. Similarly, Leo Buscaglia had enormous popular success, but is virtually never cited in the work of serious scholars on close relationships. Webber and Buscaglia are enormous successes in one respect, and not in another. But so is everyone else. What successful people have in common is that they decide what their field is, and then seek to succeed within it. Probably no one can please everyone, and the sooner one learns that, the better. There is no single criterion for success, and people who are gifted, in a large sense, are ones who can find personal success in a field of their own choosing, and sometimes, their own making.

In sum, the tendency today is to look beyond IQ to identify intellectually gifted individuals. There are many ways to be gifted, and scores on conventional intelligence tests represent only one of these ways. Indeed, some of the most gifted adult contributors to society, such as Albert Einstein or Thomas Edison, were not top performers either on tests or in school during their early years. Einstein did not even speak until he was 3 years old, and many other remarkably gifted persons have even shown characteristics associated with mental retardation, which we consider next.

1.2 Mental Retardation

Mental retardation refers to low levels of intelligence. Simple enough. Much less simple is determining how we conceive of mental retardation, and whom we label as being mentally retarded. The American Association on Mental Retardation (AAMR) includes within its definition of mental retardation two components: low IQ and low *adaptive competence*, the latter of which refers to how a person gets along in the world. In other words, to be labeled as retarded an individual not only would have to perform poorly on an intelligence test, but also would have to show problems in adapting to the environment. A child whose performance was normal in every way except for low IQ would not, by this definition, be classified as mentally retarded. There are different levels of mental retardation in the ordinarily accepted classification scheme.

People with mild retardation have IQ's of 50–70. They constitute about 85% of the population of retarded persons, and about 2% of the general population. They may acquire academic skills and demonstrate academic mastery in a number of domains, but usually at the sixth-grade level or below. They are generally helped by special education designed especially for their needs. They are likely to acquire social and vocation-related skills, given adequate training and appropriate environment. Given sufficient support and assistance, especially during times of stress, they may achieve independent living and occupational success.

People with moderate retardation have IQs in the range of 35 to 55. They constitute 10% of retarded persons, and about 0.1% of the general population. They have considerable difficulty in school, but may acquire and demonstrate mastery of academic tasks at or below the fourth-grade level if given special education. Given appropriate very structured environmental support and supervision, they may be able to engage in unskilled or possibly highly routine semiskilled vocational activities that lead to self-support. They are able to engage in many personal self-maintenance activities. Typically, a sheltered home and work environment are desirable, with opportunities for supervision and guidance.

People with severe mental retardation have IQs in the 24 to 40 range. They constitute about 4% of retarded persons, and are less than 0.003% of the general population. They may learn to talk or at least to communicate in some manner. They are unlikely to profit from vocational training, but given adequate full supervision and highly structured environmental support, they may be able to perform simple tasks required for personal self-maintenance (including going to the toilet) and possibly even some very limited vocational activities. Some custodial services may be required, in addition to a carefully controlled environment.

People with profound mental retardation have IQs below 25. They constitute less than 2% of the retarded population, and a very very small fraction of the general population. They have limited motor development and little or no speech. They are generally unresponsive to training, but may be trained to participate in some self-maintenance activities (not including going to the toilet). They require constant supervision and assistance in performing fundamental self-maintenance within some kind of custodial setting.

In thinking about mental retardation, it is important to keep in mind that people can have adaptive skills despite a low IQ. Edgerton (1967) cites the example of a man with low IQ who was unable to tell time — an indication, certainly, of some kind of cognitive deficit. However, the man employed a clever compensatory strategy. He wore a nonfunctional watch, so that whenever he wanted to know the time, he could stop, look at his watch, pretend to notice that it was not working, and then ask a nearby stranger (who would have observed his behavior) to tell him the correct time. How should we assess this man's adaptive competence — in terms of his strategy for determining the time or in terms of his inability to tell time by looking at a watch?

Edward Zigler (1971) believes that some mentally retarded children simply develop at a slower rate mentally than do children with normal intelligence. Only a small proportion of the mentally retarded, according to Zigler, have organic deficits that result in their being qualitatively different from normal individuals. Most investigators, however, seek not only to look at quantitative differences in rates of development but also at qualitative differences in performance in all the retarded. A key qualitative difference centers on metacognitive skill — that is, understanding and control of cognition. There is fairly widespread agreement that mentally retarded individuals have difficulty with the executive processes of cognition, such as planning, monitoring, and evaluating their strategies for task performance (Campione, Brown & Ferrara, 1982).

Even when retarded persons have been taught specific metacognitive skills for tackling specific tasks, such as learning a list of words, they often do not transfer these skills to any tasks other than the specific one for which they learned the skills. Nonretarded persons demonstrate much better ability to transfer strategies from one task to another. For example, retarded children do not spontaneously rehearse (practice silently) lists of words they are asked to memorize (Brown et al., 1973); even when such children are trained to memorize a given kind of list, they do not transfer that strategy to memorizing other kinds of lists (Butterfield, Wambold & Belmont, 1973).

We usually think of certain persons as mentally retarded and others as not. Reuven Feuerstein (1979, 1980; Feuerstein, Rand & Rynders, 1988), however, has refused to label such individuals, referring instead to "retarded performance". In his view, it is the performance rather than the individual that is retarded. Moreover, he has shown that we can remediate with such individuals so that their level of accomplishment begins to approach or even equal that of those showing noretarded performance.

My own view is that some individuals do show mental retardation as an attribute, but that we can remediate, nevertheless. Feuerstein makes an important point in any case: Labels can do a great deal of damage. Once a person is labeled in a certain way — whatever way — the label tends to stay with the person, and sometimes to have more effect than the person's actual performance.

Curiously, fewer and fewer children are being labeled mentally retarded these days, and more and more, learning disabled. Perhaps the latter label is seen as less pejorative. Moreover, because funding for special services is often linked to children being identified as learning disabled, schools are often eager to label children in this way so as to receive greater special-education funding. Even some parents hope that their children will be so labeled so as to be entitled to special services. We are in a strange position as a society when we try to have our children assigned labels indicating problems in order to have more attention paid to them. Perhaps we were better off when we recognized that terms such as "mental retardation" and "learning disability", although they may bring special services, also can stay with the child throughout his or her life.

Although we do not understand well the subtle influences of heredity on intelligence, we do know that some genetic syndromes clearly cause mental retardation. For example, one of the more common genetic causes of mental retardation is Down Syndrome, once called "mongolism". This syndrome results from the presence of extra chromosomal material on one of the chromosomes. The extra material disrupts the normal biochemical messages and results in retardation and other features of this syndrome.

Sometimes, hereditary factors interact with environmental ones to produce mental retardation. Although we cannot yet prevent these diseases, we can try to block the environmental contribution to mental retardation. For example, we now know how to minimize the likelihood of mental retardation in phenylketonuria (PKU), a rare hereditary disease that results in mental retardation if environmental intervention is not imposed. Essentially, children with this disease do not produce an enzyme needed for properly metabolizing the amino acid phenylalanine. As a result, if PKU is not quickly discovered after birth, and the infant consumes food containing complete proteins or other sources of phenylalanine, by-products of the incomplete metabolism of this amino acid will accumulate in the bloodstream. These by-products will cause progressively more severe brain damage and permanent retardation. In PKU, the interactive roles of nature and nurture are clear, and we can specify clearly these roles.

PKU also shows how even a disease that is completely heritable can be susceptible to environmental effects. Very often, people confuse heritability with modifiability. They assume that if a trait is heritable, it therefore cannot be modifiable. This view is wrong. PKU is 100% heritable, but also highly modifiable in its effects by eliminating intake of phenylalanine.

There are many examples of attributes that are highly heritable but also modifiable. Height is another one. Height has a very high degree of heritability, over .9 on a 0 to 1 scale. Yet, through better nutrition, heights have been increasing in recent generations, and may well continue to increase. These increases have been especially dramatic in Japan. Similarly, various kinds of diseases of childhood, such as parasitic infections, can result in stunted growth.

2 Modifiability of Intelligence

At one time, it was believed that intelligence is fixed, and that we are stuck forever with whatever level of intelligence we may have at birth. Today, many and perhaps most researchers in the field of intelligence believe that intelligence is malleable — that it can be shaped and even increased through various kinds of interventions (Detterman & Sternberg, 1982).

For example, the Head Start program was initiated in the 1960s as a way of providing preschoolers with an edge on intellectual abilities and accomplishments when they started school. Long-term follow-ups have indicated that by mid-adolescence, children who participated in the program were more than a grade ahead of matched controls who were not in the program (Lazar & Darlington, 1982; Zigler & Berman, 1983). Children in the program also scored higher on a variety of tests of scholastic achievement, were less likely to need remedial attention, and were less likely to show behavioral problems. Although such measures are not truly measures of intelligence, they show strong positive correlations with intelligence tests of the conventional kind. A number of newer programs have also shown some success in environments outside the family home. The Abecedarian Project of Ramey (1994) is a notable example: It has succeeded in raising intellectual abilities of school children in a number of different instances.

The importance of the home environment is shown in work done by Bradley and Caldwell (1984) in regard to the development of intelligence in young children. These researchers found that several factors in the early (pre-school) home environment may be linked to high IQ scores: emotional and verbal responsivity of the primary caregiver and the caregiver's involvement with the child; avoidance of arbitrary restrictions and punishment; organization of the physical environment and activity schedule; provision of appropriate play materials; and opportunities for variety in daily stimulation. Further, Bradley and Caldwell (1984) found that these factors more effectively predicted IQ scores than did socioeconomic status or family-structure variables, such as number of children.

Home environment is most important in cases of severe deprivation. For example, Dennis (1973) showed that children from certain Iranian orphanages who were not adopted by the age of 2 were, for the most part, mentally retarded. Those who were adopted were not. There was no particular intervention at all, just differences in intellectual stimulation and the nurturance of the respective environments. We are talking about major differences here, with an average difference in the order of 50 points. As you can see, when there is enough range in quality of environments, environment can be very powerful. In effect, even a decent environment becomes a powerful means for increasing IQ, and probably other aspects of intelligence as well.

One of the most impressive of the intellectual-skills training programs has been Project Odyssey (Adams, 1986), which was instituted in Venezuela during a period in which there was a Ministry for the Development of Intelligence, a unique enterprise in human history in which an entire ministry of a national government was devoted to the improvement of human intellect. The program covered a wide variety of analytic and creative skills, and was carefully evaluated. Indeed, the evaluation of the program was a model for how to evaluate such programs, because it used such a wide variety of different kinds of cognitive measures to evaluate the program's success. The results were published in one of psychology's most prestigious journals.

I mention this program especially because of the authors of the careful evaluation, namely, Richard Herrnstein and his colleagues (Herrnstein et al., 1986).

Herrnstein is the same individual who later, in *The Bell Curve*, would say that attempts to increase intelligence have been a resounding failure — an example of overblown claims that have never been materialized in concrete results. At one level, it is puzzling how a co-author on a successful program and the senior author of the evaluation of the program would later conclude that such programs are doomed to failure. At another level, it is not surprising.

Many fields of science have such powerful political overtones that it becomes difficult to discuss these fields without politics entering in. The field of intelligence is almost certainly one of these fields, especially when we come to issues of modifiability and group differences. The political arguments come from both sides: right and left. Thus, much as *The Bell Curve* can be read as a political treatise from the right, many of the replies were little more than political treatises from the left — many by people who obviously had not read the book. Indeed, a whole issue of a popular magazine was composed of articles by individuals who were asked to write the articles in a hurry, and before most and perhaps any of them had time to read the book.

The danger of politicization is that the scientific issues get lost in the noise. The controversy surrounding *The Bell Curve* was a good example, as was the book itself. Even the most conservative scientists might have trouble seeing what the social-policy recommendations had to do with the rest of the book. The book was more like two books — one a statement of statistics interpreted to make a certain, right-wing case — the other a right-wing political treatise with recommendations for society that had nothing really to do with IQ or the data presented in the book. Intelligence can be studied scientifically, and it is important we do so, lest we confuse scientific arguments, such as those of the article by Herrnstein and his colleagues (1986), with political arguments, which are so prevalent in Herrnstein and Murray's (1994) book, *The Bell Curve*.

We need to distinguish genuine teaching of intellectual skills from routine test preparation. For example, there are a number of books and courses available that may increase scores on tests, because they give practice in types of items found on particular tests, but that do not necessarily produce generalizable gains in intelligence. This is not to knock such books or courses. My own children were once of the age where they would be taking the *SAT* soon, and I bought them both a book, and would have been delighted if they wanted to take a course. My goal was not to improve their intelligence, but to improve their test scores so they could get into the college of their choice. And, on average, such courses do result in small to moderate gains on standardized tests (Messick & Jungeblut, 1981).

At the same time, there is an issue of equity with such books and courses: Not everyone can afford the time or the money. And the people who cannot afford to read the books or take the courses find themselves at a disadvantage, on average, in comparison with those who do have the time or money. Moreover, people with the time and money are unlikely to be randomly distributed across the population. Rather, they are likely to be people in the middle- to upper-middle socioeconomic classes. Once again, the tests work in favor, on average, of those who are better off to begin with.

This common finding — both with regard to tests and other measures of success in society — is sometimes called the Matthew Effect (Merton, 1968), referring back to the Bible, in which Matthew pointed out that, in simple terms, the rich tend to get richer and the poor, poorer. And he was not referring only to money. Matthew Effects tend to result in increasing polarization in the resources of society, which we are seeing right now in the United States as well as in other countries, and also result in increasing misunderstandings between the haves and the have-nots.

Curiously, schools, at least at the high school level, are increasingly becoming glorified classrooms for test-preparation courses. On Parents' Day, I attended my daughter's English class, which consisted largely of the students memorizing and then spitting back definitions of difficult English-vocabulary words. The class was a thinly disguised preparation for the *SAT*. It is hard to blame the schools exclusively: They are under pressure from parents as well as district personnel to improve test scores. But students often forget the vocabulary soon after they memorize it, because it is never well integrated into their minds. They never really actively learn to use the words and to relate the words to what they already know.

We did a study that looked at an alternative approach to improving vocabulary-related skills (Sternberg, 1987). Rather than having children memorize vocabulary words, we taught students in three different instructional groups how to learn meanings of words from context. In other words, they would see a word whose meaning they did not know in a natural context, and would be taught how to use context clues to figure out the word's meaning. Thus, if they read that "the mother looked at her child through the oam of the bubbling stew," they would be taught how to figure out that *oam* probably means steam or possibly smoke. In this case, oam is something that arises from a bubbling stew and is transparent or translucent, making steam and smoke likely meanings.

In addition to instructed groups, we had two control groups. One group got practice on figuring out meanings of words from context — the type of practice the children would be likely to have gotten if they took a test-preparation course. The other group got nothing — no treatment at all. We then compared the performance of the instructed groups to the performance of the two control groups. We found that all of the instructed groups increased significantly more than did either of the control groups from pre-test to post-test on measures of the ability to figure out meanings of words from context. The two control groups did not differ from each other. In other words, just practice is not particularly effective. People need instruction in how to figure out the meanings of the words.

I believe that instruction of this kind is superior to memorizing lists of words, because in the type of instruction we gave, we are teaching children to figure out meanings for themselves. Long after we are gone, they will have skills that they can apply to the learning of new vocabulary, rather than a memorized list of vocabulary words that they will quickly forget. If you want to develop intelligence, you need to teach people to think with content, not just to memorize it.

We can also teach seemingly more intangible skills, such as insight skills (Davidson & Sternberg, 1984; Sternberg & Davidson, 1982). We devised a program to teach three major kinds of insight skills in two domains. The insight skills were selective encoding — recognizing relevant information embedded in irrelevant information; selective combination — putting together this relevant information; and selective comparison — recognizing past information that you can bring to bear on a current situation. We taught the skills in two domains, verbal (as in the learning from context above) and quantitative. An example of a quantitative insight problem would be: If you have blue socks and brown socks in a drawer mixed in a ratio of 3 to 4, and the room is dark, how many socks do you need to withdraw from the drawer to be assured of having a pair of the same color?

Half the students received our insight training program and half received alternative instruction (the control group). All students received a pre-test and a post-test, and the measure of interest was pre-test to post-test gain for experimental versus control students. We showed that when the program was infused into school teaching for fourth- to fifth-grade (9 to 11-year old students), it was possible to get significant and substantial increases in insightful thinking abilities (Davidson & Sternberg, 1984). Thus, we can modify thinking even in its most difficult aspects, including insightful and creative as well as analytical thinking (see also Sternberg & Spear-Swerling, 1996; Sternberg & Williams, 1996).

In yet another program, we showed that it is possible to obtain substantial increases in practical intelligence as well, or what we have called children's *practical intelligence for schools*. Practical intelligence for schools refers to the practical skills that are needed to adapt to the demands of the school. Many children are bright, but do not quite understand what the school expects. They are undersocialized with respect to the value system of the school. Such students are not limited to those in impoverished neighborhoods. Many middle-class students also lack such under-standing, in greater or lesser degree. I grew up in a middle-class neighborhood myself, but it was not until I went to college that I learned that one reads mathematics assignments in a very different way from the way one reads novels. And my son, growing up in a middle-class neighborhood, did not realize that teachers expect course papers to be neat until I emphasized this fact to him.

In a series of studies, 8 to 10-year old children showed increased ability relative to controls effectively to do homework, take tests, read, and write when they received our program for increasing school-based practical intelligence (Gardner et al., 1994; Sternberg, Okagaki & Jackson, 1990; Williams et al., 1996). These results held up across a variety of kinds of assessments of performance. In sum, the available evidence suggests that we can, in fact, teach people to think better (Baron & Sternberg, 1987).

3 Heritability of Intelligence

Today, the large majority of psychologists and behavior geneticists — people who specialize in the effects of genes on behavior — believe that differences in intelligence result from a combination of hereditary and environmental factors. The old nature-nurture controversy continues, however, in regard to intelligence.

The contribution of heredity to intelligence is often expressed in terms of a *heritability coefficient*, a number on a scale from 0 to 1 that expresses the proportion of variation among individuals that is alleged to be due to heredity. A coefficient of 0 would mean that heredity has no influence on variation among people, and a coefficient of 1 would mean that nothing but heredity has any influence. It is important to remember that the coefficient indicates variation in measured intelligence. The more similar people are in terms of the gene pool from which they come, the lower the heritability coefficient will tend to be because there just is not much variation in genes; the more similar the environments from which people come, the higher the heritability coefficient will tend to be, because of lack of variation in environments (see Herrnstein, 1973). Heritability can thus vary over place and time.

Current estimates of the heritability coefficient of intelligence are based almost exclusively on performance on standard tests of intelligence (see Sternberg & Grigorenko, 1997). The estimates can be no better than the tests, and we have already seen that the tests define intelligence somewhat narrowly. How can we actually estimate the heritability of intelligence, or at least that portion of it measured by the conventional tests? Several methods have been used. It is important to understand these methods in order to understand what all the fuss is about, and what conclusions can be drawn from it. The main methods that have been used are the methods of separated identical twins, the method of identical versus fraternal twins, and the method of adopted children.

3.1 Separated Identical Twins

Identical twins have identical genes. No one knows exactly why identical twinning occurs, but we do know that identical twins result when a sperm fertilizes an egg, and then the newly formed embryo splits in two, resulting in two embryos with identical genes. Suppose that a set of twins is born, and then one of the twins is immediately whisked away to a new environment, chosen at random, so that no relationship exists between the environments in which the two twins are raised. The two twins would have identical genes, but any similarity between their environments would be due only to chance. The problem, of course, is that twins are randomly assigned to environments. They typically are put in environments that are at least somewhat similar to each other, resulting in a confound in the conclusions drawn from this method. Because variation in environments is restricted, correlations in environment tend to result in overestimates of the contribution of heredity to variation in levels of intelligence.

If we had a number of such twin pairs, and they truly were assigned to environments at random, we would be able to estimate the hereditary contribution to intelligence by correlating the measured intelligence of each individual with that of his or her identical twin. The twins would have in common all their heredity but none of their environment (except any aspects that might be due to chance). In fact, some circumstances have created instances in which twins have been separated at birth and then raised separately. In studies of twins reared apart (e.g. Bouchard & McGue, 1981; Juel-Nielsen, 1965; Newman, Freeman & Holzinger, 1937; Shields, 1962), the various estimates tend to fall within roughly the same heritability-coefficient range of 0.6 to 0.8.

Also, it has consistently been found that heritability tends to increase with age. Because studies of identical twins reared apart tend to be of older individuals, heritability coefficients will tend to be somewhat larger than those obtained with other methods. This result might seem counterintuitive: After all, with time, environment would seem to have had more time to have had an effect. But what seems to happen, in fact, is that the effects of heredity start to dominate the environment over time. In the early years, differences in environment matter more, but as the individual ages, environmental effects have more time to average out, leading the individual to show more effect of the genes.

It is also important to realize that just as what appear to be genetic effects may be due to environment; similarly, what appear to be environmental effects may actually be due to genetics. Suppose, for example, we find a high correlation between socioeconomic status and intelligence, a correlation that in fact exists. Such an interpretation cannot be taken as wholly supporting an environmental interpretation, because people may reach the socioeconomic status they reach in part because of the effects of genes: They inherit tendencies that lead to greater or lesser success. Moreover, we know that people shape environments. Scarr and McCartney (1983) have referred to *experience-producing drives*, by which they mean that genes may lead people to seek out certain experiences or others, experiences that may lead to increased or to decreased abilities.

For example, someone who inherits a tendency to prefer passive kinds of mental activities, and especially learning activities, may spend a lot of time in front of the television, watching shows that require little mental processing. Someone else who inherits a tendency to prefer more active kinds of mental activities may read and write more, leading to more mental processing, and ultimately to higher scores on tests of abilities. In these instances, genes lead to environmental effects, which in turn led to differences in cognitive abilities. Thus, we must always remember that so interactive are the effects of genes and environment that it is almost never a straightforward matter to separate the effects of the two.

I cannot emphasize enough the need for caution in interpreting the results of studies of separated identical twins, or any other studies of heritability of intelligence. In many cases, the twins studied in the research on intelligence were not actually separated at birth, but at some point afterward, giving the twins a common environment for at least some time before the separation. In other cases, it becomes clear that the supposedly random assortment of environments was anything but random. Placement authorities tend to place twins in environments that are relatively similar to those the twins had left. These tendencies may inflate the apparent contribution of heredity to measured variation in intelligence, because variation that is actually environmental is included in the correlation that is supposed to represent only the effect of heredity.

3.2 *Identical Versus Fraternal Twins*

Another way to estimate heritability is to compare the correlation of IQs for identical versus fraternal twins. The idea is that whereas identical twins share identical genes, fraternal twins share only the same genes as would any brother or sister. On average, they share only 50% of their genes. To the extent that the identical and fraternal twin pairs share similar environments due to age, we should not get environmental differences due merely to variations in age among sibling pairs. According to a review by Bouchard and McGue (1981), the average correlation between IQs of fraternal twins is 0.61, compared with 0.86 for identical twins reared together.

These data suggest an environmental contribution to IQ of $(0.86 - 0.61) \times 2$, or .50, leaving us with a heritability coefficient of $1.00 - .50$, or .75, again suggesting a high level of heritability. Unfortunately, these data are affected by the fact that fraternal twins do not share environments to the same extent that identical ones do, particularly if the fraternal twins are not same-sexed twins. Parents tend to treat identical twins more nearly alike than they do fraternal ones, even to the extent of having identical twins dress the same way. Moreover, the twins themselves are likely to respond differently if they are identical, perhaps seeking out more apparent identity with their twin. Thus, once again, the contribution of environment may be underestimated.

3.3 *Adoption*

Yet another way to examine hereditary versus environmental contributions to intelligence is by comparing the correlation between the IQs of adopted children, on the one hand, and those of their biological and adoptive parents, on the other. To the extent that heredity matters, the higher correlation should be with the intelligence of the biological rather than the adoptive parents; to the extent that environment matters, the higher correlation should be that with the intelligence of the adoptive rather than the biological parents. In some families, it is also possible to compare the IQs of the adopted children to the IQs of either biological or adoptive siblings.

When we review the uncertain and mixed results of adoption studies, we must conclude that we still do not know how heritable intelligence is. Many psychologists have concluded that it is probably about 0.5, with a somewhat greater value with increasing age. However, there is no one heritability. Indeed, changes in distributions of genes or environments can change the estimates, and those distributions vary across time and place. We know, for example, that heritabilities differ for groups: For example, heritability is higher for whites than for blacks (Sandra Scarr, personal communication). This brings us to the question of group differences.

4 Group Differences

One thing is not in doubt: In the United States, different racial and ethnic groups have different average IQs. The fact of such a difference is not in itself evidence of a bias in the tests. Bias is not a function of differences in scores between groups. It is a function of prediction. A difference between groups would be evidence of bias only if whatever the tests are designed to predict did not show similar differences.

The literature on test bias has been reviewed in great detail and *ad nauseam* (e.g. Jensen, 1980). The general conclusion from this literature is that tests are not biased, at least in the traditional sense. We need to think about what, exactly, this finding means.

What it means is that if Group A does worse than Group B on a test of intelligence, then typically, it will also do worse to about the same relative degree on whatever it is that the tests are used to predict, if indeed the tests do predict it. Thus, if Group A does worse on conventional intelligence tests than does Group B, then Group A is likely to do worse as well in, say, school achievement. For example, blacks score about one standard deviation (15 IQ points) below whites in the United States, on average. They also achieve at lower levels in school. *Voilà*, according to Jensen, Herrnstein and Murray, and others: The tests are unbiased. Japanese and other Asian Americans tend to do somewhat better than whites on many tests, and also tend to do somewhat better in school. *Voilà*, no bias. But wait a minute.

Are differences between racial groups inherited? Herrnstein and Murray (1994) imply they are. The data, however, just do not support their conclusion. Herrnstein and Murray, as well as others of their ilk, point to the heritability of intelligence as suggesting such heritability. In fact, the data available are what are called *within-groups* heritability estimates. They tell us about sources of transmission of intelligence within, not between groups. Thus, a study of predominantly white twins tells us about sources of variation between individuals who are white twins, not about sources of variation between groups of individuals, some of whom are white and some of whom are black.

The difference is not just a matter of statistical fine points. To use a frequently cited example, one which Herrnstein and Murray themselves use, suppose we have a large handful of corn seeds that show the normal variations in the corn. We plant half the seeds in cornfields in Iowa, and the other half in barren land in the Mojave Desert. Although the attributes of the corn will be highly heritable, the differences in development between the two sets of corn seeds will be due wholly to the environment. How does this logic apply to black–white differences, say?

Even if intelligence is moderately heritable, such heritability as determined within groups does not tell us anything about causes of differences between groups.

That is the point of the corn example. Moreover, when we compare groups, we have to be clear about the groups we are comparing. For example, in the United States, it is downright silly to talk about pure races. African-Americans represent, for the most part, interbreeding between predominantly black individuals of African descent and predominantly white individuals of European and other descent. The racial groups used in psychological investigations are socially, not biologically comprised. In other words, people are the race they are because of what they say, not how they were born.

There is evidence suggesting that, in fact, black–white differences are predominantly environmental rather than genetic in nature. For example, children of several hundred German children fathered by black GIs in World War II had average IQs within a half point of those fathered by white GIs. Moreover, children of black–white unions have IQs seven points higher if the mother is white, consistent with socialization rather than genetic effects (Nisbett, 1995).

Nisbett (1995), in a review of the literature, has found seven published studies that compare genetic versus environmental origins of differences in black–white IQs. These studies, unlike the twin studies, directly seek to find the source of the differences between blacks and whites. Six of the studies failed to find any evidence for genetic effects. One study (Scarr & Weinberg, 1976) was equivocal. It is just not clear how the results should be interpreted, although the authors of the study themselves interpret the results as failing to support a genetic explanation. Interestingly but depressingly, Herrnstein and Murray discuss only the one equivocal study at any length, and predictably, interpret the results in the way that is opposite to the interpretation of the authors. Here and elsewhere, evidence that fails to support their hypotheses is largely ignored, and evidence that is open to alternative interpretations is interpreted to fit their sociopolitical agenda.

Is IQ what is behind group differences in various kinds of success in society? Herrnstein and Murray (1994) certainly think so: Their whole book is aimed at making this point. They are not alone. Jensen (1980) and others believe the same. But curiously, Herrnstein and Murray's own data fail to support this claim. In one set of analyses, Herrnstein and Murray equate blacks and whites for average IQ. Thus, whatever is causing the difference between blacks and whites in this analysis, it cannot be IQ. They find that compared to whites, blacks of the same average IQ are twice as likely to be living in poverty, five times more likely to be born out of wedlock, three times more likely to be on welfare, more than twice as likely to have lived in poverty during the first three years of their life, and twice as likely to have low birth weight. These findings fail to support a view of IQ as causing differences in these various aspects of adaptation, because the IQs of the two groups were equated!

Since the beginning of the century, alarmists such as Herrnstein and Murray have pointed to group differences in IQ, and have warned that these differences are most threatening not because they exist, but because the differential reproduction rates of those in the various groups inevitably will result in a decline in the level of our intelligence as a nation. If, as these individuals point out, people who are lower on the socioeconomic as well as IQ scales reproduce faster, then whether intelligence is genetic or environmental, IQs will go down, because the bad genes and the bad environments provided by the bad parents with low IQs will result in a downward drift.

This downward drift hypothesis is accepted by the alarmists, despite the fact that over the past 30 years or so, IQs have risen very dramatically, to the tune of 60% of a standard deviation (about 9 points of IQ). Herrnstein and Murray recognize this fact, called the "Flynn effect" after its discoverer (Flynn, 1984, 1987). They have a great deal of difficulty dealing with it, and never satisfactorily resolve it. The Flynn effect is not limited to any one country. It has occurred in many countries throughout the world. Indeed, what would get someone an IQ of about 82 today would have gotten the same person an average score — about 100 — just a couple of generations ago.

There have been many speculations, but no resolution, as to the cause of the Flynn effect. Better education, better nutrition, more schooling — all are possibilities, but we just do not know. What we do know is that contrary to the prediction of downward drift, abilities have been, on average, rising.

However, we do have a problem of another kind, and it is a sort of downward drift. At the same time that IQs have been rising, scores on various kinds of tests used for college admissions have been declining. Of course, these tests measure only a part of a person's abilities. But the signs are there of decreasing academic skills: Many professors, including myself, have noted a downward drift in students' verbal skills over the years. The drift was so substantial that after many years of maintaining the same norms on the *SAT*s, the Educational Testing Service finally recentred the test once again to set the averages at 500, the middle score. They did so because scores had drifted so low.

These low scores are not due, as one might think, to declining skills of those at the bottom. Although there have been more low scores, this difference is due largely to differences in the populations of children taking the tests. Many more students now take the tests than took them during the 1950s or 1960s or even 1970s, when scores were higher. Before, only the better students took the test — now students of all stripes do. The real problem is the decline in high scores. Until the test was renormed, what was most notable was the decline of scores in the 700s and 600s, that is, near the high end of the scale.

Why are scores at the high end declining? One cannot blame people at the low end of the IQ scale, simply because, in general, they are not the ones responsible for the decrease. Rather, it is the group of people who have been pointing the finger at others — the privileged few. Why the decline? I think there are three reasons.

The first is our national preoccupation in the U.S. with the disadvantaged, and here I agree with Herrnstein and Murray (and it is about all I agree with them on!). Those at the low end of the abilities scales deserve special services, but so do those at the high end. But our national priorities are shown by the fact that 99.9% of the special-education budget goes to the low end. And that is plain stupid. Our gifted children — and I mean gifted in the sense of all the talents that constitute intelligence, not just IQ — are probably one of our most precious national resources, whether in the U.S. or elsewhere. They are our major hope in an increasingly competitive and dangerous world. At the elementary and secondary levels, we pay far less attention to them than we do to those who have various difficulties. Gifted children, it is thought, can fend for themselves. But this view is wrong. Gifted children need services as much as those at the lower end. The kind of schooling they get often bores them and makes them hate school. One of my own children, by no means a mathematics genius, spent about two-thirds of a year in middle school reviewing mathematics that he already knew. That is a waste of time and a disgrace. In turn, these children never learn how best to utilize the gifts they have.

Second, we are "dumbing down" our textbooks. Sally Reis (Reis & Renzulli, 1992) has shown that if you compare textbooks in the U.S. at a given grade level now to those used even when I was in secondary school, 30 years ago, the levels are about three grade levels lower than they were then. Elementary texts are also at a lower level. As a textbook author, I find I am never under pressure to raise the level of what I am writing: The pressure is always to lower the level.

It is easier to blame the publishers. Why are they doing this to our children? The problem is not with the publishers, however, but with the schools. The publishers publish what the schools buy. If the schools want high-level texts, that is what the publishers will produce. If the schools want pretty colored pictures, that is what the publishers will produce. The publishers are in business to make money, and so they will give customers what they demand.

We talk in the U.S. about high standards, and we have produced governmental and foundation reports ad infinitum talking about the need for high standards. But with respect to high standards, we talk a lot, but do little. When publishers produce texts at a relatively higher level, the texts do not sell. The big market is downmarket, and everyone in the publishing industry knows it. When school districts buy — even when college professors buy — they buy easy so that their students do not get too upset. And their students also do not get much of a challenge.

Our hypocrisy is not limited to education, of course. I have visited perhaps two dozen countries, and there is no country I have visited that has more overweight people than the United States. What's the U.S. solution? Raise the levels of weight regarded as acceptable at a given age. Meanwhile, more people die of heart disease than ever before. What did clothing manufacturers do recently when they discovered that small sizes went begging, and that more and more women were buying large sizes, leaving them depressed? They changed the sizing so that women would have lower sizes, and feel better about themselves. We can change the way we label things, but changing labels obviously does not change the things themselves. We can call a text "sixth-grade level", but the true reading level is what it is, and the level is on the downswing, not only at sixth grade, but at all grades.

Stevenson and Stigler (1992) have pointed out the paradox, in comparing Japanese with American parents, of how parents in this country are more satisfied with the achievements of their children than are Japanese parents, despite the considerably lower achievements of their children. They believe things are going quite well. Our national capacity in the U.S. for self-delusion is a marvel. Unfortunately, travel almost anywhere else, and no one is deceived.

Unless we start challenging children's minds, we can renorm our tests however often we want, we can pretend our children are reading at grade level when they are reading fluff, and we can resize our dresses too. The cost of our self-deceit is our failing to give all children the opportunities they deserve. It is a stiff price to pay, and it is getting stiffer. We need to make the most use of all the talent we have in all our societies, a point that has been made most eloquently by Reuven Feuerstein, whom we honor in this volume.

Note: The work reported herein was supported under the Javits Act program (Grant #R206R950001) as administered by the Office of Educational Research and Improvement, U.S. Department of Education. The findings and opinions expressed in this report do not reflect the positions or policies of the Office of Educational Research and Improvement or the U.S. Department of Education.

6

To Be, To Have, To Do: an Integration and Expansion of Existing Concepts

Yaacov Rand and Abraham J. Tannenbaum

The nature of human personality has always been a puzzle to any observer interested in comprehending the individualities and commonalties among people. In countless attempts to unravel its mystery, behavioral scientists have produced many theories, some of a comprehensive variety and most others relatively limited in scope, focusing on selected aspects of human nature. Although speculation regarding personality has always figured significantly in modern psychology, its origins are rooted in belief systems of much earlier eras, albeit not in formalized psycho-social paradigms as they are expounded today.

The seemingly endless variations in human behavior, anchored within its continuous dynamic flow, emanate from cradle-to-grave changes within each distinctive organism, and from its often unpredictable environment. It is therefore difficult to capture personality in a comprehensive theory. One way to deal with this complexity is to limit focus to one or another of its components. This is done by carefully observing and describing some personality phenomena, and justifying their choice in a conceptually meaningful manner. Such an approach has its glaring limitations, of course, including the tendency to oversimplify and over-generalize, as when personality typologies are posited.

Classifying people as either altruists or misanthropes, for example, is a little like dividing humanity into two types: those who divide others into two categories and those who do not. Nevertheless, typologies can be useful in clarifying part of the nature of personality, provided they are viewed as fairly habituated tendencies, inclinations, or orientations, not as rigid categories of belief, attitude, and behavior.

Hypothesizing Personality Types, Historical Background

Ancient classifications of human personalities can be traced as far back as the theories of ancient Greek philosophers, including Plato (427–347 BCE). Although Plato's point of departure was to understand universal Truth, and the human being as a part of the universe, his ideas are of interest even to modern differential psychology. According to Plato, the human soul is composed of three basic faculties: (a) "reason", i.e. the cognitive function, located in the Head, (b) "spirit", i.e. the connotative function, located in the Thorax (heart), and (c) the "appetitive" impulses, i.e. the physiological metabolic functions, located in the lower body

In his well known book *The Republic*, Plato also applies this triadic model to the ideal state, by dividing human society into three major classes: (a) Producers, i.e. slaves and peasants, reflecting a predominance of the "appetitive" impulses; (b) fighters, i.e. soldiers, reflecting a predominance of emotions and aspirations, and (c) governors, i.e. the ideal leaders of society, reflecting a predominance of "reasoning" intellectual faculties. This model illustrates also the concept of predominance. Human beings possess by nature all three basic faculties, or functions, but they vary as to the intensity by which these faculties manifest themselves in both implicit and explicit behavior, as well as by the predominant features characterizing a particular individual.

Closely related to the principle of *predominance* is that of *Modifiability*. Feuerstein and his colleagues (Feuerstein R., Rand Y., Hoffman M. & Miller R. 1980; Feuerstein, Klein & Tannenbaum, 1991) demonstrated through extensive experimentation with low functioning children and adults, the effects of mediating. The interface of an initiated person between the individual and his/her environment can have a profound effect on the individual's self image, value system and basic orientations, as well as the ongoing behavior. The Mediator is an individual who has both ability and dedication to help others shape, frame, understand and appreciate their surroundings more insightfully and independently. Thus, the modifiability of a human being through mediation makes it subject to change in the predominance of any of the three human faculties. Thus, the Mediator can facilitate personal change, and may generate diversity, rather than homogeneity, among those who undergo that process of change. Indeed, with the help of mediation, the predominance of any particular orientation, can be strengthened, weakened, or replaced by another one. Thus, predominance does not necessarily mean immutability. Ultimate assignment of a given individual to one or another category is determined by the intra-psychic proportional relationship among basic, sometimes antagonistic, human tendencies. But, according to Plato, people may become modified by education and experience and change their predominance and consequently their social class and status.

The principle of modifiability, or mutability, was not, and is not necessarily, of general acceptance, as reflected by the model of Hippocrates (460–477 BCE), combining physiological and psychological aspects. Hippocrates advocated a fourfold typology, according to which individuals are classified according to the predominance of certain body fluids ("humors"), considered as basic determinants of both the physical and psychic life of the individual. A predominance of blood leads to a character type called *Sanguine*, marked by cheerfulness and sturdiness. A predominance of mucus leads to a *Phlegmatic* apathetic personality. A predominance of the black bile leads to a *Melancholic*, depressive and pessimistic personality. Finally, yellow bile abundance leads to a *Choleric* personality, characterized by anger and violence. According to such views, human personality characteristics are almost exclusive derivatives of the bodily fluids composition, implying that they are both hardly subject to any external influence.

Ancient Judaic sources also deal frequently with the classification of individuals. The earliest recorded section of the Talmud, the Mishna, which was written about 2000 years ago, reflects the basic Judaic thoughts in the juridical, moral, ethical, and social areas of life. It also includes various categorizations of individuals, as illustrated by the following text:

> [Temperamentally,] there are four kinds of individuals: (a) One
> who is angered easily and pacified easily ..., (b) one who is
> difficult to anger and difficult to pacify ..., (c) one who is difficult
> to anger and easy to pacify ..., and (d) one who is easily angered
> and difficult to be pacified ... (*Ethics of Our Fathers*, ch. 5:14)

The same chapter includes various other typologies, each of them pertaining to some essential aspect of the individual's value system and modes of cognitive functioning, such as types of students according to their mnemonic functions, or in reference to their analytical level of investment, within the context of learning and teaching.

These typological systems, use metaphoric representations in order to offer some meaningful organizational frames of reference. Thus, the metaphor "Sponge", is used to represent the non-analytical mind who "absorbs everything", as opposed to "Sieve", representing a student who "separates the fine flour from the bran". Although these terms are observational homilies, lacking in neologisms or in supportive evidence, their typological formats, if not their contents, may well be precursors to modern tendencies to posit differences in personality according to theoretical or research-based typologies.

In the 19th century, the ancient Greek belief in the relation between the physical and psychological characteristics of the individual was revived by the school of phrenology (Gall & Spurzheim, 1809; Gall, 1818; Spurzheim, 1815). It was suggested that the individual's character traits and potentials are "located" in specific brain areas, affecting also the exterior shape of the skull. Accordingly, personalities may be assessed, described, and categorized by analyzing such physical aspects. This theory was also advocated by Combe (1864). Although these theories illustrate human propensities to achieve systematic organization of personality phenomena, and to reduce some of the mystery and confusion about their nature, their assertions aroused considerable controversy, to the extent that the Austrian Emperor prevented Spurzheim from delivering lectures on the subject, on the grounds that they were "anti-religious".

Modern psychological typologies, which emerged during the 20th century, are more elaborated, more encompassing, and anchored within more scientifically oriented models. Often they rely upon the systematic analysis of behavioral phenomena, leading towards more sophisticated conceptual frameworks. Broadly analyzed, these theories can be fitted into two basic groups: (1) those emphasizing underlying physical variables; (2) those which classify traits along intra-psychic and social lines.

1 Theories Based Upon Physical Variables

As a result of his observations of mentally ill patients, Kretschmer (1925) formulated a theory linking types of body structure with basic personality orientations, ranging from what is considered normal to neurotic and psychotic traits. Similar to Hippocrates, Kretschmer described three major kinds of human physiques, each associated with a particular temperament. The *pyknic* (short and stout) type was linked with an extroverted personality, more susceptible than other body types to manic-depressive mental disorders. The *asthenic*, or *leptosome* (tall and thin) physical type, is more prone to introversion and schizophrenia, and the *athletic* (muscular) type, is supposed to have a relatively greater tendency toward physically aggressive behavior. Years later, Sheldon with his associates (Sheldon, Stevens & Tucker, 1940; Sheldon & Stevens, 1942; Sheldon, 1944; Sheldon, Dupertius & McDermott, 1954), used empirical methods to test the associations between types of temperament and physical characteristics, similar to those observationally suggested by Kretschmer. Their data confirmed to a great extent Kretschmer's theory and general orientation (see Diamond, ch. 7, 1957; and Winthrop, 1957). It seems that these approaches, despite their ingenuity and systematic research, are deemed to remain limited to their historical value.

2 Intra-psychic and Psycho-social Typologies

Personality classifications originating in the psyche and in the individuals' interaction with the environment, far outnumber those based on physiological differences. Only a small sample will be referred to, sufficient to illustrate the widespread practice of positing such typologies among behavioral and social scientists.

Some of the better known theories are bipolar in nature. Jung (1933), for instance, emphasizes the "introversion"–"extroversion" dichotomy of attitudes. Within the framework of the concept of "Archetypes", he also distinguishes between the "public" personality, on which social status and reputations are conferred, and the "private" one, which is free of poses and inhibitions. In another vein, Jung regards human beings as essentially bisexual, due to the constant interaction between the sexes. Femininity in males is called the "anima", and the masculine archetype in females is identified as the "animus".

Based upon the work of Guilford and Zimmerman (1956), Thorndike (1966) suggested a more elaborate model, asking respondents to describe themselves on a continuum with respect to ten pairs of contradictory characteristics, ranged from (1) sociable to solitary, (2) ascendant to withdrawing, (3) cheerful to gloomy, (4) placid to irritable, (5) accepting to critical, (6) tough-minded to tender-minded, (7) reflective to practical, (8) impulsive to planning, (9) active to lethargic, and (10) responsible to casual. This reflects an essential step forward from models relating to broad, rather global, personality dimensions to a much more differentiated view of human phenomena.

Murray (1938) lists about twenty basic needs, or "goals" as Stagner (1961) prefers to call them, which are steeped in his theory of motivation as well as his empirical evidence drawn from intensive studies of relatively few subjects. Besides stating clearly how needs can be inferred from individual behavior, Murray classified them as primary, or *viscerogenic* needs, relating to physical satisfactions; secondary, or *psychogenic* needs, mostly satisfied in a social context through achievement, recognition, acquisition, and the like; *overt* needs that are allowed open expression without delay; *covert* needs requiring constraint and sometimes repression; *focal* needs, concentrating intensively on just a few objects; *diffuse* needs, which are far more generalized; *proactive* needs to take initiatives to produce stimuli; *reactive* needs to respond to external stimuli; and *modal* needs to perform as best one can, often for its own sake, often without regard for external reward.

From the few examples offered thus far, it is apparent that typecasting (*not* stereotyping) people according to their natures and needs has a long history in psychology. None of these classifications is meant to reveal more than a small aspect of personality, nor does it intend to characterize an individual by a single trait to the exclusion of all others in any typological system. The emphasis, instead is on relative dominance, or personal inclinations, while acknowledging that the other traits in the categorical system also figure in every personality structure.

It is also important to note that some typologies represent outcomes of theory, or of research, or both, while others are largely speculative, but bolstered by close insightful observations of people's behavior before subjecting the typologies to formal validation. The Modes of Existence (MoE) paradigm to be exposed in the forthcoming section derives partly from existing theory, which has been synthesized and subsequently expanded. It is designed to reflect the ways in which people define their identities along dimensions that may predict behaviors in daily life, working places, or other social milieux.

One of the major issues in respect to psychological typologies, is to what extent they reflect stability, or liability to be modified by environmental intervention. Psychological traits are supposed to show high levels of stability. This is particularly true, in reference to typologies based upon physiological correlates, or anchored within biologically determined psychological theories. Theories advocating for approaches based upon bi-polar continuities, or predominance, usually admit the possibility to reach meaningful levels of modifiability, as a result of powerful life events, or determined by well-oriented methods of intervention. It is under this latter perspective that the MoE model has to be referred to.

2.1 Modes of Existence (MoE): Current Concepts

In 1976, Erich Fromm published his book *To Have or To Be?*, in which he tried to "bridge over" between certain philosophical schools and reality, as perceived in various spheres of existence. His basic contention was that, beyond the endless variability of human behavior, individuals show high consistency to the manner in which they react to their internal and external world. This stable individuality is strongly influenced by a basic attitudinal system adopted through, and based upon, life experience.

The conceptual framework of Fromm's ideas reflects a re-examination of some aspects of human behavior which had often been neglected. His objectives were governed by the belief that only through knowledge, awareness of problems, and scientific research can one hope to meaningfully modify the quality of life of both the individual and society. Reality and human experience are by far more complex than many observers are able to fathom, without having at their disposal a comprehensive theoretical paradigm that can attribute meaning to the dynamic "waves" of stimuli, continuously impinging upon the organism and demanding its reaction. Ultimately, Fromm's interest is anchored in idealistic aspirations to create a better world and to transmit its basic values to future generations.

The title of Fromm's book is almost identical to those of two other authors, who may be viewed as predecessors of his theoretical model. In the foreword to his book, Fromm alludes to the French philosopher and existentialist Marcel (1965), as well as to the German scientist Staehelin (1969). Each published a volume which referred to the propensity of the individual to insist upon *Being* or *Having*. Marcel's book, published in the early thirties, was essentially a diary written between the years 1928–1933. It reflects basically a theistic view, as opposed to the atheistic existentialism advocated by Jean Paul Sartre and others of this school.

Although Marcel's fundamental orientation is mostly towards *Being*, he dedicates an entire chapter in his diary to the philosophical analysis of the phenomenon of *Having*. He refers also to the basic difficulty in determining the boundaries between *Having* and *Being*. In Marcel's own words: Everything really comes down to the distinction between what we have and what we are. But it is extraordinarily hard to express this in conceptual terms (Marcel, 1965, p. 155). Marcel was not an empiricist, but as a theoretician he insisted upon the difficulty in conceptualizing principles of human behavior, or in applying to their development scientific research methods. Staehelin, on the other hand, was deeply committed to analyzing reality in the light of a materialistic *Weltanschauung*. Thus, his work was more empirically oriented than was Marcel's. Despite this difference, both Staehelin and Marcel refer to *Being* and *Having* as basic traits of humanity and its development.

Inspired by Marcel and Staehelin, Fromm deals with *Being* and *Having* within a psycho-social frame of reference. Fromm presents a combination of empirical observations with a humanistic–optimistic view of life. The purpose is to create, through knowledge and insight, a new person and a new society. Despite being philosophically orientated, Fromm does not remain in the realm of the abstract, but is rather concerned with the individual's daily life. His illustrations are taken from the obvious and easily observable behaviors, and are re-interpreted in the light of the To Have–To Be theoretical framework. It seems to us that both orientations (being and having) do not cover essential aspects of human behavior. It seems to us warranted to add an additional major aspect to these choices, namely the To Do orientation, since it fits justifiably into the paradigm. Once the rationale is established, the entire paradigm can then be scientifically tested for validity.

3 Basic Definitions

For purposes of clarity it is appropriate to define and briefly explain the following three notions: (a) *Mode of Existence* (MoE), (b) *Being*, and (c) *Having*. By *Mode of Existence* we refer essentially to a basic attitude or style of behavior, by which the individual reacts to his/her inner or outer world of stimuli. It entails a great variety of behavioral dimensions and areas of activity. The MoE does not refer to any specific contents of experience, i.e. the "What", but rather to the "How", i.e. the manner one acts and sets priorities to life goals and personal experience. It is assumed that the MoE has its origin in early life stages, showing relative stability over life, and is expressed under a wide spectrum of life conditions. The term *Being* refers to a basic propensity of the individual to enhance self-knowledge, and to adhere to beliefs and value systems, that make life meaningful. It refers to the inner authentic existence of the individual, which governs all, or most, of his/her feelings, thoughts and deeds, reflecting a consciousness of one's fundamental orientation towards life, self, and the world. *Being* also reflects an aspiration to "become", in the sense of realizing oneself through the process of cultivating productive inner capacities, beyond specific domains of activity in which the individual may become involved. The term *Having*, reflects a basic motivation and major aspiration of the individual to possess and accumulate things, as reflected, for instance, in a strong desire to earn money and accumulate wealth. Yet, *Having* MoE does not solely refer to material possessions, but also to non-material "assets", which are approached in a possessive manner, such as having a wife or children or accumulating a wide-ranging fund of knowledge, or a respectable social position in the community.

4 A Proposed Addition to Existing Concepts: (To Do)

Utilizing the *Having* and *Being* modes of existence as starting concepts, Rand (1993) proposed that a third category should be added, namely, *Doing*. This Mode of Existence emphasizes a basic propensity of the individual to become involved in active accomplishing, in the broadest sense of the term, in order to materialize his/her aspirations. It reflects a basic orientation to do things that will meaningfully change the quality and nature of one's life, as well as the environmental conditions that have to be coped with, as boldly stated by Allport: *Personality **is** something and personality **does** something*. (Allport, 1937, p. 48).

The *Doing* mode of existence contrasts with the mode of *Being*, in which the individual shows a powerful preference for a rich, meaningful inner life. It also differs from *Having*, in which the individual's capacities and resources are strongly focused upon acquisition of material wealth, or of knowledge, or of social status. *Doing*, on the other hand expresses the individual's tendency towards playing an active role, and acquiring satisfaction, in transforming the environment. This Mode of Existence prompts also the individual to engage other people in productive action, mostly geared towards materialization of goals beneficial to themselves, to broader groups of people, and even to society at large.

Paraphrasing the well-known Cartesian aphorism *"Je pense–Je suis"* ("I think, therefore, I exist"), it may be argued: *"I act, therefore, I exist"*, *(J'agis– Je suis)*. A significant attribute of such individuals is defined by personal achievements which leave significant traces upon their own lives and upon the lives of others. The addition of the third basic orientation (c), offers ample possibilities for a broader perspective upon human behavior, and elaboration of a more meaningful paradigm for empirical investigation.

5 Rationale for a Triarchic Model

Fromm's basic two-part model may benefit from an expansion of the concept of Modes of Existence into the world of the *Doing* for a variety of reasons. *First*, by allowing for a more refined description, assessment, and categorization of individuals, leading to more adequate socio-educational intervention. *Second*, it offers possibilities to account for a greater variability of human behavior and personality development. *Third*, the added dimension may describe important segments of the population whose *Doing* orientation helps fit them for specific social roles, and particular human services.

Modes of Existence in their expanded form may have broader practical implications for clarifying socio-cultural lifestyles, elements of character education, group organization, and career choices and qualifications. They may also prove valid for marriage counseling and matching potential mates, students and teachers, helping professionals and clients, and doctors and patients. Similarly, the MoE paradigm can also be used to assess socio-cultural and ethnic differences, such as those existing between segments of the North American cultural groups, which appear to have traditions based upon the *Being* MoE, in contrast to middle class advantaged American populations which are often characterized as being more governed by *Doing* and *Having* Modes of Existence. The triarchic MoE paradigm may thus contribute to a widespread legitimization of various forms of behavior within a given society. It is also important as an instrument by which specific ways of cultural transmission can be evaluated and defined, according to their basic predominant orientations, as reflected by the To Be, To Have, To Do paradigm.

Finally, it is possible to investigate whether Modes of Existence are differentially distributed according to gender, within the same cultural context, or across cultures. Also, what are the predominant characteristics among career-minded women, in comparison with more traditional homemakers? Empirical scrutiny of such questions may serve a dual purpose: (a) to better describe and understand basic human functioning, and (b) to help test the validity of the MoE paradigm within the context of diverse social groups and environmental conditions.

6 Modes of Existence Expressed in the Wisdom of the Ages

The main purpose of referring to antecedent ancient and modern sources of the suggested triarchic MoE paradigm, is to demonstrate that these orientations have persistently influenced human life and philosophy. Moreover, they were reflected in a variety of ways, depending on the historical era, the social context, and the belief system in which they were rooted. It should be noted, that the attribution of any particular MoE to specific value systems or social groups is only meant to reveal their existence, not to express any value judgment about them. The choice of source materials is also meant to indicate the universal nature of the hypothesized model, beyond cultures and historical movements.

7 Judaism

Ancient Judaic scriptures frequently advocate a code of behavior to be internalized and materialized in daily life. Their rules, observances, and admonitions emerge from a clear perception of what the individual and human family are, and can become. Therefore, they are meaningful in depicting underlying modes of existence. After recording Israel's response to the divine covenant: "*All that the Lord hath said we will do, and be obedient*" (Exodus, 24:7), with its emphasis on *Doing* ahead of *Being* or *Having*, the Pentateuch formulates 613 commandments, divided between precepts that require, and those that prohibit, *doing* certain things. It is the *conduct* of the individual that is regulated by Judaic canons, while relatively few commandments refer to the belief system, or to any internalized mental processes.

Perhaps the first traces of an explicit reference to all the three MoE can be found in the book of Jeremiah, who predicted and witnessed the end of Judea as well as the destruction of the first temple of Jerusalem. While advocating for comprehending the Lord and following His precepts, he said:

> Let not the wise man glory in his wisdom,
> neither let the mighty man glory in his might,
> let not the rich man glory in his riches ... (Jeremiah, 10:13)

These verses refer, in essence, to the *To Be, To Do, To Have* Modes of Existence. The wise man is depicted as reflecting a life priority of *Being*, the mighty man — a life style of *Doing*, and the rich man — a basic orientation of *Having*. This short verse of Jeremiah's prophecy refers in a most concise way to the suggested triarchic model of basic human tendencies. A similar passage can be found in the Talmudic tractate of *Ethics of Our Fathers*, in which many fundamental Judaic values are expressed in the form of maxims, aphorisms, and advices, formulated by more than 70 ancient sages, who refer to various areas of human activity and life conditions. It can therefore be considered an encapsulation of pivotal components of traditional Jewish thought, which developed subsequently across the centuries and millennia. The following excerpt presents all the three basic life orientations:

> Ben Zoma says:
> Who is wise? He who learns from every person ... (*Being*);

> Who is strong? He who subdues his personal evil inclination …
> (*Doing*);
> Who is rich? He who is happy with his lot … (*Having*);
> Who is honored? He who bestows honor upon others … (*Ethics*,
> 4:1)

In essence, this text emphasizes an ethical–moral belief system, but at the same time it expresses in a most "condensed" way all the three basic human tendencies, fitting the above suggested paradigm of *To Be*, *To Have* and *To Do*.

While all three orientations are prominent in traditional Judaism, its predominant emphasis is mostly inclined towards the Being and Doing modes of existence, as can be illustrated by a number of texts (see: Ethics, 1:2, 2:2, 3:13, 3:22).

8 Christianity

As is well known, ancient sources of Christianity are deeply anchored within Judaic traditions. Similar to Judaic faith, it is considered a monotheistic religion and sanctifies the Old Testament. This is also expressed frequently by the various apostolic books included in the New Testament (see Luke, Matthew and others). Ancient Christianity tried to maintain strong ties with the precepts and principles of the Mosaic laws of the Pentateuch and its subsequent biblical prophets, but, since that apostolic era, and across centuries, Christianity has shown a significant departure from its Judaic origins, frequently manifesting strong antagonism towards both Judaic values and conducts. At later stages, it acted to create an integration among selected biblical texts, the Hebrew philosophy of Philos the Alexandrian, and the teaching of Plato the Greek (Tillich, 1952). Thus, Christianity developed independently, and it has generated moral and ethical dogmata which remain at its core today.

Similar to Judaism, Christianity appears to preach against striving for excessive material. Instead, its disciples are educated to consider the terrestrial world as an "antechamber" to the fundamentally spiritual "world to come". Although Christianity has strongly relinquished Judaic Talmudic traditions, which are mostly built upon rigorous behavioral control, there are some Biblical commandments, such as charity, which became a pivotal part of Christian dogmas, requiring active involvement in extending a supportive hand to those in need.

Missionary activity is another salient aspect of Christianity, rooted in the *Doing* MoE. Perhaps more than any other religion, Christianity aspires to bring "under its wings" as many people as possible. Although initially advocated as a spiritual dogma, aiming to help each individual benefit from Christian religion and value system, it eventually expanded to encompass politically oriented strivings, which persisted over many centuries.

Basically it may be assumed that Christian thought reflects a combined orientation of *Being* and *Doing* MoE, with more heavy emphasis upon the *Being* orientation associated with spirituality (see Tillich, 1952). *Having*, on the other hand, is less emphasized in Christian doctrines, inspite of reflecting one of the basic human aspirations. Asceticism, practiced in the catholic church, is perhaps the best illustration of defying basic human instincts and needs.

9 Oriental Tradition: Buddha

The Far East is the cradle of many philosophies and religions. Among the most lasting and influential traditions are those of Buddha (563–483 BC?) and of Confucius (551–478 BC), who created comprehensive philosophies and succeeded in gaining wide influence in many oriental societies. Their philosophical approaches centered heavily upon the essence, place, and mission of the human being in this world and in the next to come.

Historically, both philosophies emerged at the same time (around the 6th century BC). But they developed different basic orientations, contingent upon variations in social currents and life conditions, as well as upon personality characteristics of these two great spiritual masters. Although Buddhism originated in India, it succeeded more in other Asian countries than in its birthplace, probably because of its basic antagonism with the social caste system practiced in Indian society.

Buddhism attributes great importance to spiritual values and to personal perfection, vehemently opposing accumulation of material possessions. Basically, it repudiates hedonistic pleasure, physical enjoyment, and gratification of human desires. At the first steps of his revelation, Buddha himself lived for, and advocated, an ascetic lifestyle. But even at later stages, after he adopted more balanced views, as expressed by the principle of the "Middle Path", he still affirmed that "the root of human troubles is thirst or desire or attachment to objects of sense" (Hackmann, 1910).

Kyokai (1980, p. 34) claims that: "Buddha ... trained himself to keep free from greed, and then by this virtuous deed he wished that all people might know the peacefulness that would go with freedom from all greed."

In essence, Buddhism is a philosophy of *Being*. It denies the value of possessing, or *Having*. It also puts the spiritual life of the individual at the core of human existence in both the terrestrial world, and the world to come. It aspires to reach tranquillity of the mind, which can best be obtained by detachment from active contact with worldly things. It is probably significant that the meaning of the name Buddha is: "He who has attained the complete spiritual awakening" (Lillie, 1900, p. 4).

To illustrate the emphasis on spirituality as opposed to material and worldly possessions, a parable ascribed to Buddha himself deserves citation: "Certain subtle questions were proposed to Buddha, such as: What will best conquer the evil passions of Man? ... Where is true happiness to be found? Buddha replied to them all with one word: DHARMA (heavenly life) ..." (Lillie, 1900, p. 62).

It is the heavenly life, the spiritual aspects of the universe, which have to prevail over all other human desires and aspirations. Intrinsic morality and self-perfection are emphasized over social and material achievements. Thus, Buddhism places greater value on *Being* than on *Doing* or *Having*, which are not ends by themselves, but instruments to become more spiritual and to reach heavenly goals.

10 Oriental Tradition: Confucius

The philosophical approach of Confucius originated in ancient China and is deeply rooted in that society's ways of life. As compared to Buddhism, Confucianism seems to be less complex and much more bound to the "physical" material world. Its fundamental ideas are mainly geared towards the practical and daily life situations, strongly emphasizing socio-political issues, and how its rulers should behave for their own sake and on behalf of society at large.

Confucius was basically against metaphysical concepts and refused to deal with issues which cannot be observed or applied in daily life, or illustrated by personal example. In a way, he even resented spirituality, as expressed in his own terms:

To give oneself up earnestly to the duties incumbent upon men, and while respecting spiritual beings, to keep aloof from them, may be considered wisdom ... (Beck, 1942).

Beck's studies of oriental philosophies reveal a number of most instructive biographical anecdotes and statements of Confucius. One of them is directly relevant to the issue of MoE: So, for three years he worked, sowing good seed, but always with the hidden hope that the prince of his state might call upon him to help with more than advice, with ***practical*** power in its government ... (id. p. 242).

According to Cornin (1952), Confucius's teaching has left China more materialistic and less spiritual than any other of the great nations. Confucius's preaching, as well as his own life style are based upon honesty and morality, to be kept and implemented by both society and the individual. But, paradoxically, it led to despotism and to inhibition of progress.

The philosophy of Confucius may be viewed as basically reflecting an extreme *Doing* Mode of Existence. Compared with Judaism, for instance, Confucianism is much more uni-directional. The emphasis upon the *Doing* MoE in Judaism is by far more heavily loaded with a *Being* orientation (see Kook, 1985a, b; Soloveitchik, 1975, 1981). It also neglects, and sometimes even explicitly opposes, the *Being* MoE. This approach was usually less emphasized in other ancient religions and social currents of the Orient. Thus, it presents an opposite view to most of the existing Middle East and western religions.

11 First Nation America Potlatch Culture

Another illustration of an extreme Mode of Existence as a cultural approach, may be found in the Potlatch culture practiced by various First Nations of the Northern Pacific coast, especially the North American Kvakiutl tribes. Potlatch means literally a "gift", but this term refers to a ceremonial festival which lasts for several days, usually organized by a member of the group who aspires to become its leader. It consists of distribution of numerous and most valuable gifts, offered to the members of the community. Property is destroyed by its owner in a show of wealth that the guests later attempt to surpass.

In essence, this social event is a ritual in which the prospective leader manifests control over material assets and a capacity to "burn", or give away wealth. The more he possesses, the greater his prestige and chances to become the official leader of the tribe. The crucial and ultimate determinant of leadership is possession of material assets. Such a life style reflects predominantly a *Having* Mode of Existence. Social infra-structures and community frameworks are heavily geared towards creating the necessary conditions for competing for social status. Moreover, the supporters of the prospective leader contribute to his capacity of "showing wealth", so that during the intermediate time periods between the Potlatch festivities, many influential members of society are engaged in a process of accumulating wealth for political purposes. Thus, the MoE of both the individual and the social group is significantly affected, generating a general *Having* social orientation.

12 Modern Sources

The roots of Modes of Existence can be divided roughly between: (a) Sociophilosophical schools, such as the Marxism and Existentialism, and (2) psycho-behavioral theories, such as Freudian school or Victor Frankel's foundations of logo-therapeutic approach. As in the case of ancient sources, only a small sample of well-known modern constructs were chosen for explication and demonstration.

12.1 Pantheism of Benedictus (Baruch) Spinoza

The school of Pantheism (*Pan* means "all", and *Theos* means "God") has its origins in ancient Greek philosophy. It is a doctrine which deals with the identity of God and His relation to the material universe. In modern times, this philosophy is mostly connected with the name of the Dutch-Jewish philosopher Baruch (Benedictus) Spinoza (1632–1677). His basic philosophy is anchored within a belief in the existence of one, absolutely independent and all-embracing whole of substance which expresses itself in different forms of existence. This substance is the only absolutely independent *Being*, which includes, and determines itself in, all things, through the necessity of its own nature.

These views are similar to those of classical Pantheism which likewise considered the unity of the Universe as all-embracing. From this, one can infer the existence of a supreme *Being* essence upon which all elements of the whole depend, from which they proceed, or in what they subsist. According to some Pantheistic schools, God is the essence of both the material world and the animate species, including humans. God is viewed as the "imminent cause" of the entire universe. Power, wisdom, and love are His attributes, and He is in all things which exist. God is the "Supreme Being" who conceived and created nature and makes nature work according to His will (Fischer, 1909; Joachim, 1964).

Doubtless, Pantheism is a credo predominantly anchored within a *Being* Mode of Existence. We may suppose that individuals who succeed in reaching profound insight into this rather complex philosophy and identify with its basic concepts of Deism, will become activated by a lifestyle and basic orientation of *Being*. It is the internalized, perpetually acting, divine forces that are at the core of the very existence of the universe and human life. They are also the target of the individual's process of knowing, and the ultimate determinant of his/her normative value system and daily conduct.

12.2 Socialism and Marxism

The basic origins of socialist life conceptions can be traced back to ancient biblical scriptures. Judeo-Christian doctrines emphasized social justice, society's responsibilities for the weak and the needy, and abolition of oppression, subjugation, and other forms of human tyranny. Prophets preached frequently against injustice, corruptive accumulation of material wealth, as well as against a life of treachery and amoral debauchery.

Modern socialism presents a historical and philosophical approach which tries to interpret human history and social phenomena as being forcefully affected by socio-economic factors. The historic-materialism doctrine was basically formulated by the German socialist Karl Marx (1818–1883), in collaboration with Friedrich Engels (1820–1895). Their main ideas were formulated in the famous *Communist Manifesto* (1847). According to this doctrine, growth and distribution of material assets and financial capital, are among the pivotal determinants of society, hence, they must be under its control. Other main issues of this ideological current are differences between production cost and market value, methods of production and exchange, and relations between the exploiting capitalist class and the exploited proletarian one.

Socialist philosophy focuses heavily on the dysfunction of the capitalist social organization. It has an idealistic view of society, emphasizing aspirations to restructure itself in a way that its accumulated wealth, as well as the material fruits of its continuous labor and production, will be redistributed more equally among its members. Social history is determined by inexorable materialistic developments, transcending national or social boundaries. Consequently, the imminent and predictable social changes are of a universal nature.

In modern times, socialism reached practical implementation in various countries and under various social conditions. Social revolution generated and shaped powerful regimes. Its basic ideas reflect a deep aspiration for a "better world", based upon equality and justice. But, essentially socialism remains profoundly rooted in the *Having* Mode of Existence. Material possessions and their distribution are at the core of social dispute and in major political orientations of society.

The aspiration and struggle for a better and more just distribution of material assets led to the legitimization of inter-class conflict and to the establishment of highly totalitarian socio-political regimes. Dogmatic basic ideas were intensively diffused and imposed, and socio-political actions were generated and forcefully implemented. Strong emphasis was thus bestowed upon the *Having* Mode of Existence, which was continuously propagated and reinforced, significantly influencing the individual's basic value system and daily life. Unfortunately, social injustice was not alleviated and in most cases, political regimes based upon power and dictatorship were generated.

12.3 Existentialism

Existentialism is a philosophical trend of the early 20th century, although its origins may be traced to the Danish philosopher, Soren Kierkegaard (1813–1855). Among its most prominent leaders were Martin Heidegger and Karl Jaspers in Germany and Jean Paul Sartre and Albert Camus in France. Their philosophical writings considerably influenced modern cultural life, leaving many traces in both literature (e.g. Franz Kafka, Simone de Beauvoir) and drama (e.g. Jean Paul Sartre, Jean Anouille).

Despite the fact that Existentialism may be viewed as a reaction to the pre- and post-war political realities in Europe over the first half of the 20th century, it has had only a limited impact upon political and social systems in western society. Basically, Existentialism can be viewed as a reaction against both religious and philosophical idealism, which derive their authority from transcendent sources, to which the *individual* has to adhere in a most holistic way. In counter-distinction, Existentialism considers the individual as the ultimate determinant authority as to what is "right" or "wrong." According to Sartre, there are no universally binding moral laws. People are free to act at their will, and are responsible only to themselves.

Jean Paul Sartre (1957) laid out the fundamental principles of his philosophy in his capo d'opera "L'être et le néant". There he expresses the following three basic notions of his existentialist approach: (a) Being for himself (L'être pour soi), (b) Being in itself (L'être en soi) and (c) the liberty of act. Whereas the first notion (a) refers to the inner intentions of the individual which gives significance to life and to experience, the second one (b) refers to the world of objects which derive their value from their mere existence, not possessing any autonomous capacity of self definition, or attributing meaning to their existence.

The terms "L'être pour soi" and "L'être en soi" can be linked to our terms of Modes of Existence. Whereas "L'être pour soi" reflects mostly the *Being* MoE, "L'être en soi" relates more to the *Having* MoE. The tension between these two opposite life forces requires bridging activities which are performed by the acts of the individual. According to J. P. Sartre, the individual's actions are not predetermined by situational elements. Humans are endowed with unlimited capacities to act according to their free choice, defining both goals and the means to achieve them.

Although considering the person as a powerful source and measure for judging conducts and beliefs, Existentialism also presents a strong departure from the idealistic views of Humanism. By totally denying ideals, and by attributing importance only to the *act* itself, it reflects a strong orientation towards the *Doing* Mode of Existence, as well as a strong belief that individuals are capable of abiding to self-regulatory mechanisms that are mostly anchored in their own desires as well as in society's common interests. Consequently, individuals can be judged only by themselves, according to how their *acts* correspond to their self-imposed normative precepts.

13 Sigmund Freud's Emphasis on the Intra-Psychic Dynamics

Freud's psychoanalytic theory, as exposed in a great variety of his books (Freud, 1923, 1926, 1940, 1954) has had a lasting impact upon psychology, education, sociology, and literature, among other disciplines in humanities and social sciences. It is doubtless one of the most comprehensive and heuristic modern theories of personality and human development, and its influence has expanded into the realm of shaping universal thought about human nature. The Freudian approach refers mostly to the inner dynamics of the human being and to the specific ways by which individuals elaborate upon, and cope with, their inner and outer environment. In comparison with classical psychology of the second half of the 19th century, Freud boldly shifted emphasis from the manifest cognitive fields of the individual's conduct to the more "hidden" unconscious aspects of the human psyche, considered to be the key determinants of the individual's emotional and cognitive life.

Freud's revolutionary views also represent a transition from fragmentary reductionist approaches to a holistic conception of the individual and his/her intra-psychic dynamics. It is reflected, among others, by an attempt to explain all human behavior in relation to psychic energies. Thus, heavy emphasis is placed upon the individual rather than upon environment. It is the individual's ego-strength forces which affect, mold, transform and ultimately determine both personality development and coping abilities. These latter are supposed to play a primary role in determining the nature, quality, and integration of various tendencies, motives, and desires of the person, as well as the idiosyncratic ways of handling frustrations and conflicts. Likewise they influence the individual's capacity to find appropriate ways to reach instinctual gratification in a realistic way, in accordance with internalized norms and values, social requirements, and reality oriented limitations.

It is beyond the scope of this paper to fully elaborate upon this most intriguing and challenging theory. But emphasizing emotional dynamics, and the ways one copes with intra-psychic conflicts and frustrations, indicates a basic orientation towards the *Being* Mode of Existence. Major Freudian concepts, such as the male Oedipus and the female Electra complexes, are supposed to be of universal nature by virtue of philogenetic channels of transmission. Ego strength, often fostered by psychoanalytical treatment, is another Freudian term that reflects a strong emphasis upon the inner life of the individual.

The revolutionary impact of Freudian theory on the understanding of the human psyche, has rarely, if ever, been matched in theory and research on To Be, To Have and To Do aspects of personality. Under psychoanalysis, the person defines his or her essential being, specially, what To Be means, which in turn affects inclinations of To Have and To Do. The Ego is perceived as a mediator between primary instincts and the regulatory power of society's expectations. All in all, Freud viewed people from a clinical perspective, striving to penetrate to the bedrock of personal identity, or the nature of To Be, as he saw it.

14 Victor Frankel's Emphasis on the Need for a Meaningful Life

Victor Frankel is another prominent representative of the *Being* Mode of Existence in modern psychology, although his orientation is different from Sigmund Freud's. In his book, *Man's Search for Meaning* (1970), he exposes the basic principles of his theory and the psychiatric intervention method. Based upon his own traumatic life experiences in the Nazi concentration camps, and his observations of the daily struggle for moral and physical survival, he came to the conclusion that this struggle reflected an intensive effort to find meaning in life. Meaning is therefore referred to as one of the most activating and powerful motives of the individual and is crucial for survival, reaching saliency under most adverse life conditions. It may make the difference between perishing and surviving.

Frankel's Logo-therapy (*Logos*, translated literally means "meaning") focuses mostly upon finding the essential meaning attributed to life by the respective individual. It is the internalized value system which steers the individual's acts and thoughts in all major life events. It explains why people may sacrifice their life for the sake of an ideal with which they identify deeply. "Emptiness" and "boredom" are major negative etiological factors, causing mental disturbance and neurotic tendencies, whereas the search for, and the feeling of, meaning, lead to empathy, social communication and adaptation to life.

The central position of the concept of Meaning as the major energetic determinant of psychosocial life, reflects an idealistic approach to both humanity and life. It is not striving towards accumulating wealth or material assets. It also does not reflect a tendency to do things constructively or even destructively. It is through human beings themselves and via changes introduced into their very existence and aspirations that individuals may be elevated to a sense of purpose in life anchored in the *Being* Mode of Existence (MoE).

15 Alfred Adler's Emphasis on the Prestige of Power

Adler's major postulate is that social strivings of the individual, more than sexual desires and biological needs, are of primordial importance, rather than sheer

gratification of biological needs. Psychological adjustment and maladjustment should be examined essentially in terms of the individual's role and level of functioning in society. This led Adler to formulate his theory, called "Individual Psychology", and to more practically oriented psycho-therapeutic methods, based upon concepts such as "inferiority complex", striving for superiority, power and social status, and so forth.

Adler (1930, p. 398) himself relates to the individual's striving for superiority as follows:

> "It is an intrinsic necessity of life itself. It lies at the root of all solutions of life's problems, and is manifested in the way in which we meet these problems. All our functions follow its direction; rightly or wrongly they strive for conquest, safety, increase ... The urge from 'below' to 'above' never ceases."

Adler's views doubtless reflect a *Doing* Mode of Existence. Intra-psychic processes are strongly colored by the social interactions of the individual and his/her acts to gain social recognition. It is through *acting* that the individual is supposed to solve psychological problems. It is perhaps best to refer to Ansbacher and Ansbacher (1956, p. 23), who discuss the differences between Freudian and Adlerian theories as follows:

> "Whereas Freud spoke of the individual's behavior as a function of latent conflicting forces, Adler described man as a *doer*, striving towards perfection."

16 Gordon W. Allport's Emphasis on Mastery and Adaptation

Allport (1937) emphasized the importance of the *Having* and *Doing* aspects of life as major social orientations of the individual. According to his view, each individual develops an adaptational configuration of schemata, which find their expression in the manner one acts both cognitively and socially. Life's daily tasks are interpreted and treated as functions of such schemata which are mostly culturally determined. The *Doing* aspects of this view concerns, among others, the individual's efforts and investments to modify his/her own existing schemata for purposes of adaptation to the demands of both environmental and intra-psychic dynamics. In Allport's (1937, pp. 49–50) own terms:

> "The adjustment of 'men' contains a great amount of spontaneous creative behavior toward the environment. Adjustment to the physical world as well as to the imagined or ideal world ...."

This statement lends itself to a dual interpretation. It can be seen as an expression of *Being*, which aspires to reach adaptation oriented intra-psychic changes. It also reflects heavy emphasis upon the *Doing* Mode of Existence, combining internally and externally oriented *Doing* processes.

Vernon and Allport (1931) postulated the basic value system of the individual, based on the assumption that it leads to considerable energetic investment, determining to a great extent not only *what*, but also *how* and *how much* effort will be invested in a given direction or field of activity. This paradigm reflects the individual's tendencies and propensities to embrace the following six fundamental values:

a. Theoretical — expressed by search for truth and knowledge for their own sake.
b. Economic — expressed by acting towards reaching practical, financial and property goals.
c. Aesthetic — expressed by striving for beauty, art, music, literature, etc.
d. Social — expressed by charity, philanthropy, generosity, helpfulness, humanitarianism.
e. Political — expressed by search for power, dominance over others, commanding, self-assertion.
f. Religious — expressed by a belief in a Supreme power, ethical values, spiritual considerations.

This multi-dimensional model, originating in empirical data, attempts to cover what the authors consider the predominant human value orientations. These can be grouped under the MoE "umbrella", as follows:

• *Being* — Theoretical, Aesthetic, and Religious
• *Having* — Economic
• *Doing* — Social and Political.

According to this grouping, the Vernon and Allport model encompasses all three Modes of Existence. It adds meaningful support to the MoE paradigm as a useful means of describing predominant tendencies in humans. To some extent it opens up additional options for further differentiation within each MoE, not only between them.

17 Krech, Crutchfield and Ballachey's Explication of Basic Wants

In their work on human motivation, Krech, Crutchfield and Ballachey (1962) divide human motivations into six major tendencies, called "wants", as follows: (a) Affiliation, (b) Acquisitive, (c) Prestige, (d) Power, (e) Altruistic, and (f) Curiosity.

Although this paradigm does not necessarily converge with the MoE model of *Being*, *Having*, and *Doing*, there is still a close resemblance between the two theories. The concept of "want", is basically of energetic nature, expressing strong propensities of the individual in a given direction. Some of them are embedded in the individual's needs for survival. In anticipation of the Krech, Crutchfield and Ballachey thesis, Trotter (1920) lists the Affiliation want among the four most important instincts of the human being, in addition to self-preservation, nutrition, and sex. We may therefore relate to these wants as basic energetic powers, deemed to ensure the individual's existence and perpetuation.

The Curiosity and the Aesthetic wants, may be viewed as reflecting a *Being* MoE. Some authors (e.g. Welker, 1956) consider curiosity a biological component not limited to human beings. With humans it is mostly of cognitive nature, through which the individual tries to penetrate into the unknown and to enlarge comprehension of both internal and external aspects of life. It is through curiosity that the individual may attain self-enhancement through adequate activation of capacities.

The Aesthetic want is also closely linked to the *Being* MoE. Artists, for instance, often show high readiness to ignore material or prestige rewards in favor of high levels of self actualization, as expressed by their art. Naturally, exceptions may be found among artists in this respect, but most often the stronger their aesthetical aspirations, the weaker their readiness to seek other gratification that might compromise their artistic impulses.

The Acquisitive want obviously expresses a *Having* MoE. This want is strongly dependent upon cultural orientations and is more salient in Western cultures, as compared with other cultures, such as the ancient Essenes' (around 100 BC to 100 AD) way of life, or even the modern Kibbutz settings in Israel (Spiro, 1975). Despite the great time gap between them, both cultures are characterized by attitudes, social norms and organizational structures which emphasize community responsibility, and show profound antagonism to accumulation of wealth, or private property, except for the most basic human needs.

The Altruistic and the Affiliation wants, reflect a social orientation of the individual to identify with others. They are anchored in basic needs for both individual and social survival. Whereas the Affiliation want is geared towards the well-being of the individual, the Altruistic one is of a broader nature and refers to the well-being of society, or even mankind as a whole. These basic motivations seem to combine both the *Being* and *Doing* modes of existence. Altruism reflects also a profound humanistic orientation, emphasizing the importance of each individual, as well as potent feelings of responsibility towards the weak and the needy.

The last two components of this paradigm are the Prestige and the Power wants. Both reflect a strong desire of individuals to manipulate their environment. Obviously, prestige may be acquired in relation with each mode of existence. In an acquisitive society, for instance, accumulation of wealth may lead to social prestige. But this usually requires a strong inclination toward *Doing*, except for those fortunate to be born to wealth. Similarly, the want of Power is basically anchored in intensive and persistent *Doing*, reflecting a strong need to control people as well as environment. It strives for efficiency, and it characterizes many socio-political leaders across generations.

18 Nancy Cantor

In her discussion of the *Having* and *Doing* approaches to behavior, Cantor (1990) emphasizes a process oriented approach explicating not only how the individual's basic dispositions are activated and maintained, but also how they undergo adaptational changes in light of needs created by various life situations and pressures. Underlying dispositional structures are cognitively expressed and maintained in a wide spectrum of the individual's social and adaptive activities. Cognitive process oriented theories, such as Cantor's, help translate abstract psychological structures or dispositions into behavioral outcomes. Whereas Fromm's approach is mostly "extroverted", referring basically to the differential ways by which the individual acts upon environment, Cantor, as well as Zirkel and Cantor (1990) enlarge the meaning of the MoE concepts by referring them to the ways the individual acts upon him/herself in both daily life and under specific stressful situations or transitional time periods of life.

19 Robert Sternberg's Triarchic Model

In several well-circulated publications, Sternberg (1985, 1988, 1997) focuses on one aspect of To Be, namely, human intelligence, which can be understood as a significant indicator as how much a person is To Have and how well he or she is To Do. Three abilities are identified: (1) *Analytic*, or skills required to analyze problems and to respond to them effectively, (2) *Synthetic*, or competence in handling novel situations creatively, and (3) *Practical*, which required application analytic and synthetic aptitudes to everyday, pragmatic situations. In order to assess strength in these three domains of ability, Sternberg (1997a,b) argues against traditional static ability measures, or "snapshot" assessments of the individual's status of functioning in narrow cognitive domains. He opts, instead, for what he calls tests based upon system theories, such as his Triarchic Abilities Test, which includes several subtests found in other measures of IQ, but also adds such sections as "practical–verbal", practical–quantitative", "practical–figural", "creative–verbal", "creative–quantitative", and "creative–figural". The purpose of such an extended test battery is to broaden insights into human intelligence, as an aspect of the To Be component of personality.

20 Gardner's Multiple Intelligence Theory

In his view of human abilities, in the context of To Be, Gardner (1983) proposes a theory of multiple intelligences, each of which satisfies eight criteria for inclusion, as follows:

> (1) Potential isolation by brain damage; (2) the existence of "idiots savants", prodigies and other exceptionalities; (3) an identifiable core operation or set of operations; (4) a distinctive level of prenatal history; (5) an evolutionary history and evolutionary

plausibility; (6) support from experimental psychological tasks; (7) support from psychometric findings; (8) susceptibility to encoding in a symbol system.

For some 15 years, Gardner listed the following seven intelligences as identifiable on the basis of the above mentioned criteria: (a) linguistic, (b) logical-mathematical, (c) spatial, (d) bodily-kinesthetic, (e) musical, (f) interpersonal, and (g) intrapersonal. As of this writing, Gardner (1998) is soon to announce the discovery of three additional intelligences that he calls "naturalist", spiritual", and "existential". If research and clinical evidence confirm the viability of these ten discrete intelligences, then the understanding of To Be and its cognitive dimensions will be significantly advanced.

20.1 Final Thoughts on Theories Antecedent to MoE

The MoE triarchic model is anchored in belief systems that have been influential throughout the history of both eastern and western civilizations. This is illustrated by a variety of basic orientations and fields of activity which are related to the *Zeitgeist* of their respective historical and geographical conditions. Ancient sources are mostly of religious nature, encompassing several major currents in both occidental and oriental cultures. Many modern philosophies diverge from ancient religious orientations, but all the three Modes of Existence (BHD) are still heavily emphasized in various social ideologies and and psychological theories.

The concept of relative predominance has also received ample support. The MoE classifications were mostly conceived in terms of human predilections, not as rigid category classifications, since life is far from uni-dimensional. Its inherent complexity and the imperative needs for adaptation, oblige the individual to adopt a certain degree of flexibility, leading to significant diversification of reactions, attitudes, and life conceptions. Still, the predominant life orientations are at the core of daily human activities and crucial for predicting individual behaviors and interactions in various contexts.

Through empirical validation, the concept of MoE can contribute to an improved understanding of personality. Erich Fromm is one of the pioneers in this direction, by enumerating a variety of behavioral domains and showing that the predominant MoE generate differential behavioral styles. More remains to be done in the empirical areas of activity, by developing and validating adequate instruments, geared towards testing various hypotheses which relate to the MoE theory. Reichenberg (1995) is a pioneer in this direction.

21 Applications of the Modes of Existence (MoE) Theory

Erich Fromm (1976) postulates that in order to better understand the concept of Modes of Existence (MoE), it has to be analyzed not only with respect to its theoretical and ethical aspects, but also in relation to its practical relevance to the understanding of human attitudes and daily behaviors. Specifically, he writes:

> "... these two concepts (Having and Being) are rooted in human experience. Neither one should be, or can be, examined in an abstract, purely cerebral way; both are reflected in our daily life and must be dealt with concretely ..." (Fromm, 1976, p. 17).

Just as MoE may be present in various degrees within each individual, they also differ in their proportional frequency within a given culture. For instance, current western culture may be strongly inclined toward the *Having* MoE. As Fromm suggests:

> "... Because the society we live in is devoted to acquiring property and making a profit, we rarely see any evidence of the Being Mode of Existence and most people see the Having Mode as the most natural mode of existence, even the only way of life ..." (id. 17).

Fromm's view of western culture may be contested, as well as any uni-dimensional view of a given culture. But such a view reflects a sense of predominance. Empirical investigation may perhaps yield more solid information as to the relative strength of a given MoE within a given social or cultural framework.

More recently, Dittmar (1992) expressed agreement with Fromm's comments that individual ownership of material possessions is deeply rooted in western culture. But she considers *Having* in a more complex way. According to her, *Having* does not fulfill instrumental functions only, but also significant symbolic ones. Consequently, material possessions do not relate only to external inter-personal dimensions but also to intra-psychic dynamic structures, such as self-image, locus of control, and identification processes. Dittmar refers basically to the socio-psychological models of Abelson (1986) and Prentice (1987) who suggest a functional dichotomy concerning material possession (see also Abelson & Prentice, 1989): (a) fulfillment of instrumental functions, such as providing means for existence, control, facilitating entertainment or other pleasurable activities, and (b) fulfillment of symbolic expressions of personal and social identity.

In order to sharpen the understanding of the concepts of *Being, Having* and *Doing*, it is necessary to describe some of their differential values and behaviors. This may become extremely helpful for purposes of: (1) clarity in conceptual definitions and analysis; (2) initiating empirical studies as to their applicability in investigating individual functioning; and (3) facilitating the elaboration of didactic and educational intervention methods, so as to assist the individual in his/her endeavors to reach adaptation. Primary attempts were made to differentiate between the individual's behaviors, according to the predominance of the MoE. The following three major areas were analyzed: (a) the cognitive, (b) the emotional-affective and (c) the social domains of activity.

22 Cognition

22.1 Learning Processes

Ancient thinkers debated the issue of what is more important: accumulation of knowledge, or creation of new knowledge by self-activated insights. This debate can be translated into modern terms as a differential view concerning learning processes. People oriented to a *Having* MoE, will tend to store knowledge, either by keeping strict records of different contents, or by memorizing contents as they are, without really integrating them within their thinking system. Such people may well remember what other people said, without adding any personal analytic or critical thought to such statements. It is the possession of knowledge that characterizes such individuals, as illustrated by persons who master a great deal of trivia and frequently demonstrate these "possessions" without really attributing to them meaning beyond sheer "knowledge". People activated by a *Being* MoE, on the other hand, may invest in absorbing a variety of ideas with a more analytic orientation. As Fromm (1976, p. 18) points out: "… Instead of being passive receptacles of words and ideas, they *listen*, they *hear*, and most important, they *receive* and they *respond* in an active, productive way.… They do not simply acquire knowledge that they can take home and memorize…".

The *Doing* MoE expresses itself in a different approach to learning. Internally oriented people, for instance, may study just for the sake of obeying an inner urge, without any ulterior purpose. It is the act, rather than its outcome, which is important. Self image and social status are mostly determined by the *amount of doing*, rather than by its quality. Such differential approaches can be found in academic activities, or in any other non-formal behavior.

22.2 Metacognitive Processes

An additional differential aspect of cognitive behavior refers to the utilization of metacognitive processes, as built-in structures of the individual's thinking activities.

Metacognition is basically defined as: "knowledge or cognition that takes as its object, or regulates, any aspect of any cognitive endeavor" (Flavel, 1978, p. 4). As such, metacognition is a completely internalized mental process, activated as a self-regulating or self-analyzing device, in order to generate more adequate problem solving behavior. The quality of such processes is determined by the individual's intellectual capacities. But the propensity to make use of them is strongly rooted in a variety of non-intellective factors, such as self-assurance, tolerance of frustration, and the need for novelty.

Metacognition can also vary in contingence with the specific contents and goals of learning. Whereas contents may depend on the task one copes with, learning goals may often be geared towards gaining efficiency, or clarification of a normative or moral dilemma. To some extent, metacognition can also be linked to creative processes, albeit based upon accumulated and stored knowledge, but free to design original ideas or to find new connections for existing ideas.

Intensive metacognitive mental activities may be associated with individuals who lean toward the *Being* MoE, on account of their general need to play an active role in regulating their own thinking processes and the choice of contents to be integrated. This inclination leads also to critical thinking and to heavy investment in coping autonomously with internal conflicts and moral dilemmas or contradictions.

Individuals with a predominant *Having* MoE, would be expected to make less use of metacognitive processes than would be those who are more of a *Being* MoE. To some extent they may even deliberately avoid such internalized "dialogues", because such self-monitoring activity could cast doubts upon their ability to generate and efficiently use their own strategies. Persons with a predominant *Doing* MoE, may often use metacognitive processes, but mostly in order to increase their efficiency in coping with specific tasks or reaching practical goals they have set forth for themselves. As opposed to those with a predominant *Being* MoE, their metacognitive processes will tend to be of a more pragmatic nature. Indulging in self criticism, based upon ethical or moral standards or geared towards solving internal conflicts and dilemmas, are usually less frequent with such individuals. Still, they may be more inclined to activate metacognitive processes than would be those with a *Having* MoE.

23 Affective–Social Processes

23.1 Love

Fromm (1978) elaborates upon the different ways one person may love another person. According to his basic dichotomous model of *Having* and *Being*, he makes a distinction between the state of "falling in love" and "loving". Falling in Love usually reflects a profound internal state of *Being*. It is characterized by a potent strive to put into evidence one's most beautiful internal feelings and positive personality traits, in order to gain the other partner's sympathy and affection. Loving is related to Falling in Love but often continues in a different manner. Some persons may develop relationships which are of a possessive nature, reflecting a *Having* MoE. In such cases, the other partner is considered a "piece of property" which can be imposed upon, restricted, and strongly controlled, as any material object or asset.

Individuals with a predominant *Doing* MoE, may be more oriented towards demonstrating love actively, without indulging too much in creating and developing meaningful affective connections with the love-partner. Relations may be of a practical nature, sometimes geared towards increasing the individual's capacities to perform tasks in various fields of interest and preferred activities. Whereas individuals with a *Having* MoE, may use "love" as an instrument to increase their material possessions, those motivated by a *Doing* MoE will consider love as a tool to increase their performing capacities.

23.2 Authority

The nature of relationships between human beings can be schematically described according to the following triad model:

$$A > B; A < B; A = B.$$

Simply stated, in the interpersonal relationship of A and B, sometimes A exercises authority over B. This relationship is depicted by $A > B$; sometimes the situation is reversed: B exercises authority over A, as represented by $A < B$. And of course, $A = B$ demonstrates equality between two interacting individuals. Usually, such relationships are of a dynamic nature, changing from one to another in different situations or at different times. Changes also occur because of how they view each other's competencies and values in various circumstances. Social flexibility and adequacy are part of the normal person's adaptation, as manifested by emotional acceptance of all three basic social roles as legitimate and self satisfying. Such an approach facilitates frequent changes in social positions without experiencing discomfort or feelings of frustration, and generates feelings of contentment and well-being.

Fromm (1978) makes a clear distinction between *Having* authority or *Being* an authority. *Having* authority is relatively unstable, because it is based mostly upon situational challenges which require that the individual possess particular competencies to cope with them. The existence of such competencies in a given individual may cause the other to accept his/her authority, as long as the respective conditions persist.

Accepting and exercising authority may be either rational or irrational. Whereas rational authority is based upon the dominant figure's qualities to help the other person to cope autonomously with given tasks or problems, irrational authority is mostly based upon power and subjugation of the "weaker" partner. Therefore, it is also frequently loaded with external symbols of power. The following metaphor is presented by Fromm to illustrate this kind of authority: " The king — to use this title as a symbol for this type of authority — can be stupid, vicious, evil, i.e. utterly incompetent to BE an authority, yet he HAS authority. As long as he has the title, he is supposed to have the competence. Even if the emperor is naked, everybody believes he wears beautiful clothes ... (Fromm, 1978, p. 27).

The *Being* kind of authority is of a different nature. It is based mostly upon the individual's personal attributes, considered as reflecting a value system, which is accepted by large segments of the respective social group, as expressed by Fromm:

> "*Being* authority is grounded not only in the individual's competence to fulfill certain social functions, but equally so in the very

essence of a personality that has achieved a high degree of growth and integration." (id. p. 26).

Such authority requires high personal value standards, which enable its possessors to serve as a role-model for those who admire his/her personality and ways of life. Buddha, for instance, can be viewed as a classical representative of a *Being* authority.

A *Doing* kind of authority is deeply embedded in the pursuit of goals posited by a dominant individual or a social group. The aims may be temporary or rooted in long term needs, depending on the nature of the task. Such authority is usually task-bound and may be most differentiated. It may be exercised with vigor in a highly desired task, but totally absent in less arousing activities, and expressed by shyness or withdrawal.

Basic propensities towards one or another kind of social relationship ($A > B$; $A < B$; $A = B$) may also depend upon the prevalent Modes of Existence, as reflected by a "specialization" in one of these patterns of behavior. Individuals with a predominant *Being* MoE, will act to acquire and exercise authority by manifesting competencies and by serving a behavioral model figure of the value system and "Weltanschauung" characteristic of their personality. Whereas individuals activated by a *Having* MoE, will strive to rule over other people and acquire leadership, regardless of their genuine competencies. Their main interest will be in the ruling itself, and less in attaining some specific goals. It is the $A > B$ model of interaction which will prevail in such cases.

Individuals dominated by a *Doing* MoE, will be oriented to pursue in the most efficient way the materialization of well defined pragmatic goals, as found indispensable by them in the respective area of activity. Exertion of authority will, therefore, be more situational oriented than reflecting a general aspiration and a tendency to rule over other persons.

23.3 Family relations

Another important social area of activity connected to the individual's MoE refers to the pattern of interactions established within an intimate, relatively small social group such as the family. Family composition may differ on many variables, including parental age, number of children, social status, historical background, etc. Such variables play an important role in establishing the nature and intensity of the family's internal interactions. They may determine the relations of the parental couple between themselves, those between the parents and their offspring, as well as the emotional and social connections among siblings or other members of the extended family.

Parental Modes of Existence, as well as those of other family members, may also be a potent determinant of the nature, development and intensity of the intra-familial relationships. A parental *Being* MoE, for instance, may develop and foster similar basic orientations within the psychological outfit of their descendants. Their educational messages, transmitted, through both manifest and latent channels of communication, may strongly emphasize self-materialization and aspirations for developing intra-psyching coping mechanisms. On the other hand, persons with predominant *Being* MoE, are often heavily centered around the development of their *own* personality, struggling continuously to reach optimal materialization of their capacities and abilities. Thus, such parents may often pay less attention to the cognitive and emotional needs of their children.

In addition, they may encourage their children's scholastic orientations which are more directed towards arts, literature, education and the like, than to more materialistically oriented subject matters and professions. The main criteria for professional choice may be to what extent they offer possibilities and opportunities for self-expression and for development of sophisticated internalized thinking capacities.

A *Having* parental MoE may come to expression by directing the children towards professions and life orientations, based upon financial and economic value, such as lawyers, doctors, etc. Significant parental efforts may be invested in offering high level scholastic opportunities for their children. By the same token, they may set high-level academic demands from their children, in order to facilitate opportunities to reach higher levels of socio-economic status. Parents themselves may also heavily invest in developing their own professional careers, even when detrimental to the intra-family relationships.

A *Doing* parental MoE will tend to educate the children towards a most active, often cooperating, style of life. Intensive and frequent contemplation may be negatively viewed and sanctioned as reflecting laziness and inefficiency. Professional choice may be heavily determined by the amount and nature of requirements imposed by the job. Parents may act as "workaholics", and may require similar attitudes from their children, regardless of their personality characteristics and specific areas of activity.

24 Measuring Modes of Existence

As earlier exposed, the Being, Having and Doing (BHD) triarchic paradigm relates to particular life styles, occupational choices and successes, marital decisions, educational approaches, social affiliations, and other idiosyncratic behaviors. In order to determine its practical application, the theory needs to be placed under empirical systematic, scientifically oriented scrutiny. If indeed, it helps to better understand human motivation and action in various domains of it, it may meaningfully contribute to socio-educational decision-making processes, differential manpower selection, and so forth.

Measuring Modes of Existence may be a challenging task due to the complexity involved in such a multi-directional paradigm, as well because of its primary nature, and lack of previous empirical studies. For illustrative purposes, the following paradigmatic procedure for developing such an assessment instrument is suggested:

(1) Present a lecture on the MoE (HBD) model, to a group of graduate students in education or psychology (group A).
(2) Request each member of the group to formulate 8–10 short "statements" which would faithfully reflect each one of the three Modes of Existence.
(3) Present the same lecture to a second group of graduate students (group B).
(4) Following this lecture present at random all the "statements" formulated by group A (par. 2) to the group B (judges), without specifying to them the specific relation between the "statements" and their respective MoE.
(5) The task of the judges will be a dual one: (a) To classify the statements according to the *Having*, *Being*, and *Doing* paradigm, (b) To rate each statement in terms of its loading to the respective MoE, on a scale running from *1* (very low) to *5* (very high).
(6) According to these ratings, the ultimate composition of the instrument's items will be finalized, taking into account the following criteria: (a) A minimum of 75% of the judges attributed the respective "statement" to the respective Mode of Existence. (b) An average loading rating score of the "statement" of 4 (high) and above.

Reliability can be assessed by test–retest, or by split-half procedures. The test composition procedure, as suggested above, may in itself constitute construct validity. Predictive validity may be assessed by confirming research hypotheses and by differentiating between groups or individuals. The above suggested assessment device may be applied to various adult or adolescent populations. Patterns of MoE clusters may be found characteristic to specific populations such as prospective teachers, social workers and other social agents. Admissions to various vocational and professional programs can be oriented by the individual's position on the three Modes of Existence dimensions.

24.1 Concluding Thoughts

Some of the most enduring social-psychological insights are truisms that the lay public senses intuitively. The human heart and mind often attain understandings of people that behavioral scientists struggle to reveal in theory and research. In these instances, hard-won discovery becomes a matter of confirmation rather than revelation.

Such is the case of the Modes of Existence triad. Although rooted in pronouncements of immortal ancient sages of various cultures and in modern theories of Allport, Fromm, Tillich, Sartre, and Cantor, among others, it has the ring of popular familiarity and consensus. Who hasn't seen individuals doing whatever they consider clearly essential and constructive in their lives, or, conversely, engaging in counterproductive behavior? Who doesn't know of people preoccupied with acquiring ownership of goods and services because they believe it will help strengthen the economy for everybody's benefit, or, on the contrary, because they are power hungry, greedy, or just plain self-indulgent? And who doesn't know or hear of men and women dedicated to becoming the kinds of people they aspire to be — self-fulfilled and at peace with themselves, or unfortunately, turning out to be the worst possible role models any decent human being would want to emulate or follow?

Toward the positive end of the continuum, the *Having* person is not only the traditional capitalist bent on owning material riches; there are those in the *Having* mode who display an insatiable Faustian need to seek out and absorb every appealing cultural, aesthetic, and scientific treasure, or to "own" the hearts of men and women. The *Being* person calls to mind Jean-Christophe, Romain Rolland's fictional image of Beethoven, in all of his emotional striving to reach beyond the reachable, who is adjured to face up to life, or even death, by being what he was meant to be — a Man — a paragon of dignity, integrity, adequacy, security, and whatever else it takes to rise to the level of a true humanist? Finally, the *Doing* person is vivified in Rank's theory on traumas of life and of death. To him, the means of conquering death, and thus achieving immortality, is through creative production (Rank, 1932). What haunts the person is the finiteness of being, the fear of leaving nothing behind, nothing to indicate that he or she spent a lifetime in this world. Some create literature, art, music, or science that is codified for all time. Others strive to leave their lasting mark on people by educating, curing, or caring for them, or even "just" by bringing offspring to life. When individuals dedicate themselves to the *Doing* MoE, they may succeed in imprinting their identity on eternity, thereby banishing the kind of death or non-being that is associated with anonymity.

In a practical sense, MoE is in line with other personality classifications, such as the Allport, Vernon and Lindzey (1960) *Study of Values* and the Thorndike (1966) *Dimensions of Temperament*, which likewise do not pretend to divide people into rigid categories or groupings. Instead, they provide insights into particular idiosyncrasies that distinguish individuals from others in the crowd, while acknowledging considerable overlap among them in the targeted traits. The Allport, Vernon and Lindzey (1960) categories are labeled "Theoretical", "Economic", "Aesthetic", "Social", "Political", and "Religious". MacKinon (1963) refers to these attributes as "values of Man" and reports his own evidence that research scientists favor the Theoretical highest, followed by the Aesthetic, while acclaimed architects reverse this order of highest preference. For creative mathematicians, both the Theoretical and the Aesthetic are also rated highest, but equally so. It is therefore clear that the way people see themselves reveals something about the domains of productive activity they choose and qualify for, in their life's work.

Through self-report, MoE likewise attempts to probe human values, albeit from its own unique perspective. Not only does it spotlight traits that form important parts of the mosaic of human personality; but it is also designed to help evaluate the goodness of matching between a person's preferred Mode of Existence and his or her choice of education, career, spouse, and friends. Construction of the instrument for assessing MoE priorities is based on a variation of Thorndike's (1966) method of designing his *Dimensions of Temperament*. Adapted for research, the MoE paradigm promises to inform both hypothesis building and empirical testing on the link between values and behaviors.

Most of the empirical work implemented in the field of human modifiability is anchored in performing skills and activities, while elaborating upon tasks which require from the individual both cognitive and adaptational solutions. Although reported cognitive modifiability has been proven to be of structural and durable nature, hence, meaningfully affecting the individual's personality, very little, if at all, has been done in the area of assessment of modifiability in relation to most encompassing basic personality characteristics. The following chapter (Reichenberg & Rand) represents a first attempt to empirically investigate the MoE model, as to its possibilities and significance in the area of social fields and educational frameworks. It reflects the heuristic value of the paradigm, and it opens up meaningful "avenues" of interest for differential assessment as to the individual's basic life orientations, as well as a potent instrument to be used in various areas of activity, covering a wide spectrum of pragmatic issues as well as of social policy and decision making.

7

Reflective Teaching and its Relation to Modes of Existence in Practical Teaching Experience

Rivka Reichenberg and Yaacov Rand

Research conducted on Co-operating Teachers (CT) and their role in qualifying prospective teachers indicated that the CT are one of the dominant factors in the teacher training process. This article describes a pilot study which referred to the following two focal points of influence of the interaction between Co-operating Teachers, who guide the prospective teachers in their practical teaching experience, and their respective students: *one*, in the cognitive area, represented by Reflective Teaching, and the *other* in the area of basic personality inclinations, represented by Modes of Existence (Fromm, 1976; Rand, 1993). One hundred and nine students and seventy-six Co-operating Teachers from two different teacher training colleges participated in the study.

The student population was divided according to the following variables: (a) year of study; (b) the college's approach to teaching experience (Theoretical versus practical orientation). Findings suggest a significant relationship between MoEs and reflective teaching components. The contribution of the former (MoE) in explaining the latter, i.e. Reflective Teaching is differential with respect to both the orientation and the intensity of the effect.

1 Introduction

In recent years changing perceptions of the professional nature of teaching have made teacher training a central issue in educational research. Practical experience, as an integral part of the teacher training process, occupies an important place in forging the professional character of the teacher–student.

In the course of acquiring this experience, students learn to practice educational and pedagogical judgment regarding their teaching procedures and methods; to apply didactic principles and methods to impart knowledge and study skills; to develop their own analytical ability towards both themselves and their pupils; as well as to develop reflective cognitive habits; take stands on issues in education; and consolidate their professional identity and self-image with regard to education and teaching (Ziv, 1991; Kremer, 1978, 1982; Kremer & Moore, 1979; Hersh, Hull & Leighton, 1982; Zeichner, 1980 and others). Three major partners collaborate in this process: the *Pedagogical Mentor*, the *Co-operating Teacher* and the *students* themselves.

Numerous research studies conducted over the last decade on teacher training, focused primarily on the following issues: (a) Work characteristics and self role perception of the Pedagogical Mentor, (b) Role of the Co-operating Teacher in the training process of the prospective teachers, and (c) the perception of teaching as a reflective activity.

In recent years the latter two topics have become pivotal in teacher training research due to their importance and paramount effect on the teacher students' professional development (Ziv, 1990, 1991; Ziv et al., 1995; Zilberstein, 1994, 1995; Louden, 1992; Ross, 1990; Ross et al., 1993; Zeichner, 1988).

Studies done on the role of the Co-operating Teachers within the teacher training process indicated, that they play a most determinant role in the framework of this process. The centrality of the Co-operating Teachers, and their impact upon the teacher training process is implemented by both the direct mediation of teaching skills and the indirect mediation by serving as a behavioral–professional model (Feiman-Nemser, 1990; Enz & Cook, 1990; Zeichner, 1983, 1988; Schwebel et al., 1992; Odell, 1990).

The perception of teaching as a reflective activity has also gained wide acceptance in both the theoretical and empirical fields. Among others, it is embedded within the long-lasting controversy as to the nature of teaching: Is teaching more idiosyncratic than generic in nature, or, is it more an art of self-expression rather than an applied science? (Kagan, 1993, in Zilberstein, 1994b, p. 12). This controversy only serves to reinforce the need for studying the roles of reflection with regard to the attitudinal-position variables anchored within the interaction between the Co-operating Teachers and their respective students. The research of these mediation dimensions is still at its initial stages, and has yet to be systematically studied.

We have chosen to concentrate upon a number of variables which reflect the interaction between the Co-operating Teacher and the prospective teachers. These variables present a combination of both cognitive and non-intellective components, which, according to existing literature, bear a significant influence and impact upon the practical qualification process and the entire training process of the future teachers. In this respect we will address two major variables: (a) *Reflective teaching*, which pertains to the cognitive area of the individual's functioning, (b) *Modes of Existence* (MoE), which belong to the non-intellective area of functioning, considered by Fromm (1976) and Rand (1993), as most important determinants of human behavior in general and of teaching and learning in particular.

Another aspect of our study refers to the issue of constancy versus modifiability of the above mentioned variables. In other terms are Reflective thinking and Modes of Existence liable to become modified by environmental intervention, as generally postulated by the Structural Cognitive Modifiability (SCM) theory (Feuerstein, Rand & Hofmann, 1979), or are they constant personality attributes, albeit showing individual differences. Assuming that modifiability is found to be possible, further studies will have to focus upon the specific Mediated Learning Experience (Feuerstein & Rand, 1974) modalities and methods needed to be activated in order to achieve modifiability goals, beyond sheer exposure to needs inherent in educational realities.

For purposes of clarity, we would like to elaborate briefly upon some major concepts of our study. Reflection in teaching refers to the development of critical thinking, which the students, or the teachers, employ when considering the educational or teaching activities they are involved in, by using self-judgment and self-control processes. By virtue of this critical introspection, teaching becomes a calculated and controlled cognitive act which prevents impulsiveness, routine and purely technical functioning (Ross, 1987; Kemmis & McTaggard, 1982; Dewey, 1933; Ross et al., 1993).

Such reflective processes can develop mostly when broad guided professional interpretation is made of the student's teaching. Such interpretation exposes the students to the analysis of didactic events and interactive processes which took place during the teaching activity. Likewise, it enables the students to exercise their own judgment and self-control mechanisms, by noting to what extent the goals they set for themselves, were fulfilled by their respective actions.

It is assumed that guided experience, provided with direct reference to the student's teaching activity in the training class, tends to increase the Co-operating Teachers' possibilities of directing students toward employing autonomous reflective processes over their own teaching, both during and after it takes place (Louden, 1992; Ross et al., 1993; Schon, 1987 and others). As stated above, reflective teaching in training activities has yet to be systematically, empirically investigated.

The contribution of our study is manifold. It emphasizes the importance of Reflective Teaching as a highly necessary didactic component of teaching and education. It also sheds light upon a new set of variables, such as the MoE, which was never empirically studied before in relation to educational processes. Both variables may become critical in both teacher formation processes, as well as among those which will have to be considered in various educational and policy making decisions. It also leads to the development of an innovative evaluation tool, by which differential reflective components may be identified, as they show presence during on-going basic interactions between Co-operating Teachers and their students, during their common feedback conferences. These joint activities make it possible to achieve repeated mutual clarifications of various teaching situations, from a retrospective-intuitive and/or analytical viewpoint (Ross, 1990; Ross et al., 1993; Stoddart, 1990; Zeichner, 1990).

The MoE notion belongs to the non-intellective realm. It is a theoretical concept suggested by, and anchored within, Fromm's philosophical approach. Originally, this concept referred to two basic Modes of Existence: (a) The *Having* mode, which reflects an inclination, or an aspiration, to "have", i.e. to possess something. This refers to the basic attitude of the individual, expressing a need for possessing and owning, on both material and non-material levels, in various spheres of life; and (b) the *Being* mode, reflecting the individual's inclination, or aspiration, to "be" something, expressing a profound need for self-actualization and self-development. MoEs are reflected in the individual's primary behavior patterns, determining the differential way in which one is likely to respond to sets of stimuli in relation to their predominant MoE.

Rand (1993) added a third Mode of Existence — the *Doing* one, reflecting the individual's propensity to act upon, and to change, the environmental conditions which he/she is living in. By combining Fromm and Rand's conceptual frameworks a triadic model was elaborated, encompassing all three above mentioned MoEs: *Having, Being, and Doing* (H.B.D).

2 Modes of Existence — their Essence and Meaning

The triadic MoE model is based upon the assumption that all three Modes of Existence exist concurrently in each human being. Individual differences in this respect stem from the predominance of one of the three MoEs and the structure of their relative potency, resulting in the development of personality character traits, and largely determining one's behavior and manner of coping with reality.

Figure 1 presented below reflects a *schematic* paradigm depicting the various MoEs in different constellations of predominance. It should be noted that the dynamic inter-relationships between these inner potencies are actually highly diverse, and ultimately determine the individual's unique patterns of conducts, manners of coping behavior, and level of adaptation.

In a comprehensive paper on this subject, Rand and Tannenbaum (1995) refer to the social-philosophical sources of these three basic human tendencies. Their analysis shows that these orientations have existed since the dawn of time, serving as major orientation and regulation mechanisms for both the individual and human society. The major religions which have evolved throughout history differ in their respective emphasis on one or another of the three basic tendencies (H.B.D). For example, Buddhism stresses the tendency of *Being*, as opposed to the basic outlook of Confucian doctrine which emphasizes the *Doing* tendency. Judaism, despite the

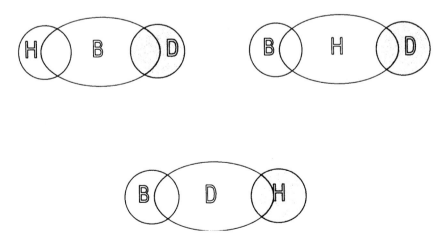

Figure 1: Triadic Model of MoEs according to unique H.B.D. dominance

variegation of its streams, is in essence a most complex conjunction of *Being* and *Doing*.

In order to facilitate analytical comprehension and insight, as to the suggested MoE paradigm and its basic premises, some basic definitions and elaborations are offered in the following section.

Modes of Existence (MoEs) represent fundamental attitudes or characteristic ways of behavior, according to which the individual responds to the world of external and internal stimuli. The latter refer to a wide variety of behavioral dimensions and spheres of activity. They do not refer to any specific content, hence, they are not related to the "what", but rather to the "how", i.e. to the manner in which the individual reacts to a wide variety of stimuli, occurrences, circumstances and conditions in life. Due to their holistic nature, they may serve as an important parameter to describe human beings and systematically differentiate between them, as well as to predict their behavior according to the specific predominant Mode of Existence.

Another aspect concerning the above presented triadic model refers to the issue of the manner in which the MoEs are formed. Their consistency beyond situational components indicate, that they take form during a lengthy and ongoing process, having its origin in the earliest ages of the individual's life, and continuing into adulthood throughout the various developmental stages.

Children's behavior, usually patterned according to their motivational tendency to act in line with a given mode, strengthens the power of the latter, by virtue of materializing it in practice. Thus, it ensures, in fact, a relatively high level of stability and its continuous long-term existence.

Similar to any psychological structure, the Modes of Existence are characterized by self-perpetuation and self-regulation. Self-perpetuation is achieved by virtue of the repeated use of the same, or similar, behavioral patterns. When the latter meet with success, they are internally reinforced, which streamlines the structure with regard to both the degree of response accuracy and the speed with which it is performed. Thus, it also becomes more parsimonic, requiring less energy for utilization. This latter is characteristic of primordial supreme adaptive importance.

In addressing the concept of MoE within an adaptation context, we may assume that individuals acquire their own unique MoE pattern based upon their individual life history and subsequent adaptive needs and goals. These needs are determined by prevalent environmental conditions as well as by a set of socio-cultural determinants comprising meaningful frames of reference and of belonging. According to our triadic model (see Diagram 1), individuals are characterized by their unique MoE composition, in which one mode is usually the predominant one, and the other two, although less salient, still have an impact upon their conducts and coping behavior. Thus, the *Being* mode, for instance, may show predominance, whereas the *Having* and/or *Doing* MoEs exert a much lesser influence upon the individual's behavior and life orientation.

2.1 The Being Mode of Existence

The term Being refers to a set of basic tendencies in individuals, directing their activities as well as the amount of energy to be invested, in developing their own personality and towards optimal self-actualization. This proclivity reflects a basic orientation towards life and self, dictating most of the individual's actions, thoughts and emotions.

This tendency expresses a deep desire to "be", through materializing the hidden potential in the individual's personality. The essential meaning of life, reflected by this MoE, is grounded in a perpetual, comprehensive process expressed by inner abilities transcending any specific realm. These tendencies usually characterize creative people in a wide variety of artistic and scientific realms, but they exist no less in people functioning in regular working areas and levels of proficiency, in relation to their specific skills and their main motivational aspirations and inclinations (Fromm, 1976).

Fromm also views the individuals' deep desire to "be", as expressing their willingness to relinquish things evincing "ownership", in exchange for the opportunity to develop their ability to express and fulfill themselves. There are two prerequisites for self-actualization: (a) perceiving oneself as a psychologically independent person, and (b) being able to use logic-based control mechanisms. These conditions help people ground themselves in adaptation processes requiring decision making judgment and effective utilization of their inner capabilities.

2.2 The Having Mode of Existence

The term Having reflects a basic human tendency to accumulate and acquire things and wealth, making them one's personal property. In this context, the term "acquisition" should not be considered as pertaining to material assets only, but as reflected in the widest possible sense. This inclination is undoubtedly manifested in extreme stinginess, but it can also relate to acquiring non-material "assets", such as gaining control over knowledge, data or over people with whom they develop social or other relationships.

In this context, Rabbi Yochanan Ben Zakai makes an interesting comment in the Mishnah: "If you have learned much Torah, do not keep the "good" for yourself only" (Ethics of the Fathers 3:9). This saying reflects a clear stand against the "materialistic" approach of studying Torah, in effect, it is a warning against the basic tendencies of the Having MoE. It illustrates just one of the completely non-materialistic realms in which an individual's Having tendency may be expressed. Such individuals mainly direct their energy and efforts into controlling "things" or other people, as often happens in hierarchical work structures, and to a great extent in family life as well.

According to Dittmar (1992), this basic human tendency also characterizes the contemporary consumer society, especially in the western world, which is frequently described as a society based upon materialistic and possessive aspirations. Social status is often gained by the monetary value of the individual's property and assets. The latter become heavily loaded by symbolic values and social importance. They also have explicit behavioral expressions, such as the public demonstration of the accumulated wealth, which is highly determined by social reactions and additional possibilities for further accumulation of property. These attitudes are well reflected in MacPherson's following comment: "Materialistic relations, to many people, have increasingly become the most important relations determining their freedom" (MacPherson, 1962).

McCraken (1990) considers materialism as a kind of language by which people communicate with one another. Belk (1991), on the other hand, criticizes Western society's materialistic orientation and emphasis on amassing possessions, since the prevailing individualism linked to such tendencies precludes the development of a more idealistic, socially-oriented society, which is essential for the proper development and progress of society as a whole.

2.3 The Doing Mode of Existence

The Doing MoE proposed in Rand's triadic model (1993) reflects the individual's basic tendency to act and to be involved in activities directly, or indirectly, related to achieving pragmatic goals, through changing environmental conditions and life circumstances. Besides the religious and cultural roots that may be found for this tendency, it is also emphasized in a variety of modern psycho-social and economic doctrines (Allport, 1937).

Doing tendencies are strongly contrasted with Being aspirations, in which individuals display a fundamental preference for the development of an intense inner life, basically orientated towards their "inner" personalities. Doing also differs from Having, in which the individuals' energy is mainly directed towards "acquiring" material or other assets, primarily expressing an outward orientation and a desire to control external frameworks and make them their exclusive property. People functioning in accordance with the Doing MoE, seek — and usually find — their satisfaction in the very process of doing, and in their ability to alter their environmental conditions, according to their personal goals. Moreover, such individuals are most prone to motivate other persons to become involved in actions geared towards materializing their aspirations and achieving the objectives set before them. This Mode of Existence generally encompasses high performance ability, and is characterized by constant striving to enlarge the scope of their personal and organizational activities. It is by the very fact of doing that such individuals feel positive about themselves, creative and socially valuable.

The conceptual elaboration on Fromm's binary model posed by Rand's triadic model has great significance not only from the theoretical point of view but also for various pragmatic areas of activity. This model enables a more precise and more diversified description of the individual in terms of characteristic behaviors. The model also enables assessing wider segments of the population, whose lives and basic attitudes do not comply solely with the binary model Having and Being MoEs.

The expanded triadic model is also of significant heuristic value. Potentially, it may become an effective tool in manifold decision-making processes, it opens up possibilities for follow-up research studies on teacher and in-service training, and it could effectively be used in admitting candidates to teacher training programs and planning training activities for employed teachers, thereby increasing their job performance and chances for success.

This model is still at the "beginning of the road" and has not yet been comprehensively and empirically researched with regard to the potential target population and various professional occupations. We consider research of this kind to be of vital importance for testing the value of the model in general, and its possibilities and significance in various specific realms, in particular.

3 Components of Reflection in Teaching

One of the most essential tools in developing practical experience with prospective teachers is the "feedback conference", which takes place after the student has given a lesson under supervision. Co-operating Teachers and Pedagogic Mentors use this procedure as a means of mediation to impart to students professional attitudes and various didactic methods, nurturing, thus, their reflective thinking concerning their own teaching processes within their inherent complexity and diversity of contexts.

For the purpose of our study, we used Louden's model on reflection (Louden, 1992), in order to analyze the "feedback conference" to identify the basic components of reflection, and to differentially assess their intensity and hierarchical relationship. Louden's model reflects a combination between Schon's theory on reflection (Schon, 1983, 1987) and Habermas' "action research" orientation (1971), as well as with the approaches of other education researchers, such as Ross (1987) and Ross et al. (1993). What makes the model suggested by Louden so unique and innovative, is its two-dimensional structure and the very process of its construction. The model developed over the course of "action research" in which Louden himself participated as a member of the research team, both as a "participant-observer" intervening in the teaching act upon its implementation, and as a "spectator", reflectively analyzing the act of teaching, in combination with the performing teacher herself. Thus, Louden became an active partner throughout the entire research process, collaborating in the various stages of both planning and critically evaluating the teaching act after its implementation.

Louden's model is mainly directed toward analyzing the reflective processes of the teacher, according to their essence and nature. It may be viewed as an integrative paradigm, liable to help us understand the differential aspects of reflection and the various forms in which teachers use it in their work. The model's conceptual framework has two basic dimensions: (a) Interest areas and (b) Forms. Each one of these two dimensions has four components, giving rise to a model

Interest				
Forms				
Technical	Introspection	Rehearsal & Replay	Inquiry	Spontaneity
Personal				
Problem-solving				
Critical				

Figure 2: Matrix of reflective process dimensions according to Louden's model.

constructed on a 4×4 matrix (see Diagram 2). According to it, each reflective act can be defined according to the above-mentioned two dimensions (interest area and form). The interest areas determine the content of the reflection and its basic direction, whereas the form determines the way in which the reflection is materialized.

Due to the model's complexity we chose to focus only on the dimension of forms. This choice is inherent in the empirical orientation of our study, which concentrates on the "how" of the reflective teaching. The combination of the "how" and the "what" is supposed to be the subject of one of the follow-up studies we are planning to implement. For the sake of clarity, we will briefly define the four components of the form dimension.

The four forms or components of Louden's model of the reflective processes are defined as follows:

Introspection. Introspection is a conscious process, usually performed when people contemplate their own qualities, thoughts and feelings, or when they assess their own reactions to some experience which they underwent. This kind of thinking implies an explicit interiorized control process, which may ultimately be expressed in a change of behavior and/or change in the individual's schematic and conceptual system in relation to the given subject under scrutiny. This process can be of a short-term or prolonged nature, depending on the degree of importance attributed to the specific issue which is the object of contemplation. Basically, Introspection is distanced from the act itself, and in Schon's terms, it is considered as a "Reflection on Action".

Rehearsal and Replay. This form of reflection is also removed from the action itself, but it focuses specifically on a given action, either already performed or to be performed in the future. It can take on two basic forms: (a) *during the planning* stages of the teaching activity, as an anticipatory simulation of what should, and could, occur during the forthcoming lesson (Rehearsal), and (b) focusing specifically on the drawbacks and successes of the lesson *after* the teaching act was actually performed (Replay). This is a classical example of Reflection on Action. The bi-directionality of this reflective form is most compatible with the teacher's work and needs stemming from the use of various teaching procedures, and the need to check their differential efficiency.

Although teaching realms vary in content, they share principles regarding the didactic processes and the best ways of conveying the respective contents to the student audiences. This form of reflective thinking may be seen as a vital tool in the teacher's professional development and "repertoire" of behaviors. Reflective thinking generates constant feedback between past and planned experiences, and between performance and future planning. The "feedback conference" between the student and the Co-operating Teacher, on one hand, and between them and the Pedagogic Mentor (the teacher of didactic), on the other, can serve as a most efficient teacher formation process, reinforcing autonomous interiorized control over what happened during the lessons under observation. Thus, fostering such kind of Reflective Teaching may be considered as a most useful instrument of teacher training procedures.

Inquiry. The element of inquiry consists of a combination of performing a given teaching activity and discussing it, with constant interplay between the action itself and the verbal analysis of it. This type of reflection may be described as reflecting connections of a "spiral" nature, in which the four basic actions of reflection are represented: (a) planning, (b) action, (c) observation and (d) control.

Inquiry is a process which requires great mobility from one function to the other, and the integration of the "spiral" links between them actually helps the teacher to assess the efficiency of the changes adopted as a result of an anterior reflective thinking process. Inquiry can include not only the student doing the teaching, but also outside participant observers, involved in the training process.

Spontaneity. The element of spontaneity characterizes the essence of reflection while doing. It takes place during the teaching act itself, when the teacher encounters difficulties, whether real or imagined, stemming from the didactic needs and goals of the teaching action, or from classroom interactive processes. Due to the immediacy of this form of cognitive reflectivity, it is primarily directed towards subsequent action. This kind of reflection is to a great extent of intuitive nature, but through repeated experience, it often enables the teacher to efficiently cope with classroom difficulties by making rapid methodological changes and by venturing into new directions, not previously planned or considered.

4 Research Layout

The results presented below comprise only a part of a more comprehensive study, conducted in order to assess a number of possible connections between: (a) Cognitive elements, such as the different aspects of reflective teaching, (b)

Attitudinal factors, such as Traditional versus Modern educational stance, and (c) Non-intellectual, personality-related factors, such as Modes of Existence (MoE). The research was carried out among a population of prospective teachers, in different stages of their professional training, as well as among more experienced educators, working as Co-operating Teachers, involved in guiding students to become qualified professionals.

In the following section, we will address only the following research question:

> *Is there a dominant Mode of Being pattern among the prospective teacher population, and what is the effect of employing various reflective processes while teaching?*

The importance of this research is anchored, among others, in the area of the individual's professional choice, basic orientations in decision-making processes, institutional orientations regarding teaching student admissions, and the planning and implementation of teacher training programs leading towards professional acquisition and development.

Based upon the theoretical literature, we hypothesized that educators charac-terized by a predominant Being MoE, including, among other things, the inherent tendency toward self-actualization and the search for insight, will be more prone to utilizing reflective components in their teaching activities. Our contention was that the reflective processes are of great importance in raising the level and efficacy of teaching processes.

The subjects were chosen randomly out of the student roster in two teacher training institutions in central Israel. For purposes of comparison the subjects were divided into two groups, according to their seniority and teaching experience, as follows:

(a) Prospective Teacher Students ($N = 109$).
(b) Co-operating Teachers ($N = 76$).

By definition, the Co-operating Teachers have no less than five years working experience and are also considered as extremely good teachers and professional educators.

The student population was further divided according to the following vari-ables:

(a) Year of study (2nd or 3rd).
(b) Basic preferential training method activated by the college (theory-oriented method versus practice-oriented method).

This research design applies to the entire study. In order to assess the relation between reflective elements and MoEs, we randomly selected 50 students and their respective Co-operating Teachers, whose "feedback conferences" were recorded for analytical analysis and investigation.

The research instruments included two innovative devices which were specifi-cally designed and evaluated for the purpose of this research (Reichenberg, 1995), as follows:

(a) **MoE Evaluation Scale (MES)** — referring to the three Modes of Existence of Rand's triadic (H.B.D) model (Rand, 1993). This scale is composed of a number of statements which the respondents have to grade in terms of the degree by which they adhere to those statements, and consider them as reflecting their basic tendencies.

The scale's reliability was tested on a population of university students in education, ($N = 62$) by means of Cronbach's Alpha factors for internal consistency. The reliability coefficients ranged from 0.74 to 0.86. In another evaluation of the MES reliability, conducted on a population of prospective teachers ($N = 160$), Cronbach's Alpha coefficients ranged between 0.74 to 0.84, indicating a relatively high reliability level for this type of a questionnaire. Structure validity of the MES was also reported, based upon clear distinction between the MOEs (Reichenberg, 1995).

(b) **Reflection Evaluation Scale (RES)**:

The scale for evaluating reflective processes (RES), was developed according to Louden (1992) basic model (see p. 9). It is based upon an item-analysis of the contents of the "Feedback Conferences", usually held between the Co-operating Teachers and their students. These discussions were taped and analyzed by three independent judges, according to the four form-related components of Louden's model (Introspection, Rehearsal and Replay, Inquiry and Spontaneity). The coherence coefficients between judges yielded a reliability score around 0.92 for Spontaneity and Rehearsal/Replay, and even higher for Introspection and Inquiry.

The above-mentioned research instruments were administered twice, namely at the beginning of the school year (before) and at its end (after) of the school year. Comparisons were made by means of Analyses of Variance and Multiple-steps Regression Analyses.

5 Findings

In order to assess the eventual connections between MoE and the four forms of reflection, in Pearson correlation coefficients were calculated between the three MoEs (H.B.D) and the four elements of reflection, at the beginning and the end of the experiment. These correlations are shown in Table 1.

The table shows a significant positive correlation between the MoE Being and all four reflective components among the students, for both the "before" and "after" assessments. These correlations indicate that the higher the level of the subject's Being MoE, the higher the level of all components of reflection.

In contrast, no significant correlations were found between the other two MoEs (HAD) and the active components, except the correlation between Having and Introspection ($r=-0.32$; $p<0.05$). This negative correlation indicates that the higher the subject's level of the Having MoE, the lower the level of introspective reflection.

Table 1: Correlation factors between MoEs and elements of reflective forms at the beginning (before) and end (after) of the school year among the students ($n = 50$)

	Introspection	Rehearsal	Inquiry	Spontaneity
"Before"				
Having	0.21	0.5	−1.4	0.04
Being	0.25*	0.33*	0.26*	0.48**
Doing	−0.04	0.24*	0.04	0.25*
"After"				
Having	−0.32*	−0.02	−0.19	0.04
Being	0.22	0.33*	0.37**	0.19
Doing	−0.09	0.16	0.14	0.07

*$p < 0.05$ **$p < 0.01$

In order to determine how much of the variance of the reflection components may be explained by each of the three MoEs (H.B.D), and whether there is an additional explanatory contribution by all the three MoEs, when combined together, hierarchical regression analyses were performed in two steps, with the four reflective components as the dependent variables. Entered in the first step of the regression were the measures of the three MoEs; and in the second step the interactions between them. These analyses were conducted separately for the "pre" and "post" assessments.

The following table (Table 2) presents the regression analyses of the four reflective components: Introspection, Rehearsal/Replay and Inquiry, with reference to the first step only, because no additional explanatory values were found for the MoE interactions. For Spontaneity, the second step of the regression analysis is also presented.

The above presented data indicate that the total explained variance of the three MoEs vary from 24% for Spontaneity to 12% for both Rehearsal/Replay and Inquiry. (Introspection = 17%). These percentages are moderate although higher than what is usually found in this type of research.

Adding the MoE interactions, as a second step of the regression analysis, significantly increased the percentage of the explained variance, but only for the component of Spontaneity.

The data presented in Table 2 shows that the Being MoE is the strongest explanatory contributor of the variance of all the reflective components. The higher the level of Being, the higher each one of the four reflective components (Introspection, Replay/Inquiry, and Spontaneity). In contrast, negative Beta factors were found for the Having MoE, for all the components, although significance was found solely for Introspection. We may conclude generally that the higher the

Table 2: Hierarchical regression analyses: contribution of the three MoEs to explaining the variance in reflective elements

	Introspection	Rehearsal	Inquiry	Spontaneity	
				Step 1	Step 2
Having	−0.29*	−0.11	−0.24	−0.15	−0.19
Being	0.39**	0.29*	0.35*	0.47**	0.41**
Doing	−0.11	0.14	−0.03	0.09	0.20
Being & Having	—	—	—	—	−0.38**
Being & Doing	—	—	—	—	0.40**
	0.17	0.12	0.12	0.24	0.44

$*p < 0.05$ $**p < 0.01$

person's level of the Having MoE, the lower his or her level of reflection in general, regardless of the specific nature of the reflection. Thus, the research hypothesis that the Being MoE will have a higher positive correlation with the components of reflection than the other two MoEs (H, B) was fully supported.

The reflective component of Spontaneity is the only one that benefits from an explanatory addition due to the inclusion of the variables of the second step (interactions). Since the explained addition of the two interactions is about 20%, the total variance of Spontaneity explained by the MoEs is about 44%. This figure is doubtless most meaningful, when considering the fact that the MoEs are non-cognitive variables, and reflection is a purely cognitive one.

In order to investigate more accurately the effect of these interactions on the Spontaneity component, the subjects were divided into two groups (High/Low), according to the level of their Being MoE. In each of these groups a regression analysis was performed separately for the Having and Doing Modes of Existence. The following diagram (Figure 3) shows the relation between these two MoEs and Spontaneity according to the subjects' level of Being.

The above-presented diagram indicates that the effect of the Doing MoE on Spontaneity is actually highly conditional on the level of the Being MoE. The findings show that, among subjects characterized by a high level of Being, Doing has more of an effect. The higher the level of Doing, the higher the level of Spontaneous reflection. On the other hand, the findings are reversed for the Having MoE, among subjects characterized by a high level of Being. The higher the subjects' level of Having, the lower their level of Spontaneity. Among subjects with a low degree of Being, it was found that the higher the level of Having, the higher the level of Spontaneity. We may therefore conclude that the impact of the Having and Doing MoEs also depends largely on the level of the individual's level of the Being MoE.

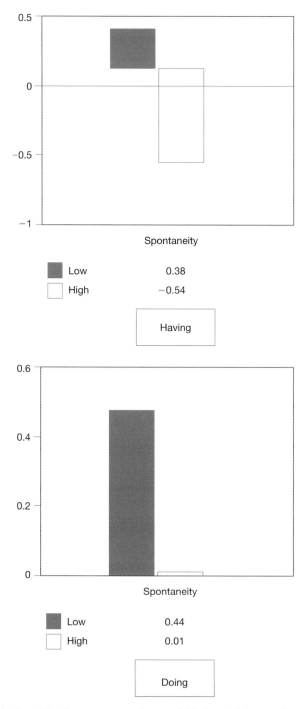

Figure 3: Relationships between Having and Doing MoEs and Spontaneity to the level of Being MoE.

These findings emphasize the central effect of the Being MoE, not only due to its direct relation to reflective Spontaneity, but also because it serves as a mediating factor concerning the relation between the Having and the Doing MoEs, with the individual's level of reflective functioning.

Hierarchical regression analyses regarding the relation between the three MoEs and the four reflective forms, were also conducted at the end of the school year. These regression analyses show a significant contribution of the interactions to Introspection, Inquiry and Spontaneity. Rehearsal/Replay was the only reflective component which remained not affected by adding the interactions into the regression analysis.

The essential nature of the triadic MoE model, as well as its differential impact upon the various forms of reflective thinking, as postulated by Louden (1992) within the context of education and teaching, may be briefly summarized as follows:

(a) The Modes of Existence are highly related to the individual's general tendency to use reflective mental activity.
(b) The explanatory contribution of the Modes of Existence as to the various reflective components is not uniform. Each one of them affects these components differently, both as to the individual's general inclination to use them, as well as to their intensity.
(c) The Being MoE is the major and most potent contributor to the reflective components. This explanatory contribution of the Being MoE is of both direct and indirect nature, acting in combination with the other two MoEs (H,D).
(d) The contribution of the Doing MoE is relatively lower than that of the other two MoEs (B,H). Its impact expresses itself mostly in interaction with them. An interesting phenomenon is that the level of probability of reflection, in connection with the Doing MoE only, is the lowest of all the MoEs. Yet, in conjunction with Having and Being, this Mode has a differential effect, as expressed in two main situations: (a) when Being is high and (b) when Having is low.
(e) The Having and Being MoEs make contrasting contributions to affect the individual's orientation to make use of reflective thinking. Whereas the Being MoE strengthens the general tendency to use reflective functioning, the Having MoE weakens such tendencies.
(f) The interaction between the three MoEs are also determinant factors as to reflection in general and as to Spontaneity in particular. The findings show that the influence of Having and Doing greatly depends upon Being. This latter (B) acts probably as a moderating factor upon the other two MoEs. The more dominant the Being MoE, the smaller the influence of the other two MoEs (H,D).

The above-reported data, and in particular the differences found in the level of reflectivity between the Prospective Teachers on the one hand, and the Co-operating Teachers, on the other hand, reported by Reichenberg (1995) are also relevant concerning the issue of human modifiability, in this respective area.

Reflective teaching is basically a cognitive way of functioning, albeit also includes a series of non-cognitive components, such as readiness, or anxiety, to indulge in this kind of behavior, or capacities to come with the feelings of frustration, often connected to such inner-control processes. The well known hereditary approach to intelligence, which rejects the modifiability postulate concerning this major human function, can easily be attributed to reflective thinking too. This is mostly due to the inherent links between intelligence and all kind of higher level thinking processes. One may consider both of relatively immutable nature, and their existence, or activation, to be very little affected by environmental intervention, be it via direct exposure to the need to use reflective thinking, or by induced need systems.

Following our findings, we may postulate that producing reflective thinking processes, can be acquired, either by experience, or by systematic intervention processes. Experienced success in this respect may reinforce this kind of behavior and make it become habitual and highly efficient in leading the teacher to reach his/her educational and teaching goals.

6 Discussion

The major objective of the research reported here was to study the eventual connections between Modes of Existence and reflective teaching, in populations of Prospective Teachers. The findings indicate a strong relationship between the MoEs and various components, or forms, of reflection. The contribution of the MoEs in explaining these latter indicates significant differential impact upon them, in terms of both the individual's general orientation towards using them, and the potency of their influence upon reflection.

Our hypothesis that significant positive correlations will be found between the Being MoE and the various components of reflection was completely substantiated. The correlation coefficients presented (see Table 1) clearly indicate that the Being MoE has a significantly higher correlation with the reflective components than the other two MoEs (Having, Doing). This finding was found to be true both in measures taken at the beginning of the scholastic year (pre) and at its end (post). This emphasizes the unique importance of the Being MoE as a determinant factor upon the development of all forms of reflection, as specified in Louden's model.

This finding may have highly significant implications for a number of main areas of functioning in the area of teaching and education. It may produce meaningful changes as to the process of selecting candidates to enroll in teacher training activities, and may also highly affect the content and nature of various teacher training activities. Attitudinal education, for instance, which is currently marginal to the prevalent teacher preparation programs, may become much more central to these latter, due to its heavy impact upon the acquisition of, and the readiness to use, reflective teaching.

Regarding the other two MoEs, consistent correlations were found between the Having MoE and all the four reflective components. These correlations were all negative, i.e. the higher the MoE score, the lower the scores of reflective teaching.

Statistical significance was found only with Introspection. We may assume that the negative correlations are anchored in the fact that "Having", is generally of exogenous nature, i.e. directed outwards, whereas reflection is of a more endogenous nature, i.e. directed towards the inner interactions of the individual. This interpretation is at this stage of speculative nature and requires further systematic and well-directed investigation, in order to verify this hypothesis. We may find some support to it, in the fact that the correlation of Having with Introspection shows statistical significance. Introspection is doubtless heavily directed towards the interiorized processes of the individual's mental activity.

The summarized findings highlight the existence of a significant positive correlation between the Being MoE and the four components of reflective thinking. Our hypothesis was rooted in the essential similarity between these two variables, characterized by the individual's orientation towards internal processes. As stated in the definition of the Being MoE, it stresses self-fulfillment and high involvement, both cognitively and emotionally, in the processes of personality self-formation, skill application. Thus, by its very nature, this Mode requires higher reflective ability both as an ongoing control process, and as a means of solving different dilemmas anchored in daily life. Consequently, there is a intrinsic connection between the two; suggesting mutual reinforcement.

We may postulate that an increase in the individual's level of identification with the Being MoE, will result in a parallel (albeit non-linear) rise in reflective thinking. Likewise, increased reflective thinking, may be connected with an augmentation, or amplification, of the individual's orientation towards the Being MoE. The relatively high correlation between the two, i.e. the predominant Being Mode of Existence and the tendency to indulge in reflective teaching, among prospective teachers and/or Co-operating Teachers, presumably increases the short- and long-term efficacy of the educational and teaching processes, regardless of specific situational levels which they have to cope with.

According to these views, both variables have not to be viewed as given and immutable components of the individual's behavioral repertoire. The person's reflective ability, as well as the Being Mode of Existence, may grow and develop due to both experience and systematic goal-directed intervention. The implications and meaning of these empirically supported assumptions, are manifold and complex. They should be seriously taken into consideration, on both the theoretical and the pragmatic levels. To demonstrate just some possibilities, we suggest the following:

(a) To assess the predominant MoE composition of both students enrolled in teacher training programs, and the prospected Co-operating Teachers, in order to work out the specific assignment of a given student to a specific Co-operating Teacher.

(b) Using the assessment instruments and procedures as a tool to work out and activate training curricula with regard to the fostering and development of teacher oriented patterns of MoEs.

(c) Elaboration and systematic application of curricula destined to foster and develop the teachers' reflective ability. Such programs will tend to reinforce the student's, or teacher's, awareness as to the importance of such teaching orientation and its connection with the individual's basic tendencies, as expressed by the MoE pattern.

The intensive process of interaction between Co-operating Teachers and their respective students, still needs to be theoretically formulated, and empirically investigated and studied in depth. Questions like "what degree of correlation between the Co-operating Teacher's and the student's MoE pattern, is optimal for the efficiency of the training process?" illustrate the pragmatic importance of our conceptual framework and empirical findings. The research described in this chapter is to be viewed as a preliminary study, and naturally opens up new channels of thought, leaving us with many questions to be investigated, so as to enable us to raise the quality of teacher training processes, and subsequently that of teaching and education.

Considering the frequently observed predominance of the Being MoE as more adequate for educators, bears consequences also for predominance of the other two MoEs. The consistent, albeit insignificant, negative correlations between the Having MoE and the basic components of the reflective forms of thinking, can be helpful in the processes of admitting and assigning teaching candidates. According to these findings, the more dominant the Having MoE in students, the less their tendency to use reflective processes. This phenomenon may also be explained by the specific characteristics of this MoE. The Having MoE is deeply anchored in a basic orientation to own and accumulate assets which are exogenous to the individual's personality. Thus, such individuals may have difficulties in relating to the teaching process from other viewpoints, opposed to their possessive tendencies. They may also experience difficulties in coping with a variety of teaching situations, by employing internalized thinking processes, which often require dissociation from external factors and scrutiny of one's own character and behavior.

Assuming that reflective cognitive processes are of primary importance in the teacher's work and effectiveness, inclusion of assessment procedures to determine the candidates' MoE predominant MoE pattern, may become pivotal to the criteria determining their suitability for Teacher Training institutions. By the same token, it would be worthwhile to study the possibilities and didactic ways to significantly modify and shape the hierarchical pattern of the individual's MoE system, via a systematic, and well guided intervention program.

Additional studies may be directed towards inquiring the etiologic and correlative aspects of both the MoE patterns and the reflective processes. Such studies might offer new perspectives as to the teacher's work and the Teacher Training processes. Teaching is, without a doubt, a highly complex activity. The difficulty in predicting the interactions liable to develop during the course of teaching activities, the interpersonal involvement of teachers and their respective pupils, the number and nature of unexpected classroom occurrences, and the prolonged time during which educational acts is performed over the years, all emphasize the need to develop the teacher's reflective ability and flexibility of thought. These realms may not be presumed to develop of their own accord, neither can their development be left to chance only. The turn of educational thinking in these directions is bound to be a blessing and will benefit us all if it leads to substantial changes in the complex area of teacher training.

8

Questioning as a Form of Mediation

Shmuel Feuerstein

1 Questioning as a Form of Social Communication

In any conversation, in either oral or written form, partners in the communication process decide and plan what they will convey to each other. "At the basis of their planning is their ability to know what their partners already know and what their partners need to know so that the communication will be effective" (Kraut & Tory Higgins, 1984, p. 88). Exchange of information is thus based on an assessment of the best way the message can be conveyed. This requires careful planning on the part of the speaker, and adequate perception of his audience's ability to comprehend the message. "In sum, social cognition — beliefs about others — is at the root of communication and communication itself can influence social cognition." (Kraut & Tory Higgins, 1984, p. 88).

All the components of successful communication need to be co-ordinated and structured by the quality of mediational interaction, which in turn is orientated and determined by the parameters of MLE (Feuerstein & Feuerstein, 1991) and particularly the first three: (a) intentionality and reciprocity, (b) the mediation of transcendence and (c) the mediation of meaning. The other parameters are situationally, culturally and personally determined.

Speakers and listeners continually adapt as the conversation proceeds. Listeners know to make what are termed "authorized inferences" (Clark, 1977), by drawing on lexical or stylistic elements in the conversation to infer further information which is not stated explicitly in the conversation. Learning to make these "authorized inferences" is both a linguistic and a paralinguistic skill. Gestures or tone of voice help people acquire the ability to make most inferences.

Written texts adhere to the same rules, in that the writer plans to address an audience with certain characteristics, and develops his text to transmit his message coherently to them. One major tool used in the particular case of written communication is word categorization. Meanings are derived from the way in which readers or speakers assign attributes or emphasis. Writers use context to prompt readers to understand the particular meaning they have in mind.

The linguistic bases of transmission of knowledge must be set within the context of the learning situation, as related to socio-cognitive dynamics. Tomasello, Kruger & Ratner (1993, p. 495) while discussing the ways in which humans (as compared to other social animals) learn, state: "Human beings are able to learn from one another in this way because they have very powerful, perhaps uniquely powerful forms of social cognition. Human beings understand and take the perspective of others in a manner and to a degree that allows them to participate more intimately than non-human animals in the knowledge and skills of cospecifics."

2 Collaborative Learning

Tomasello et al. (1993) then suggest three main types of learning according to the perspective of the agent involved in the transmission of information. These three types of learning are as follows: (a) *imitative learning*, which involves reproducing an act, an object, or a function; (b) *instructed learning*, where there is a deliberate effort and intent on the part of the agent to transmit given information; and (c) *collaborative learning*, in which both partners in the process work together towards the goal of acquiring knowledge.

"Imitative learning and instructed learning are means of cultural transmission: by modelling or instruction the adult passes on to the child valued elements of the culture. Collaborative learning is different. Collaborative learning takes place when neither interactant is an authority or expert; the intersubjectivity is symmetrical." (Tomasello et al., 1993, p. 500).

MLE as a quality of interaction is present in all three above-mentioned forms of learning. This quality again turns any type of learning into a collaborative experience. Mediated imitation, animated by intentionality and reciprocity, is very different from the imitation produced by direct exposure to models of imitation. When the mediator attempts to act as a model, he renders the mediatee-imitator aware of his intention to have him learn from him as a model by changing the amplitude of his behavior. (Reciting a blessing, for example, for purposes of imitation is performed more loudly and more slowly so as to render the mediatee able to imitate.) In the process of imitation MLE will change the three components of the interaction: the *stimulus*, which is modified by repetition for instance; the *mediatee*, who is rendered alert and motivated by mediation of meaning, and finally the *mediator* who will change himself in order to become an accepted model or object of imitation.

By the same token, instruction is not necessarily and not always animated by a mediational quality. Instruction may act more as an exposure to a source of stimuli presented by the teacher, a book or television and be effective in transmitting the message or unit of information, but will have a very limited effect on the learning capacity of the learner. The degree of efficiency of the interaction will depend on the sensitivity and receptivity of the learner.

Collaborative learning is a quality of MLE inasmuch as intentionality implies a reciprocity in the interactive process. This reciprocity generates a true collaborative interaction. The mediator initiates the mediatee in his intentions and turns him into an active partner in the elaboration of the behavior. This will manifest itself in a variety of ways. For instance, both the teacher and the student discuss a problem or an experiment and search together for a solution. The uniqueness of collaborative learning in comparison to the other two modes lies in the fact that in collaborative interaction there is a process of creative learning and not only mere transfer of previously known information.

In collaborative learning, both participants — regardless of age differences between them — help each other. The student may at times teach the teacher or the father, as part of a genuine partnership. This type of learning is described in the Jewish book of *Gemara*[1] by the following words of Rabbi Chanina: "I learned a great deal from my fellows, more from my friends than my fellows and from my students most of all." (Taanit, 7/1)

It is also echoed in the statements of one of the Jewish religious thinkers of the 19th century, who said: "I don't call my students 'students' because I have never called a person a student, because I do not know who learned more from whom ...".

The following parable of Rabbi Eliezer (1965) is also illustrative of this same idea. In this story, the sage turned to his student to quote the Jewish Bible (Torah) on the issue they were dealing with. The student responded by making the following comparison: "This well cannot give more water than it has given; thus I cannot say Torah more than I received from you." The rabbi responded by saying that a fountain that is flowing and gives water has the power to give more than it receives; thus the student could produce more Torah than his teacher. The interpretation of this parable is as follows: The well is passive and receives, there is no renewal but there may be evaporation and ageing. The fountain is flowing and active; the flow creates new paths which are connected to the fountain but are different as well. The flow makes for creative individuals, and sometimes unconventional paths. All this takes place with the encouragement of the teacher, the wise man, adult or parents, and all are examples of collaborative learning.

3 Modes of Questioning in the Learning Process

The way a question is formulated (open-ended or closed) is of critical importance to the successful outcome of learning. Open-ended questions have many possible answers. These include such general questions as: What would happen if ... Is this true for all cases ... Can you give me another problem with the same answer?, etc. Closed questions do not necessarily have one right answer but are more circumscribed. For instance, Which row has the most fruit? is a closed question. Obviously both types of questions are appropriate depending on the circumstances. Whether questions are open or closed, the intention and the perception of the questioner is extremely important. Teachers need to have question strategies that

---

[1]Gemara — compendium of discussions and analyses of the Jewish Oral Law (*Mishna*) carried out by the interpreters who worked in the 3rd–5th centuries AD. Sometimes the term Gemara is applied to the *Talmud* as a whole.

are clear and adapted to their students. Without this, students will ask "Why do questions have to be answered so fast in school … Why does the teacher ask all the questions … Why I am supposed to have the answers … Why are there so many little questions in school?" etc.

According to the medieval Jewish thinker Maimonides, the teacher needs to provoke questions in order to sharpen the students' mind (Hilchot Talmud Torah, IV, par. 4–8). Students also need to ask questions. When students get no answer or an unsatisfactory answer to their questions, they may not have the knowledge to ask the right question or they do not understand the way to phrase a question to obtain the information they need. However, when students are empowered to ask the right kind of question, they will then tend to ask much more sophisticated questions.

The awareness that an unanswered question can be a satisfaction is a lesson in itself. Learning to ask questions and to answer them satisfactorily enters into what are termed higher order skills, which include critical thinking, logical reasoning, meta-cognitive and cognitive strategies (see Resnick, 1987, pp. 1–59).

When instruction is not motivated by mediational principles, a form of Socratic, irony-based "teaching" may at times occur. Socratic teaching is characterized by:

1. Feigned, ironic innocence which serves to undermine the false confidence of the teacher's dialogue partner.
2. A breakdown in the students' argumentation, leading them to confess their lack of knowledge.
3. Short answers indicating agreement or disagreement from the teacher.
4. Shaping of these answers into the learner's conclusions (Simon, 1949).

The "Socratic" teacher may often be dissatisfied and explicitly manifest his dissatisfaction not because the answer was incorrect but because it was not the type of answer he wanted to hear. The solution is forced out of the student. Socratic agreement with the terms the student uses tends to be ironic and is designed mainly to prove the students' lack of knowledge so that he can lead him to accept his own opinion (Simon, 1949; Lives, 1960).

This technique is similar to a maze that has one entrance and one exit. Within the labyrinth there are many false alleys that the student is allowed to enter, only to be misled and guided back to the same exit. The lesson is clear for modern Socrates: Socrates is not willing to change and he comes with a predefined answer. He does not authorize his students to deviate from the path that leads to this solution. If there are any attempts by the students to express their own opinions, they receive initial acknowledgement followed by rejection. The students are not taught to think independently, resist or criticize others' opinions. They are not given permission or even the liberty to make a mistake. The individual is virtually pushed aside, discounted, his opinions ignored — to extract the definition. Clearly Socratic dialogue is characterized by conflict. When irony is used to produce conflict alone it is not effective teaching.

4 The Role of Questioning in Jewish Studies

The Jewish Bible (Torah) is said to teach in all domains, both abstract and concrete. As such "it seeks the essence of all things" (Steinsaltz, 1989, p. 2). One of the hallmarks of the Torah is its dialectic, which consists almost entirely of arguments dealing with laws, religious teachings, ethical concepts, etc. The interpretations of Torah in Talmud[2] captures differences of opinions, and their mode of resolution. It reports the commentaries of the Jewish Sages, and how the conclusion was reached as stages of logical proof. The Talmud uses a coded form to introduce the nature of the argument to follow, and students of Talmud learn to anticipate forms of reasoning from them. "From the Talmud we have studied records, not only laws, but the processes by which laws are uncovered. By describing those processes, the rabbis propose to resolve the tension between ordinary life and logic" (Neusner, 1984, p. 271).

Neusner (1984, pp. 2–3) points out that the Jewish Bible contains sustained arguments that prefigure the arguments of the Talmud. As early as in the discussion about Eve, we find such complex propositions as:

> "Did God really say you shall not eat of any tree of the garden …?" (Genesis III, 1).
> Abraham pleads with God to save Sodom using the hypothetical construction: "What if there should be 50 innocent within the city …?" (Genesis XVIII, 24).
> Moses predicts failure with a question: "What if they do not believe me and do not listen to me but say …?" (Exodus IV, 1).
> Balak scolds Balaam: "What have you done to me? Here I brought you to damn my enemies …" (Numbers XXIII, 11).
> Job's detractors say: "Would you discover the mystery of God? Would you discover the limit of the Almighty?" (Job XI, 7).

Whatever the intrinsic interest of each of these questions and the answers they receive, it would be insufficient to interpret them as pure literary devices. Rather, one of the most important modalities of mediation in Jewish studies, especially in those which do not deal with simple transmission of information, is the use of questions, which are shaped in such ways as to mediate higher mental processes to the individual. This forms a particular mode of thinking and a way of elaborating the information that has been transmitted to the learner. Hence it enriches his repertoire of thinking. This is particularly true in cases in which implicit questions are easily detected from the nature of the interpretation. Each interpretation is based on a specificity of the text, and the given information. Thus, one of the most important ways of involving the individual and letting him or her practically construct the answer alone is detecting the question which underlies the text, and which of necessity leads to a particular form of interpretation. This was one of the

[2]Talmud — The compendium of Jewish Law including *Mishna and Gemara*. Talmudic texts were written in Israel and Babylon until the 5th century AD.

most important contributions to the didactics of teaching the Jewish Bible made by the late Nechama Leibowitz (1941–1970).

In the framework of the MLE, the student is in the center of the interaction, and the interaction is designed to enable him or her to adapt and change — become an independent learner, be critical, form his or her own opinion, and control cognitive and emotional behavior. Biblical study involves dealing with canonical text. The text, although it is limited to a certain form, is essentially a learning framework and the mediator must organize the relevant material and guide the mediatee's behavior. In this perspective, questions involve analyzing and organizing the text, discovering its literary structure, its contradictions, logical or historical consistency, and bridging with previously learned material. Questions also involve introducing different concepts and evaluations, asking the student to explain or base various concepts on the text, highlight strengths or weaknesses in each view.

Biblical study blends a variety of methods. The commandment for each individual to renew a study of the Jewish Bible mediates the feeling of competence to the student. The teacher is an active partner in the learning process and the students' questions prompt the teacher, father or adult to re-examine his knowledge, position, way of teaching, etc. — in short to change. The question is also designed to elicit the reasons for various events, their meaning and relationships to other elements. This prompts the mediatee to construct possible alternatives or reasons and helps him construct the historical, theological and causal relationships involved, as is discussed in detail below.

4 Talmudic Argumentation

Talmudic argumentation is a powerful mediational tool. Otherwise there would be no reason to explore the minute details of the ancient Jewish Law which has no direct applications in our time. If there were no underlying power of transcendence in the Talmud, there would be no reason to scrutinize the ways in which the sages of the past reached their conclusions. According to the commentary of the Sages in *Kiddushin* (30/2) the following verse is related to methods of Talmudic study: "Happy is the man who has his quiver full of them, they shall not be ashamed but they shall speak with the enemies in the gate" (Psalm 127, 5):

> "What enemies in the gate? Rabbi Chia bar Abba said: A father and his son, a teacher and his student who are studying Torah in one gate, become enemies of one another, but they do not move from there until they become friends of one another" (Kiddushin, 30/2).

In other words, the Talmud is often depicted as a battle of the minds. There are two basic types of argument structures found in the Talmud, which can be examined in terms of their mediational thrust: *informative* (proximal) inquiries deal with a search for facts in the text, whereas *formative* inquiries mediate modalities of thinking and awareness. These arguments fall into three major categories of questions:

1. Information questions ("When?", "Whose argument is this?", "How is it done?", "How can you find it?", "What is the general rule?", "What is he trying to tell us?", etc.);
2. Directional questions affecting the flow of the argument ("How is this so?", "Why did he ask it?", "The reason is X but if ...?", "According to your opinion, is it not the case ...", "We have found A, what is B?", "Shall we disagree about this?", etc.);
3. Refocusing questions ("Is that so?", "Are you still at this?", "Does he really have to go on reckoning like a peddler?", "Did he take the trouble to teach us?", "Are you casting one man against another?", and other questions that suggest another approach.

One of the most interesting phenomena is the way in which the question is shaped as a mediating element — not only by its structure, but also by the way the question has been introduced. There are about twenty or more ways of introducing questions, each one having a different connotation. Each prepares the listener or the reader for the specific structure which the question to follow has as its goal. The various modalities of questions and the specific labeling prepare the listener for the differential goal of the question and the particular role which the partner will have to play in answering. This prompts the learner to scan mentally for those elements he will need to be able to answer the question. Thus, the question becomes a real challenge for the respondent and does not allow him to simply seek a ready-made answer. Instead, it creates conditions that will enable him to elaborate the given information, and to look for other information which may help him in constructing the particular answer. The quality of interaction which develops between the Talmud teacher and the learner should ideally be a form of collaborative learning and the form and content of questions in the Talmud are in fact designed for this purpose.

5 Examples of Question Functions

There are a variety of terms depicting different forms and goals of questioning in the Jewish studies, each of them related to different functions.

- The term *Maitaivai* is usually considered to be a question which is meant to seek, or orient the respondent towards an understanding of the differences between two attitudes, approaches, and meanings in the Talmud and Mishna.[3] In other words, the search is re-oriented towards understanding a discrepancy created by a statement of Talmudic sources, and the sources which may exist in a Mishnaic

---

[3]Mishna — The Jewish Oral Law constituting the most ancient part of *Talmud*. Codified by Yehuda Ha-Nasi in the 3rd century AD.

statement. Since there is a difference in hierarchy between the Talmudic source and the Mishnaic source, the need to find the reasons for the discrepancy not only has practical meaning in terms of the way the Jewish Law will ultimately be determined, but also serves to identify a subordinated hierarchy where the lower source become contradictory or discrepant with a hierarchically higher level source. This creates a particular need to find a way to explain the contradiction. One could for example shift the particular answer to an area in which it is not relevant anymore, and in this way solve the contradictory nature of the question sources. Alternatively, it may under certain circumstances be associated with a re-interpretation of the Mishnaic source. When the sources are clearly discrepant and contradictory, the problem is to what extent can one detect the more hidden, structural reasons for the dispute, or differences of opinion, not just as a local issue, but based more on generalized, universal principles, whose effects will be felt in a variety of other areas. This is another very important issue made feasible by the mediated question. It orients the individual to the search for more generalizable rules by which differences may be explained and understood.

The opening words *"Rami Veriminu"* in many of the sources mean a difference of opinion between sages of equal standing. In other words there is no hierarchical relationship. The Talmud and Mishna texts form a very intricate system of reconstruction of certain basic assumptions which have been either transmitted orally or traced back to Biblical sources of discrepancy — whether in the Biblical text itself, or among equals in the Mishna or Braita.[4] This makes a great difference — not only in terms of the practical outcomes of the Jewish Law, but also as regards the need to create an equilibrium between these two antagonistic sources, because we cannot assume contradictory views on this level of the sources without finding the reasons or a proper explanation for it. In the case of "Rami Veriminu", there is a very great need to re-establish the equilibrium. One of the most important goals of this type of questioning is the creation of divergent thinking. In addition, these questions orient the respondent towards the understanding, formulation, and application of abstract relationships, rather than simply dealing with units of information. The search for the relationship between various and contradictory units of information reflects an attempt to re-establish the equilibrium between two contradictory sources of information by according a legitimacy to this diversity of views, and enabling the learner to suggest and advocate his own solutions. Those elements which lead to a generalized rule are given priority. The rules or answers which relate to the specific or local elements are of lesser importance than those which will lead to more universal or generalizable rules by virtue of which many more questions can be answered.

In many cases, rather than searching for a specific response, the question is raised to prompt the respondent to produce responses whose validity applies to a larger number of questions in the same category, or in certain cases, to types of questions

---

[4]Braita — Discussions of the Jewish Law that were not included in *Mishna* codified by Yehuda Ha-Nasi in the 3rd century AD.

which have only tangential relationships to the particular issue. An individual who is confronted with such questions will have to scan all the knowledge he has accumulated, and all the information which he has, in order to find those areas in which this particular question may become relevant and in which the response to the particular case will be acceptable and relevant to a variety of other situations.

Extensive cognitive activities are involved in the questioning process. The first is the retrieval of information, based on the search for a certain affinity between the various situations that can be answered by the same response. The nature of the affinity then needs to be defined by comparative processes, which will produce relationships of commonality and difference. Only those parts of the situation that are relevant to the question will be accepted. If a situation cannot be taken into consideration because it deals with a different type of component which is not akin or not alike, or eventually even totally contradictory to the particular question, a decision must be made. What are the elements which can be considered to be related to this particular situation? Which elements are not? Contradictions may arise from differences in views by different authorities at different periods, under different conditions, the irrelevancy of the situation, or the fact that it needs to be related to a different source of commandments or source of Biblical texts.

MLE focuses and requires a more systematic approach to the data. The information must be both retrieved but also organized in a way that it points to the relationships between these sources of information by progressively detecting the various characteristics of each. A mediating question is one which orients the individual to react in a more precise and a more accurate way, rather than formulating the answer in a way which is satisfactory to him. It mediates a more appropriate response from him. In particular, it requires answers buttressed with logical evidence, based on a precise analysis of the particularities of the element under scrutiny. The question, whether it attempts to reintroduce an equilibrium or not, will always induce in the individual the need to deal with multiple sources of information. In order to better be able to respond to the question, the respondent will have to obtain information from various sources that will confirm his hypothesis and give it strength and structure. In other situations the question will make the individual look for additional sources or reasons for the differences which have been found. In order to do this, the multiple sources of information have to be defined in terms of the time, place, situation and configuration in which these particular contradictory sources were produced in order to formulate hypotheses as to the reasons for the differences.

- The question such as "What could be the good reason for it?" (The contradictory nature of the elements under study again prompts the respondent to look for those elements in the data that may yield the meaning and reason for the existing response.) The elaboration principle, as well as the elaborational stage of the mental act are defined in many cases by the attempts that the questioner will make to orient the respondent towards a formulation of the problem.
- "What is the particular reason for this problem?" This term is used when

questions are primarily related to the elaboration system and do not just attempt to identify facts or events. The mediator must relate the events to specific conditions or to use multiple sources of information to combine different answers, promote tasks designed to find ways the respondent can answer and look for the appropriate strategies, eventually inventing them to find an answer to the particular question. There are many questions which actually require the mediator to set a goal and well-intentioned strategy. This is meant to activate the mind of the respondent to become able to answer. These types of questions create sharpness in all the three phases of the mental act.

- "What does he want to let us know?" What kind of meaning does he want us to derive from these sayings? The respondent must first correctly decode the quotation, saying, or event: What does this event inform us about? What kind of meaning does it want to impart to us? Information needs to be gathered on the input level, elaborating the relationships which this may have with a variety of other areas. The elaboration process thus determines the nature of the input level — in other words, what kind of questions to ask, localizing the information, where to take the information from, and what kind of relevance to give to the information, as a function of the task.

- "What does this want to tell us?" is a typical question meant to activate the three phases of the mental act and to create the modalities by which the specific reasoning processes will become the point of departure for a variety of theoretical and practical modes of reasoning.

- Similarly, questions such as, "From where are these words, meanings, conclusions?" "How and where did you derive them?" also call for major elaboration activity implying a search in a variety of other areas. The solution to this question is to look for all the sources where one can eventually find the traces of reasons which are related to the particular event described in a given statement.

- The question, "What do you learn from it?" or "What is derived from it?" functions in the same way. It encourages a search for various meanings, significance, and the reasons for a variety of areas. Attempts to find the basic controversy in conflicting views and not just a casuistic event which may have limited meaning may also lead to defining different hierarchies in the Talmud but less contradiction with biblical sources. In this case the problem is to define the principles underlying these opposing views. The search for higher order levels of thinking, the principles, rules, and modalities of interacting with particular data, is an attempt to find parsimonious modalities of interacting with events, and solve problems with greater scope. For instance, the question as to the difference between two groups of thinkers ("Bet Hillel" and "Bet Shamai"[5]) concerning the way to light the Hanukkah candles (in progressive order, one more a day or the reverse order, one less a day) is not just treated as an isolated difference between the two schools with episodic meaning. Rather, understanding this

---

[5]Bet Hillel and Bet Shamai — Two schools of exposition of Oral Law named after Hillel and Shamai who lived at the end of the 1st century BC and the beginning of the 1st century AD.

question helps relate it to a variety of other differences between the Bet Hillel and Bet Shamai schools. The mediated question therefore generates higher mental processes which search for the rules providing economic ways to deal appropriately with categories of events. The need for logical evidence is sharpened to the extreme by these challenging, attacking questions which require the individual to make use of all the data possible and all the reasoning he can muster to respond.

Mediated learning questions are a source of the individual's awareness that not all answers will be accepted. In order for these answers to be accepted, they must contain acceptable rules, principles, and laws. The role of these questions go far beyond the simple, practical, or pragmatic issues. Even when the two views are consonant in terms of their components, questions still remain, such as "What are the differences between the two?" as a way to better understand why these two processes are mentioned in two different ways, or by two different verses in the Bible. "Why do we need two different sources?" "Why cannot we rely only on one source?" All these questions are exercises in higher mental processes, and in particular, in sharpening the need of the individual to use logical evidence as a way of interacting with his questioner, and later on with himself through a process of internalization. The message is: Do not just accept each answer at its face value. Do not accept the answer such as, "Because", without having the reason given for this "Because". Do not accept, "That is the way." Make it understood. Do not accept simple aesthetic reasons or simple fantasy as sources for decisions. The logical or empirical reasons must dominate and will have to be used in order to make something acceptable to the audience or to the questioner.

Thus, overall, questions in Jewish studies deal primarily with higher order reasoning. Questioning everything, questioning every event, questioning every reason is geared towards identification of more general rules which lead to a more efficient way of thinking. The major goal is to generate within the individual a critical approach that can be used in a variety of ways, in a generalizable, transferable, and explanatory way. The MLE in Judaism is the source of knowledge of the Jewish Law. It transcends the practical, pragmatic sense of this Law to the commandments of the study of the Jewish Bible, that itself transcends by far the specific needs of the Jewish Law. It is an important source of learning and understanding, even when the pragmatic, practical elements no longer prompt this need. All these are the building blocks of the mediational interaction in Judaism.

PART 2

9

Dynamic Cognitive Assessment and the Instrumental Enrichment Program: Origins and Development

Rafi S. Feuerstein

The purpose of this chapter is to reconstruct the origins and trace the development of the two applied systems created by Reuven Feuerstein to whom this volume is dedicated. The theory and method of dynamic cognitive assessment (Learning Potential Assessment Device — LPAD) and the Instrumental Enrichment cognitive intervention program (IE) have become the most popular embodiment of the Feuersteinian approach in education and psychology. The following analysis of these systems is based both on written sources and on personal communication with Reuven Feuerstein.

1 The Quest for a New Assessment Method

The LPAD program has been in use since the end of the 1950s. One of the factors leading to its creation was an objective social and educational need associated with mass Jewish immigration to Israel in the1950s and 1960s (Feuerstein, R., Richelle, M., 1963). The country's population doubled during this period. Many of the new immigrants came from traditional communities of North Africa and the Middle East, who showed varying degrees of difference to the culture of the European-born inhabitants prevailing at the time in Israel. One of the pressing needs was to provide psycho-educational assessment to immigrant populations that, despite the high level of their intellectual abilities, functioned on the conventional psychometric tests at a low level due to their cultural difference. Thus there was a clear need for the design of a method that could reveal thinking ability and modifiability of the immigrant children and youth, beyond the mere registration of low functioning as expressed in their manifest performance. This innovative attempt was made at the time when the majority of educational psychologists viewed the child's basic cognitive functions as being determined by the maturational process and his/her basic intellectual abilities as largely predetermined genetically. The role of educational intervention was seen as adding more specific skills and content knowledge. The concept of LPAD, on the contrary, was to construct such an assessment procedure that would indicate the conditions leading to the enhancement of individual modifiability and change in the individual's basic cognitive functioning so that he/she could adapt to the demands of the new culture. Those conditions had to be manifested by acquiring learning skills and thinking strategies which would allow the integration process. In addition, such a procedure would have to assess the amount of investment required to achieve this change.

The specific socio-political conditions existent in Israel at that time rendered the question of integration of low functioning new immigrants an acute one. The general public, professionals, politicians and the press vehemently debated the ability of the fledging state to absorb a large number of new immigrants whose skills did not measure up to the demands of Israeli society. The young state's poor educational and rehabilitative resources were the major factor in these doubts. It was presumed impossible to increase the low functioning of these youngsters by normal educational processes, even the most intensive ones. Therefore, in the eyes of the professionals, the 14–15-year-old youth that failed to attain the educational achievements anticipated for his/her age was at severe risk of being unable to integrate either educationally or socially.

Reuven Feuerstein, at that time a research student studying under Jean Piaget and Andre Rey at the University of Geneva, was approached by Youth Aliyah organization leaders with a request for him to examine the issue of the possible adaptation of new immigrant youth in Israel. Responsible for the residential education of immigrant youth, Youth Aliyah faced public pressure to exclude some of the low functioning youth from the immigration process. It was argued that the existent screening procedures indicated that the low functioning youth would not be able to adapt to new conditions, unlike many others who acted normally and regarding whom no doubts whatsoever were raised in relation to their immigration and successful absorption in Israel. Youth Aliyah leaders were in search of an optimistic scientific approach that would justify the immigration of these low functioning youth to Israel.

Initially immigration candidates were tested using a variety of standard tests including so-called culturally-fair non-verbal tests (Raven's Matrices, Cattel's tests), development tests (Bender Gestalt test, draw a person test), Rey's practical intelligence tests, and Piaget assignments. The results simply confirmed the fears — namely that the children's functioning was much lower than their age-referenced norm (Richelle & Feuerstein, 1957). In many cases the test performance of 14-year old adolescents was on the functioning level of 4–6-year-olds. Reuven Feuerstein recalls receiving an urgent telegram from Israel reporting the conclusion reached by psychologists who examined immigrant youth using the Bender Gestalt test, whereby 300 performed at the level of people with brain damage and demonstrated a severe lack of visual-graphic-motor maturity.

This harsh reality created a pressing need to find appropriate instruments for assessing this population so as to reveal the adolescents' real potential, and evaluate their modifiability. During this quest it became absolutely clear that it was not sufficient to replace the assessment instruments. Rather it was essential to change the whole method of assessment. Not even the most sensitive assessment instruments, if administered in a static form, could reflect more than the youngsters' present functioning. It was therefore essential to find a method of evaluating the adolescent's capacity for change by creating models of change by means of intervention. This necessity caused Reuven Feuerstein to renounce the static method of assessment, namely all the methods that gauge a person's intelligence without using intervention. As a substitute for the conventional methods Reuven Feuerstein began to develop the dynamic cognitive assessment procedures aimed at the evaluation of the learning potential rather than a manifest level of functioning. This search eventually led to the development of the LPAD — the Learning Potential Assessment Device.

Later, at the beginning of the 1990s, Reuven Feuerstein decided to change the name from that of *potential* to *propensity*. The reason for this change was his conviction that the concept of *potential* or capacity reflects a limited entity, which may theoretically be quantified, even if it has not yet reached full realization. On the other hand, he believes that the concept of *propensity* conveys the meaning of thrust or energy, which cannot be quantified, *inter alia* because it is likely to lead to the creation of new and different effective behavioral cognitive structures in the individual. For this reason I will henceforth use the term *propensity* in describing LPAD, in spite of the fact that it was introduced at a later stage.

2 The Characteristic Features of LPAD

The characteristic feature of LPAD (Feuerstein et al., 1979; Feuerstein et al., 1995; Feuerstein et al., 1997; Feuerstein et al., 1998) is that it is designed to evaluate the process of change occurring in the examinees and not just their present level of functioning. The assessment process is composed of three stages:

- **The first stage** (test) is designed to examine the present level of the examinees in varied cognitive fields and to reveal processes responsible for their success or failure.
- **The second stage**, (intervention) which expresses the change in approach much more acutely, is the intervention stage, which is designed to correct the deficient cognitive functions discovered during the first stage of the test. Naturally the intervention stage is not supposed to rehabilitate the examinees' overall functioning, but to create samples of change in the fields revealed as defective.
- **The third stage** (post-test) again contains a series of assignments conducted in a static form without intervention which are designed to examine the extent of the influence of the intervention provided during the second stage. Are the changes stable? What is the range of the influence of the changes? Does a change in one area influence other areas? In other words; to what extent is the change structural? The samples of change are supposed to supply information in several areas:

1. Initial deficient cognitive functions and their modifiability;
2. Identification of the most successful modes of intervention;
3. The examinee's profile of modifiability.

The LPAD deviated from the static assessment approach in five areas:

1. *A change in the assessment's objective.* Static assessments focus on the product

of the assessment expressed in the cumulative score. LPAD is concerned with the thinking process, i.e. the quality of the process and the main difficulties (the deficient cognitive functions) experienced by the examinee. The following parameters of examinees' learning changes are examined: The extent of the change; its significance for the examinee (i.e. the distance between the initial performance and the functioning following the intervention and the degree of centrality of the area which has changed); the conditions required to generate a change of this kind. It is important to note that contrary to the static tests, which compare the examinee to normative functioning, the LPAD compares the child to him or herself, while characterizing the unique components in the individual thinking process.

The LPAD does not restrict itself to the exposure of potential, but when necessary endeavors to create it. In this respect LPAD differs from some other learning potential assessment procedures that seem to be concerned with the exposure of the existing potential and not of the creation of new potential (see Lidz, 1987; Feuerstein et al., 1995; Feuerstein et al., 1998). The LPAD, on the other hand, examines the possibility of reinforcing the potential and even the creation of sets of new thinking structures.

2. *A change in the assessment instruments*. The instruments comprising the LPAD were selected to meet two conditions:

- **they demand the mediational process**
- **they must be sensitive to the direction of every slight change in the subject's functioning.**

The instruments were constructed so that the examinees feel the need for external mediation in order to successfully cope with the assignments. Furthermore, the instrument must be able to reveal how the cognitive structures contained in it may be learned: cognitive functions, principles, the strategies required for the solution of problems, which permit control over other assignments. The LPAD instruments are not of an informative character, and they do not address the crystallized intelligence. Contrarily they address the fluid intelligence associated with thinking strategies. The instruments permit mediation leading to rehabilitation of the thinking processes discovered to be defective during the first stage of the assessment. The LPAD instruments must be structured in such a way so as to permit sensitive identification of even minimal changes occurring in the examinee's functioning. The instruments must function as a "sieve" to pick up any change. The "filaments" of such a cognitive "sieve" are composed of assignments addressing the various operations, and are presented in different modes, and at graded levels of difficulty. This device is aimed at locating the change following the success in solving an assignment in which only one parameter has changed. For example, an examinee who has not done well in an analogical assignment in the performance mode, is likely to succeed in an assignment demanding use of the same operation in the verbal mode. An examinee who has not succeeded in the recall assignments in the verbal mode is likely to succeed in the visual-motor or the auditory mode. This model also permits the gradual changes generated in the examinee to be monitored throughout the graded assignments.

3. *A change in the assessment situation.* In the static assessment the examinee is guided to preserve a fixed situation, so as not to create a difference which is likely to affect the possibility of comparing the examinee's results with the group norms. In the LPAD the examinees are compared to themselves which allows us to manipulate the assessment situation. The focus of the assessment objective is not on what is the examinees' level in relation to the population but on how they learn, on how they think, and on the conditions required to create the necessary change in them so as to improve their functioning.

4. *Emphasis on process.* The characteristics of the LPAD as described here in brief shape the LPAD as an assessment which is focused on the process of change undergone by the examinees following their exposure to the mediated experience. The LPAD does not dwell on the final product but on the factors which enabled the examinees to arrive at a given product. The thinking process is described by the cognitive functions and the cognitive map, permitting its process analysis and the identification of specific stages where difficulties occurred.

5. *Interpretation of the results.* The LPAD takes into account a wide range of data regarding the examinee's baseline functioning and test performance. These include initial IQ scores, intelligence age, developmental age, and a comparison of pre-intervention to post-intervention LPAD achievements. A general scoring characteristic of static tests is replaced by an active search for the examinees' abilities and comparison of their pre- to post-mediation achievements. Revealed at the first stage of the assessment, on the basis of the cognitive map, are the examinee's defective cognitive functions and their level of severity, as well as the cognitive nature of the assignment, where the defective functions appeared in comparison to the nature of the assignments, where the functions appeared to be relatively normal. The deficiencies become targets for the intervention during the second stage of the assessment. The assessor attempts, by probing, to rehabilitate the various deficiencies of the examinees while they are working with the assignments. During the third stage, the examinee receives a series of assignments in order to examine the influence of the mediated intervention on the examinee's functioning.

The change in the examinee's functioning is analyzed with the help of the Profile of Modifiability. This instrument enables the degree of structural change observed to be analyzed in relation to each one of the functions revealed to be defective, and to evaluate the examinee's general modifiability profile. It is important to emphasize the principle of comparing the examinees to themselves, while closely observing the manner in which they act from the cognitive point of view. The individual profile of modifiability supplies information regarding the examinees' readiness to grasp the principles on which the problems facing them are based. The profile also includes the quantity and quality of the investment required to create a structural change in relation to the various types of assignments, according to the parameters of the cognitive map. Even if the examinees' functioning is low, the LPAD tests demonstrate the degree of modifiability demonstrated by them in relation to their initial performance, and the structural degree of the change. Such an analysis serves as a basis for the development of optimal conditions required for generating future change in the various environments in which the examinees operate: home, school, the company of children etc., while creating a bridge from the results of the evaluation created in the assessment environment, and the examinees' actual environments.

3 The Theories of Structural Cognitive Modifiability and Mediated Learning Experience

The application of LPAD with large groups of low functioning children and youth created a feedback informing the original theoretical foundations of this approach. As a result an important circle was created with theory informing application and the application data enriching the theory. A number of principles were formulated reaching beyond the task of dynamic assessment and ranging to a more general theory of structural cognitive modifiability and mediated learning experience (Feuerstein, 1991; Feuerstein et al., 1977; Feuerstein et al., 1990; Feuerstein, R., Feuerstein, S., 1991; Feuerstein et al., 1997). The application of LPAD with different populations of children and youth demonstrated that many of them apparently failed to benefit from their rich everyday experience. The remarkable expression of this regrettable phenomenon is the fact that people who had been exposed to various activities over a long period of time revealed very limited performance ability when they were required to perform the same activities themselves. Their concept of reality remained episodic and concrete without any organization and association processes leading to a lack of "learning from experience".

Reuven Feuerstein was faced with the following questions: Do these observations reflect a fixed and unchangeable, or a temporary and modifiable condition? Were the problems of those youth related to the fact that they had not acquired the appropriate operations due to the lack of maturity or lack of appropriate stimulus, and was their condition therefore irreversible because the "critical period" had elapsed?

The answer to these questions demanded a broad theoretical attitude regarding the human thinking potential from the dynamic viewpoint. As mentioned above, this approach was established and developed following the development of the LPAD, its extensive use with different populations and the results thereof. The LPAD led to the identification of three sets of concepts: The concepts of deficient cognitive functions, the Cognitive Map, and the criteria of Mediated Learning Experience.

Instead of referring to a high or low intellectual level, Reuven Feuerstein proposed an alternative conceptualization of deficient performance. He observed that the adolescents frequently lack extremely specific thinking functions, whose lack or deficiency was sufficient to hinder the entire thinking process. For example, impulsive behavior at the input stage was sufficient to cause the examinee to input the question in a defective and/or distorted manner, and thereby fail in the assignment. Or, the examinees' lack of a spontaneous tendency to compare two sets of data was sufficient to cause the examinee not to compare well various possible answers, thereby denying him/her the opportunity of correctly answering the assignment demanding analogic thinking. Examinees whose need for precision was insufficient because their childhood environment did not require them to be precise, are prone to errors arising from that fact that they do not examine the assignment in detail but only "roughly". The failure of such examinees in the regular tests is pre-assured. Does such a failure in an assignment demanding the operation of selection, analogic thinking or logical repetition, indeed mean that the examinees are not capable of exercising these operations, not even after the learning stage? Do specific processes which are defective or missing in the peripheral input and output stages fail to permit the central processing stage to perform its action, since the data does not reach it properly, or does not flow from it in an exact form? Even defective cognitive functions revealed in the processing state are often specific and not general.

These observations led to the formulation of the list of deficient cognitive functions. The cognitive functions are the set of basic cognitive activities essential for the whole thought process to exist properly. In other words: the cognitive function describes the quality of the functioning of the intelligent act. It is important to emphasize the "state" nature of the function and not its being a rigid thinking structure. This concept arises, inter alia, from the dependency between the level of functioning (defective-normal) for a particular assignment in which the particular cognitive act occurred. It is a common occurrence to meet an adolescent pupil whose study achievements are extremely low, but who is a good actor. Why does he have difficulty relating to two sources of information simultaneously in a mathematical question? On the other hand, he is capable of analyzing the state of movement while relating to the four directions of the vehicle, the weather at that time, the mechanical condition of the car, the speed of the journey, etc.

The list compiled by Reuven Feuerstein includes about thirty *deficient cognitive functions* in the input, elaboration and output stages of the mental act. These functions permit the thinking process of every person to be described in an extremely precise manner, due to the great amount of detail and the sharp distinction between them. And indeed, to put forward a defined target for the cognitive rehabilitation process, instead of the sweeping use of labels in relation to particular deficiencies (such as dyslexia, dyscalculia, dysgraphia and so forth). The description of a child as "dyslexic" should raise the question of whether there is a particular function which is directly responsible for the child's difficulty. For example, there could be a problem of spatial concepts associated with the reading process. Likewise, one may ask whether two children who are described as dyslexic do indeed suffer from the same defective function. The deficient cognitive functions are not defined on the basis of their affinity to particular content unlike the elements of intelligence defined by Thurston, Gilford and particularly by Gardner. This content-neutral nature permits them to be attributed to each one of the fields of thinking content, so that the application of the comparison between them is very broad. Another important advantage arising from this concept is that low functioning does not necessarily testify to a broad and irreversible cognitive injury, but could reflect a deficiency in one of the essential conditions for the processing process, yet not the processing process itself.

One of the important implications of the definition of the defective functions and their formulation was the exposure of the mode of intervention essential to rehabilitate them. Reuven Feuerstein insisted that in fact the adolescents who he examined by LPAD needed to acquire varied thinking principles. In order for them to benefit from the various worlds of content, it was essential that they be given appropriate forms of perception and generalization. But it was not just a question of abilities that they must acquire. Also necessary was the adoption of an active-changing tendency vis-à-vis the revolving world contrary to their passive-receptive approach. Their passive approach led to the absence of organization processes and consequently to an episodic perception of reality. Reuven Feuerstein suggested that what was missing was the Mediated Learning Experience.

4 Mediated Learning Experience

Mediated Learning is defined as one of the two modalities of interaction with the world:

- The first modality is the *direct learning* of a person from the stimuli appearing in his environment. A person absorbs varied knowledge from his physical and social environment.
- The second modality, *mediated learning*, is the one responsible for the existence of a person's modifiability, namely, the creation of the thinking processes responsible for a person's adaptation to the environment. And indeed, mediated learning is responsible for a person's cognitive and emotional development. Furthermore, the *Mediated Learning Experience* is responsible for the creation of the cognitive functions in particular and a person's thinking structures in general. *Mediated learning* is the mode of communication between human beings (parents-children, teachers-pupils), which causes the recipient of mediation to acquire varied methods of organization of the large amount of information continuously flowing to him from the world. And indeed, he will acquire the tendency to organize the large amount of information in an active manner and thereby turn it into knowledge.

Three parameters are required to define a particular interaction as *mediation*:

1. *Intentionality and reciprocity*. The mediator is responsible for the stimulation reaching the recipient of mediation. The direction to mediation causes the

mediator to change the three elements of the interaction; the mediator, the stimulation and the recipient of mediation.

2. *Transcendence (transfer)*. The mediator goes beyond the particular objective of interaction. There are two levels to this transfer. First, the creation of a web of cognitive connections which link the specific content of the interaction with other contents. For example, mediation of a feeling of achievement given to a child in a reading lesson endows the child not only with confidence in his ability in the lesson, but also with a very valuable cognitive instrument, which also enables him to appraise his ability in completely different areas. Second, the creation of the pupil's tendency to constantly increase the repertoire of his cognitive and emotional functioning. The recipient of mediation is supposed to change from a passive observer in the world of stimuli, to an active absorber constantly organizing the stimuli he absorbs and attempting to produce the maximum amount of information from them.

3. *Mediation of Meaning*. The mediation of meaning answers the question "What is my purpose in mediating to you ...?" in an attempt to shape the energetic aspect of the recipient of the mediation. That is to say, to endow the recipient of mediation with the feeling of necessity and essentiality in the adoption of the substance contained in the mediation.

Beyond these three parameters, there are additional parameters which do not constitute an essential condition, but which characterize various types of mediation interactions, whose appearance is not essential and is even modifiable in accordance with the various states, and the cultural modalities characterizing human beings (Feuerstein, 1991).

5 The Cognitive Map

The third conceptual tool developed by Reuven Feuerstein is the cognitive map, whose importance is attributed to the connection it creates between the examinee's functioning and the substance of the assignment in which he is being assessed. The cognitive map analyzes the mental act required to perform the assignment by means of seven parameters. The manipulation of the elements of the map in the assessment process is an important part of the assessor's ability to raise various hypotheses in relation to the examinee's functioning. The seven parameters are:

1. *The content of the mental act.*
2. *The modes or the language* in which the assignment is expressed.
3. *The main thinking stage (input, processing or output)* in which the assignment occurs.
4. *The cognitive operations* required for the purpose of performing the assignment.
5. *The level of complexity* of the assignment (the quantity and quality of the elements of the information from which the assignment is composed and the degree of the examinee's acquaintance with them).

6. *The level of abstraction* required to perform the assignment.
7. *The level of effectiveness* required in the assignment defined by three factors: the speed required to perform the assignment, the level of precision which the assignment imposes on the person performing it in order to successfully carry out the assignment, as well as the feeling of effort which performance of the assignment creates in a person. This parameter is closely associated with the preceding parameters mentioned above.

The cognitive map played an important role in the development of the *Instrumental Enrichment* tools, in that it covers varied fields of thinking and the various levels, and the modalities in which they operate. The cognitive map also helps to view the *deficient cognitive functions* as "states" and not as "traits", since it indicates the various cognitive characteristics of the assignment as being potentially responsible for the high or defective functioning of a particular function. In other words, the *cognitive map* fulfills the presumption of the interaction between the assignment and thinking, as responsible for a person's level of functioning.

6 Cognitive Modifiability

The first principle of cognitive modifiability is that the differences in the functioning of human beings should be described as a function of the level of their propensity to change. Furthermore, the level of modifiability is not conceived as a fixed psychological entity, not as a "thing" but as a state, which is itself modifiable with a possibility of increase or decrease, expansion or contraction.

For example, a high level engineer required to work in an absolutely new technological environment is likely to encounter difficulty in learning effectively, similarly to a child with Down Syndrome who, due to chromosomal–neurological reasons, has trouble learning something quickly. These two people are likely to be similar to a normal, but culturally deprived, child who due to a mediational deficiency learns slowly and in a defective manner. It may certainly be said that there are human beings in a state of lower modifiability, but the very fact that such a state is likely to appear in every person shows the fluid and changeable nature of these phenomena. For this reason, Reuven Feuerstein considers it justified to define learning difficulties of various kinds as a "state" and not as a "trait". This definition is based upon the presumption that all these phenomena reflect one basic propensity — "the propensity to change". Accordingly, the degree of human beings' propensity to change, in situations requiring change, is the basis for the distinction between human beings. This definition leads to the concept of the person as being much more flexible and indeterminate than often presumed. The person is seen here through numerous changing states rather than the fixed traits, whose origin is perceived as fundamentally genetic.

This perception also has clinical implications. The methodological approach prevailing in educational and clinical psychology is to identify the stable traits in a person's functioning in various fields. This task is not easy since human functioning is of a fluid nature. On the other hand, the Feuerstein theory of modifiability views the absence of stability in the human functioning as its most prominent feature. The significance of viewing the lack of stability in functioning as a permanent factor leads to the description of the mode of the person's functioning as a "state" and not as a "trait".

From this it transpires that the tendency to change is itself also subject to change, since it is a "state" and not an "object" that can be defined according to criteria of quantity or quality. Notwithstanding the fact that Reuven Feuerstein's work focused mainly on cognitive aspects, the above approach is not limited to cognition, but also includes the emotional, motivational and energetic factors. One may say that the only thing possible to predict of people is that they are not predictable.

The observation of significant changes occurring in originally low functioning youth who underwent LPAD led to the formulation of the second principle: increased modifiability is capable of removing blocks generally considered to be unsurpassable.

The first block is *the etiology of the low functioning.* Burt, Jensen and some other psychologists claimed that the factors determining the level of a person's functioning are fundamentally endogenous: hereditary and genetic. As such, problems perceived as arising from these causes are naturally unsurpassable. The Feuerstein theory of Structural Cognitive Modifiability does not ignore the existence of factors of this kind, but it views them as distal factors. According to this theory, these factors constitute blocks to the external mediation process. Since mediated learning experience is essential to the development of the thinking processes, a block of this type is likely to cause abnormal cognitive development in the child. For example, autistic children, or those suffering from other kinds of communications problems, have difficulty forming relationships with other people and are therefore blocked from receiving the intensive mediation they require. This block is likely to lead to cognitive difficulties and poor modifiability.

Children afflicted with Down Syndrome are likely to find it difficult to follow rapid stimulation in their early years, e.g. rapid speech, rapidly changing pictures, etc. If the human interaction these children are exposed to does not adjust itself from the outset to the required speed and perceptual acuity, it simply will not penetrate in full, and once again normal cognitive confidentiality will not occur following the absence of or deficiency in mediation.

Culturally different new immigrant students are likely to have a block because their native culture does not use that many super-ordinate concepts for the organization of data as their new culture. Furthermore, these students are likely to have different learning and behavioral habits, typical of their country of origin. For example, they would not admit their lack of understanding out of considerations of politeness toward the person speaking to them. The block interfering with mediation may result in turning these students from "culturally different" into "culturally deprived". Outward behavior in the cognitive tasks may even resemble that of an organically impaired individual, but this state can be explained as a result of the block preventing adequate mediation experience.

The distal etiological factors may have a different nature but their role is secondary because they only support, or on the contrary, interfere with the proximal factors responsible for the mediational process. This model significantly changes our view of the etiology and impairment because instead of a direct link between the distal factors and the outcome, it offers an intermediate process of a mediational nature ultimately responsible for the outcome. It thus opens up wide perspectives for treatment even when distal factors cannot be alleviated. For example, the mediator will slow down the pace of speech addressed to the Down Syndrome child, and will even repeat the message several times so that the child can absorb it well. In this way the child's receptive ability previously directly linked to his or her chromosomal impairment becomes moderated by the mediation. Mediation can be effective even with children who suffer from autistic behavior and communicative problems. For example, instead of viewing the echolalia of such children merely as a clinical syndrome, one may use it as a channel for the development of child speech so that they repeat, again and again, the message conveyed to them. The theory of structural cognitive modifiability postulates that every person is modifiable, regardless of the kind of distal factor responsible for the impairment, and of the fact that the developmental outcome depends on the proximal factor, namely adequate experience of mediated learning.

The second block is *age*. Age is perceived as an extremely important developmental factor determining a person's functioning. Hebb (1949) and Hunt (1961) emphasized the interaction of endogenous-hereditary and exogenous-experiential factors in shaping human intelligence. The direct interaction of the organism and its environment plays an important role here. The response to the environmental stimuli leads to the creation of a group of brain cells responsible for the formation of higher thinking processes. Therefore Hebb asserted that the formation of intelligence is dependent upon cerebral maturation processes which have so-called "critical periods". During these periods the brain is particularly sensitive to external stimulation. Once the critical period is over the brain is no longer capable of benefiting from experiences. Naturally advanced age is perceived as a block for further modifiability due to the termination of the maturation and the beginning of the global decline.

Reuven Feuerstein et al. (1980) argue against the "critical period" approach to modifiability both in regard to childhood and to old age. In a number of case studies it was shown that children who "missed" their critical period for development of communicative and cognitive functions are capable of catching up if proper mediation is provided. Somewhat similar results were obtained with the older individuals who, under proper conditions, demonstrated considerable cognitive modifiability (Blatt, Shaya et al.). It was also shown that the performance of older individuals strongly depends on the type of intelligence tests administered to them; when the assignments took into account the influence of life experience on intelligence the elderly performed even better than the college students.

The third block is the severity of the functional difficulty. Logic suggests that the more severe the condition, the less optimistic the developmental outcome. Once again Reuven Feuerstein suggests that the level of severity does not constitute an unsurpassable obstacle in the way of modifiability. For example, ordinary educational practice perceives a condition such as combined blindness, deafness, and lack of speech as being unmodifiable. On the other hand, it has been proved during the last hundred years, by cases such as Helen Keller and others, that even such multiple obstacles can be overcome.

One important aspect of modifiability is that human beings are apparently the only creatures that not just receive mediation, but also, become mediators to themselves. Here the relationships between cognitive functions and emotional motives are circular. On the one hand emotional factors are shaped by cognitive functions: We ask "*With whom and why* are you angry? *Did she do it intentionally? How do you know this?*" On the other hand emotional factors motivate the development and use of cognitive functions.

The application of Feuerstein's model of mediated learning experience converged with other theoretical trends such as that of Vygotsky (1978, 1986). This led to the conclusion that the factor responsible for the universality of a human modifiability is the presence of mediated interactions in the transmission of culture from generation to generation. Human beings, unlike other living beings, do not learn, i.e. change, merely as a result of their direct and unmediated exposure to the world, but also through some kind of human mediator placed between the recipients of mediation and the world. By means of deduction and inference the mediators convey their stances, approaches and particularly the manner in which they perceive the stimulation and the methods of connection between the various stimuli and the manner of creating the information to the recipient of the mediation.

In fact the experience of mediation appears as a process of transferring culture from generation to generation, which includes the transfer of the past, of accumulated experience and in particular skills which have developed, values and so on. The culture transmitted has a kind of cognitive skeleton that determines the manner in which the accumulated knowledge is represented and organized. This cognitive "skeleton" is transferred together with cultural content and is imprinted in the next generation by means of the positive experience in mediated learning. In this way not only the world of knowledge and values of the new generation, but also its cognitive structure is organized. The inter-cultural differences in the manner of thinking observed in different societies are the product of the various methods of organizing and processing knowledge. Mediated knowledge leads to a cognitive design that is different in different societies. At the same time it is important to emphasize that the mediation process has a universal structure represented by the existence of the three fundamental parameters of mediation: Intentionality and reciprocity, transcendence and mediation of meaning. The difference between the cultures, on the other hand, arises from the differences in other parameters of mediation.

Mediation is considered to be responsible for a person's learning potential, which for its part leads to the enormous developmental changes which have occurred in human society, and which occur in the human individual throughout his lifetime. Mediation leads to learning potential since it shapes people's thinking structures enabling them to process given information and create new information not absorbed directly from the world.

7 Instrumental Enrichment

The *Instrumental Enrichment* program (Feuerstein, 1968; Feuerstein et al., 1980; Feuerstein et al., 1999) was designed to develop and reinforce modifiability with persons who for various reasons lacked the tools for coping with learning and cognitive tasks. As described above, an adaptation block can be found in people functioning at a low level, or even the ones functioning at a high level but who face a rapid qualitative change in their position associated with a new environment and new assignments that require a new type of response. For this reason the program is applied to a wide range of recipients functioning at lower as well as higher levels.

Instrumental Enrichment, as an intervention program, is designed to structurally reinforce the learning potential of individuals in order to make them become capable of benefiting from the formal and informal learning processes available to them. The main problem in the adaptation process arises from the difficulties benefiting from the learning processes available to individuals during their experience with various events. This phenomenon, i.e. a lack of permeability of the individual in the face of the learning processes, as well as the lack of resistance to the learning processes that occurred — is not coincidental. It arises from the person's lack of cognitive flexibility, dependent upon the absence of appropriate tools and means of thinking, effective perception methods, use of time and space relationships, significant organization of information, causal relationships, etc.

The objective of the mediated intervention is to create in people — through mediation attuned to age and level of experience — the flexibility required to benefit from the various learning processes to which they are exposed.

The concept of modifiability was first applied with low functioning adolescents in French transit camps on their way to Israel. The intervention based on this concept was continued with similar populations of students in Israel in the framework of the Youth Aliyah organization. In 1958 Reuven Feuerstein founded ten alternative educational programs, which absorbed a population of students who, due to their defective educational-cognitive functioning and behavioral problems, failed to be integrated into regular Youth Aliyah boarding schools or had been removed from them. Equipped with the concept of modifiability in every person beyond the severity of their condition Reuven Feuerstein and his colleagues embarked upon a struggle against the segregation trend in the absorption of immigrants with difficulties. The goal of integration was not acceptable by everyone and Reuven Feuerstein and his colleagues had to come up with a creative solution regarding the low functioning adolescents at risk of being placed in special institutions.

The first alternative created was named ***The Third or Therapeutic Class***. This setting, established in a few kibbutzim and youth villages, was intended to absorb youth whose functioning and educational achievements were low but who had no primary mental or neurological problems. The educational program included the use of mediated learning and certain tasks and activities, which later became integrated into the Instrumental Enrichment program. The assumption was that the integration of low-functioning children into a heterogeneous setting would advance more advantageously than if they were to stay in a homogenous special education environment. Eventually this alternative was abandoned in favor of more effective *Preparatory Programs* described below.

The second alternative established by Reuven Feuerstein and his colleagues was the **Therapeutic Groups**. This was intended for children with primary mental disturbances (organic or emotional) and whose educational difficulties were the result of this, unlike the above settings, which focused on children and youth whose cognitive problems were secondary to their educational failure.

Furthermore, an **Advisory Network** was set up, which supported the efforts of the teachers and educators in the youth villages and kibbutzim. This helped them to treat their pupils' problems and they were consequently in increasingly less need of being transferred from regular framework to special institutions.

These three settings (*Third Class*, *Therapeutic Classes* and *Therapeutic Groups*) were established with the clear objective of preventing the isolation of low functioning children in the special settings which existed at the time. Following the opening of alternative settings the population in the special institutions declined and eventually they were closed.

Even at an early stage, in 1958, the **Preparatory Programs** were established in Youth Aliyah, at the initiative of Reuven Feuerstein and under his leadership, and they were designed to train pupils for full integration into normal frameworks in the kibbutzim and youth villages. The establishment of **Preparatory Programs** within the framework of Youth Aliyah boosted the development of tools and methods leading to the Instrumental Enrichment program. The fact that as the Director of the Youth Aliyah Psychological Services, Reuven Feuerstein almost completely stopped placing the "abnormal" population in special institutions, led to their closure. This situation created the need for the development of new placement, teaching and educational methods to ensure the integration of low functioning youth in regular frameworks. The trend was to train them in the institutions mentioned above, and from there, following a preparatory period, to transfer them to normal institutions.[1]

8 The Consolidation of the IE Theory and Application

The year 1963 saw a breakthrough in the development of the Instrumental Enrichment program. That year Reuven Feuerstein was invited to present his theory of structural cognitive modifiability and mediated learning experience at the series of seminars at the New York Medical College.[2]

---

[1]Worthy of mention is Professor Reuven Cohen-Raz's experience on Kibbutz Palmachim which absorbed a group of boys from "Kiriyat Ya'arim" under the guidance of Israel Goralnik. This experience was described in Cohen-Raz's book *As All the Other Boys*.
[2]Under the direction of Professor Alfred Friedman and Martin Deutsch, who were joined by Professors A. Tannenbaum and H. Passow from the Columbia University, and Professors M. Hamburger from New York University and M. Shoval from Rutgers University.

This experience enabled Reuven Feuerstein to wrestle with various conceptual orientations and to clarify the significance of intervention based upon the theory of structural cognitive modifiability and mediated learning experience. This encounter highlighted the great urgency for the development of a program designed to assist low functioning youth to adjust to normal educational frameworks both in the US and in other countries. Worthy of note is the fact that at the seminar Reuven Feuerstein was given the opportunity to meet McVicker Hunt who was one of the main opponents of the concept of intelligence as a fixed entity. Hunt was among those who saw the necessity for the development of intervention programs aimed at changing the thinking structures of these students whose failure to adapt to the demands of technological culture prevented them from benefiting from the educational processes required for integration into the culture.

Shortly afterwards the N.I.C.H.D., via T. Jossem and M. Begab, decided to create a program that would permit the "translation" of Feuerstein's theory and the accumulated practical experiences into research language. The objective of this initiative was to expand the theory, operationalize it, and disseminate the product. The following psychologists and educators participated in the project: Abe Tannenbaum, Davis, Deitsch, Martin Hamburger, Harry Passow, Mendel Hoffman and J. McVicker Hunt, who contributed his experiences of working with emotionally and culturally deprived populations. At certain stages of the project it also received support from Lee Cronbach.

9 The Characteristics of the IE program

The program is composed of 14 sets of paper and pencil exercises called "instruments" containing about 300 pages. Every single instrument is built around a specific subject such as: organization of dots, orientation in space, comparisons, temporal relations, etc. Each page contains a set of assignments that "repeat" themselves while gradually changing. The distinctive feature of the assignments is that the content is not subject oriented but constitutes a means for providing formal, cognitive, conceptual and logical tools to the student. The IE program realizes the content-free approach which avoids anchoring the teaching of the cognitive processes in a specific content. As such, the IE program differs from other cognitive education programs that design the study contents according to principles of formal thinking and convey them to the pupil in the course of teaching specific contents. IE does not teach reading, mathematics, history or physics as a specific objective, but creates in the students the necessary infrastructure and the essential pre-conditions for the study of all content subjects.

The content–neutral approach used in the IE program is derived from the analysis of the three features of the learning situation: the content learned, the student, and the teacher.

Firstly, Reuven Feuerstein et al. (1980) argued that the study content has a special unique structure, which dictates the internal pace and organization of the contents learned, in accordance with its modal properties. When one introduces the content "from the outside" for the purpose of achieving additional targets such as the acquisition of cognitive processes, a conflict is created between the central target — the acquisition of the contents, and the additional target — the acquisition of thinking processes. In any event the structure of the syllabus does not always permit the program to be designed for the development of thinking. Furthermore, anchoring the thinking processes and the cognitive activities by making it conditional on a specific content is liable to cause difficulties in the ability to convey what is learned from the content studied to new contents. "Abstraction" of the thinking processes from the contents is necessary, permitting them to be linked in principle to more varied contents which are also greatly removed from the areas learned directly.

The second factor is the student. Frequently students are oriented exclusively toward the content material in which they expect to attain achievements and any discussion "above" the material is perceived by them as irrelevant to the area of knowledge which they wish to acquire. Any attempt at extracting the formal principles from the study content, observes Reuven Feuerstein, encounters the pupil's objections. This is particularly true in relation to the population for whom he constructed the IE program, i.e. low-functioning students.

The third factor is the teacher. Those who propose teaching thinking through content expect the teacher to know how to develop didactic principles necessary to achieve this objective. But the teacher usually has neither the time nor the tools required to do this. As he developed the IE program Reuven Feuerstein hoped that teachers themselves would design assignments and exercises on the basis of the samples given during the training course. However, years of experience proved this to be impossible. The teacher must be given the complete set of IE tools to be able to mediate students' thinking.

10 Initial Evaluation of the IE Program

As a result of fruitful research and development activity in the US described above, the Instrumental Enrichment program research was launched in four "Youth Aliyah" institutions in Israel: Two boarding schools "Kiryat Ya'arim" and "Ramat Hadassah", which were used as *Preparatory Programs* for very low functioning populations and two day youth centers in Ashdod and Ashkelon. The research examined the influence of the Instrumental Enrichment program as opposed to the influence of general enrichment programs. It also examined the influence of the type of the institution — i.e. boarding school as opposed to day youth center — on the students' progress (see Rand, Tannenbaum & Feuerstein, 1979). All four groups of students received 300 extra hours of enrichment in addition to their regular educational program over a period of two years. Two groups, one residential and the other at the day centers received 300 hours of Instrumental Enrichment, while two other groups, one residential and the other one at the day centers, received 300 hours of general enrichment including basic learning skills, reading, writing and arithmetic. All the groups included low functioning youth whose school performance showed a lag of 4–6 years. The participating students were 12–16-year-olds whose level of functioning had been defined as slight-borderline retardation (60–85), and their level of basic skills was similar to children in Grades 1–3. Children with better functioning were not accepted into these frameworks. The program was aimed mainly at basic skills, which would enable the pupils to be integrated into regular educational frameworks of the Youth Aliyah or community schools after a stay of two years in the *Preparatory Programs* framework.

The research hypothesis of Reuven Feuerstein and his colleagues was that the boarding school group that received the IE program would show the greatest change in various aspects of their performance. It was further hypothesized that the achievement of those boarding school students who received only general enrichment would be higher in comparison to the students attending the day centers even if the latter received the IE program. Finally, it was hypothesized that the day center students who received no IE would have the lowest achievements.

The findings showed that the IE program indeed had a strong influence in students' performance, while the nature of the educational framework, that is boarding school versus day center did not have a significant influence (see Rand, Tannenbaum & Feuerstein, 1979). Furthermore, students at the day center who received the IE program demonstrated better results than the boarding school students who received no IE. The IE program recipients performed better not only in cognitive but also in content subject tests. This result was particularly interesting, since these students, unlike the general enrichment group, received no special support in language, mathematics, and any other school skills.

The follow-up study was conducted three years later, when the students from the IE and general enrichment groups were recruited into the Army and took the Army psychometric tests (Rand et al., 1981). The results of the Army tests showed that the difference between the IE and general enrichment groups not only did not diminish as usually happens with specific intervention programs but also actually continued to increase. The interpretation given to this finding was that the changes created in the students following their participation in the IE program were of a structural character. The structural change is defined by Piaget, among others, as a change that continues to develop beyond its initial effect achieved by intervention. The IE program apparently supplied the students with tools for organization of the data at the input level, the methods of elaboration and processing, and the output strategies, which enable them to benefit from the variety of learning situations to which they were exposed. Although this is not our purpose here, it is important to note that the theory and the instruments have come far from their starting point. On one hand they have been used to treat severe cases of functional delay and on the other have been implemented in high-tech industry and sophisticated organizations.

11 Conclusion

Reuven Feuerstein's contribution to psychology and education is extensive and multifaceted. It includes wide-ranging clinical experience that influenced the development of the theory and the application methods derived from it — i.e. the LPAD and the IE program. The theory itself includes the concept of Structural Cognitive Modifiability (SCM) which postulates the human being's ability to change, the notion of Mediated Learning Experience (MLE) and the elaboration of mediation parameters, deficient cognitive functions, and the cognitive map. Some readers may perceive these components as unconnected independent entities and so in previous articles (1997, 1999) I have discussed the necessity of the conceptual–theoretical cohesion of these components. In this article, dedicated to my father and teacher Reuven Feuerstein, I have attempted to expound on the elements of the theory and their historical and philosophical links to each other. I have also endeavored to determine the developmental trend, characterized on the one hand by the on-going research and on the other by continuous practical application, which greatly influenced the programs themselves as well as their internal connection. In addition the article highlights the critical junctions in the development of the theory at which it was influenced by clinical experience and vice versa.

10

Theme and Some Variations on the Concepts of Mediated Learning Experience and Dynamic Assessment

Carol S. Lidz

I entered my doctoral studies knowing exactly what I would do for my dissertation. I had been a practicing school psychologist for a number of years, and had developed deep dissatisfaction with the tools of my trade, particularly those involving diagnostic assessment. My dissertation topic would be: "Alternative Approaches to Assessment for the School Psychologist." This would launch my quest for a better way to approach assessment of school children. There just had to be a better way.

When the time to write a dissertation finally approached, one of the faculty on my committee asked if I had ever heard of Reuven Feuerstein or of learning potential assessment. I had not. By way of introduction, the professor connected me with a participant in one of the workshops, who kindly agreed to share a copy of his workshop materials (I assume it is safe to admit this now). And so began my entry into the world of dynamic assessment. This was a revelation. I had never heard of anything like this approach. This was the path I was seeking. I was hooked. And, so I remain.

Lest this begin to sound like a testimony for a "Dynamic Assessment Anonymous" meeting, I shall use the remaining space of this chapter to review and discuss my applications of the central concepts of Feuerstein and his collaborators in my work; however, I shall maintain a somewhat informal tone, as this seems appropriate to the nature of this book, which bears witness to the broad and significant influence of Feuerstein's ideas and efforts.

1 The Mediated Learning Experience Rating Scale

While all of the theory and instrumentation discussed in the many workshops and training opportunities were exciting and of interest, it was the concept of Mediated Learning Experience (MLE) that most captured my attention. It seemed to me that it would be useful to operationalize MLE into a scale so that interactions could be described with some precision, interventions developed to address the specific components, and research designed to investigate the impact of this concept. As a school psychologist, I was also interested in the diagnostic potential of an MLE scale. To be useful for school psychologists, the scale would need to be portable, easy to administer and to learn. These were the motivations that spawned the Mediated Learning Experience Rating Scale.

1.1 The Scale

In designing what was to become the MLE Rating Scale, there were some assumptions and presumptions to be incorporated and addressed. On the one hand, I wished to reflect the original MLE components as closely as possible. On the other hand, I also wished to ground the content of the scale in the current research literature. Therefore, my first effort was to survey the research available, primarily on the topic of parent-child interactions that related to child development and cognitive functioning. Some of these findings were published in Feuerstein, Klein and Tannenbaum (1991). There was substantial research support for most of the components. What also emerged from this search was the importance of interactions that were not explicitly represented as components of MLE, namely, "responsivity" and "affective involvement." The evidence regarding the relationship of these two parameters with children's cognitive and social development far outweighed the evidence for any other dimension of interaction. Therefore, I added these components to the conceptualization of MLE as operationalized in the Scale.

I also wished to design the Scale as a measure of the mediational repertoire of the adult. We found from early research that reciprocity functioned independently of adult mediational behaviors, that is, did not correlate highly with the other components. If the reciprocity score had been added into the total MLE score, this could have resulted in considerable distortion of the findings. Conceptually, it seemed to me possible that an adult could be engaging in a number of potentially effective mediational behaviors that are not "received" by a child whose reciprocity is damaged or dysfunctional. While it could be claimed that MLE was not happening under these conditions, it seemed useful for both diagnosis and research to have separate (though, certainly not totally independent) measures for the mediator and mediatee. I also found it difficult to know when in fact a child was reciprocal, and did not want to confound the parents' intent with the child's particular way of showing or not showing reciprocity. I had seen too many active, inattentive children who, while bouncing off the wall or hiding under the table, nevertheless, were absorbing what was said and happening. Thus, another deviation from the original conceptualization of MLE was that this would be a measure of the mediator. (I have developed a beginning conceptualization of a scale for the child's reciprocity that has been tried out in the research of Diny van der Aalsvoort in The Netherlands. Also, the child's reciprocity is included in the new dynamic assessment procedure developed with Ruthanne Jepsen; see below.)

I have also deviated from the Klein scale, an alternative approach to assessment of MLE, and from published statements by Feuerstein in the consistent use of 11 to12 components rather than remaining restricted to the recommended 3 to 5. Each component seems to make an important and unique contribution to adult–child interactions, and the more comprehensive view allows more sensitive patterning of a variety of mediators in a variety of situations, for example, in differentiating the mediational patterns of mothers and fathers (Zambrana-Ortiz & Lidz, 1995). I do not as yet have a research basis for selecting some as being more important than others, and do not feel that any component at this point in our knowledge can be dismissed or weakened in relation to the others. In my view, one of the powerful contributions of the conceptualization of MLE is its comprehensiveness, and the inclusion of components of interaction that have not previously received adequate attention.

Designing a scale also required work to reduce inference so that the components would be as clearly defined and independent from each other as possible. I also had concerns about differentiating means from ends in the original conceptualization of MLE. It seemed to me that some of the original components represented the means toward MLE, while others represented the desired outcomes. I reconceptualized the outcomes in terms of facilitation of self-regulation, representational thinking, active learning, and strategic problem solving. These became the criteria of the components; that is, a component deserved to be included as an aspect of MLE if it was in the service of one or more of these criteria.

The idea of using a rating scale rather than frequency ratings again reflected my desire to use the scale as a practitioner and the need to connect assessment with intervention. I wanted to be able to show growth on the part of the mediator in response to intervention. Thus, the definition of MLE relies on the summation of the highest ratings on the scale, but there is an assumption of a continuum, where caregivers may have some beginning elements of MLE already in their repertoires and could be shown that they are "on the road" even if not fully there. It also seemed that a rating scale could provide measurement sensitivity because it would produce a fair amount of variance. I also have no idea what "more" of any component means. Are two occurrences better than three? I therefore sought to capture the qualitative rather than the quantitative aspects of the interaction, though, clearly, some of the ratings do involve quantity and consistency of occurrence. It may well be that quantity counts; that is an issue for further research, and frequency information can easily be added to the qualitative ratings.

The Scale itself is included and elaborated in the Lidz (1991) book, but I shall review the definitions of the components here, as included in the Scale. My intent is to promote some general consensus of the definitions:

1. *Intent*: the extent to which the mediator engages the child and maintains the child's involvement in the interaction. The mediator would have to make it clear to the child that the child's involvement is desired. The primary process addressed is attention, that is, elicitation and maintenance of the child's attention. To obtain the highest rating, communication of intent must induce self-regulation in the child.
2. *Meaning*: the attribution of value and importance to the content of the interaction. The primary process addressed is perception and the referents

must be perceivable to both child and mediator; the mediator highlights, activates, enhances, elaborates the perceptual properties of the tangible content of the interaction.

3. *Transcendence*: the connection of the current situation with past or present experiences of the child. The referents are not perceivable in the current situation, but require mental imagery by the child. At the highest level, this would involve encouragement of if-then or cause-effect thinking that helps the child go beyond the perceptual properties of the content.

4. *Task Regulation*: manipulation of the task or content to promote the child's ability to succeed and develop competence. This could include verbal directions or non-verbal manipulations that make the task accessible to the child. At the highest level, mediation of task regulation would promote the child's ability to develop strategies and think planfully about the content. Task regulation would also include communication of a basic or underlying principle that facilitates task solution.

5. *Praise/Encouragement*: includes positive remarks that provide feedback to the child about what went well or what needed more thought or practice. Exclamations of praise alone do not obtain the highest, mediational, rating.

6. *Challenge* refers to the creation of Vygotsky's notion of "zone of proximal development" with the child. Mediation of challenge requires selecting and presenting content in a way that is ahead of the child's current level of functioning, yet within the child's reach of competence in collaboration with a more experienced guide.

7. *Change* involves communications that document the child as learner to the learner, that demonstrate that the child is performing at a more advanced level in relation to the interaction that has occurred.

8. *Joint regard* reflects demonstrations of the ability of the mediator to see the situation or experience from the child's point of view. This can be expressed in empathic statements that verbalize what the child is not fully able to express. Joint regard also refers to evidence that the experience is a shared learning experience, through references using "we" or "us."

9. *Shared experience* occurs when the mediator communicates a personal experience or thought to the child that relates to the content of the interaction. This experience or thought would refer to the mediator and not to experiences previously shared with the child (those are covered under transcendance). These experiences are used to elaborate and enhance the content of the interaction and give the child access to information the child would not otherwise derive from direct experience.

10. *Psychological differentiation*, as the "intrusion factor," refers to the ability of the mediator to maintain the role of facilitator of the child's learning, without injecting the mediator's needs into the interaction. The mediator would not co-opt or take over the learning experience from the child.

11. *Contingent responsivity* is the ability of the mediator to respond in a timely and appropriate way to the child's initiations and responses; this requires accurate reading of the cues of the child.

12. *Affective involvement* is the "warmth factor." This component reflects the
mediator's communications of affection and positive regard to the child. This
can be done verbally or non-verbally, within whatever style the mediator
employs, but the mediator's enjoyment of being with the child should be
evident.

The application of the Scale involves setting up a direct observation situation
between a mediator and a child or within a classroom, in relation to an instructional
activity. In the case of parent (caregiver)–child interaction assessment, the parent
is asked to engage in two to three activities with the child. The first activity would
be free play, where a standard, age-appropriate set of toys is made available, and
the parents are requested to "play with your child with these toys". Then the toys
are removed and replaced with a set of plastic leggos, and the parent is asked to
"teach your child to build a house with these". Finally, the parent may be asked to
read a short book with the child.

When making the ratings, the assessor attempts to be unobtrusive, and scores
each interaction set on the Scale; that is, the full Scale is applied to each situation
(free play, structured teaching and reading). For research, the interactions are
videotaped, and independent scorers are trained to score the segments. When
applied in the classroom with teachers, the assessor views one entire lesson as it
naturally occurs, and rates the entire activity on each of the components. Both
parents and teachers are debriefed following the observation to ascertain how
typical this interaction was and in what, if any, it deviated from the usual.

There are now a number of studies using the MLE Scale that have documented
its positive psychometric properties and usefulness for inclusion in studies requiring operationalization of adult–child interaction. The earliest studies, by Glasier-
Robinson (1986, 1990) and Lidz, Bond and Dissinger (1991) were included and
summarized in the text that offers a manual for the Scale (Lidz, 1991). Since that
time, additional studies, mostly dissertations, have added evidence regarding both
reliability and validity (Alvarez-Ortiz, 1996; Green, 1996; Weinblatt, 1993; van der
Aalsvoort, 1997; Zambrana-Ortiz & Lidz, 1995). The Scale has been translated into
Dutch (including Flemish) and Spanish (Puerto Rican), and has been modified into
versions with specific applications for parents, teachers, and literacy-development
(from author).The availability of this Scale allows me, when functioning as a school
psychologist assessor, to expand my repertoire to include parent–child and teacher–
child interaction evaluation as a regular aspect of most assessments. Moving from
focusing just on the child to the referred child's contexts has received increasing
support in the literature, but few diagnosticians are adequately prepared to do this.
It is one thing to say that the context of behavior must be considered, and quite
another to know how this can be done. The MLE Rating Scale provides a very
concrete, specific guideline to help diagnosticians describe the interactional components of the home and school environments, and, more importantly, helps the
assessor link these observations to recommendations for intervention.

It is possible that different scales are needed for different purposes and that
there is no need for just one procedure. The fact that there are somewhat differing

operationalizations (therefore, definitions) of MLE from researcher to researcher, however, does present some difficulty, at least to interpretation of the data and to attempts to explain the MLE concept to others. Resolution of these definitional differences remains a challenge.

2 Dynamic Assessment

I was first attracted to Feuerstein's work mainly because of his ideas of dynamic assessment. However, it soon became clear to me that I could not apply the specific procedures of learning potential assessment in my work. Though beginning as a generalist and continuing to see children of all ages, I had become a pre-school specialist. Three-year-olds just cannot draw complex figures, find squares in dots, or solve the stencil designs. The discrepancy between existing procedures and the needs of my population was, in my view, good, because it forced me to think about what I really wanted to do and how I could do it. My first attempt to design a dynamic assessment for young children involved a modification of one of the subscales of the Kaufman Assessment Battery for Children. This appears in my 1987 book, in a chapter with Thomas (Lidz & Thomas, 1987).

I had become increasingly convinced that assessment, at least for those of us who were practicing school psychologists, needed to get close to the curriculum of the child who is experiencing learning difficulty. I agreed with Feuerstein that dynamic assessment was not tied to any particular procedure, but, along with Instrumental Enrichment, was a way of delivering MLE to children as a means of facilitating cognitive functioning. It therefore seemed to me that dynamic assessment could be conceptualized generically, and not in relation to any specific procedure or instrument. With this in mind, I developed the ideas related to "curriculum-based dynamic assessment", that are described in my 1991 book. It was the idea of a generic approach that characterized most of my workshops and course teaching during the early and mid 90s.

I also had the good fortune to become involved as a consultant to Greenberg's COGNET project at the University of Tennessee. The focus of this consultation was the development of a group dynamic assessment procedure that could then be used as an assessment tool within this project (though not necessarily limited to this use). Again, an adaptation of an existing measure was used, this time, the Das-Naglieri Cognitive Assessment Scale. After much piloting, three research projects demonstrating the utility of this procedure were completed (Lidz & Greenberg, 1997; Lidz, Jepsen & Miller, 1997; Jepsen & Lidz, accepted).

Becoming increasingly frustrated with the paucity of evidence of use of dynamic assessment by practitioners (Lidz, 1992), and wishing to develop a more structured approach to assessment of pre-school children, and one closely related to pre-school curriculum demands, I developed the most recent procedure in collaboration with Ruthanne Jepsen: *The Application of Cognitive Functions Scale (ACFS)*. This Scale represents a compromise, in that the interventions are more scripted and prescribed than I would ordinarily advocate for a dynamic assessment. However, it seemed to me that, on the one hand, beginning users needed the support of such scripts, and, on the other hand, such specificity (allowing scoring) was necessary for research studies. It is always possible for diagnosticians to deviate from any script, and this would be encouraged when there is no concern for generation of quantitative data.

2.1 The Scale

The Application of Cognitive Functions Scale attempts to be referenced in relation to the typical demands of a pre-school curriculum, but to the processing rather than content demands of the curriculum. The question was posed of what children really need to be able to do that is generalizable across content and that would provide a foundation that characterized a variety of specific curricula. The intent was to provide information that, on the one hand, described important learning charac-teristics of the child, while, on the other hand, offered information to the teacher that related to instruction.

The ACFS has six subscales:

1. Classification: sorting blocks into categories based on an abstract characteristic (color, size or shape), and the flexibility to change the basis for the sort.
2. Perspective Taking: the child-as-teacher communicates to the assessor-as-learner in a way that conveys awareness of "other" during the course of a drawing task.
3. Auditory memory: retelling details of a story read to the child, and maintaining the sequence of the story's events.
4. Visual memory: recalling a number of toys presented to the child and demonstrating the application of memory strategies.
5. Planning: communicating the steps and sequential order of a familiar complex activity.
6. Sequential Pattern Completion: noting and completing increasingly complex patterns involving shapes, and creating an original pattern.

Each of these activities is offered with a pre-test–intervention–post-test format, with a prescribed intervention that addresses the processing demands of the task. The child's behavior during the intervention phase of each activity is rated on seven dimensions: self-regulation, persistence, frustration tolerance, flexibility, motiva-tion, receptivity, and interactivity. Thus, while MLE is built into the assessment tool itself and is expected to characterize the behavior of the assessor during the course of intervention, there is now a rating and operationalization of the child's reciprocity that allows research into the relative contribution of this dimension of the interaction to outcomes such as the child's competence in school.

Research that has incorporated my earlier approaches to dynamic assessment of individual children has included two unpublished dissertations (Reinhart, 1989; Thomas, 1986) and one published project (Jitendra & Rohena-Diaz, 1996). Research on the ACFS is in process; however, preliminary research with a cohort of 29 normally developed pre-school and kindergarten children has documented the appropriateness of the tasks for this age group as well as the responsiveness to intervention of most of the subscale tasks.

3 The "Let's Think About It" Parent Program

Ever the school psychologist who is trying to connect assessment with intervention, my next concern became the transfer of the ideas of MLE to those most significant to children's development: the caregivers. Although we knew that parents could be taught the components of MLE from Glasier-Robinson's data (1990), it seemed to me that the more important question was: what is it that we think the children need to learn, or, what would be the best outcomes for the children who experience optimal MLE? The specifics of MLE could then be embedded into a program and used as the means to an end, but we needed to be clear about this end and "go for it," rather than just hope that it happens. This gave birth to the parent program, "Let's Think About It", designed in collaboration with Lisa Chase Childers, a talented pre-school teacher from St. Luke's School in New York City.

3.1 The Program

The "Let's Think About It" parent program includes six units and involves homework and discussion meetings with parents. The units reflect a combination of the types of processes addressed in the dynamic assessment and mediated learning experience measures. These include the following:

1. "Noticing Our World": focuses on the perceptual properties of the environment, helping children not only to look, but to see; not only to listen, but to hear.
2. "Looking Back": helps children make connections between their current and previous experiences, and offers an explicit opportunity for cultural transmission. This unit also addresses cause–effect relationships.
3. "Let's Make A Plan": helps children connect the present with the future and focuses on generating goals and strategic plans to reach those goals. This unit is an opportunity to develop "if … then" hypotheses.
4. "That's Fantastic!": focuses on fantasy and imagination; in this unit the children are encouraged to free themselves from their perceptual world and develop their "what if …" thinking.
5. "What's The Big Idea": is an opportunity for focusing on rules, main ideas, and general principles.
6. "The Nimble Symbol": is the most explicit focus on literacy and numeracy. The activities help develop the child's ability to become a symbol user and maker.

Initial research with highly educated parents demonstrated high levels of parent satisfaction with the Program, as well as highly significant improvement on a self-rating scale reflecting components of MLE. Aspects of the program have been abstracted and translated for use with parents of Head Start children in Puerto Rico by Zambrana-Ortiz (personal communication), with reportedly positive response. We are currently seeking opportunities to use this Program with a variety of caregivers, including parents of children with disabilities, as well parents with low socioeconomic status. A project with parents of deaf children is currently underway at the Lexington School for the Deaf in Jackson Heights, New York.

4 Conclusion

Clearly, many of us have been stimulated and energized by the ideas of Feuerstein and his colleagues. The concepts of MLE and dynamic assessment have been true catalysts for a large number of studies and approaches. My last search of Psychlit generated 150 entries on the topic of dynamic assessment, and I know there are even more out there in journals not covered by this source. The numbers of people in this quest and the domains within which they work are ever increasing. Indeed, one of the values I have experienced is that the central concepts permit and encourage discussions across domains and across disciplines. MLE is meaningful and relevant to all members of an interdisciplinary team, and dynamic assessment can be designed for applications by psychologists, speech pathologists, educators, and others. It has been an exciting and interesting journey, and one I hope that will continue for us as individuals and as a group who share the desire to improve the lives of children and our ability to contribute to this improvement.

The inspiration to engage in this continuing and growing work is the true legacy of Feuerstein.

11

Learning Test Concepts and Dynamic Assessment

Jürgen Guthke and Jens F. Beckmann

On an international scale, the dynamic testing approach is being discussed as an alternative or complement to the conventional static intelligence test. While many theoreticians and practitioners approve of the fundamental aims of dynamic testing, there is restrained (Snow, 1990) or even harsh criticism that bears chiefly on methodological aspects. Most of the criticism relates to lack of standardisation of tests and to inadequate validation. We have examined these critical voices. Feuerstein's arguments against the customary psychometric procedures are well known. In our so-called Diagnostic Programs we try to combine his demand for more individualisation of the testing with the requirements of psychometry and standardisation. The authors review more recent evidence on the validity of learning tests compared with conventional intelligence tests. In doing so, they emphasise a more experimental validation on the basis of learning experiments. They also discuss the material to be used in learning tests (e.g. curriculum-related vs. curriculum-unrelated material), the arrangement of the training phase and problems of analysis. In addition, they point out that the principle of dynamic testing is not confined to intelligence assessment.

1 Learning Test Concepts and Dynamic Assessment[1]

1.1 Criticism of the Conventional Intelligence Test and the Emergence of the Learning Test Approach. Preliminary Remarks Highlighting Auto-biographic and Historical Aspects

The senior author (J. Guthke) requests the reader's permission to start with a somewhat personal introduction. After completing my psychology course in 1961, I set up a psychological guidance centre for children and parents in a rural district in the former German Democratic Republic (GDR). In my practice I used a variety of tests, including traditional intelligence tests. It should be noted that as a consequence of the 1936 Soviet "pedology decision" that banned psychological

[1] A modified version of this article was published in Educational and Child Psychology (1997, 14, 17–32) and is dedicated to Professor R. Feuerstein on the occasion of his 75th birthday as a token of deep respect. Many thanks to Jerry Carlson (Seattle, U.S.A.) and Julian Elliot (Sunderland, UK) for their helpful suggestions to improve the translation.

testing, such tests were officially prohibited in East German schools at the time. We practitioners knew that we would incur political criticism and massive objections of school inspectors if they learned that we were using illegal "bourgeois or Western tests". We were also aware, however, of the massive objections raised against intelligence tests not only by Soviet-influenced academic psychology (especially during the 1960s) but also by "progressive representatives" — as they used to be called here — of Western psychology. What I and many other practitioners particularly liked about these tests and what caused us to adhere to them, despite the "theoretician's" criticism, was the fact that the tests were standardised, that they specified norms and hence a yard-stick that reduced at least somewhat the diagnostician's subjectiveness and arbitrariness, while increasing the comparability, replicability and communicability of assessment results. This was especially important to those who were new to the profession who did not have the opportunity to develop, on the basis of decades of experience, some kind of "implicit statistics" about the normal and deviant behaviour of subjects in a test situation. We needed the yard-sticks provided by "explicit statistics", that is, standardised tests and norms. But, when administering tests I soon grew uneasy about the impossibility of responding flexibly to a child's level of competence and needs, because I was not allowed to give a child who had come close to solving an item even the slightest clue, and because I never learned how children might improve their test performance after an extended, built-in intervention phase. Occasionally I gave children who came up with not entirely wrong solutions a slight hint although it was against the test directions, and gave me a guilty conscience. Later I came across Vygotsky's work (cf. Vygotsky, 1964), and was especially impressed with his notions of assessment and of the "zone of proximal development". All at once I had found a theoretical justification for my "deviant behaviour" as a test administrator, one that came from a Soviet psychologist who happened to be rediscovered. However, I could not entirely soothe my conscience because I found my approach to be too subjective, not adequately susceptible to making comparisons and inadequately founded theoretically and methodologically. So when I returned to the university in 1966 the idea that haunted me in my research work was the possibility of combining the psychometric paradigm with Vygotsky's views on assessment (see my first monograph on the subject, Guthke, 1972) — a topic that increasingly attracts the attention of researchers world-wide and which is currently the focus of substantial debate and controversy. It is also an issue we will discuss below.

A point of major importance is that nowhere in my reading of Vygotsky did I find evidence that he considered the psychometric paradigm inconsistent with his views of assessment, instead, in his oft-quoted example (Vygotsky, 1987) relating to the definition of the "zone of proximal development", he explicitly used terms employed by Binet, in particular the term intelligence age (mental age or in German: "Intelligenzalter"). For Vygotsky, the difference between the intelligence age attained in the Binet test by using the customary test procedure (the "zone of present development") and the intelligence age a subject can attain when given prompts, represents the operational definition of the "zone of proximal development". Paradoxically enough, a recent, most instructive publication by the

Jerusalem Feuerstein Institute (Kozulin & Falik, 1995) advanced the thesis that Feuerstein's Learning Potential Assessment Device (LPAD, cf. Feuerstein, Rand & Hoffman, 1979), originally developed as a non-psychometric, more qualitative and individual-oriented ("clinical") procedure, paid more heed to Vygotsky's positions (even though Feuerstein traces his academic lineage back to Piaget and his pupil Rey but hardly to Vygotsky) than to various learning test approaches, such as those of Campione and Brown (1987), Budoff, Meskin and Harrison (1971), Hamers, Sijtsma and Ruijssenaars (1993) or our learning test approach, which all invariably refer to Vygotsky. For a review of all of these approaches, see Guthke and Wiedl (1996), and Haywood and Tzuriel (1992). Theoretically, the learning test concept or the dynamic testing approach can of course be traced back not only to Vygotsky but also to many other cognitive and developmental psychologists of the '20s and '30s and to the pioneering work of Wilhelm Wundts pupil Ernst Meumann (cf. Meumann, 1922). Even psychometricians (e.g. Kern, 1930, a diagnostician who carried out vocational aptitude tests, for a historical review see also Wiedl, Guthke & Wingenfeld, 1995) called for "dynamic tests" (cf. de Weerdt, 1927) long ago. But only in the '60s did researchers systematically set about providing a theoretical rationale for "dynamic assessment", mainly in Israel (work by the Feuerstein group), in the United States (cf. Budoff, 1967), the Soviet Union (e.g. Ivanova, 1973), in Hungary (Klein, 1970), in Great Britain (Hegarty & Lucas, 1979) and in East Germany (Guthke, 1972). Since then substantial development in the theory and practice of dynamic assessment have occurred world-wide (cf. Hamers et al., 1993; Haywood & Tzuriel, 1992; Guthke & Wiedl, 1996; Lidz, 1991).

1.2 Criticism of the "Dynamic Testing" Approach and a Definition of "Dynamic Testing"

Even though substantial advances have been made, practitioners still tend to be reticent in their use of dynamic assessment procedures. In particular, they deplore the fact that the new procedures are so time-consuming, the lack of standardisation of some of them, and the lack of conclusive evidence that learning tests lead to more sound decisions and better suggestions for appropriate therapeutical interventions. For example American researchers (Snow, 1990; Glutting & McDermott, 1990; see also the new overview by Grigorenko & Sternberg, 1998) believe that although the new procedures represent an innovative departure in assessment, several issues need to be addressed. These are summarized in Box 1.

We, as well as other teams of researchers, try to meet the criticisms that dynamic procedures deviate from standardised approaches by combining the psychometric procedure with the new approach whenever this seems appropriate (see below). We would gladly assent to the second criticism if we could think of a better term to describe the new assessment approach aptly and, at the same time, cover all its variants. In a monograph on "Dynamic Testing" (Guthke & Wiedl, 1996) that has just been published, Wiedl and the senior author attempt to provide proof that the "dynamic testing approach" is not to be restricted to intelligence assessment

BOX 1

Criticism of the "dynamic assessment" approach (cf. Glutting & McDermott, 1990; Schlee, 1985; Snow, 1990; Büchel & Scharnhorst, 1993)

1. The term "assessment" is generally applied in science to standardised and quantifiable surveys (measurements). The critics point out that some "dynamic assessment" procedures do not heed the APA standards that require that "directions to a test taker that are intended to produce a particular behaviour sample (often called a "prompt') should be standardised, just as the directions are standardised for any other test" (American Psychological Association [APA], 1985, 3.23, p. 30). In the absence of such standardisation there is a danger that when testing the same child different psychologists will obtain different results because there is too much variation in the prompts presented.

2. The term "dynamic" is at least misleading because in the test administration or analysis (course analysis) even a "static test" (e.g. a so-called motion picture test) can be "dynamic". As Snow (1990, p. 1135) put it, "There is a bright future for the concept of learning assessment, but no future for terms like dynamic and static in it".

3. Proof of the higher validity and relevance to therapy of Dynamic Assessment, compared with conventional measures of intellectual status, is still inadequate. Mostly, the differences between pre-test and post-test correlations with external criteria (like success in school) are negligible. It is not certain whether from the way subjects tackle curriculum-unrelated intelligence test items one can really derive recommendations for use by the teacher. A German educationalist (Schlee, 1985) questions generally whether it is possible to derive from psychological tests — even if they are committed to the "dynamic testing" approach or treatment-oriented assessment (Förderdiagnostik) — recommendations for interventions suited to the school setting, stressing that this is a task to be accomplished not by psychological testing but by didactics.

and to the learning aspect and that it represents a far-reaching experimental assessment strategy that can be applied successfully to almost all assessment issues in the fields of educational, clinical and work psychology — in relation to both performance and personality characteristics. (Incidentally, as Bourmenskaya (1990) observed, Vygotsky had already pointed out that the concept of "Aneignung" (acquisition of culture) and the "zone of proximal development" should not be confined to cognitive characteristics but should relate to the development of the whole personality.) Intelligence learning tests thus represent just one variant of assessing the "zone of proximal development" that Vygotsky had contemplated evolving and that came to be used most widely internationally. Therefore, in spite of some hesitations, we decided to go on using the word "dynamic testing" as a generic term that covers the variety of new assessment techniques designed to

BOX 2

An attempt to define "dynamic testing"

"Dynamic testing" is a collective term that subsumes various assessment procedures, such as Testing the Limits, Learning Potential Assessment, Interactive Dynamic Assessment, Learning Test Concept, "pure" repetition of tests and repetition of tests involving systematic variation of conditions ("experimental psychodiagnosis", stress assessment), which, by systematically eliciting and determining intraindividual variability during the course of a test, are designed to identify more validly the current status of a mental trait and/or its modifiability.

systematically elicit intraindividual variance during the course of testing (see Box 2). Especially with regard to clinical application it also includes procedures that cannot be justified on the basis of Vygotsky's conception, for example procedures that deliberately make test items more difficult, instead of easier, by using interfering or complicating material to ensure early detection of persons at risk and to improve differential diagnosis (cf. Wallasch & Möbus, 1977), and by using time pressures in order to assess intellectual performance under stress (Krypsin-Exner, 1987). As was suggested above, when providing a theoretical rationale for "dynamic assessment" one can point not only to Vygotsky but also to Zubin (1950) and to contemporary trait theoreticians (Epstein & O'Brian, 1985; Schmitt, 1990; Steyer & Schmitt, 1992), who think the determination of the "range" (Zubin, 1950) of any trait by using multiple measurements is inevitable, and who therefore frown upon the conventional one-time administration of test procedures in assessment work.

Due to space restriction the next Box (see Box 3) can only provide a rough summary of the great variety of methods, issues and areas in which the "dynamic testing" approach is currently applied (for a more detailed description, see the various chapters on application in Guthke & Wiedl, 1996). "Dynamic procedures" have been tried out not only in intelligence, concentration and memory tests, but also in experimental games and questionnaires and even in interviews.

Each item of the survey could be discussed at length, something that is impossible here. The following survey of basic options in "dynamic testing" is not complete either, nor can it be explained here in detail. Nonetheless, we hope it will stimulate the discussion in some small measure.

1.3 Basic Options in "Dynamic Assessment"

One basic issue upon which we have already touched is whether the so-called learning phase should be more qualitative, child centred and clinical, as is the case with the LPAD (cf. Kozulin & Falik, 1995), or more quantitative, standardised and

BOX 3

Issues in and areas of application of "dynamic testing"

1. Assessing the intelligence of children and adolescents, especially disadvantaged individuals, ethnic minorities, children who require special support
2. Assessing "reserve capacities" (plasticity) of "healthy intelligence in old age" on the basis of learning test-like procedures
3. Curriculum-related learning tests within the framework of treatment-oriented assessment, to ensure educational career decisions and to improve interventions
4. In neuropsychology, assessing the "rehabilitation potential" of patients with organic brain disease and of schizophrenics
5. In clinical learning tests, to carry out differential diagnoses in adults (e.g. to differentiate between organic and neurotic performance deficits)
6. Trainability tests and Learning Assessment Centres for assessing vocational aptitudes
7. "Experimental psychodiagnosis" through systematic variation of instruction, task or general test conditions in aptitude and achievement
8. Repetitions of measurement and variation of the application of questionnaires, e.g. standard instruction vs. maximal
9. "Social learning tests", e.g. for examining children with behaviour problems and whether therapy is indicated
10. "Progressive Learning Interview" for the "dynamic measurement of attitudes", e.g. attitude toward environmentally responsible behaviour

psychometric (as in the learning tests developed by our research group). We hope that R. Feuerstein, whom we highly esteem, will note — at least with sceptical interest — how in our Diagnostic Programs (Guthke & Wiedl, 1996; Guthke & Wingenfeld, 1992) we attempted to combine his all-important demand that the testing should be individualised with the requirement of standardisation. To that end, the learning test concept is combined with the principle of adaptive testing. For this kind of learning test we used the term "Diagnostic Program". Each subject is given prompts or additional items tailored to his errors but he is always led back to so-called target items that all subjects must tackle. The recently published "Adaptive Computer Assisted Intelligence Learning Test Battery" (ACIL; Guthke et al., 1995; see also Beckman & Gathke, 1999) was constructed with this principle in mind. This test procedure is designed to identify, among pupils between 12 and 16 years of age, the "core factor of intelligence", i.e. the reasoning factor, in three domains (in the verbal domain — analogies, in the numerical domain — series of numbers, in the figural domain — series of figures). We will succinctly explain the procedure, using the Adaptive Figure Series Test, a subtest of the battery, as an example (see also Figure 1).

The abscissa plots the individual areas (areas of complexity) of the test and their degrees of difficulty which were obtained not by means of the test statistics but by the structural information theory (cf. Buffart & Leeuwenberg, 1983), a theory originally developed in psychophysics that allows for determination of the "objective difficulty" or complexity of the individual item. At each level of difficulty sets of two items are presented, e.g. 1 and 2; 3 and 4. At the beginning and the end of the individual areas of the test are so-called target items, for example, 1, 2; 7, 8; 13, 14; 19, 20. If a child solves a given set of target items correctly, s/he will proceed to the next set of target items, e.g. from 7, 8 straight to 13, 14. If, however, the child makes any errors — for example, if s/he fails to solve item 7 and item 8 (or if s/he solves only item 7 or only item 8), s/he has to return to the easier item 3. If the child fails again on that item, prompts depending on the kind of error made will be given, and s/he will be given an equally difficult item (item 4). However, if item 3 was solved without help, the next item will be presented on a higher level of difficulty (item 6). The child must now confront the target items 7 and 8 once more. If s/he fails again, s/he will receive additional prompts. This test strategy guarantees highly individualised testing and training as demanded especially by Feuerstein et al. (1979). The consistent presentation of target items also ensures that all subjects tackle these items. There is a wide variety of ways to move through the program. It is important to note that there were children with the same initial performance who differed in their final levels. On the other hand, there were children whose final levels were the same, but who had started off differently. This is evidence of different learning paths in spite of the same initial or final levels.

Even this procedure does not enable a concrete curriculum-specific description of the subjects cognitive "potentials" and "deficits", nor can "psychoeducational recommendations" (Kozulin & Falik, 1995) — something the LPAD is said to provide — be derived from it. We must take into consideration that in his LPAD Feuerstein primarily uses conventional curriculum-unspecific intelligence test items, as we do in our learning tests (for similar reasons). In light of the current theory of "situated cognition" (Cole, 1991; Resnick, 1991; Greeno, 1992), which can be traced back to Vygotsky, it is very doubtful whether evidence on cognitive deficits and potentials obtained when using abstract intelligence test items will permit generalisations about how subjects cope with curriculum-related tasks. As early as 1985 Schlee had expressed doubt — with reference to the treatment-oriented assessment technique (cf. Kornmann, Meister & Schlee, 1983) developed in Germany and based chiefly on learning test-like procedures that use curriculum-related items — that it can lead to suggestions on how to assist children because, he argued, teaching can be improved not on the basis of assessment but only with an idea of the didactic goals in mind. Of course, that point can be criticised too, but no doubt the criticism Schlee expressed in 1985 must still be taken seriously as it has not yet been possible to prove that teachers were more successful in teaching children who had been studied using treatment-oriented assessment than children studied using conventional assessment procedures.

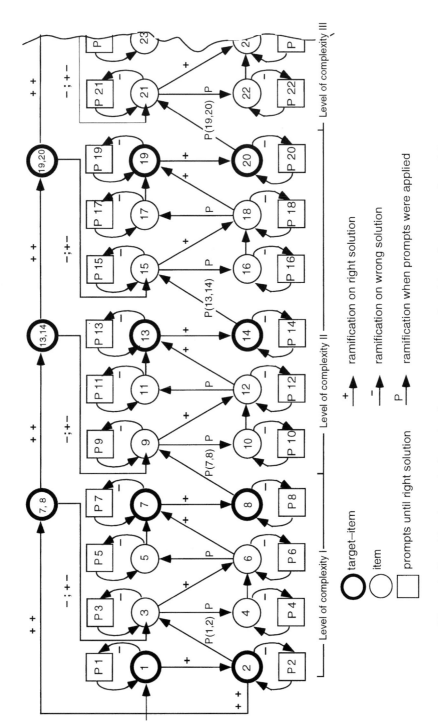

Figure 1. Ramification rule for adaptive computer-assisted learning test series of figures

BOX 4

Options one has when using "Dynamic Testing" in achievement situations

1. Standardisation/psychometrisation (Budoff et al., 1971; Campione & Brown, 1987; Carlson & Wiedl, 1980; Guthke, 1972) vs. individualisation/clinical, qualitative approach (Feuerstein, "treatment-oriented assessment", e.g. Kornmann et al., 1983; Probst, 1979)
2. "Abstract", curriculum-unspecific vs. curriculum-specific items
3. Variants of the "learning phase". Emphasis on different aspects
   3.1. "Imitation" (Vygotsky), feedback, prompts (with short-term learning tests) vs. demonstration of the item-solving strategy between pre-test and post-test (with long-term learning tests)
   3.2. Training of cognitive operations or paying more heed to the "orienting basis" (van der Heijden, 1993)
   3.3. Learning is more heavily guided or more heavily self directed (Wiedemann, 1993)
4. Problems of test administration and analysis
   4.1. One test session only or use of a pre-post-test design on the basis of one or several post-tests (Campione & Brown, 1987; Hamers et al., 1993)
   4.2. Determining the number and kind(s) of prompts, additional items and feedback information, or determination of the learning gain in a post-test compared with the pre-test
   4.3. Use of difference scores (pre-test–post-test, absolute or relativised scores) or post-test scores, use of goal attainment or learning success criteria
   4.4. Determining learning gains only quantitatively or determination of qualitative "types of change"
   4.5. Assessing only learning gains or "learning processes"

In the Netherlands interesting efforts have been made recently to develop highly curriculum-specific learning tests for use with lower-grade pupils (cf. Guthke & Wiedl, 1996, chap. 3.1, 3.2), especially with reference to reading and the potential for learning mathematics. In Box 4 some options of using dynamic assessment in achievement situations have been outlined.

The question of how the so-called learning phase in dynamic test procedures should be arranged falls within the provinces of instructional psychology (Lompscher, 1972; Ewert, 1992) and didactics. Vygotsky contended that if a child is capable of imitating a solution shown him by adults, that solution will already be in his "zone of proximal development". For a variety of reasons, we, as well as other researchers, set less store by imitation but concentrated on the extent to which a child can derive benefit from variously designed prompts and feedback information, or from built-in strategy training when solving tasks presented on a post-test. Mostly the invitation to a child to "imitate" something is only the last massive prompt in a well-dosed system of prompts. The question of how feedback information, prompts and training programs should best be arranged cannot be answered in a general way but only with regard to the specific items and target groups. In connection with so-called adaptive instructional systems, Leutner (1992) showed how differently feedback information can be arranged and how feedback effects can vary with target groups. The voluminous but ultimately barren research on aptitude-treatment interaction at least showed that it is exceedingly difficult to assign particular intervention techniques to particular target groups.

Of course, test designers cannot be expected to solve the problems instructional psychology and didactics have so far failed to solve, and to devise ideally suited intervention strategies for all testees within the framework of dynamic testing. However, we must bear in mind that inferences about "learning ability" are always made on the basis of a specific intervention strategy used with a particular learning test. Generalisations about a "global learning ability" will therefore have to be called into question not only by the specificity of the item material used (as in conventional static intelligence tests) but also by the specificity of the intervention. Some of the forms interventions can take in dynamic test procedures are also outlined in Box 4.

With regard to the analysis of dynamic test procedures, some of the points listed in Box 4 have to do mainly with the measurement of change (on this, cf. Guthke & Wiedl, 1996, chap. 5) and with the assessment of learning gains vs. learning processes. At first sight these seem to be purely methodological/statistical problems relating to the highly complicated problem of utilising difference scores. The assessment of learning processes, instead of simply "learning gains" — the procedure that has predominated thus far — is still in its infancy. Using cluster analysis and latent cluster analysis techniques, the Osnabrück- and Leipzig-based research groups have identified "types of learners" that have yet to be validated against "external criteria". In the recently published Adaptive Computer Assisted Intelligence Learning Test Battery (ACIL, Guthke et al., 1995; see also Beckmann & Guthke, 1999), subjects are assigned, on the basis of cluster analysis, to categories representing "types of learners".

This cue sets the scene for the last part of this article, the problem of validation.

1.4 New Validation Strategies. Some Findings

As we said at the beginning (see Box 1), those who are critical of "dynamic testing" point out that it has not yet been shown to have higher validity than the conventional intelligence test. It must be emphasised, however, that the designers of conventional intelligence tests also can hardly point to conclusive validity studies. Even the manuals of the most popular and frequently used variants of the Wechsler test, for example, do not list predictive validity coefficients.

In common with other research teams with a more psychometric bias, we originally tried to compare the validity of learning tests with conventional intelligence tests by correlating test scores with school grades and teacher ratings. Although we were aware that this was a highly problematic approach there appeared to be no better criteria available. It is well known that grades do not represent dependable "criteria of intelligence" because many other factors other than intelligence impinge upon them. Published meta-analyses repeatedly showed that post-tests or learning tests mostly had slightly higher validity coefficients than the static intelligence test versions. Often the differences were insignificant, however (cf. Glutting & McDermott, 1990). The main findings that emerged when the validation was performed in the traditional manner are as follows:

1. The validity coefficients of the learning tests were at least no worse than those of the conventional static tests.
2. Especially in longitudinal studies and in studies of low-achieving subjects, learning tests usually had higher validity coefficients (cf. Guthke & Gitter, 1991).
3. In adaptive, individualised teaching, compared with the usual in-front-of-the-class teaching, learning tests were superior to static tests regarding the prediction of the success of learning (Wiedl & Herrig, 1978).

Because of the weakness of the "traditional criterion-oriented validation" against school grades and teacher ratings, during the last few years we have focused more attention on so-called construct validation. The "building blocks" of that validation are described in a number of publications (for a summary, see Guthke & Wiedl, 1996). In developing our "new learning tests", the so-called Diagnostic Programs (see above) we made a great effort to derive the item pool from basic research in cognitive psychology. Unfortunately, due to space limitations, content validation or task analysis, an important aspect of construct validation, cannot be discussed here.

In conclusion, we will discuss recent evidence concerning more appropriate forms of criterion-oriented validation. Researchers demanded long ago (cf. Guthke, as early as 1972) that in validating dynamic test procedures primarily "dynamic criteria", rather than "static" external criteria should be used. In a study conducted in the '70s, Guthke (1972) found that a number series learning test was a better predictor of change in the mathematicss grade across one year than the static test version.

Hessels (1995) reported recently that on the so-called Learning Potential Test for Ethnic Minorities (LEM), a learning test devised in the Netherlands for use mainly with foreign children, many children who on the RAKIT, the most familiar Dutch conventional intelligence test, were classified as "mentally retarded" had normal scores. At first, the concurrent validation based on school achievement tests, which are regularly used in the Netherlands as meticulously constructed Rasch scale procedures, yielded only similar static test and learning test scores. Then so-called residual gains, based on regression analysis and serving as measures of the progress of learning, were calculated between the individual school achievement tests and correlated with the preceding static tests and learning tests. Using this statistical approach, the learning tests displayed higher predictive validity than the static test. The trend toward improved ability of the learning tests to differentiate became even more noticeable when in an ANOVA-procedure static test performance groups and learning test performance groups were compared with respect to their learning gains in the repeated school achievement tests.

Of course, there are many factors in classroom learning environments which are not easily controlled. Therefore, some time ago our research group began to investigate the extent to which learning tests and static intelligence tests predict success in experimentally standardised, i.e. comparable learning procedures. The tests involved were subtests of the Computer-Assisted Intelligence Learning Test Battery (ACIL) described above and static test versions that require subjects to do the same things. At first, in a complex, dynamic scenario — of the kind used in the complex problem-solving paradigm in cognitive psychology (Frensch & Funke, 1995) — knowledge acquisition and knowledge application processes were generated. During an exploratory or knowledge acquisition phase, the subjects (14-year-old pupils) were asked to uncover, by performing systematic manipulations of the control devices and indicators of a fictitious machine (Beckmann, 1994), the latent causal structure of relations between the control devices and the changes that occurred in the displays (feedback). Then, during a control or knowledge application phase the causal knowledge acquired was to be used for attaining a goal (setting the displays to a particular value). It is assumed that the more the subjective causal model acquired corresponds to the objective model, the more appropriate the manipulations will be. Table 1 shows the correlations of the subjects' performances in complex problem solving with their performances on conventional intelligence tests, on the one hand, and on the corresponding learning test versions, on the other.

The conventional static intelligence tests were not correlated with knowledge acquisition (although they capture the reasoning factor that in other work proved highly relevant to complex problems; on this cf. also Beckmann & Guthke, 1995), and they were correlated with control performance. By contrast — and as expected — the learning test versions used were correlated at higher levels especially with knowledge acquisition.

Again, it may be objected that the subjects were asked to engage in curriculum-unspecific learning that has not much to do with everyday reality. To meet that objection, we also utilised standardised computer programs based on curriculum-related material, e.g. Schrettenbrunner and Leutner's geography program "Famine in the Sahel" (cf. Leutner & Schrettenbrunner, 1989), and a "combination theory" computer program developed by our co-workers Vahle and Riehl.

In addition to being given a learning test battery (ACIL, see above), the corresponding static test versions of the test were administered to all subjects (series of figures, series of numbers, and verbal analogies). When the subjects set about the curriculum-related program we recorded, like in a pre-test, their prior domain-specific knowledge. When they had completed the "Combination Theory" program they were retested for domain-specific knowledge, on a post-test. The measure of learning gain we calculated was the so-called residual gain. It is based

Table 1: Correlations between performances on learning tests and static intelligence tests and performances in complex problem solving

Predictors	Complex problem solving MACHINE, $N = 40$	
	Knowledge acquisition	**Knowledge application**
Static intelligence tests		
Series of figures	0.07	0.32*
Verbal analogies	0.13	0.30*
ST	0.11	0.36*
Learning tests		
Series of figures	0.42*	0.39*
Verbal analogies	0.36*	0.50*
LT	0.52*	0.57*

Note: * = $p \leq 0.05$ (one-tailed). ST and LT are aggregated measures of the two static tests and the two learning tests, respectively.

on the individual difference between the expected post-test score determined by regression analysis and the truly obtained one. This makes it possible to control the influence of initial score level on the amount of change. Accordingly, a positive residual gain reflects more post-test improvement than would "normally" be expected with the corresponding pre-test score; conversely, a negative residual gain is recorded for a subject who improves less than would be expected on the basis of his/her pre-test score (with reference to the entire sample).

Table 2 presents the results of logistic regression analyses performed to predict, on the basis of learning test scores on the one hand and of static test scores on the other, whether subjects fall into the subsample of those with positive residual gains (i.e. those who show "above-average" improvement and hence excellent learning ability), or into the subsample of those with negative residual gains (i.e. those with "below-average" improvement and hence poor learning potential). The first two columns of Table 2 illustrate the predictive ability of the learning test (column 1) and of the static test (column 2) on the criterion mentioned. The individual predictive performances were similar, with the hit-rate when learning tests were used, almost 79%, compared with 65% for the static tests. There is a slight increase in the hit-rate when both predictors are included in the regression analysis (see column 3). It is of particular interest that in this "competing situation" the learning tests were superior to the static tests. When partial correlations were compared, it was found that learning tests can apparently account for static test-related proportions of the variance as well as additional proportions of it.

Table 2: Results of logistic regression analyses. Dependent variable: residual gain, independent variables: learning test parameter (LT), static test parameter (ST)

Predictors	Dependent variable		
	Residual gain in the "Combination Theory" program		
LT	0.36*		0.26*
ST		0.25*	0.00
df	1	1	2
Sensitivity (%)	77.3	60.0	73.7
Specificity (%)	80.0	70.0	85.0
Hit-rate (%)	78.6	65.0	79.5
χ^2	14.2*	6.4*	12.4*

Note: *$p \leq 0.05$, one-tailed. groups $n_\oplus = 20$ (positive residual gain), $n_\ominus = 19$ (negative residual gain). Sensitivity: Identification of $\ominus$ by means of regression analysis; specificity: Identification of $\oplus$ by means of regression analysis. The predictors were determined in grade 8, and the criterion was determined in grade 9.

Another mode of analysis also yielded interesting results. Employing factor analysis two criterion factors (cf. Table 3) were obtained. The first factor was called "status factor" because it was marked by school grades and prior knowledge test (pre-test). The second factor was termed "learning factor" because it is marked mainly by the results the subjects obtained on the post-tests of the curriculum-specific teaching programs. When correlating the factor scores with the static tests and the learning tests (cf. Table 4), as expected we found that the learning tests were strongly related to the "learning factor", whereas the static tests were hardly not. The correlations of the learning tests and static tests with the "status factor" are at about the same level.

Space limitations prevent us from discussing further validity studies we and other research teams conducted, a finding of particular relevance is that in a seven-year longitudinal study of "normal pupils" (begun when they started school) a Raven learning test version was not superior in predictive validity to the conventional static version (the CPM) (again, the external criteria used were the problematic school grades). However, the learning test turned out to be a much better predictor of the future scholastic progress of the low-achieving pupils than the static test (cf. Guthke & Gitter, 1991). Wieland (1991) obtained similar results. In this study a learning test version of the CPM was a significantly better predictor of the results of a one-week admissions procedure for special education for children with learning disabilities than Raven's conventional CPM.

Given findings such as these we hope that one day we will have sufficient evidence to persuade even the harshest critics that Vygotsky was correct in his

Table 3: Results of the factor analysis involving the variables mathematics and German grades and performance on the "Combination Theory" program (CT) and on the knowledge pre-test and post-test of the "Famine in the Sahel" (FIS) computer cimulation. $N = 134$, grade level 7

Variables	Factor 1 (Status of knowledge)	Factor 2 (Knowledge acquistion)	h^2
Mathematics grade	0.80	—	0.69
German grade	0.84	—	0.75
CT-port	—	0.84	0.71
Pre-FIS knowledge	0.55	—	0.32
Post-FIS knowledge	—	0.70	0.55
Variance explained	35.8%	24.7%	

Note: Loading ≥ 0.30 were incorporated as substantial loadings into the table.

Table 4: Results of linear regression analyses for factor 1 and factor 2 with the learning test parameter (LT) and the static test parameter (ST)

Predictors	External variables (external criteria)	
	Factor 1 (Status of knowledge)	Factor 2 (Knowledge acquisition)
ST	0.26 (2.0)*	0.07 (0.6)
LT	0.28 (2.1)*	0.44 (3.4)*
df	125	125
F	21.4	20.7
adj. R^2	0.24	0.24

Note: *$p < 0.05$, one-tailed. The brackets behind the standardised regression coefficients (β-weights) list the corresponding *t*-values. In the regression analyses, the individual factor scores relating to the factors 1 and 2 were used as dependent variables.

belief that the assessment of the "zone of proximal development" enables a better prediction of a person's learning in everyday life than that obtained from a conventional intelligence test. It would be even more important and satisfying if from the kind of dynamic procedures described and detailed analysis of learning processes, workable recommendations for interventions could be developed. We have already embarked upon work in this direction by identifying "types of learners" (see above) and by studying response latencies in learning tests (cf. Beckmann, Guthke & Vahle, 1997). Although we are not yet within sight of our goal, we are hopeful that it can be realised.

This research was supported in part by a grant from the "Deutsche Forschungsgemeinschaft" (DFG: Gu 297/4). Correspondence concerning this article should be addressed to Prof. Dr. J. Guthke, Institute for Developmental Psychology, Personality Psychology and Psychodiagnostic, University of Leipzig, Augustusplatz, P.O. Box 920, 4009 Leipzig, Germany.

12

Culture-Fair Assessment and the Processes of Mental Attention

Juan Pascual-Leone and Janice Johnson,
with Stacey Baskind, Samantha Dworsky, and Elizabeth Severtson

The assessment of cognitive functions and learning potential (i.e. developmental intelligence) in minority, culturally different, and exceptional populations remains a difficult problem. Classic psychological tests of the IQ variety, often used to characterize psychometric intelligence, measure primarily the middle-class socialization for school of the child's cognitive functions, rather than his or her learning potential or developmental intelligence (e.g. Samuda et al., 1989). Dynamic assessment methods (e.g. Feuerstein, Rand & Hoffman, 1979; Lidz, 1987; Tzuriel & Haywood, 1992), pioneered by Vygotsky and anticipated in the assessment ideas of the neuropsychologist Andre Rey (e.g. 1963), constitute a clear advance over classic intelligence tests, because dynamic methods aim to assess learning potential instead of knowledge or actual skill level. Reuven Feuerstein, who studied with Andre Rey in Geneva, has played a seminal role in developing these methods.

Dynamic assessment methods have limitations, however. These include their difficulty in generating valid quantitative scores with good psychometric properties, and their relative lack of explicitness with respect to process-analytical organismic foundations (e.g. the lack of a cognitive-developmental or neuropsychological theory that can explain how dynamic learning processes modify constructive processes in the learner). Constructs that might be used to explain dynamic processes include the information-processing notion of working memory, the neoPiagetian and/or neuropsychological notions of mental capacity/working memory, executive processes, central conceptual structures, etc. However, researchers in dynamic assessment usually do not integrate such constructs into a substantive theory of the process of change. Such a theory is needed in order to explain subjects' performance on tasks and to develop better tools for dynamic assessment.

We cannot address all these issues in the current chapter. Because this volume is a Festschrift to honor Professor Feuerstein, we chose to discuss one important

We thank the participating schools and the children and adults who took part in the reported research. We are grateful to Drs. E. Blackstock and D. Mason for assistance with gaining access to research participants, to R. England for programming the computer-based FIT and CSVI tasks, and to A. O'Neill for help in preparing figures. We appreciate the contributions of S. Gamgee, R. Smith, L. Guzina, C. McKenzie, A. O'Neill, and H. Stevenson, all of whom assisted in data collection.

aspect that may be a common link connecting Feuerstein's work with our own: the mechanism of mental attention, which is often called mental capacity.

Feuerstein's insightful clinical books on dynamic assessment contain many passages in which mental capacity — "capacity" for short — is mentioned and used as a construct (Feuerstein et al., 1979; Feuerstein et al., 1980). Although Feuerstein's concept of mental capacity remains unexplicated, it seems to us to provide a common link that connects our dialectical constructivist work on cognitive development and cognitive style with Feuerstein's clinical developmental work. In this chapter we summarize briefly our process-analytical view on mental attention and the mental significance of cognitive style, and we suggest how these views lead to methods of assessment that might complement dynamic methods, by affording new ways of mental-capacity measurement that are psychometrically sound and theoretically well founded.

1 A Dialectical Constructivist View of a Child's Organism

We believe that it is possible to describe an organization of processes, molarly defined, that can serve as a substantive model of the child's "psychological organism." We also believe that these processes: (1) can be described using explicit but intuitive constructs so that they serve to model children's processes "from within," that is, from the perspective of the subject (subjectively), as much as "from without," with the perspective of the observer (i.e. objectively). Further, the models generated with these constructs can: (2) describe the processes in their step-by-step unfolding (i.e. in "real time"), (3) describe the processes of change (i.e. development and learning), (4) model the organismic "processual formulas" characteristic of individual-difference variables that define human types such as cognitive styles, and (5) have a proper (i.e. experimentally testable) interpretation within neuropsychological theory. We call *metasubjective* a theory/model of the psychological organism that satisfies the five conditions above (Pascual-Leone & Goodman, 1979; Pascual-Leone & Johnson, 1991).

The particular metasubjective theory we are proposing begins by positing two distinct categories of processes and two radically different ways of coping with experience. The two categories of processes appear in Table 1 as the distinction between *schemes* and *hidden operators*.

Schemes are informational (i.e. information carrying) processes, which correspond neuropsychologically to collections of neurons — neuronal networks — that are both cofunctional (i.e. often conjointly causing performance) and coactivated (related by activatory links that cause them to be often activated simultaneously or in lawful succession). Schemes are highly active units, and they tend to become released and to apply (to determine performance) under minimal conditions of activation. This highly active condition is congruent with the principles of summation and spreading of activation in dynamic networks, which in our theory are manifested by the principle of *Schemes' Overdetermination of*

Table 1: Definition of terms

Schemes: "Software", informational processes
   Operatives = Procedural transformations
   Figuratives = Declarative states
      E = Repertoire of *executive* schemes
      A = Repertoire of *affective* schemes
   H or **H'** = Repertoire of "*action*" schemes

HIDDEN OPERATORS: "Hardware" resources or capacities
      M = reserve of *mental "energy"*, **M**-power = $e + k$
         e = Number of schemes that **M** can boost simultaneously
            in the sensorimotor period
         k = Number of symbolic schemes that **M** can additionally
            boost to hyperactivation
      I = Mental *interrupt* mechanism; central inhibition utility that
         grows with **M** growth

Mental effort is the allocation of **M** or of **I**
      C = *Content* learning (or content schemes)
      L = *Logical*-structural (or relational) learning
         LM = **L**-learning due top mental effort
         LC = **L**-learning due to automatization of C-learning
      F = Gestalt *Field* factors caused by cortical local lateral inhibition

ORGANISMIC PRINCIPLE:
      SOP = Principle of *Schematic Overdetermination of Performance*:
         Neural spreading of activation towards the "final common
         path"

Performance (SOP principle). This principle is an organismic generalization of Piaget's principle of Assimilation. Because all activated schemes tend simultaneously to apply to *inform* (in the etymological sense of "injecting" form into) the synthesized performance, the performance, at any time, is synthesized by the dominant (most activated) *cluster of compatible schemes available* in the brain at the time of responding. The probability of this performance is proportional to the relative dominance of the cluster of schemes generating it (Pascual-Leone, 1989, 1995; Pascual-Leone & Baillargeon, 1994; Pascual-Leone & Goodman, 1979; Pascual-Leone & Johnson, 1991; Pascual-Leone & Morra, 1991). This principle is analogous in connectionist models to the "relaxation" or update algorithms which in every trial of a computer-learning experiment, generate the current step of the simulation (e.g. Shultz et al., 1995; Smolensky, 1988).

   From a process-analytical perspective, schemes can be defined by three components: (1) an *organismic functional system* that describes a purpose, intentionality, or component of praxis that the scheme in question serves (e.g. "reach-to-grasp", or "identify-the-given-X-figure-in-the-figural-compound", or "recognize-the-person-in-front-of-you", etc.); (2) a *releasing component* defined by a set of *conditions* (properties or relations of any sort, which become cues inducing activation of the scheme when they match suitable features in the input); and (3) an *effecting component* defined by a set of *effects* (action blueprints, transformations, mental moves) that when they apply bring about an aspect of the behavioral or mental performance.

Schemes are our psychological units, a neo-Piagetian *and* neo-Vygotskian construct (Pascual-Leone, 1996). More explicit postulates of this theory of schemes, their neuropsychological interpretation, and a method of metasubjective task analysis useful for recognizing schemes in the context of specific task performances are outlined by Pascual-Leone and Johnson (1991). In the current chapter we simply state, as Table 1 suggests, that there are, in addition to content modalities of schemes (e.g. auditory, visual, motor, linguistic, affective, etc.), different important modes of processing that constitute, as modalities do, different natural kinds of schemes ("natural kinds" because they are prefigured in the brain by way of distinct areas where they have their innately wired projection).We mention here only the triadic classification of schemes as being *figurative* (related to "declarative," in the current sense of this word), *operative* (related to the current sense of "procedural"), or *executive* (schemes that embody processual plans and control structures — this is the current sense of executive functions). Figurative schemes, or *figuratives*, are the only vehicles for "presentation" or "representation" of mental states, distal objects, and objectified concepts. Figuratives constitute the "mental objects" on which mental computation is carried out. Such computation involves application of operatives on figuratives as prescribed by executives, to produce changes that other figuratives may categorize. Operative schemes or *operatives* embody transformations or procedures that, if applied appropriately, bring about predictable results.

The construct of scheme (or schema) is well recognized nowadays, so that we expect it not to be overly controversial. The second category of processes we will discuss, the hidden operators, is less well recognized, although related constructs already exist in the literature. *Hidden operators* are "hardware" resources or partly-innate *capacities* of the psychological organism that serve to regulate internally (endogenously) the degree of current activation of schemes and/or their qualitative (semantic-pragmatic) characteristics. We group these hidden operators, or capacities, into two categories: (1) the capacities that in their dynamic interaction constitute a mental attentional mechanism, or *mental attention*, which is distinct from the schemes (i.e. informational processes) on which it bears; and (2) the capacities that in dynamic interaction among themselves produce, often with the help of mental attention, the *learning mechanisms* of schemes and the *dynamic syntheses* of performance (i.e. truly novel perception, representation, thinking or action) that are overdetermined by all activated schemes which apply. This is what we call the principle of Schematic Overdetermination of Performance (**SOP**). The second category of hidden operators is comprised of learning mechanisms (Content or **C**-learning, versus Logical-structural or **L**-learning) and special brain functions for space and time representation (a "Space" or **S**-operator — the neuroscientists' brain processes that address the question "where" in representing input objects, *versus* a "Time" or **T**-operator — brain processes that address the question "what" in representing input objects). We do not discuss further this second category (see Pascual-Leone 1995, 1996; Pascual-Leone & Goodman, 1979; Pascual-Leone & Johnson, in press).

The capacities that constitute *mental attention* are identified in Table 1 by the letters **E**, **M**, **I**, and **F** (i.e. Executive schemes, Mental operator, Interruption operator, and Field operator) (Pascual-Leone, 1970, 1987, 1997b; Pascual-Leone & Baillargeon, 1994). Dynamic interactions among these capacities ("hardware" operators of the brain) constitute mental attention as an organismic system: ⟨**E,M,I,F**⟩. The letter **E** in this model stands for the set of *currently* (i.e. here-and-now) *dominant* (most highly activated) executive schemes in the subject's repertoire of schemes. These currently-dominant executive schemes, often referred to as "the executive" or "supervisory attentional system" (Shallice, 1982), can regulate the mobilization and allocation of **M** and **I**, as discussed below. We refer to this set of currently-dominant executive schemes as an **E**-capacity, or **E**-operator, to emphasize that (due to innate prewiring of their brain substratum in the prefrontal lobe) dominant executive schemes are effectively activated and made dominant by the currently-dominant affective/motivational schemes (the dispositional goals set by the limbic system). In turn, these executive schemes can, due to innate prewiring, regulate endogenous attentional resources, so that action schemes relevant for the goals in question become dominant and produce (via Schematic Overdetermination — **SOP**) the Performance in question.

The letter **M** stands for an endogenous attentional capacity or "mental energy" that the dominant executive schemes (i.e. the operator **E**) can mobilize and allocate to task-relevant schemes, so as to boost them into hyperactivation — a state in which they are likely, due to the Schemes' Overdetermination of Performance to determine performance. **M** is an endogenous limited resource, and only a small number of schemes can be boosted by **M** simultaneously; this number is the individual's maximal **M**-capacity or **M**-power.

M is often confused with the construct of working memory. **M** is, however, just one of the organismic capacities that enable working memory. If working memory is defined empirically as the total set of currently hyperactivated schemes in the subject's repertoire, as is often done nowadays, then working memory — a descriptive construct — can be produced by causal factors other than **M**-capacity: affective/emotional factors (the **A**-capacity of Table 1); the automatized complex schemes which we have called **L**-structures (Pascual-Leone, 1996, 1997b; Pascual-Leone and Goodman, 1979); perceptual-motor saliencies such as those described

---

[1]Notice, for example, that Baddeley's definition of working memory (Baddeley, 1992; de Ribaupierre & Bailleux, 1994; Pascual-Leone & Baillargeon, 1994) is not empirical; it is instead a non-constructivist theoretical definition of processing mechanisms, which in fact conflate mental attention with two of the modalities/modes of schemes (visuospatial and linguistic/logological).

Table 2: Predicted **M**-power values as a function of age and their correspondence to the Piagetian substage sequence

M-power (e + k)	Piagetian substage	Chronological age (Years)
e + 1	Low preoperations	3–4
e + 2	High preoperations	5–6
e + 3	Low concrete operations	7–8
e + 4	High concrete operations	9–10
e + 5	Transition to formal operations	11–12
e + 6	Low formal operations	13–14
e + 7	High formal operations	15–16

Note: In this model, e is the **M**-power that develops during the first 26–28 months of life, later used as a constant to maintain hyperactivation of the tasks' general executive. Variable k is the **M**-power emerging later, often used to activate "action" schemes.

by Gestaltists, which we call **F**-capacities (these are structural "attractors" in the language of current dynamic theories), etc.[1]

The letter **I** in our model of mental attention stands for the central (executive-driven, "top down") capacity to actively inhibit or *interrupt* activation of task-irrelevant schemes. We call this organismic factor *interrupt* or **I**-operator (Pascual-Leone, 1989). **M** and **I** are hidden organismic constructs (not just latent variables; Pascual-Leone, 1997a), and they increase endogenously with age (maturation) from birth to adolescence, in normal children. We believe that in normal children these attentional operators grow concurrently. Table 2 shows the idealized pattern of growth in **M**-power across the school years.

In tasks that demand the conjoint use of both the **M** and **I** capacities, there are stages or levels of performance that correspond to Piaget's and neo-Piagetian developmental stages (these are what we call *misleading situations* — see below). Figure 1 illustrates our model of mental attention. Note that **M, I,** and **E** are related in the brain to the prefrontal lobe, so that the prefrontal lobe metaphorically carries the "flash light" of mental attention whose "beam" can regulate (activate or inhibit) schemes from other regions in the cortex as demanded by the task.

The letter **F** in Table 1 and Figure 1 stands for the neo-Gestaltist "field" factor or capacity, which we call **F**-operator. This "field" is a closure mechanism for both the internal field and for performance, akin to the neo-Gestaltist principles of "Minimum" and "S–R compatibility" (Pascual-Leone & Morra, 1991; Proctor & Reeve, 1990). This **F** factor is a sort of minimax function generated, we believe, in the brain by neuronal "lateral inhibition" mechanisms in conjunction with the schematic overdetermination (**SOP**) principle. In process analytical terms, this minimax function can be formulated as follows: The performance produced will tend to be such that it minimizes the number of schemes that directly apply to

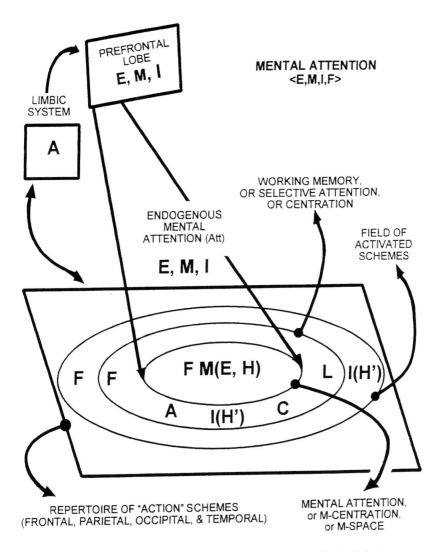

Figure 1: Model of endogenous mental attention. Capital letters represent "hardware" operators or scheme processes defined in Table 1.

inform the performance (including perception or representation); and it does so while maximizing the set of distinct, salient features of experience (activated low-level schemes) that, directly or indirectly, inform this experience (Pascual-Leone, 1987, 1995; Pascual-Leone & Johnson, 1991). For example, errors in the Wechsler (1991) picture completion subtest, such as failing to see the missing doorknob in the picture of a door, are caused by this **F** minimax mechanism, which prevents the application of low-level (local-perceptual) schemes, like the simple doorknob scheme, because automatized higher-order schemes, like the super-scheme of a standard door with its own doorknob, can also be applied and incorporate the lower scheme's representation.

As a result of non-linear dynamic interaction among all these mechanisms, a heuristic implicit "choice" and synthesis of performance (whether in action, perception, representation or mentation) takes place, which is brought about by the **F** and **SOP** mechanisms. It is within such a non-linear dynamics for constructing actual performance that the significance of mental attention, as a major developmental mechanism, becomes fully clear. By boosting (with **M**-operator) the activation of, and/or deactivating (Inhibition or **I**-operator), schemes in the field of activation, mental attention (monitored by affects via the **E**-operator) can effectively change the "choice" of performance that **F** and **SOP** will together synthesize in a given situation. Notice that endogenous mental attention is often called self-directed mental effort (James, 1961), mindfulness (Langer, 1989; Salomon & Globerson, 1987), or more loosely, working memory (e.g. Anderson, 1983; neo-Piagetians — e.g. Demetriou, 1988; Stankov, 1988).

2 Two Ways of Coping with Tasks: Strategies in Misleading versus Facilitating Situations

Vygotsky (Kozulin, 1990; van der Veer & Valsiner, 1991) and Luria (1973) spoke of two distinct forms of processing: the *high cognitive functions* (*conceptual*, logico-mathematical, logological or generic knowing) and the *low cognitive functions* (*experiential*, perceptual-motor/spatiotemporal, mereological or knowledge of particulars). Many other philosophers and psychologists (e.g. Goldstein, Piaget, Tulving) have made related distinctions. In fact, Plato was the first thinker to have formulated one dialectic of two modes of knowing/processing in humans — two distinct worlds of human existence — whose dynamic interactions constitute conscious experience and thought (Pascual-Leone, 1996). We characterize these two modes of processing (learning, thinking, coping, etc.) as *high-road* versus *low-road* thinking/processing (Pascual-Leone & Irwin, 1994). This very apt metaphor was originally introduced by Salomon and his coworkers (Salomon, 1992; Salomon & Globerson, 1987; Salomon & Perkins, 1989).

Low-road processing, like the metaphor that "low-road" (narrow local road) traveling suggests, is rich in content learning. It is efficient and occurs easily in facilitating situations, that is, in situations in which the available salient cues guide the adaptive performance of the subject. In this sense, low-road learning is driven by the situation ("data driven") and yields much content and experiential detail. With repeated experience, it easily produces habituation and automatization. Organismic resources used here are predominantly of two sorts: (1) content (**C**-capacity) associative learning — the natural capacity of schemes elicited by cues in a situation to adapt (Piaget's accommodation) by incorporating patterns from recurrent (relatively "invariant") aspects of the situation; and (2) exogenous (often *not mental*) attention — curiosity, arousal, content saliency, etc., strongly elicited by the situation. Albeit slower in acquisition than the high-road variety, low-road processing is highly efficient in facilitating situations.

A situation is *facilitating* when all the schemes it activates are compatible with the task at hand. A situation is *misleading* when it elicits schemes that interfere with the task at hand. For instance, in Piaget's Conservation tasks the situation elicits perceptual-global schemes of quantity that make the "sausage" appear to have more substance than the "ball" of clay. This is a misleading Gestaltist "field effect" (S–R Compatibility: the appearance makes you think that there is more amount — this is an **F** factor in our theory) that supermarkets use very effectively in their packaging. Facilitating situations, because the schemes they elicit contribute to (or do not interfere with) the subject's task, are optimal ones for examining learning abilities, and traditionally have been used in this way by learning theoreticians, from Behaviorist to Vygotskian.

When development is studied using facilitating situations (as learning theoreticians and perceptionists often do) it appears as continuous, a linear growth function being its characteristic curve. *Misleading* situations, in contrast, are characteristic of problem-solving paradigms, because they elicit (often via salient "cues") schemes that hinder progress in the task at hand. These are the situations unwittingly used by Piaget and others to investigate cognitive development. In these situations development appears as discontinuous, in the sense of exhibiting a non-linearly growing, at times stepwise, characteristic growth curve as a function of chronological age. This is found predominantly in cross-sectional studies, where there is no contamination with learning by virtue of repeated testing. The stages of development described by Piaget and neo-Piagetians are found reliably only in misleading situations. In these misleading paradigms subjects' performance often conforms to what non-linear system theories like catastrophe theory (Molenaar & van der Maas, 1994; van der Maas & Molenaar, 1992), would predict, which has led to claims that development is explained by non-linear system theories (Thelen & Smith, 1994).

Misleading situations (but not facilitating ones) are a source of internal conflicts — dialectical contradictions — between or among alternative processing strategies elicited by the task. These alternatives strategies draw on different processing resources (schemes or capacities) of the organism. Stages of development appear in misleading situations, because learned habits (or innate automatisms) — i.e. "low-road" processing — become obstacles for good performances. This is why in misleading situations subjects use problem-solving — non-automatized "high-road" processing — to cope with task demands and do so by way of *dynamic syntheses*. Dynamic syntheses are brought about by the tendency (this is Piaget's "assimilation") of dominant compatible schemes to apply together and *overdetermine* (this is the **SOP** principle — Pascual-Leone & Johnson, 1991; Pascual-Leone & Morra, 1991; Rappaport, 1960) subjects' performance or mentations. Influenced by (although critical of) Gestalt psychology, Piaget (1969, 1970) and Vygotsky (1978; van der Veer and Valsiner 1991) saw equilibrations/dynamic syntheses as the main organismic cause of "creative" problem-solving coping with situations (i.e.

"high-road" processing). In these syntheses, task-relevant schemes not activated by the situation are internally activated by the subject's *mental attention* (Houde, 1992, 1994; Luria, 1973; Pascual-Leone, 1970, 1980, 1987; Pascual-Leone & Baillargeon, 1994).

High-road processing/learning is normally found in misleading situations. As Salomon's analogy to "high-road" traveling (by car on expressways, or by airplane) suggests, this is a processing/learning that minimizes the acquisition of detailed and perhaps irrelevant content, focusing instead on the structural elements that are essential for the intended component of praxis (the chunk of action and/or representation) that is being addressed. Because it abstracts only the infrastructure of the praxis, high-road learning leads to the formation of what Piaget might call "operational structures", and Case (Case et al., 1993) currently is calling "central conceptual structures". These are superschemes, that is, systems of schemes, that can be transferred across types of situations, because they embody essential structural characteristics of the intended praxis as totality, and they are less affected by interference from situational cues (because these cues are often selectively excluded, via the Interrupt operator, when misleading). Consequently, high-road schemes can be used with advantage in a top-down manner to cope with misleading situations. High-road processing/learning is quite selective in the information it retains: Its schemes do not incorporate initially much of the relevant content on which they bear. Only the essential structure of the relevant context and its meaning for praxis — perhaps a plan of action — is retained. For this reason, the use of high-road schemes to produce concrete performance often demands the prior dynamic synthesis of all the schemes involved: the main high-road schemes themselves, other relevant content (low-road) schemes, and even some other less abstract high-road schemes embodying subordinate structural details. Thus the first essential resource for the abstraction and use of high-road schemes is the availability of the endogenous mental attention we have already discussed, with its various hidden operators or general-purpose capacities.

A second very important ingredient of high-road processing/learning is the planful foresight and hindsight (Pascual-Leone, 1984) which come with having a rich repertoire of executive schemes and more abstract meta-executives. Meta-executives are executive schemes that often have a conscious or preconscious representation and carry the gist or plan for a given praxis (Pascual-Leone, 1983, 1984, 1990a, 1990b; Salomon & Globerson, 1987).

As compared with low-road learning, high-road learning is much more generalizable across different contexts (types of situations). Salomon and Perkins (1989) attribute this generalizability to the fact that this category of processing takes place at a higher mode of mindful abstraction, retaining only what is common, or just what is relevant, across all instances of application; often aided by a linguistic, symbolic, or propositional rule formulation. These two kinds of processes are subject to individual differences, both developmental and stylistic.

Figure 2 gives a flow chart of the fundamental steps involved in high-road and low-road processing. In this chart, and following Pascual-Leone (1989; Pascual-Leone and Baillargeon 1994), we call *x-strategies* the effortful strategies that are

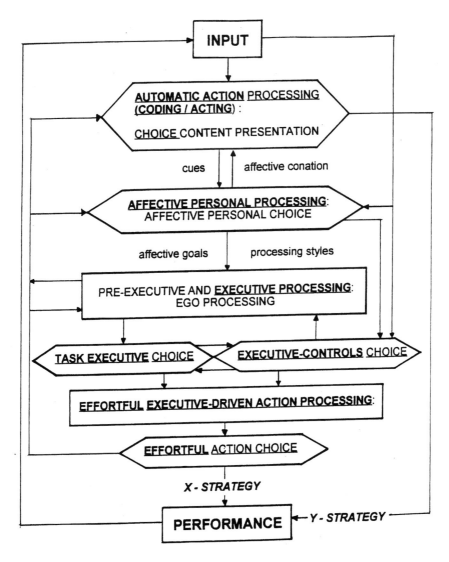

Figure 2: Flow chart of the fundamental steps involved in high-road (*x*-strategy) and low-road (*y*-strategy) processing. Misleading situations are ones in which *x*- and *y*-strategies are in conflict.

characteristic of high-road processing/learning; these are represented in the Figure by the arrowed paths down the centre of the diagram. We call *y-strategies* the often automatized, two-step strategies that constitute much of low-road processing/learning; these are represented by the arrow-path down the right-hand side of the diagram. We wish to emphasize that the probability of a child generating *x*-strategies versus *y*-strategies is not just a function of developmental maturity (growth of **M**-power), but is also a matter of executive repertoire and cognitive style. For instance, the type of subject (child or adult) that Witkin (Witkin & Goodenough, 1981) called field independent tends to produce more *x*-strategies than *y*-strategies, whereas field-dependent subjects do the reverse (e.g. Pascual-Leone, 1989; Pascual-Leone & Morra, 1991; Pascual-Leone & Baillargeon, 1994; Baillargeon, Pascual-Leone & Roncadin, 1997).

3 Low-Road Processing (Y-Strategies) can Hinder Reasoning: An Illustration from Elementary Mathematics

Consider research done by Severtson (1994); Severtson, Johnson & Pascual-Leone, (1995) on adult and child solutions to multiplication problems. We mention only findings that contrast performance on two different Area problems. The first task was to solve the following word problem: **"A window is 11 cm long and 7 cm wide. What is the area of the window?"** This task presents a facilitating situation, because all aspects of the verbal formulation elicit schemes that are useful for the intended solution. The mental demand of this problem can be estimated from either of formulas (1) or (2) below:

$$\text{ADD (mapping}^{\#}, \text{side1*, side2*)} \Rightarrow \text{area*} \tag{1}$$

$$\text{MULT(lookuptable}^{\#}, \text{side1*, side2*)} \Rightarrow \text{area*} \tag{2}$$

The formulas represent schematically mental-multiplication operations that children must perform in tasks such as calculating the area of a rectangular figure — two sides whose length values must be multiplied. We take the formulas as simplified models of the operations, schemes, and/or mental computational constraints demanded by the task solution.

Formula (1) represents the way children initially understand the multiplication operation: as a special form of addition (i.e. repeated addition). ADD (in capitals to indicate an operative scheme) stands for the scheme of addition; this operative scheme applies on the schemes that stand for the values of each side of the rectangular figure, i.e. side1* and side2*. The asterisks indicate figurative schemes. There is also a parameter (marked by #); this is a special sort of figurative that stipulates the special procedure to be used when the operative ADD (or MULT in formula 2) is applied to figurative schemes side1* and side2*. In the case of ADD, the procedure is to do some sort of cartesian mapping of side1* onto side2* and add the results; in MULT the procedure is to look up in a table (or retrieve from memory) the product of the numbers assigned to the sides. Clearly, formula (2) represents the mature procedure, when multiplication is understood as an operation different from addition.

Assuming that children have in their repertoire all the symbolic schemes represented in the formulas, each formula indicates the four schemes (stipulating processual or situational constraints to be satisfied) to which subjects must mentally attend. That is, subjects must apply **M**-capacity to boost the activation of these four

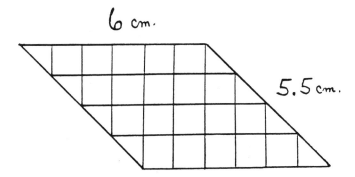

Figure 3: Area of a rhomboid problem: The participant is shown a diagram of a rhomboid divided into 1×1 cm panes and with the lengths of two sides labeled. "What is the area of this window?"

schemes, while interrupting (**I**-operator) other irrelevant competing schemes; this mental act will ensure that the operation is synthesized and the problem solved. Consequently, the mental demand (**M**-demand) of the task should be at least equal to $e + 4$, where "e" is the mental capacity needed to activate the task executives, and 4 is the number of, operative and figurative, symbolic schemes needed to carry out the operation. A child with an **M**-power equal to $e + 4$ (i.e. 9- or 10-years old, as indicated in Table 2), should solve this task — but only if he or she has the necessary executives. A child should, therefore, be in school grade 5 to have a fair chance of solving the word problem.

In the Rhomboid problem, children were shown the rhomboidal window illustrated in Figure 3, and asked **"What is the area of this window?"**. In contrast to the word problem (or to a visual presentation in which the window is an actual rectangle), the rhomboid problem presents a misleading situation. Misleadingness comes from a mismatch (S–R incompatibility — a misleading **F**-factor) between the canonical *area multiplication formula* as interpreted in the case of a rectangular window, and how this formula must be applied in the case of a rhomboid. Students learn and automatize the area formula "Area = Base × Height" and tend to assimilate Base and Height to side1 and side2. In the rhomboid problem, the Base is properly given by a side1, but the Height is not explicitly given and must be measured or computed. The fact that the rhomboid in Figure 3 has the lengths of both sides explicitly marked introduces another misleadingness, a content-learning one, due to the automatized low-road processing cued by this information (i.e. multiply the two values given to obtain the solution). To avoid these pitfalls[2] subjects must be mindful of (i.e. keep within mental attention) the need to perform the Height-obtaining operation. Formula (3) below gives a correction to formula

---

[2]Wertheimer (1959) the great Gestalt psychologist, anticipated this idea of situationally induced errors with his concept of "B solutions" to geometric problems.

(2) that achieves this goal, and so should solve the Rhomboid task.

$$\text{MULT(lookuptable}^{\#}, \text{side1*}, \text{HEIGHT(side2*)}) \Rightarrow \text{area*} \qquad (3)$$

Notice that the **M**-demand of formula (3) is equal to $e + 5$ (5 symbolic schemes plus the executives). This is the **M**-power of 11- or 12-year-olds (see Table 2), and, therefore, there should not be a high probability of children solving the rhomboid problem until school grade 6. Notice, further, that the **F**-factor and the content-automatization factor (what we have called **LC**-learning — e.g. Pascual-Leone & Goodman, 1979; Pascual-Leone, 1995, 1996), are the misleading causes (low-road processes!) that force the need to use a high-road processing strategy such as that of formula (3). Without these misleading factors a lesser, simpler strategy, such as that of formulas (2) or (1), would suffice.

To test these predictions, Severtson tested a sample of 20 children (half girls) in each of grades 2 through 7 (age range 7 to 13 years). An adult sample was comprised of 21 university students selected from a group of 37 previously tested with the Group Embedded Figures Test (GEFT; Oltman, Raskin & Witkin, 1971). The GEFT is a measure of field-dependence-independence, and the sample was chosen so that 15 of the subjects (11 females) scored as being field dependent (i.e. below the full-sample mean and median on the GEFT); the remaining 6 subjects (3 females) were field independent, scoring at the top of the GEFT distribution for the sample. We were particularly interested in the field dependent adults. Children below grade 5 showed little familiarity with the concept of area and could not cope with the task. Our results, therefore, focus on children in grades 4 through 7 and the sample of field dependent adults. Responses were scored both for correctness and for the strategies used to obtain a solution. Scores were assigned for subjects' initial responses as well as for their final responses, following prompting by the interviewer.

Figure 4 shows the percentage of correct initial responses for the two area tasks. It is apparent, as the models of formulas (1) and (2) predict, that grade 5 (but not grade 4) children have a high probability of passing the area Word problem. About 50% of the grade 4 children incorrectly added two or four of the sides of the window to obtain the area; and even after prompting by the tester, grade 4 children continued to use simple addition of the sides to obtain the final answer. By grade 5, the vast majority of children used multiplication to solve the problem, as did all the adults.

Further, as predicted by formula (3), grade 6, but not grade 5, children pass with a high (i.e. percentage correct >0.60) probability the Rhomboid problem (grade 4 children did not receive this item, because they showed little understanding of area on the simpler problem). More striking, however, and in accord with our analysis of the misleading (**F**- and **LC**-) factors in the Rhomboid situation (factors that pertain to low-road processing/learning that appear stronger in field-dependent subjects), the field-dependent adults fail the Rhomboid task rather catastrophically! The adult subjects uniformly multiplied the two labeled sides, rather than the actual base and (unlabeled) height. Overall, very few participants applied multiplication correctly in their initial response. In contrast to adults, the children used

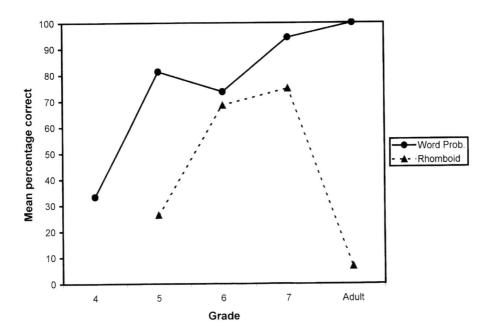

Figure 4: Percentage correct responses to two area problems, as a function of school grade.

lower level strategies with some success (e.g. counting the cells marked-off on the rhomboid; or a combination of multiplying to get the area covered by complete cells and adding on the remaining halves).

Prompting by the tester often involved leading the subject to count the cells and to note the contradiction between the number of cells and the value obtained by multiplying the labeled sides. Following prompting, there was increased successful use of multiplication by the children, but not by the adults. Successful adults tended to fall back on counting to obtain a correct answer. Thirty-three percent of the field-dependent adults continued to insist that one must multiply the sides and that, therefore, counting the cells gave the wrong answer. In fact, when pressed by the tester to resolve the contradiction between the number of cells and the result obtained by multiplying the labeled sides, only 3 of the 15 field dependent adult subjects (i.e. 20%) were able to discover the correct multiplicative formula. This contrasts with the 6 tested field independent subjects: One used the correct formula initially; of the 5 who did not, only 1 could not discover the correct formula when pressed by the interviewer — i.e. 83% of our small sample of field independent adults could figure out the correct multiplicative formula.

These results highlight our theory's contention that failure in misleading situations, which demand high-road processing, can be due to at least three sets of factors: (1) insufficiency of mental attentional "energy" (**M-power**), as illustrated here by the grade levels at which the two tasks are passed; (2) insufficiency of executive know-how (**E-level**), which could lead subjects without enough schooling in multiplication problems and procedures to fail these problems at any age; and (3) insufficient attentional interrupt capacity (**I-power**), as illustrated by the field-dependent adults whose cognitive style is characterized by a disposition not to use the interrupt capacity (that they in fact have) to control misleading low-road processes — for instance, **F-factor** and automatization, i.e. **LC**-learning (Pascual-Leone, 1970, 1989; Pascual-Leone & Morra, 1991; Baillargeon et al., 1997). These three factors of our dialectical constructivist model of mental attention are important, because they may help to redefine what is needed for better culture-fair assessment.

4 Culture-Fair Assessment as Executive-Controlled M-Measurement

Pascual-Leone and Ijaz (1989) argue that tasks that suitably assess mental-attentional capacity (i.e. **M-power**) in a relatively pure fashion — what we have called **M**-measurement — are, both theoretically and empirically, culture-fair tests. Such tasks should be regarded as ways of "assessing the process of *creative/dynamic syntheses* in cognitive functioning (i.e. the processing mechanisms themselves) rather than the possession of strategies, knowledge and skills" (Pascual-Leone & Ijaz, 1989, p. 170). This is in sharp contrast with ordinary cognitive or intelligence testing. After six years of research on the foundations of **M**-measurement, we are in a position to clarify this statement and present some new conclusions about culture-fair testing. The analyses conducted in the previous section can help us to understand how to obtain a relatively pure measure of **M**-capacity, which is maximally culture-fair. We summarize in six **M**-Measurement (MM) points these conclusions:

(MM1) Such a task will have to tap high-road processes that require the use of mental attention, but at the same time minimize the executive demand (**E**-level) of the test items. Executive demand can be minimized in a number of ways, for example: (1) by using learning as a control in an introductory section prior to testing; (2) by keeping constant the executive processes used in all items, even when mental-attentional complexity (i.e. **M**-demand) of items is increased from one class of item to the next, so as to facilitate intra-task learning at the executive level; and (3) by creating valid alternative forms of a given **M**-measurement paradigm and testing subjects twice. The initial testing can serve as self-administered executive-learning experience, before subjects receive the second alternative form (to which they automatically transfer the acquired executive know-how), which is used to evaluate the subjects' **M**-power uncontaminated by executive-knowledge differentials.

(MM2) The task should be constituted by an ordered set of *classes* of items (homogeneous scales), each class indexing one given **M**-demand value (and thus discriminating the corresponding **M**-power in subjects). The task should contain as many different item classes as needed to ensure that all possible/relevant values of **M**-demand are present, each represented by a different class of item.

(MM3) Items within one class should be homogeneous in the sense that all have the same theory-based *processual formula* (i.e. mental-strategy formula; Pascual-Leone, 1989; Pascual-Leone & Goodman, 1979; Pascual-Leone & Baillargeon, 1994). This means that all items in a class have the same balance and configuration of task-facilitating and task-misleading organismic features (hidden operators/capacities, executive strategies, etc.) and the same relationships among these features. Within a class, all items should also have the same configuration of facilitating versus misleading features. Notice that, in this dialectical constructivist approach, since processual formulas are constituted by organismic processes that the task elicits from subjects, item features are, in fact, mental subjective constructs — *subjective* in the "objective" sense of pertaining to the subject.

(MM4) The same processual formula should ideally be found across classes of items within the test. The only processual difference among items from different classes should be the graded value of their **M**-demand parameter. This ideal, never completely attained, is approximated by minimizing differences other than **M**-demand among across-class items, and doing so in a theory-guided manner with empirical verification (e.g. Pascual-Leone, 1970, 1978; Pascual-Leone & Sparkman, 1980; Pascual-Leone & Baillargeon, 1994).

(MM5) Classes of items are ordered in terms of a purely structural, theory-guided measure: the number of discrete schemes that must simultaneously be boosted with **M**-capacity in order to implement the task-solving strategy. When there is construct validity, this number corresponds to the cardinal measure of the largest set of schemes in the subject's activated repertoire that can be boosted in its totality with **M**-capacity (i.e. it corresponds to the subject's hidden parameter **M**-power). If the hidden variable that underlies **M**-measurement is general-purpose and develops endogenously by virtue of maturation, as we believe, then the measure of **M**, when validly obtained, should be invariant across methods of assessment. This unusual feature suggests that **M**-measurement holds promise as a means of culture-fair assessment. The hidden parameter that **M**-measures are designed to assess is a purely structural set-measure. For this reason, when method and content variance are different in two different **M**-measures, their intercorrelation should not be expected to be overly high — possibly of the magnitude found in the area of cognitive styles (which are also structural constructs), that is, often no higher than a Pearson correlation of 0.60.

(MM6) **M**-measurement tasks can be constructed in facilitating situations or in misleading situations. Facilitating **M**-tasks do not require that subjects use active mental-attention inhibition (the *interrupt* mechanism, which we call **I**-capacity). Misleading **M**-tasks do demand the use of the **I**-interrupt, because in this case, irrelevant or misleading schemes activated by the situation (i.e.

low-road processing, *y*-strategies) must be actively inhibited in order to permit the synthesis of a correct *x*-strategy (Pascual-Leone & Baillargeon, 1994). Note, however, that to optimize measurement of **M**, the task's demand on **I**-interrupt capacity (i.e. the stress on the child's power of central, active inhibition) should be minimized. Although requiring active interruption when they are misleading, good **M**-measurement tasks must not unduly tax the subject's interruption capacity.

With the background provided by these **M**-measurement postulates, we can now state an important conclusion about culture-fair testing to which our recent research has led us. *The culture-fairness of a task for assessing developmental intelligence or learning potential can be maximized if the task is constructed as a misleading* **M***-measurement instrument* (MM6), *and its executive difficulty (**E**-demand) is minimized using the methods given in* (MM1). This is a counter-intuitive conclusion from the perspective of common sense: One might think that a facilitating task, by providing more task-relevant cues, should in fact be easier for children who are culturally different or culturally deprived; but this is not so. An instrument is culture-fair only when it is not biased in favour of any subcultural group of subjects; but the superior repertoire of schemes of subcultural groups that have had a richer executive learning environment (Feuerstein's mediated learning experience) will be better able to take advantage of the task-relevant cues in facilitating situations. In contrast, in misleading situations, subjects must use active inhibition (the attentional **I**-operator) to interrupt activation of misleading schemes and must use mental capacity to boost the activation of task-relevant schemes. In testing situations, there may in fact be contextual cues that can prime relevant executives. In a misleading situation, however, when the contextual cues are not actively attended to, they will be interrupted; and once interrupted, they cannot be used to advantage by children whose experience has led them to acquire a superior repertoire of schemes. Suitably misleading situations, therefore, should be more culture-fair.

5 An Initial Confirmation of Our Constructivist Principle for Culture-Fair Testing

We have begun to test these conclusions using exceptional populations. We summarize below results from research that compared performance on **M**-measures of "mainstream" hearing schoolchildren with that of age-matched children from two special populations: Deaf children and academically gifted children (Baskind, 1997; Dworsky, 1996; Pascual-Leone et al., 1997). An ideal **M**-measure should not discriminate among these groups. To the extent that current **M**-measures do exhibit group differences, one can infer that experiential factors impact unduly on performance.

Research on academically gifted children suggests that they do not necessarily differ from their mainstream peers in mental capacity or developmental intelligence. Where gifted children may differ is in sophistication of executive processes, such as those found in good learning, speed of processing, imagination, creativity, and divergent thinking (e.g. Colangelo & Davis, 1991; Porath, 1992; Runco, 1986; Segalowitz, Unsal & Dywan, 1992).

Similar in some respects are conclusions reached regarding deaf children. It seems clear that they do not differ in mental capacity from hearing children, but may have characteristic patterns of weakness (e.g. low spontaneous use of rehearsal in memory tasks; Bebko, 1984; Marschark, 1993) and/or superiority in some executive schemes. In particular if they are signers, deaf children often exhibit superior executives and performance in visuospatial skills, such as simultaneous processing (e.g. Emmorey, Kosslyn & Bellugi, 1993; Parnasis et al., 1996; Todman & Cowdy, 1993; Todman & Seedhouse, 1994). This may not be so, however, when their hearing parents are non-signers (Marschark, 1993).

Our samples were comprised of 19 9- to 12-year-old mainstream hearing children age-matched with 19 academically gifted hearing children and 19 deaf children. Deaf children attended a school for the deaf; at school they communi-cated in American Sign Language (ASL). All but four of these children were profoundly deaf, and the majority had hearing parents. Gifted children had been identified as such by their School Board, on the basis of standardized test performance and teacher recommendation.

We focus here on two **M**-measures. The first is the Figural Intersection Test (FIT; Pascual-Leone & Ijaz, 1989; Pascual-Leone & Baillargeon, 1994). This is a well-validated, misleading **M**-measure. Previous research has shown the FIT to be relatively culture-fair, particularly in a second testing (Miller et al., 1989; Niaz & Caraucan, 1996). FIT items require the child to locate the one area of intersection of two to eight overlapping, geometric shapes. Figure 5 shows an item with six overlapping shapes (on the left-hand side of the figure). Note that the overlapping shapes create a gestalt that makes it difficult to locate the area of intersection of the six target shapes (which are presented discretely on the right-hand side of the figure). This is what makes the task a misleading one. The **M**-demand of an item corresponds to the number of shapes to be intersected; the **M**-score is the highest item class (defined by number of intersecting shapes) that the subject passes reliably. Children were tested twice using alternative FIT forms, first with a computer version and then with a paper-and-pen version.

The second task was the Compound Stimuli Visual Information task (CSVI; Pascual-Leone, 1970, 1978), a well validated, facilitating **M**-measure. Children were trained to associate a number of individual visual cues (e.g. square, red, large, *x*-in-the centre) with discrete button presses on a button panel. The cues were presented on a computer screen. Once the stimulus-response units had been acquired to criterion, test items (compound stimuli) were presented that contained two to eight relevant cues, and the task was to respond to as many cues as were present in each item. A well supported mathematical model is used to assign **M**-scores as a function of item class (number of relevant compound cues) and number of cues correctly responded to (Pascual-Leone, 1970). This task is facilitating, because all the information present in the compound stimulus is relevant for the correct response.

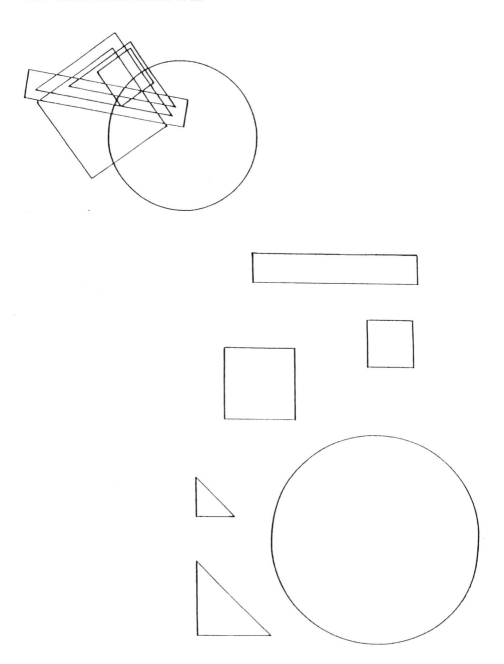

Figure 5: FIT test item that includes six figures to intersect (i.e. **M**-demand = 6).

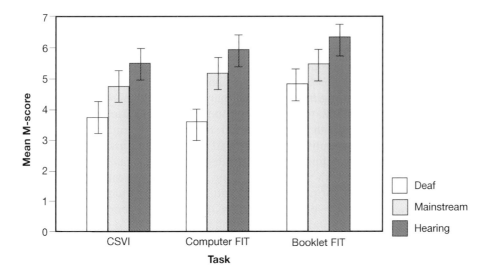

Figure 6: Mean **M**-scores on CSVI and FIT as a function of group. Bars indicate standard deviations.

Children received each task in a separate session and in the following order: Computer FIT, CSVI, booklet FIT. All testing was individual, except for the FIT booklet which was administered in small groups for the hearing children. Deaf children were tested in ASL by two native signers.

Figure 6 displays mean **M**-scores on the CSVI and FIT. The theoretically expected mean score on both tests is 4.5–5.0, given the developmental **M**-growth predictions (see Table 2). We focus first on the FIT. Analyses revealed that in the first (computer) FIT testing, mainstream hearing children performed significantly better than deaf children, but did not differ from gifted hearing children. On the second (booklet) testing, deaf children performed at the same level as mainstream hearing children. This result replicates findings mentioned above, with children from economically or socially deprived backgrounds (Miller et al., 1989; Niaz & Caraucan, 1996). It suggests that the executive demand of FIT initially puts some children at a disadvantage, but that (consistent with MM1 above) this advantage can be eliminated with practice. Only the deaf sample showed a significant improvement in performance from the first to the second FIT testing. The gifted hearing sample performed significantly better than mainstream hearing sample only on the second, booklet, FIT testing. The existence of a gifted advantage on the booklet FIT, but not on the computer version, replicates findings of Roncadin (1996) and Sedighdeilami (1996). More recent studies suggest that FIT does discriminate giftedness, albeit with less differential variance than standard achievement or intelligence tests (e.g. Raven).

Consistent with our claims regarding facilitating tasks, the deaf sample scored significantly lower than the hearing samples on the CSVI. Gifted and mainstream

212 Juan Pascual-Leone et al.

hearing children did not differ, however, on this task.

Our results suggest that, with reference to **M**-capacity, gifted children are like mainstream children, but with a superior executive repertoire that gives them an advantage on certain kinds of tasks. Results for the CSVI are consistent with those obtained by Globerson (1983) with Israeli children, and suggest that the superior executive repertoire of gifted children may prove less of an advantage on **M**-measures than on standard tests of psychometric intelligence.

The deaf children in our sample appear to be like the mainstream hearing children, but with an executive repertoire that is inferior in some respects. Results for the FIT suggest that this executive-strategy deficiency can be eliminated by practice, via pretesting with an alternative form of the FIT. A subsequent study in our lab has shown a similar practice effect with alternative-form pretesting for deaf children, when the order of FIT testing is reversed (i.e. booklet followed by computer FIT). These findings were replicated also by results for another misleading **M**-measure used in the current study, but not reported here (Baskind, 1997; Pascual-Leone et al., 1997). Using a modified span (consonant recall) task, we found that under misleading testing conditions (i.e. conditions that interfere with application of executive — e.g. rehearsal — executives) and after practice via pretesting with alternative test forms, performance differentials between deaf and hearing (including gifted!) children were eliminated. It is important to note that the majority of deaf participants in the current study had hearing parents. Marschark (1993) has pointed out that problems in early communication between deaf children and hearing parents may have a disruptive effect on the child's parent-mediated learning experiences.

Our results are consistent with our claim that misleading **M**-measures are more culture-fair than facilitating ones. Since children were tested only once with the CSVI, however, we do not have a firm test of this claim. We have in fact collected CSVI retest data for deaf and hearing children, but these data have not yet been analyzed. Based on past research (McFarland, 1972; Pascual-Leone, 1970; de Ribaupierre, 1975), we predict that the performance of all children will improve on a second testing with the CSVI, so that group differentials should be maintained.

6 Is Executive-Controlled M-Measurement a Solution for Culture-Fair Assessment of Learning Potential?

In this chapter we have argued that endogenous mental attention can be measured (**M**-measurement) and that this form of measurement can yield culture-fair ways of assessing learning potential. Indeed, Globerson (1983) showed in Israel that the CSVI task is more culture-fair than Raven's Progressive Matrices. Subsequently, in studies with gifted and mainstream children in Toronto, Roncadin (1996) and Peressini (1996) found that the FIT and CSVI distinguish less strongly between gifted versus mainstream groups than does Raven's. Our research on exceptional populations, summarized in this chapter, indicates that when testing culturally different children, subjects' prior knowledge of requisite executive schemes (in our case, produced via pretraining with an alternative form of the task) is a mandatory requirement. This finding is convergent, using a quite different methodology, with the theses on Dynamic Assessment that Feuerstein has pioneered.

Can our approach, which easily lends itself to quantitative measurement (Baillargeon, 1993; Pascual-Leone, 1970, 1978, 1980, 1987; Pascual-Leone & Baillargeon, 1994; Pascual-Leone & Ijaz, 1989; Baillargeon et al., 1997), replace dynamic assessment and dynamic testing, or is it rather intended to clarify these methods theoretically and complement them empirically? A careful consideration of *what* is being assessed in **M**-measurement, and *how* culture-fairness is achieved in it, clarifies the nature and limits of our form of assessment; and shows the second alternative to be correct.

A quote from Andre Rey can help to place the issue in its proper perspective: "The results from a test that isolates an activity, a simple reaction, or at least a phenomenon that seems elementary (sensorial threshold, perceptual time, reaction time, speed of free association, short-term memory, etc.), serves, without a doubt, to differentiate individuals; nonetheless these differentials are not too valid for a parallel classification of these same individuals at the level of high mental processes, which imply symbolic activity and the abstraction of concrete knowledge and relations" (1963, p. 215, translated by JPL).

Those who would confuse **M**-measurement with the traditional assessment of short-term memory might read this quote of Andre Rey as implying that our tasks should lack predictive power at the level of high cognitive functions. But we have emphasized in this chapter and elsewhere (e.g. Pascual-Leone, 1987; Pascual-Leone & Baillargeon, 1994) why **M**-measurement is a distinct form of fundamental measurement and not just the empirical measurement of a simple, isolated skill or ability. **M**-capacity, and the endogenous mental attention of which it is a part, is a construct standing for a hidden, general-purpose, content-free organismic function which is central for processes of symbolization and high cognitive functions in general; and so **M**-tasks have been shown repeatedly to have considerable predictive power for children's and adults' high cognitive functions (e.g. Johnson, Fabian & Pascual-Leone, 1989; Johnstone & El-Banna, 1985; Niaz & Lawson, 1989; Stewart & Pascual-Leone, 1992).

A number of researchers have found that measures of working memory predict higher level functions (e.g. Carpenter & Just, 1992; Engle & Cantor, 1993). Working memory, however, is a descriptive construct that subsumes numerous distinct causal determinants, from **M**-capacity and executive overlearning and automatization (**L** − logical/structural learning − capacity), to linguistic automatization, or perceptually/spatially facilitated recall produced by Gestaltist or other factors (**F** capacity, **S** capacity), to affective/emotionally facilitated recall (**A** capacity in the jargon of our theory). Measures of working memory, therefore, confound measurement of mental capacity with measurement of other factors, including task-relevant content. Furthermore, the concept of working memory cannot easily be integrated with the very important central, active inhibitory processes (our **I**-capacity) that are now beginning to be recognized as important for high cognitive functions (e.g. Case, 1992; Dempster, 1992; Stuss, 1992).

Most important, **M**-measurement differs radically from the ordinary testing of simple skills to measure high cognitive functions, as is described in Rey's quotation. **M**-power (the estimated measure of **M**-capacity) is a purely functional–structural variable — the measurement of a "psycho-set" (the largest set of schemes simultaneously activated by **M**) in the subject — a structural characteristic of the subjects' mental processes. Thus although **M**-measurement has a family resemblance with simple, basic skill testing, it is radically different and more fundamental. We have shown repeatedly that **M**-capacity (or rather, a given power/level of endogenous mental attention) is a necessary but not sufficient condition for the transition from one developmental stage to the next, stages that index in various ways the level of the subject's high cognitive functions. It is not sufficient because adequate executive know-how, an executive repertoire appropriate for the stage of developmental intelligence in question, is also needed; and these executives, which differ from one cognitive domain to the next, must be acquired in suitable executive learning environments — the mediated learning experience upon which Feuerstein has so much insisted (e.g. Feuerstein et al., 1980).

Appraisal of high cognitive functions should thus require assessment of the subject's endogenous mental attention (**M**-measurement), in order to evaluate in a deeper developmental way the learning potential of the subject; but it must also involve dynamic assessment of skills and abilities in relevant substantive domains of high cognitive functions. This is so because, "It is at the level of the 'superior faculties' [high cognitive functions — JPL] where the most valid differentiation among individuals is found" (Rey, 1963, p. 215, translated by JPL).

PART 3

13

Developmental Perspectives of Mediated Learning Experience Theory

David Tzuriel

1 Developmental Perspectives of Mediated Learning Experience Theory

Feuerstein's theory of structural cognitive modifiability and mediated learning experience (MLE) (Feuerstein et al., 1979; Feuerstein et al., 1980; Feuerstein, Rand, & Rynders, 1988) has emerged as a response to educational needs to understand specific environmental factors and especially socio-cultural factors that influence cognitive development, learning processes, and learning potential. Two main applied systems have been devised from the MLE theory: The Learning Propensity Assessment Device (LPAD, Feuerstein et al., 1995) and the Instrumental Enrichment program (Feuerstein et al., 1980). The MLE theory has triggered many psychologists and educators to explore related theoretical and practical issues. These issues cover a broad spectrum such as the effects of parent–child MLE processes on children's cognitive modifiability (Klein, 1988, 1996; Tzuriel, 1996, 1998, in press-a, 199a, Tzuriel & Ernst, 1990; Tzuriel & Eran, 1990; Tzuriel & Hatzir, 1999; Tzuriel & Weiss, 1998a,b), the effects of mediation on cognitive modifiability, and transfer ability of immigrant children (Tzuriel & Kaufman, 1999), the nature of learning potential and the plasticity of the cognitive system (Lidz, 1987, 1991; Tzuriel, 1997a, b, c), readiness to benefit from mediation given within and across different cultural contexts, the effects of Instrumental Enrichment on internalization of high-order concepts (*novel symbolic mental tools* in Vygotsky's terms), and the impact of intervention programs on structural cognitive modifiability (Feuerstein et al., 1980; Tzuriel, 1998; Tzuriel & Alfassi, 1994; Tzuriel et al., in press; Tzuriel et al., 1988).

The main purpose of this paper is to present several developmental perspectives of the MLE model. These perspectives are based on a series of studies in which (a) the MLE criteria were operationalized for observation, and (b) a dynamic assessment (DA) approach was used to measure cognitive modifiability of children. Most research is based on studies carried out at Bar Ilan University's laboratory (Tzuriel, 1000a,b) using Tzuriel's DA measures for preschool children (Tzuriel, 1997a, b, c, 1998, in press-a,b). In the first part of this paper the basic theoretical hypotheses of MLE will be presented with emphasis on developmental perspectives. This section includes definition of the MLE criteria and the distinction between cultural difference and cultural deprivation. The second section focuses on developmental research in which the effects of parent–child MLE strategies on children's cognitive modifiability are studied. Within this section I will discuss few methodological aspects of conducting research within the MLE theory. Finally, integrative issues will be discussed with suggestions for future research and elaboration of the MLE theory.

2 Theoretical Principles of MLE

Unlike other developmental models which conceive the parents as providers of opportunities for learning (i.e. Piaget), but basically passive in terms of facilitation of the developmental process, the MLE model conceives parents as active-modifying agents in directing and shaping the child's development. MLE interactions are defined as a process in which parents or substitute adults interpose themselves between a set of stimuli and the human organism and modify the stimuli for the developing child. In mediating the world of stimuli to the child, parents may use different strategies such as alerting the child's attention, changing the stimulus frequency, order, and intensity, relating it to familiar contexts, and regulating the order and timing of its sequence. Adequate mediators relate also to the child's motivational aspects by arousing the child's attention, curiosity, and vigilance, focusing him/her on relevant aspects of the situation, and by providing meanings to neutral stimuli. From a cognitive perspective, adequate mediation facilitates development of cognitive functions required for temporal, spatial, and cause–effect relationships. The MLE processes are gradually internalized by the child and become an integrated mechanism of change in the future. As the child develops internalized self-mediational strategies, the parents gradually withdraw from the situation and allow the child more autonomy in implementing the acquired mediated strategies. Adequate MLE interactions facilitate the development of various cognitive functions, learning sets mental operations, strategies, reflective thinking, and need systems. The acquired and internalized MLE processes allow developing children to later use them independently, to benefit from novel learning experiences in varied contexts, and to modify their own cognitive system.

Feuerstein and colleagues conceived MLE interactions as a *proximal factor* that explains individual differences in learning processes and cognitive performance. Factors such as organic deficit, poverty, socioeconomic status, and emotional disturbance are considered to be *distal factors*, which might correlate with learning ability, but they affect learning ability only through the *proximal factor*, which is the MLE interaction. Feuerstein et al. (1995) suggested 13 criteria of MLE, but only the first five criteria were operationalized in studies of infants and young children (Klein, 1988; Lidz, 1991; Tzuriel, 1996, 1997b; 1998, 1999a, in press-a; Tzuriel & Eran, 1990; Tzuriel & Ernst, 1990; Tzuriel & Hatzir, 1998; Tzuriel & Weiss, 1998a, b; Tzuriel & Weitz, 1998). These five criteria will be described here briefly. For a detailed description of all MLE criteria see Feuerstein et al. (1988, 1995).

According to Feuerstein and colleagues, an adult–child interaction can be defined as mediated interaction if it contains three basic "ingredients": *Intentionality and Reciprocity*, *Meaning*, and *Transcendence*. These criteria are considered necessary and sufficient for an interaction to be classified as MLE. Other criteria can contribute to cognitive development but are not conceived as necessary and/or sufficient in a mediated interaction.

2.1 MLE Criteria

(a) *Intentionality and Reciprocity* is an interaction characterized by efforts from a mediating adult to create in the child a state of vigilance, and to facilitate an efficient registration of the information (input phase), an adequate processing (elaboration phase), and accurate responding (output phase). The Reciprocity component is of crucial importance to the quality and continuation of the mediational process. The mediated child who responds or reciprocates to the mediator's behavior enables the mediator to adjust his/her mediation and continue the process efficiently. Intentionality and Reciprocity is observed, for example, when the parent intentionally focuses the child's attention on an object and the child responds overtly to that behavior. The parent can draw the child's attention on a specific aspect of a drawing, highlighting its specific features, and sensitively waiting and even encouraging the child's response.

(b) *Mediation of Meaning* refers to interactions in which the mediator tries, when presenting a stimulus or pointing to an event, to emphasize its significance and worth. This is done by expressing interest and affect and by pointing to its importance and value. The significance of a stimulus can be conveyed non-verbally (e.g. facial expression, tone of voice, rituals, repetitious actions) or verbally (e.g. illuminating a current event, activity, or learned context, relating it to past or current events and explaining its value). Children who experience an adequate amount of mediation of meaning internalize this interaction and will use it later in various contexts. They will be not only more open for mediation of meaning but also will initiate attachment of meaning to new information rather than passively waiting for meaning to come. A parent can express enthusiasm in the presence of an event, or explain the personal significance and unique importance of a stimulus, which to the child might look neutral.

(c) *Mediation for Transcendence* is characterized by going beyond the concrete context or the immediate needs of the child. The mediator usually tries to reach out for general principles and/or goals that are not bound to the "here and now" or the specific and concrete aspects of the situation. In mother–child interactions, for example, mothers might go beyond the children's concrete experience and teach strategies, rules, and principles in order to generalize to other situations. Mediation of Transcendence occurs usually in spontaneous family contexts (e.g. eating, bathing, playing, fighting) where the parent uses the spontaneous interaction to mediate important generalized principles, rules, values, and concepts. In formal teaching situations, the parent (or teacher) might mediate rules and principles that govern a problem or a learned subject and show how they are generalized to other school subjects or daily life situations. According to the MLE theory a child who receives an adequate mediation for Transcendence usually internalizes this specific type of mediation and will use it efficiently in other contexts. The efficient use is not limited only to provision of mediation by others but also to generation of transcendence when confronted with new situations. The child will transfer the rules and strategies learned previously to other problems that vary in terms of content domain, and level of complexity, novelty, and abstraction. It should be noted that although mediation for Transcendence depends on the first two criteria, the combination of all criteria becomes a powerful vehicle for the development of cognitive modifiability and the widening of the individual's need system.

(d) In *Mediation of Feelings of Competence* the mediator initially arranges the environment to ensure the children's success and interprets the environment in a manner which conveys to the child the awareness of the capability of functioning independently and successfully. This is done in various ways such as reorganizing the child's environment so as to ensure opportunities for success, explaining to the child the reasons for successes and failures, and by rewarding the child for attempts to master the situation and cope effectively with current problems. The mediator provides feedback not only to successful solutions but also to partially successful performances and for attempts at mastery.

(e) In *Mediation for Control of and Regulation of Behavior* the mediator regulates the child's responses, depending on the task demands, as well as on the child's behavioral style. Regulation of behavior is carried out by either inhibiting impulsive tendencies, or by accelerating inefficient slow behavior. This mediation is of critical importance in helping the child to register information accurately, delay needs for immediate gratification, and pace the inner rhythm of response as a function of task demands. Mediation of regulation affects the whole process of mental activity in input, elaboration, and output phases of the mental act. It can be carried out by analyzing the task components, inhibiting the child's acting-out behavior, delaying immediate gratification, focusing on task characteristics, and eliciting metacognitive strategies.

According to Feuerstein, the MLE strategies used in parent–child interactions help children internalize learning mechanisms, facilitate learning processes and self-mediation, give indications about future changes of cognitive structures, develop deficient cognitive functions, and provide for the ability to benefit in the future from mediation in other contexts. From this it follows that changes in cognitive structures during development are not automatic but depend to a large degree on appropriate mediation. Feuerstein focused on ways to bring about change rather than on the etiology of the manifested deficiency. Nonetheless, the biological factors are not ignored, nor are their detrimental effects denigrated. The argument is that in spite of the strength of the biological factors, there are ways to overcome them — with some individuals more easily than with others.

2.2 The Distinction between Cultural Deprivation and Cultural Difference

While the focus of this paper is on molecular (psychological) aspects of MLE one cannot avoid the wider molar (sociological) aspects. One of Feuerstein's distinctions, derived from clinical experience with immigrant populations, in Israel and elsewhere, is the difference between *cultural deprivation* and *cultural difference*. Many of the immigrants had to go through an accelerated process of integration, a process that required acquisition of sophisticated technology. The social pressures for mainstreaming posed pressures for development of new assessment methods that would take into account the immigrants' diverse cultures and allow the fulfillment of their learning potential, especially those who were misdiagnosed by conventional psychometric tests. Feuerstein has observed that the process of adaptation of an immigrant group to a new culture depend more on the group's ability to preserve cultural transmission under a new socio-cultural context rather than on the "distance" between the original and the new culture. What is important for adaptation and transfer of mediational strategies is not the content or the transmission methods of the original culture, but the experience of mediation and feelings of cultural identity. Culturally deprived individuals are those who are deprived of mediated learning experiences *within their own* culture. While culturally different individuals may manifest certain deficient cognitive functions, they are expected to overcome them rather quickly and/or with less mediational efforts. The culturally deprived individuals, on the other hand, have a relatively reduced modifiability, which is a result of insufficient mediation on a proximal level. This distinction has a great impact on developing assessment procedures imbued with mediational components and on intervention programs aimed at compensating for the lack of MLE.

3 Developmental Perspectives of Mother–Child MLE Interactions

One of the most important hypotheses of the MLE theory is related to effects of mediation within the family on development of *cognitive performance* and *cognitive modifiability*. Cognitive performance refers to the individual's manifested performance without any guidance or help whereas cognitive modifiability refers to performance after a mediation phase where the individual was taught how to register efficiently incoming information (input), process it (elaboration), and express it efficiently (output).

Mother–child MLE interactions as determinants of cognitive modifiability were examined in a series of studies by Tzuriel and his colleagues (Tzuriel, 1996; Tzuriel & Eran, 1990; Tzuriel & Ernst, 1990; Tzuriel & Hatzir, 1999; Tzuriel & Weiss, 1998a, b; Tzuriel & Weitz, 1998). The cognitive measures used in these studies included both dynamic assessment (DA) and static/conventional tests (see discussion below). The general hypothesis in these studies was that MLE interactions within the family are more accurate in predicting the DA *Post-Teaching* performance than are performance of static measures or DA *Pre-Teaching* measures. This hypothesis is based on both, Vygotsky's (1978) concept of the *zone of proximal development* (ZPD) and Feuerstein et al. (1979, 1980, 1988) MLE theory. The rationale behind this hypothesis is that adequate MLE provides children "psychological tools" which serve to expand and differentiate their ZPD. This is why the upper level of ZPD measures would be more accurate as a predicted outcome of MLE interactions than static test performance (Tzuriel, 1989). The main objectives of these studies were to investigate the hypothesized effects of distal and proximal (MLE) factors in determination of the child's cognitive modifiability and study the effects of context and subjects' characteristics in determining the relation between MLE and cognitive modifiability. Before presenting the developmental findings, a brief description of the DA measures and some methodological issues related to developmental research should be first discussed.

3.1 Methodological Aspects

The methodological aspects relate (a) to the type of cognitive measures used in research, (b) the observation system of MLE interactions, and (c) the type of statistical analyses applied.

3.1.1 Type of Cognitive Measures

In all the Tzuriel and colleagues' studies, attempts were made to measure the children's *cognitive modifiability* using a DA approach (Feuerstein et. al., 1979; Haywood & Tzuriel, 1992; Lidz, 1987; Tzuriel, 1995, 1996, 1997a, 1998, in press-a,b,c; Tzuriel & Haywood, 1992), in addition to static tests. The term *dynamic assessment* (DA) refers to an assessment of thinking, perception, learning, and problem solving by an active teaching process aimed at modifying cognitive functioning.

DA differs from conventional static tests in regard to its goals, processes, instruments, test situation, and interpretation of results (Campione, 1989; Feuerstein et al., 1979; Grigorenko & Sternberg, 1998; Guthke & Stein, 1996; Hamers, Sijtsma & Ruijssenaars, 1993; Lidz, 1987, 1991, 1997; Tzuriel, 1992a, 1996, 1997b, 1998; Tzuriel & Haywood, 1992). The conceptualization behind using change criteria measures of modifiability are more closely related to teaching processes by which the child is taught how to process information, than they are to static measures of intelligence, which relate to the end products of the learning process. The mediational strategies used within the DA procedure are more related to learning processes in other life contexts than do conventional static methods and therefore give better indications about future changes of cognitive structures. Accumulating evidence from educational research provides indications that a score reflecting individual differences in "modifiability" added substantially to the predictive power of learning in an unrelated program (Embretson, 1992) and predicted assignment to special education programs two years after the end of the intervention (Samuels et al., 1992). Developmental research showed the efficacy of DA as predicted outcome of mother–child MLE strategies (Tzuriel, 1999a, in press-a; Tzuriel & Eran, 1990; Tzuriel & Ernst, 1990; Tzuriel & Hatzir, 1998; Tzuriel & Weiss, 1998a, b; Tzuriel & Weitz, 1998).

The conceptualization behind the use of DA in relation to parent–child MLE interactions is that measures of modifiability and change are more closely related to mediational processes by which the child is taught how to process information, than they are to static measures of intelligence. The use of both, DA and static psychometric measures allows comparison of the relationship of MLE criteria scores with both measures and testing hypotheses related to the relationship of MLE processes to these measures. In all studies carried out we used the *measurement/research* version rather than the *clinical/educational* version of DA (Tzuriel, 1997a,b,c, 1998). According to the measurement/research version, Pre-Teaching and Post-Teaching phases are given without mediation and the child's responses are scored. A short-term but intensive mediation is given in-between the tests and responses are recorded and scored. It should be noted that in the *clinical/educational* version, no scores are given and assessment refers mainly to qualitative aspects of the child's performance. The qualitative aspects refer, in addition to the child's performance, to the amount and nature of mediation needed to solve a problem, the level of task difficulty in relation to the child's solution, behavioral tendencies that affect the child's cognitive responses, and affective-motivational (non-intellective) factors that affect performance (Tzuriel, 1991a, b). Mediation is adapted to the child's level and parallel item(s) are presented only after the child shows mastery level. Once the child shows adequate mastery it is possible to move to a higher level of difficulty.

Three DA measures were used in the developmental studies: *The Children's Analogical Thinking Modifiability* (CATM, Tzuriel & Klein, 1985, 1987, 1991a, b), *The Children's Inferential Thinking Modifiability* (CITM, Tzuriel, 1989, 1991b), and the Pre-school version of the *Complex Figure Test* (Tzuriel & Eiboshitz, 1992).

The Children's Analogical Thinking Modifiability Test (CATM). The CATM (Tzuriel & Klein, 1985, 1987, 1991) is composed of 18 colored (red, blue, yellow) blocks and three sets of analogical problems for Pre-Teaching, Teaching, and Post-Teaching phases. Each set contains 14 analogical problems increasing in level of difficulty. The blocks are different in dimensions of color X size X shape ($3 \times 2 \times 3$). An example problem from the CATM is presented in Figure 1.

Each of the 14 CATM items is presented in the ascribed order. The tester places the first three blocks and asks the child to find the last (fourth) block and place it in the correct position. In items 11–14 (level IV), which contain two blocks in each part of the problem, the tester places both blocks and asks the child to find the blocks of the last part. Cronbach-alpha reliability coefficients for the Pre-Teaching and Post-Teaching Phases are 0.85 and 0.89, respectively (Tzuriel & Klein, 1985). The validity of the CATM as well as its effectiveness with different groups of children, have been established both clinically and empirically (Missiuna & Samuels, 1989; Samuels, 1998; Samuels, et. al., 1992; Tzuriel, 1992a,b,c; Tzuriel & Caspi, 1992; Tzuriel & Ernst, 1990; Tzuriel et al., 1999; Tzuriel et al., 1998; Tzuriel & Kaufman, 1999; Tzuriel & Weitz, 1998; Tzuriel & Hatzir, 1999; Tzuriel & Klein, 1985, 1987, 1991).

The Children's Inferential Modifiability Test (CITM). The CITM, designed by Tzuriel (1989, 1992a) is based on the principles of the Organizer test from the

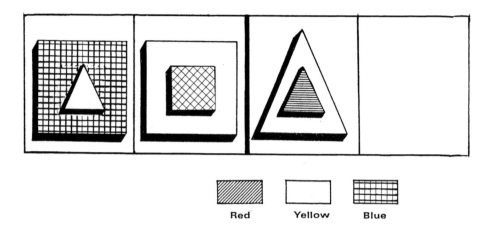

Figure 1: Example problems from the CATM test.

LPAD (Feuerstein et al., 1995). The objectives of the CITM are to assess young children's ability to solve problems that require inferential thinking as well as their ability to modify their performance following a process of mediation. The test is composed of four sets of problems for Pre-Teaching, Teaching, Post-Teaching, and Transfer phases. The child is first presented with a set of 24 familiar pictures (i.e. clothes, animals, and furniture) and he/she is asked to name them. Naming pictures is aimed at establishing familiarity with the objects. The child is then presented with two example problems, and instructed in the rules for solving them and in procedures for gathering information. The problems are composed of a set of figural "sentences". Each "sentence" presents information about the possible location of objects in houses with different colored roofs. In terms of Feuerstein et al.'s (1979) list of deficient cognitive functions, the task requires systematic exploratory behavior, control of impulsivity, spontaneous comparative behavior, planning, inferential-hypothetical ("iffy") thinking, and simultaneous consideration of many sources of information. The operations required for solving the task are related to *negation*-negative inference ("the chair is not in the red house and not in the blue house"), and inductive reasoning. The objective of the Transfer phase is to examine the degree to which a child can make a "transfer" of the strategies and principles learned in previous problems and use them with new problems. The Transfer problems cover several dimensions, such as consideration of a different aspect of the data, coping with complex presentation of information, using "negative" information, and eliminating irrelevant clues. An example problem from the CITM-Transfer phase (TR8) is presented in Figure 2.

In item TR8, four houses are presented at the top of the page with red, black, white, and blue roofs. The child is instructed to place cards with pictures into the appropriate houses at the top of the page. To solve the problem the child is given 4 rows, at the bottom of the page, with each row containing part of the

TR8

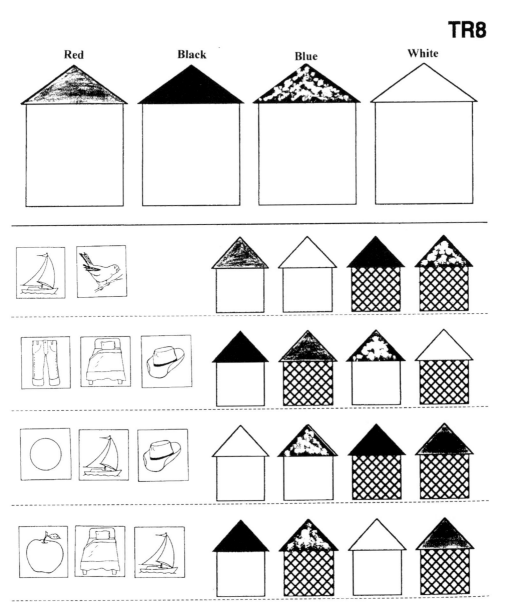

Objects on left cannot enter the meshed houses

Figure 2: Example item (TR8) from the CITM test.

information. The rules are that in each row the objects in the left *should not* enter the meshed houses to the right. In the first row, the Donkey, Circle, and Airplane should not enter the meshed houses (black and red); it is not known at this stage which object will be in which house. In the second row, the Airplane, Table, and Socks should not go into either of the meshed houses (white or black); but again one does not know which object goes into which house. In the third row, the Pants, Table, and Carrot should not enter the white or blue houses. In the fourth row the Car, Carrot, and Circle should not enter the red and blue houses. The task requires systematic exploratory behavior, control of impulsivity, spontaneous comparative behavior, planning, inferential-hypothetical ("iffy") thinking, and simultaneous consideration of several sources of information. The operations required for solving the task are related to negation–negative inference ("the chair in not in the red house and not in the blue house"), and inductive reasoning. Cronbach-alpha reliability coefficients of the Pre-Teaching, Post-Teaching, and Transfer phases are 0.82, 0.82, and 0.90, respectively (Tzuriel, 1992b). The CITM's validity has been established in several developmental and educational studies (Tzuriel 1989; Tzuriel, & Eran, 1990; Tzuriel & Kaufman, 1999; Tzuriel & Schanck, 1994; Tzuriel & Weiss, 1998a, b).

The Complex Figure Test is a dynamic assessment measure developed for young children, based on Rey's (1956) test. Tzuriel and Eiboshitz (1992) adapted the Complex Figure that is used dynamically in the LPAD for young children (Versions I and II). The versions of the Complex Figure for young children are presented in Figure 3.

The test is composed of 5 phases: (a) in the first phase, the child is asked to copy the figure and then (b) to draw it from memory. (c) In a mediation phase that follows, the child is taught how to gather the information systematically, to plan the construction (i.e. drawing first the major lines and then secondary lines, going in clockwise order), and pay attention to precision, proportions, and the quality of lines. (d) A second copy phase and (e) a second memory phase are administered exactly as in phases a and b. Comparison of copy and memory phases before and after mediation provides information about the modifiability of the child's perfor-mance. The Complex Figure has 11 components, each one given one point for accuracy and one for location, for a possible total score of 22. A third, qualitative, score, ranging from 1 to 7, is given for organization. The Complex Figure test has been used previously with different groups of pre-school children with learning disabilities and with academically high-risk disadvantaged children (Tzuriel, in press-c; Tzuriel & Eiboshitz, 1992; Tzuriel & Hatzir, 1999; Tzuriel et al., in press; Tzuriel & Weitz, 1998). It was found effective in predicting treatment effects of a program aimed at developing visual motor integration ability with these pre-school children. The reliability of the test was studied on a sample of kindergarten and grade 1 children ($n = 15$) by two independent raters (Tzuriel, in press-c). The inter-rater reliability computed by Pearson correlation for *Accuracy + Location* scores were as follows: Copy-I — 0.99, Memory-I — 0.98, Copy-II — 0.98, Memory II — 0.97. The parallel reliability coefficients for *Organization* scores were Copy-I: 0.90, Memory-I: 0.95, Copy-II: 0.48, Memory-II: 0.78.

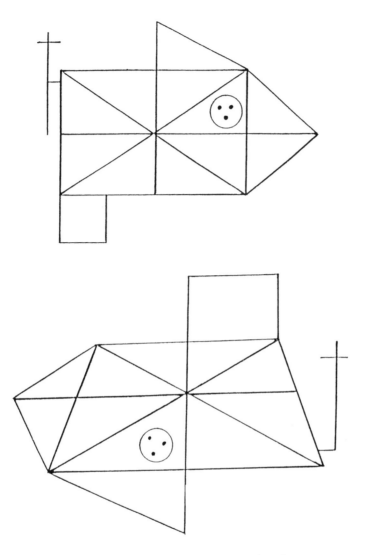

Figure 3: Pre-school versions of the complex figure test.

3.1.2 Observation System of MLE Interactions

Observations of mother–child MLE interactions were carried out in the studies reported below were carried out by videotaping mother–child interactions and analyzing them by the *Observation of Mediation Instrument* (OMI, Klein, 1988, 1996). According to Klein's method a macroanalytic rather than a microanalytic approach is preferred to assess the quality of mother–child interaction. For example, when a mother hands an object to her child and focuses him/her attention on some aspects of the stimulus, it is coded as a behavior reflecting *Intentionality and Reciprocity* only if it was reciprocated by the child's response. Whenever the mother makes an attempt to generalize a rule, suggest a concept, or a principle that goes beyond the concreteness of the situation, it is coded as *Mediation of Transcendence*, regardless of the specific content being conveyed. The basis of the observation system was an interaction "event" which might contain one or more MLE criteria. According to Klein previous attempts to measure mother–child interactions (e.g. Clarke-Stewart, 1973) "do not offer clear understanding of which behaviors occurring during parent–child interaction represent necessary and sufficient conditions for learning experience" (p. 56). The advantages of the MLE molar observational approach over others its allowance of the identification of meaningful patterns of continuity in parents' behavior across a developmental dimension. Sroufe (1983) has already mentioned earlier, that understanding of continuity in child development is not characterized by mere additions of behavioral components but rather on transformations and epigenesis. One of the advantages of this approach is that it allows comparison of similarities in behavioral patterns across time in spite of changes of contents. This approach coincides with other patterns such as emphasis on holism and the need to look at the meaning of behaviors within a psychological context rather than as isolated behaviors (Santostefano, 1978; Sroufe & Waters, 1977).

In all studies reported by Tzuriel's and colleagues the MLE interactions were sampled in two distinct situations: *free-play* and *structured*. These contexts were hypothesized to represent typical and major parent–child interactions. Vygotsky and others have made a similar distinction between these two contexts earlier (Vygotsky, 1978; van Geert, 1994; Valsiner, 1984; Wertsch, 1984). They distinguished between two sources of ZPD: *play* and *instruction*. While in play, children create their own ZPD and corresponding level of potential development, in the context of instruction, ZPD is created by a competent goal-oriented adult (Intentionality in MLE theory terms) who mediates the world to the child.

The OMI, originally developed for infants, was adapted for different ages (5- to 8-year-old children), by changing the type of stimuli presented, by using two interactional type of situations, and prolonging the interaction time (usually a period of 30 minutes). The reliability coefficients for infants ranged as follows: Intentionality and Reciprocity, 0.76–0.85; Meaning, 0.62–0.83; Transcendence, Feelings of Competence, 0.68–0.81; Regulation of Behavior, 0.68–0.81 (Klein, 1988). The reliability coefficients, based on five studies (Tzuriel & Ernst, 1990; Tzuriel & Weiss, 1998a, b; Tzuriel & Weitz, 1998; Tzuriel & Gerafy, 1997; Tzuriel et al., 1998) are presented in Table 1.

3.2 Statistical Analyses of DA Measures

One of the problems raised frequently in using DA data as indicators of cognitive modifiability is related to analysis and interpretation of gain scores. Equals Pre- to Post-Teaching gains do not necessarily indicate equal gains; high initial score is usually

Table 1: Inter-rates reliability coefficient of MLE criteria and MLE — total scores

MLE Criteria	Tzuriel & Ernst (1990)	Tzuriel & Weiss (1998)	Tzuriel, Kaniel, Zeliger Friedman & Haywood (1998)	Tzuriel & Weitz (1998)	Tzuriel & Gerafy (1994)
Intentionality & Reciprocity	0.54	0.42	0.75**	0.95***	0.90***
Meaning	0.85**	0.73*	0.78**	0.86**	0.85***
Transcendence	0.80**	0.83**	0.98***	0.86***	0.53
Feeling of Competence	0.87**	0.94***	0.80**	0.86**	0.58
Regulation of Behavior	0.55	0.85**	0.81**	0.95***	0.83**
MLE — Total	0.93***	0.93***	0.94***	0.85**	0.72**

$*p < 0.05$ $**p < 0.01$ $***p < 0.001$

associated with lower gain then low initial scores. A possible statistical solution is using hierarchical regression analysis in which the prediction of a children's Post-Teaching (high ZPD level) score by MLE mother–child interactions is estimated in a *second step* after it had been explained, in a *first step* by the Pre-Teaching (low ZPD level) score. In this way, the variance of the Post-Teaching score predicted by the mother–child MLE interactions, had been "washed out" from the initial cognitive performance. The second step prediction reflects the "pure" variance that can be explained by mediation effects within the DA testing situation. This analysis provides an important indication of the effects of mothers' mediational strategies to the children's cognitive modifiability within the DA context.

Another possibility for data analysis that was used in two studies (Tzuriel & Ernst, 1990; Tzuriel & Weiss, 1998a, b) is the *structural equation modeling (SEM)* analysis. The use of SEM allows designing complex models with intermediate variables and latent constructs. Another advantage is the possibility to infer causal relations among variables without having to use experimental designs. Also the nature of the variables involved in testing the theory are not always given to experimental manipulations, and the accumulated effects that several variables have on outcome variables are not easily given to manipulate simultaneously. The holistic approach used in SEM contributes to understanding of the conceptual whole more than the sum of fragmentary separate analyses.

4 Mother–Child MLE Interactions and Child's Cognitive Modifiability: Current Research

In one of the earliest studies on the effects of family factors on children's cognitive modifiability, a global measure of home environment was used rather than specific MLE mother–child strategies (Tzuriel & Caspi, 1992). The findings of this study showed a differential prediction pattern of the CATM-Post-Teaching scores by cognitive and family factors in both deaf and hearing groups (Tzuriel & Haywood, 1992). Using stepwise regression analyses it was found that, in the deaf group, the CATM-Post-Teaching score was predicted by the mother's occupation, the overall score of Home Observation for Measurement of the Environment (HOME) inventory (Bradley & Caldwell, 1984), and the CATM-Pre-Teaching score ($R^2 = 0.70$). In the hearing group, only one significant ($R^2 = 0.62$) predictor was found: an analogy sub-scale from the SON test (Snijders & Snijders-Oomen, 1970). For this group the similar psychometric qualities (both tests tap the analogies domain) take precedence over the family factors. Those results indicate that the contribution of family factors as indicated by the level of cognitive stimulation and emotional warmth given in the family was more critical in the deaf group, to overcome the mediational barriers and to actualize the upper level of the ZPD than in the hearing group.

In the first study with preschool children in which mother–child MLE interactions were observed (Tzuriel & Ernst, 1990), mothers from low, medium, and high SES groups ($n = 48$) were videotaped while interacting with their 5-year-old

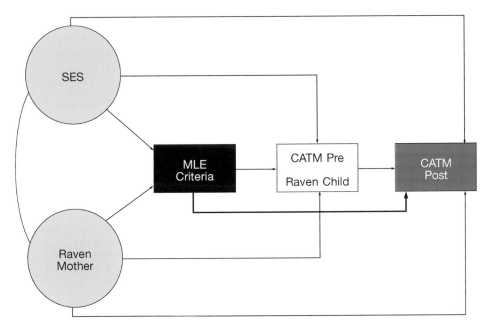

Figure 4: Structural equation analysis of distal and proximal factors of children's cognitive modifiability: a schematic model (by permission of *The Journal of Cognitive Education*).

children in a free-play and structured situations. The interactions were analyzed later using Klein's (1988) Observation of Mediation Instrument (OMI). The children were given the static and DA measures in order to study their predictive efficiency by the MLE processes. The DA measure was the CATM and the static test was the Raven's Colored Progressive Matrices (Raven, 1956). The data were analyzed using structural equation modeling with a LISREL approach (Joreskog & Sorbom, 1986). The schematic SEM model is presented in Figure 4 and the empirical findings are presented in Figure 5.

The findings indicated clearly that the *proximal* factors of MLE interactions better explained the children's cognitive performance than did the *distal* factor of mother's SES or intelligence. The mothers' SES, which explained four out of five MLE criteria, was not related to any of the children's cognitive performance measures, static or dynamic. Differential effects of MLE criteria on different cognitive performances coincide with the specificity requirement in validation of theoretical constructs (Wachs, 1992). The CATM-Pre-Teaching score was explained by *Mediation for Meaning*, whereas the CATM-Post-Teaching score was explained by *Mediation for Transcendence*. The interpretation of these results was that Mediation for Meaning is effective when the child encounters new situations and has to cope with problem solving tasks by attributing meaning to the novel stimuli. Attribution of meaning such as labeling, relating present stimuli to past experience,

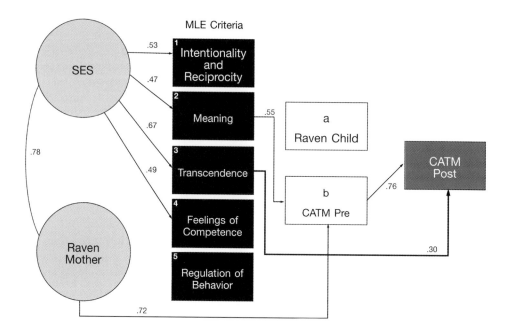

Figure 5: Structural equation analysis of distal and proximal factors of children's cognitive modifiability: empirical findings (by permission of *The Journal of Cognitive Education*).

and attaching value is crucial for first encounters with tasks such as those presented to children in the Pre-Teaching phase of the CATM. Mediation of Transcendence, on the other hand, requires learning of generalized principles, rules, and strategies. These learning skills were actually taught during the mediation phase of the CATM and were reflected in the CATM-Post-Teaching performance. The differential prediction of the children's Pre and Post scores by different MLE criteria especially the specificity of prediction (Wachs, 1992) further validates the MLE theory as well as the efficiency of the DA approach in developmental studies.

Prediction of children's cognitive modifiability by MLE processes was investigated in a kibbutz setting by Tzuriel and Eran (1990). Kibbutz mothers and their children were observed interacting with their children in a free-play situation, and their MLE scores were compared later with the children's scores on the CITM (dynamic) and the Raven's (static) tests. Since the unique kibbutz situation allows for a relative control of many environmental factors, it was assumed that relatively more variance in the children's cognitive performance would be associated with their mothers' MLE strategies than would be expected in other samples. In a series of three stepwise regression analyses, the CITM *Pre-Teaching, Post-Teaching,* and *Gain* scores were predicted, each, by Raven and MLE-Total scores. The findings revealed that the CITM-Pre-Teaching (static) was predicted only by the Raven

($R = 0.40$; $p < ''.004$), the CITM-Post-Teaching was predicted equally by both, MLE-Total and Raven ($R = 0.69$; $p < 0.002$), and the CITM-Gain was predicted only by MLE-Total score ($R = 0.43$; $p < 0.001$). These findings were explained in the following way: In the first analysis both scores are static measures and can be considered as reflecting the lower level of ZPD. This result verifies what is commonly known, that the common variance of two cognitive tests is higher than the common variance of a cognitive test with an observed behavior (i.e. MLE mother–child interactions). In the second analysis both the Raven and MLE mother–child interaction score equally predicted the *CITM-Post-Teaching* score. The CITM-Post-Teaching score seems to be composed of two components: the previously acquired inferential skills, as manifested in children's Pre-Teaching performance, and what has been learned as a result of mediation given by the examiner in the teaching phase. It is plausible to assume that the first component (Post-Teaching score) is attributed to the Raven score, and the second component (Post-Teaching score) to the MLE-Total score. In the third analysis only the MLE score predicted the Gain score. These findings indicate that the more the criterion variable (Pre, Post, Gain) was saturated with mediation effects, given within the testing procedure, the higher the variance contributed by the mother–child MLE interactions.

The findings of Tzuriel and Ernst (1990) were examined further in a third study (Tzuriel, 1996). The objectives of this study were to investigate the frequency of MLE mother–child strategies in free-play versus structured situations among low-, medium-, and high-SES, and to find out the prediction of the CATM scores by mother–child MLE interaction. For our discussion only the prediction of DA scores by MLE interactions are of interest. The children's cognitive performance on the CATM was in a series of stepwise regression analyses by MLE scores in two distinct situations: *free-play* and *structured*. Two questions were posed: (a) which combination of the MLE specific criteria is best for prediction of the children's cognitive performance, and (b) in which type of situation (free-play versus structured) will the child's cognitive performance be most predicted by mother–child MLE interactions? Using a stepwise regression analysis approach two sets of analyses were carried out, one for the Total-MLE scores and the other for the specific MLE criteria. In each set three analyses were carried out, one for each of the CATM scores (Pre-Teaching, Post-Teaching, and Gain) as criterion variables. The regression analyses revealed three principal findings: (a) In both sets of analyses (MLE-Total and MLE Criteria), the CATM scores of both the Pre-Teaching and the Post-Teaching tests were predicted by the MLE interactions of the *structured situation* and not by the free-play situation; (b) Higher predictions were found for CATM-Post-Teaching than for the CATM-Pre-Teaching scores; (c) In the second set of analyses where the specific criteria were taken as predictors, the motivational component of the MLE (Mediation for Competence) was stronger than any other criterion in predicting the CATM scores. Similar findings were reported in another study (Tzuriel & Weiss, 1998a, b) using a different measure (CITM) and a different sample (2nd graders, $n = 54$). Only the Total MLE score of the structured situation predicted the children's performance on the CITM. One possible explanation for the findings is that MLE in the structured situation samples better the quality of the mother–child interactions as a determinant of cognitive development. Another explanation is that MLE in the structured situation is more diagnostic and accurate than the MLE in free-play situations. Another possible explanation is that the predicted cognitive variable, the mediation given to children to perform better on the CATM or CITM, reflect similar mother–child MLE aspects; in both mediational contexts, the required cognitive functions and the cognitive domains that are used are similar. The findings of both studies point to the necessity of further studies in which interactions of context in interaction, cognitive domains, and specific MLE strategies will be considered simultaneously in predictions of children's cognitive modifiability.

The effects of distal factors on proximal factors (MLE) and the combined effects of both on children's cognitive modifiability was investigated further using a different set of distal variables: mothers' emotional attitudes and children's personality (Tzuriel & Weiss, 1997). Based on Feuerstein's theory, MLE interactions are conceived as a proximal etiologic determinant for differential cognitive modifiability, whereas mothers' emotional attitudes and children's personality factors were conceived as distal factors and therefore insufficient to explain cognitive development. A sample of 54 children (26 boys and 28 girls) in grade 2 were videotaped interacting with their mothers in free-play and structured situations. The interactions were analyzed with the OMI, using MLE criteria of Intentionality and Reciprocity, Transcendence, Meaning, Feelings of Competence, and Regulation of Behavior. The children were administered the Parent Affective-Rejection Questionnaire (PARQ, Rohner, 1978) and the Personality Assessment Questionnaire (PAQ, Rohner, 1978). The main dependent variables were the Pre-Teaching, Post-Teaching, and Transfer scores of the CITM.

The data was first analyzed by a hierarchical regression analysis (Tzuriel & Weiss, 1998b) in which the criterion variable was the Post-Teaching score, and the predictive variables were, in the first step the CITM-Pre-Teaching (low ZPD level) and in the second step the mother's five MLE criteria. The control of the contribution of the Pre-Teaching to the Post-Teaching performance is of most importance. After controlling for the Pre-Teaching score, the residual variation can accurately reflect the effects of mediational criteria. In other words, the contribution of MLE to Post-Teaching, after "washing out" the Pre-Teaching effects can reflects the "net" effect of mediation on children's cognitive modifiability.

The results of the regression analysis showed that in step 1, 18% of the Post-Teaching score was explained by the Pre-Teaching score (0.43, $p < 0.01$). In the second step, two MLE criteria have emerged as significant predictors: *Regulation of Behavior* (0.36, $p < 0.01$) and *Transcendence* (0.21, $p < 0.05$) in addition to the Pre-Teaching score (0.39, $p < 0.01$). The three variables explained 42% of the variance and the change from first step to second step was 24%. These results indicate that the higher the mothers' mediations for Transcendence and Regulation of Behavior, the higher the child can benefit from mediation and change his/her cognitive functioning within the DA testing situation. The results confirm the hypothesis that children whose parents mediate to them how to generalize (transcendence) and regulate their behavior can later benefit from mediation in which these learning mechanisms are required.

The data was further analysed using a model of distal and proximal factors that explain the child's cognitive modifiability (Tzuriel & Weiss, 1998a; Tzuriel, 1999a). The analysis was carried out by a *structural equation model* (SEM) using the LISREL VI version (Joreskog & Sorbom, 1986). The main findings reveal that (a) All MLE criteria were predicted by the distal factors of mothers' acceptance–rejection and the children's personality, (b) the distal factors did not explain any of the children's cognitive factors, (Pre- or Post-Teaching) (c) MLE criteria of Transcendence and Regulation of Behavior explained the children's Post-Teaching-CITM score whereas no MLE criterion explained the Pre-Teaching-CITM score. An important conclusion of this study was that while the children's personality characteristics and the mother's acceptance/rejection attitudes (distal factors) do not directly affect cognitive modifiability of the children, they do however influence them via MLE processes. The results confirmed one of the central derived hypotheses of the MLE theory that the proximal factor of MLE better explained variations in cognitive modifiability than distal factors.

It is intriguing to note that the CITM-Post-Teaching score was explained by two specific MLE criteria: Transcendence and Regulation of Behavior and by the Pre-Teaching score. The explanation for that is that the performance on the CITM-Post-Teaching is composed of two components: (a) learning of task specific principles and strategies of problem solving, and (b) the initial performance on the CITM. The first component — the CITM-Post-Teaching — was explained mainly by the mothers' mediations for Transcendence and Regulation of Behavior, both reflect a typical MLE interaction in which the mother is involved in both, mediating rules and principles and monitoring the flow of the children's behavior. Task analysis of the CITM problems reveals that mastery of the task requires several cognitive functions such as systematic exploratory behavior, planning, hypothetical thinking, applications of rules, and generalization of principles. These cognitive functions depend on adequate internalization mediational processes which consist of, among other things, regulation of behavior and application of generalized principles and rules. These processes correspond to the mediational criteria found to be as most predictive. It is plausible to assume that these two MLE components, acquired during normal mother–child interactions, were assimilated by the children and equipped them with the thinking tools and mechanisms that are required later in other tasks and learning contexts. When similar mediation for Transcendence and Regulation of Behavior are provided in other learning situations, these children can retrieve their previous mediational experiences, apply them efficiently with different tasks, and modify their cognitive structures.

One of the questions raised frequently by developmental researchers is what are the effects of early parent–child interactions on cognitive development of children at-risk. This question was investigated more specifically using parent–child MLE interactions and DA measures (Tzuriel & Weitz, 1998) with a group of 5–8-year-old children ($n = 26$) born with very low birth weight ($<1250\,g$; VLBW). The VLBW children were compared to a group ($n = 30$) of normal birth weight (NBW) on static and DA measures, but more importantly on the prediction pattern of Post-Teaching scores by MLE interactions in the two groups. The two groups were matched on variables of age, sex, and parents' educational and professional level, which constitute their SES. The VLBW children were all studying in the regular school system (kindergartens and grades 1 and 2) and had normal health conditions without any clear neurological deficiency. The static tests used were The *Visual Motor Integration* (VMI) Scale (Beery, 1986); *Vocabulary and Concept Formation* sub-scales from the WISC-R; *Auditory Sequential Memory Test (ASM)* from the ITPA; and *Draw-a-Person Test* (Goodenough, 1926). The DA measures were the CATM and the Complex Figure test. Mother–child interactions were videotaped in free-play and structured situations and analyzed later using the OMI. A one-way MANOVA on the static standard tests revealed significant Group differences ($F(5, 50) = 2.62, p < 0.05$), indicating, as expected, that the NBW children achieved higher than the VLBW children. One-way ANOVA's on the specific scales revealed that the Group differences were contributed mainly by Concept Formation, Vocabulary, and the Visual Motor Integration tests. Analyses of the DA findings showed that the NBW children achieved higher scores on the CATM Pre-Teaching in both Method-1 ($F(1, 54) = 16.54, p < 0.001$) and Method-2 ($F(1, 54) = 13.83, p < 0.001$). However, the initial differences disappeared after the Teaching phase. An ANCOVA on the CATM Post-Teaching score with CATM Pre-Teaching score as a covariate revealed no significant Group differences using either the Method-1 ($F(1, 53) = 2.06, p = ns$) or Method-2 of scoring ($F(1, 53) = 1.01, p = ns$). Thus, in spite of the initial superiority of the NBW children, the mediation given within the DA procedure has brought the VLBW children to close the gap with the NBW children. Similar analyses that were carried out on the Complex Figure test scores revealed no significant superiority of the NBW children over the VLBW before or after the Teaching phase of the DA procedure.

Analysis of the correlational patterns in the two groups revealed that a Verbal Ability and Memory factor (defined previously by separate factor analysis on the static tests) was correlated 0.44 ($p < 0.01$) with Mediation for Transcendence in the VLBW group, as compared to -0.11 ($p = ns$) in the NBW group; the two correlations were significantly different (Fisher-$Z = 2.04, p < 0.05$). This finding indicates that *Mediation for Transcendence* is more crucial in development of verbal ability and memory skills of VLBW children, than in the NBW group. The causal interpretation of this finding should be treated rather cautiously, due to its correlational nature. It might well be that within the VLBW group, mothers who tend to use more Mediation for Transcendence are those whose children show an initial higher level of verbal and memory skills.

The DA findings were analyzed by a series of hierarchical regression analyses in which the CATM (or Complex Figure) Post-Teaching score was taken as a *first step* predictor, Group as a *second step* predictor, MLE Criteria as *third step* predictors and the Group × MLE Criteria interactions as *last step* predictors. As mentioned above, the hierarchical regression approach seems to be most appropriate for analyses of the effects of MLE on cognitive DA gains. The hypothesized effects of mother–child MLE interaction on Post-Teaching (high ZPD level) score can be examined after "washing out" the Pre-Teaching effect (low ZPD level). The variance of the Post-Teaching score predicted by the mother–child MLE interactions reflects the "pure" variance that can be attributed to mediation effects within the testing situation. This analysis might provide an important indication of the effects of mothers' mediational strategies on children's *cognitive modifiability*.

The findings showed generally, that the Post-Teaching scores of the CATM and Complex Figure were significantly predicted by the MLE criteria of *Transcendence*; the higher the mother's mediation for Transcendence, the higher is the Post-Teaching score. The contribution of Transcendence above the variance contributed by the Pre-Teaching and Group variables ranged between 4% to 10%; a finding which coincides with previous results using the CATM (Tzuriel & Ernst, 1990) or the CITM (Tzuriel & Weiss, 1998a, b) tests. The interactions of *Group by MLE Criteria* across the different analyses revealed a complex differential predictive pattern — positive in the NBW group and a negative in the VLBW group. The opposite predictive pattern was found mainly for two criteria: *Intentionality and Reciprocity and Feelings of Competence* (findings differ somewhat for the different criteria and predicted variables). These interactions indicate that for the VLBW children, the *higher* their Post-Teaching score, the *lower* the MLE score, and vice versa. In the NBW group, on the other hand, the children's Post-Teaching score was positively related to the MLE score, a finding which coincides with the main study's hypothesis. The findings for the VLBW children seem, at first glance, to be contrary to what is hypothesized by the MLE theory. However, thorough examination of the theoretical concepts suggests that although MLE is considered as a proximal causative factor of children's cognitive modifiability, in some cases the children's initial cognitive level can influence parents' MLE efforts in their interactions with their children. It might well be that within the high-risk VLBW children, which evidently have lower levels of cognitive functioning then NBW children, those who show a relatively lower modifiability, require more mediation to compensate for their difficulties, whereas those who show higher levels of change require less compensating MLE efforts from their parents. In view of these findings it seems that one should conceive MLE processes, not only as an independent parental interaction mode that is necessary for the development of cognitive modifiability, but also as a behavioral parental response to the child's initial difficulties. As a matter of fact Feuerstein himself emphasized the reciprocal nature of the MLE interactions suggesting that parents calibrate their mediational efforts to the child's difficulties. Of course according to the theory, without the extra mediational efforts given to the VLBW low-functioning children, their cognitive level might be much lower than what would be shown otherwise. These results call upon more research in which parental mediation will be experimentally manipulated with different groups of high-risk children using various static and DA measures. Our hypothesis is that mediation will be more effective, and therefore more predictive of children's cognitive modifiability, as a function of severity of children's condition.

5 Conclusion

The results from developmental studies confirmed the MLE theory by showing that the MLE proximal factors are more predictive of the children's cognitive modifiability than the distal factors. The use of DA within this research framework proved itself as more useful than the static tests. The predictive power of MLE processes is much more powerful when a DA approach, with its inherent learning processes, is implemented. Comparison of the MLE paradigm with other cognitive-developmental approaches (i.e. Bornstein & Tamis-LeMonda, 1990) points to three main advantages of the MLE model. First, the MLE model is *explicitly* based on philosophical assumptions about the nature of cognitive modifiability, and the active role of the change agents in shaping up the development of the child. Second, unlike other atheoretical models which are based on some observed phenomena MLE theory provides us with general theoretical principles that can be applied across different domains, ages, and groups. The third advantage is that the MLE model as a comprehensive model allows practitioners to include, under the same theoretical umbrella, developmental aspects, diagnostic processes, educa-tional intervention programs, and socio-cultural aspects. Thus, MLE processes can be applied, on a *micro level* (i.e. detailed study of specific behaviors) and on the *macro level* (i.e. exploration of transmission of culture from one generation to another). The common theoretical threads across different domains permit inter-disciplinary research within a common conceptual framework.

Mother–child interactions have been studied from different perspectives using a variety of concepts (i.e. responsiveness, demandingness, and scaffolding). However, research derived from these perspectives, while being accurate and predictive of children's cognitive development, is nonetheless, rather limited in scope and nature. Even Vygotsky's theory has not produced research that explored the *specific mediational mechanisms* that contribute to children's cognitive develop-ment. Kozulin and Presseisen (1995) have already commented that "Vygotsky made no attempt to elaborate the activities of human mediators beyond their function as vehicles of symbolic tools. This left considerable lacunae in Vygotsky's theory of mediation" (p. 69).

It is important to note though that Feuerstein and his colleagues do not relate specific parental aspects of mediation to specific cognitive outcomes. According to the MLE theory the effects of mediation are conceived in a holistic way. It is the contribution of other researchers who later on followed the MLE theoretical framework and empirically specified the types of mediations as related to cognitive performance (Klein, 1988, 1996; Tzuriel, 1996, 1998, 1998a, in press-a).

6 Future Research

In this section of the conclusion several questions and cautions are raised regarding future research. First a word of caution: overgeneralization of MLE theory to explain too many phenomena may bring about only the devaluation of the theory.

It is most important, now that the effects of MLE are established, to delineate the conceptual limits of the theory.

An important aspect of the mediational process that needs to be further studied is the role of reciprocity. For example it is important to study not only the effects of mediational process on children's cognitive functioning but also the effects of children's characteristics on parental MLE strategies. The reciprocal effects should be integrated within an ecological framework (i.e. family, social and cultural contexts). Similar conceptions have been discussed in Bronfenbrenner's (1979) ecological approach and Super and Harkness (1986) concept of *developmental niches*.

Other topics which deserve more attention is the role of different family members as mediation agents (fathers, grandparents, siblings), the extent to which MLE processes are generalized across domains or contexts of interactions, whether there are prerequisite factors for becoming an efficient mediator, and the role of parents in *mediation for mediation* (e.g. mediating to the child the need to ask for mediation or provide mediation).

Parts of this manuscript were written while the author was on a Sabbatical leave at the Department of Psychology, York University, Canada. Correspondence and requests for reprints should be addressed to David Tzuriel, School of Education, Bar-Ilan University, Ramat-Gan 52900, Israel. (E-Mail: tzuriel@mail.biu.ac.il) (Fax 972-3-535-3319).

14

A Mediational Approach to Early Intervention

Pnina S. Klein

The mediational approach to early intervention has evolved from the theoretical framework of cognitive modifiability (Feuerstein, 1979, 1980) and its extension and application for use with infants, toddlers, young children and their families (Klein, 1996). Based on this approach it is possible to identify several basic criteria of mother–infant interaction which are necessary determinants of a mediated learning experience. Such experiences are considered prerequisite for young children's capacity to benefit from new experiences. More specifically, to develop cognitive and socioemotional dispositions or needs that enhance learning. These include such basic needs as the need to seek clarity in perception, to associate, compare, contrast, seek out analogies or other relations between things, quest for information beyond what is perceived by the senses, the need to please others, to experience success and to plan and regulate one's own behavior. The relationship between the criteria of parental mediation and children's subsequent development, has been examined in a series of studies, cross culturally and with populations of children with special needs. Research on a mediational approach in work with low SES families and with families of very low weight infants is presented.

1 A Mediational Approach to Early Intervention

The relationship between various parental behaviors and infants' development has been studied widely and intensely. However, available research pertaining to cognitive development does not clarify the specific elements of adult–infant interaction that constitute a learning experience for the child.

There is a theoretical base (Feuerstein, 1979, 1980) and empirical data (Klein, Weider & Greenspan. 1987; Klein, 1988, 1991; Klein & Alony, 1993) suggesting that specific characteristics of adult interaction with children constitute mediational behavior and may effect children's predisposition to learn from new experiences. Mediated learning, as distinct from direct learning through the senses, occurs when the environment is interpreted for the child by another person who understands the child's needs, interests, and capacities, and who takes an active role in making components of that environment, as well as of the past and future experiences, compatible with the child. Mediation affects the individual's present learning and may improve his/her opportunity to learn from future experiences. Basic elements of what constitutes a teaching mediational interaction between a caregiver and a child at any age were identified, based on Feuerstein's (1979, 1980) theory of cognitive modifiability, a summary of available research, and a series of studies carried out by the author. The most salient of these factors were empirically defined (see Table 1) (Klein et al., 1987a, 1987b; Klein, 1988, 1991, 1996).

1.1 How Does Poor Mediation Relate to Learning Problems?

Some differences in children's capacity to benefit from new experiences are linked to the type of interactions they have had with the adults who cared for them. These differences are apparent in the way these children approach new experiences, in the way they integrate them with other experiences, and in the way they express themselves. Some of these children lack the enthusiasm or need to explore their environment, to seek out "newness". They are satisfied with a blurred, undifferentiated picture of their environment. Their eyes and ears are not tuned to detect fine differences between various things they perceive through their senses. In cases of extreme deprivation of mediation they grow up to be uninterested, apathetic, and uninvolved. They do not search for meaning or make spontaneous comparisons between experiences. They relate to bits and pieces of reality rather than form a continuous flow of meaningful experiences. They do not form a link between a cause and its effect, between past, present, and future experiences. Fragmentation in time and space limits one's capacity to benefit from experience, because each experience is "boxed in" in one's mind in isolation from all others. They may have difficulties in bearing in mind a goal or setting a goal for their behavior, especially if such a goal requires several steps for its attainment. They seldom attempt to adjust or plan their behavior in line with the requirements of the task, and, in general, they have difficulties controlling or regulating their own behavior. Many of these children have no need to express themselves verbally or communicate in a way that will be clearly understood by others. They think and speak in an egocentric manner and are frequently unaware of the need to modify their behavior so that others can relate to it.

Some of these children are not aware of the fact that they can obtain information from adults or from other sources beyond what meets their eyes or their other senses. Lacking experiences in which someone related events from them or pointed out information about objects or people beyond what can be perceived directly through the senses, these children are not aware that something meaningful may be obtained through questioning or exploration.

Lacking experiences in which adults associate various objects, people and behavior with meaning or excitement, these children may feel excitement in relation to very few experiences or objects, in a limited range that is primarily associated with the satisfaction of basic physiological needs. Most of these behaviors have been identified by Feuerstein (1979, 1980) as deficient cognitive processes related to poor mediation experiences. Children who have these limitations may be considered as lacking flexibility of mind or as having difficulties in benefiting from new experiences.

Table: Definitions and examples of basic criteria of mediation

Definition of criteria	Examples
Intentionality and reciprocity (focusing behavior): Any act or sequence of acts of an adult that appears to be directed toward affecting a child's perception or behavior. These behaviors are considered reciprocal when the infant or child in the interaction responds, vocally, verbally, or nonverbally.	Selecting, exaggerating, accentuating, scheduling, grouping, sequencing, or pacing stimuli. Talking or handing a toy to a child is seen as intentionality and reciprocity only when it is apparent that the adult's behavior is intentional and not accidental, and when there is an observable response from the child that he or she saw or heard the intentional behavior. Examples of intentionality might include a parent making a visible effort to change his or her behavior and the environment by (a) bringing an object to the child, moving it back and forth, observing the child and continuing to adjust the stimulus until the child focuses on it; (b) by moving a bottle or a particular food item in front of the infant's eyes until he/she focuses on it; (c) placing toys in the bath water; (d) placing oneself in front of the child to obtain eye-to-eye contact; (e) placing objects in front of the child at a distance requiring that he or she will attempt to reach them.
Mediation of meaning (exciting): An adult's behavior that expresses verbal or non-verbal excitement, appreciation, or affect, in relation to objects, animals, concepts, or values.	These behaviors may include facial gestures or paralinguistic expressions (e.g. a sigh or scream of surprise), verbal expressions of affect, classification or labeling, and expressions of valuation of the child's or adult's experience (e.g. "Look, I am washing your foot now", "See how long this macaroni is", "Look at this beautiful flower", or "This cup is special, it belonged to Grandfather").
Transcendence: An adult's behavior directed toward the expansion of a child's cognitive awareness, beyond what is necessary to satisfy the immediate need that triggered the interaction.	Talking to a child about the qualities of the food during feeding is beyond what is necessary to assure provision of nutrition; exploring body parts or the characteristics of water during bathing is not necessary for bathing. Transcendence may be provided through expressions implying inductive and deductive reasoning, spontaneous comparisons, clarifications of spatial and temporal orientation, noting strategies for short- and long-term memory or search and recall memory activities.
Mediating feelings of competence: Any verbal or non-verbal behavior of an adult that expresses satisfaction with a child's behavior and that identifies a specific component or components of the child's behavior that the adult considers contributive to the experience of success.	Such identification can be achieved, for example, by careful timing of a verbal or gestural expression of satisfaction, through repetition of a desired behavior, or through verbal and non-verbal expression (i.e. saying "good", "wonderful", "great", "yes", or clapping hands and smiling when the child successfully completes a task or part of it).
Mediated regulation of behavior: Adult behaviors that model, demonstrate, and/or verbally suggest to the child regulation of behavior in relation to the specific requirements of a task, or to any other cognitive process required prior to overt action.	Behavior is regulated on a mediational basis by the process of matching the task requirements with the child's capacities and interests, as well as through organizing and sequencing steps leading toward success. For example, "It is hot; cool it first before putting it in your mouth", "Let's wash your face carefully, so that no soap will get into your eyes", "Slowly! Not so hard! it is delicate, do it gently", or "First, turn all the pieces over, then search for the right piece". Mediated regulation of behavior may be related to the processes of perception (e.g. systematic exploration, to the process of elaboration (e.g. planning behavior, or to the processes of expressive behavior (e.g. reducing egocentric expressions and regulating intensity and speed of behavior).

Table 2: MISC program: intellectual and social-emotional needs in relation to mediation

Mediation processes	Examples of the process	Intellectual needs	Social-emotional needs
1. Focusing (Intentionality and reciprocity)	Making the environmental stimuli compatible to the child's needs, e.g. bringing closer, covering distractions, repeating, sequencing, grouping, helping the child focus, see, hear and feel clearly.	Need for precision in perception (vs. scanning exploration). Need for precision in expression.	Need to focus on and decode, facial and body expressions of emotion. Need to modify one's own behavior or the environment in order to mediate to others (to make the other person see or understand).
2. Exciting (meaning)	Expressing excitement vocally, verbally, or non-verbally over experiences, objects, people, etc. Naming, identifying.	Need to search for meaningful new experiences (i.e. listen, look, taste things that remind one of past experiences). Need to respond in a way that conveys meaning and excitement (sound, look, and feel excited). Need to invest energy in meaningful activities (along the lines of intrinsic motivation).	
3. Expanding (transcendence)	Explaining, elaborating, associating, and raising awareness to metacognitive aspects of thinking. Relating past, present and future experiences. Relating to physical, logical or social rules and framework.	Need to go beyond what meets the senses. Seek out further information through exploration. Request information from other people and from other sources. Need to seek generalizations. Need to link, associate, recall past information, and anticipate future experiences.	Need to think about one's own feelings and the feelings of others. Need cause and cause-and-effect sequences in social interaction. Need to associate between experiences, recall past information and anticipate future experiences.
4. Encouraging (feelings of competence)	Praise in a way that is meaningful to the child. Clear isolation and identification of the reasons for success. Well timed in relation to the experience.	Need to seek more success experiences. Need to summarize one's own activities and determine what led to success.	Need to please others and gain more mediated feelings of competence. Need to identify what pleases different people. Need to provide others with mediated feelings of competence.
5. Organizing and planning (regulation of behavior)	Regulation with regard to speed, precision, force, and preferred sequence of activities.	Need to plan before acting, e.g. consider possible solutions prior to responding. Clarifying goals, meeting subgoals. Need to pace one's activities. Need to regulate the level of energy invested in any given task.	Need to control one's impulses in social situations. Learn acceptable ways of expressing one's emotions (i.e. regulate the pace and intensity of one's social responses to anger and joy).

In contrast to the children who have suffered from mediational deprivation, most children who have benefited from proper affectionate care and mediation are basically secure and interested both in people and in the world around them. They have developed the need to interact and to share experiences with the caregiver, to focus and perceive clearly, to associate and form links between perceptions, ideas, and behaviors: to choose an objective, to plan and organize their behavior; to seek information, to ask, to explore, and to take different components of reality into consideration. These children are better equipped to learn from other people and from new experiences and to adjust to their human and general environment in any given culture.

1.2 Summary of Research

The MISC (Mediational Intervention for Sensitizing Caregivers) was applied in work with populations of infants at risk and infants of at risk mothers (single parent families, teenage mothers, drug-dependent parents, and other risk factors) (Klein, 1996).

If was found that the factors of quality mediation predicted cognitive outcome measures up to four years of age better than did the children's own cognitive test scores in infancy, or other presage variables related to pregnancy and birth histories and to mothers' education (Klein, Weider & Greenspan, 1986). Similar findings were reported for a sample of very low birth weight infants (Klein et al., 1987a). Intercorrelations between mothers' mediational behaviors over time, when their children were 6, 12, 24 and 36 months, averaged 0.53 and the average interjudge reliability for assessing these behaviors ranged between 0.74 and 0.81 in studies of low socioeconomic status (SES) American (Klein, Weider & Greenspan, 1987b) and Israeli mother–infant samples (Klein, 1988).

Because these studies were correlational and could not lead to cause-and-effect conclusions, another study was designed to examine the sustained effects of modifying the mother–infant mediational interaction on infants' cognitive test performance and behavior. This study will be referred to as the follow-up study.

The research design of the follow-up study included a randomized assignment to the experimental and control groups; an observational assessment of maternal mediation, a "baseline" assessment of the infants' developmental status, using Bayley's Mental Development Scales, prior to training mothers in mediational strategies, and a follow-up evaluation of experimental versus control mothers and children one year and three years after the termination of training.

The total study sample consisted of 68 families in a small, low-SES urban community in Israel, who were randomly assigned at a ratio of approximately 2.5 to 1 to an experimental and control group ($n = 48$ and 20, respectively). This community was singled out for intervention by the Ministry of Education and the Office of Welfare in Israel. Large proportions of children in this community had poor school-readiness records, experienced school failure, and dropped out of school.

Activities developed for the experimental group were based on the MISC Program (Mediational Intervention for Sensitizing Caregivers (Klein, 1996). These activities were designed to improve the mother's mediation to her child. The level of mediation was defined by the frequency of appearance of empirically defined maternal mediating behaviors and their children's responsiveness. The training of mothers was carried out in the homes by paraprofessional "mediators" and supervised by professional developmental psychologists.

The intervention was carried out using a participatory approach in which a series of interactive techniques were applied through video taping and feedback. Parents (or other caregivers) viewed themselves interacting with their own child and afterwards were helped to analyze this interaction according to the basic criteria of mediation.

Intervention in both groups was terminated when mothers could verbally define the basic components of the parental behaviors targeted by the intervention. In the experimental group, these behaviors were represented by the criteria of mediation, and in the control group, by basic aspects of responsive, non-punitive yet demanding environment.

Mediation processes effect children's cognitive input, elaboration, and output processes. It was expected that maternal behaviors of focusing, affecting, and expanding would effect children's vocabulary and abstract reasoning and, in general, prepare children to perform better in situations requiring "new learning", such as tasks requiring immediate sequential memory. Thus, children's cognitive performance was assessed using the following measures: Peabody Picture Vocabulary Test (PPVT), the auditory reception, visual reception, visual association, auditory association and auditory sequential memory of the Illinois Tests of Psycholinguistic Abilities (ITPA), as well as the Beery and Bucktanika Test of visual motor integration.

Comparison of the two groups on the separate components of each mediation factor three years following the intervention, revealed that the experimental-group mothers showed significantly more mediation behaviors across all components of mediation (Klein & Alony, 1993).

Significant differences in favor of the experimental group were found on the PPVT, auditory reception, and auditory association measures. The average PPVT IQ for the experimental group was 101 (SD = 15.5), and for the control group 84 (SD = 14.1).

Of all factors of maternal mediation, *the mother's expanding and rewarding behaviors were most frequently related to children's cognitive performance.* Children's expressions of affect were related more to factors of maternal mediation than any of the other variables of children's behavior, and were mostly related to maternal encouraging behaviors, maternal expansion of ideas, maternal request for affect, and expression of feelings. Focusing behavior was positively and significantly related to all variables of child's expression of affect.

One of the most interesting findings in the follow-up was the relationship found between maternal mediation behaviors and children's test performance. *Mothers' expanding and rewarding behaviors were found to be most frequently correlated*

with children's cognitive measures. Within these two criteria, maternal request for
expansion of ideas (rather than provision of information) *and rewarding with*
explanation (rather than simply saying "good", "fine", etc.) *were singled out as*
most significantly related to the children's cognitive performance at age four. These
findings coincide with those reported by Collins (1984), identifying the variable of
"demandingness" as one of the most essential determinants of the quality of
"good" family environments. The current study provided the possibility of
exploring the effects of various types of "demandingness".

Children's expressions of affect (including naming, nonverbal expression of
feeling, and associating between things) were most significantly related to all
criteria of maternal mediation, but mostly to maternal rewarding behaviors,
maternal expansion of ideas, and maternal request for "affect", that is, for signs of
excitement in relation to some meaningful objects or events. Focusing behavior,
which was not significantly related to any of the cognitive outcome measures was
most significantly related to the child's expression of excitement (i.e. $r = 0.73$)
between maternal focusing of child's attention and the child's spontaneous naming
of objects or things, and $r = 0.58$ between maternal focusing and child's spontaneous provisions of association).

A noteworthy relationship was found between the children and the mothers'
non-verbal expression of feelings. Mothers' expression of feelings were also found
to relate to children's spontaneous provision of rewards to others $r = 0.44$). The
positive relationship of the criteria of mediation to both cognitive outcome
measures and to behavioral assessments is an important finding in itself. It supports
those (i.e. Lazar et al., 1982) who claim that a focus on cognition is not an adequate
criterion for determining the impact of parent–child interaction.

The MISC program applied in the follow-up study was not designed to improve
children's performance on specific cognitive tasks. Yet, three years following the
termination of the intervention, children in the experimental group outscored the
children in the control group with regard to language performance as measured by
the PPVT, and two measures of verbal reasoning. These findings suggest that those
low SES children who participated in the experimental group were brought well
within the normal range of verbal performance.

Mothers in the experimental group expressed higher aspirations for both their
boys' and girls' intellectual growth, but they also expressed a more flexible and
balanced view of what factors were important for their children's future development.

Provision of external rewards is frequently criticized (LeVine, 1980; Lepper, 1981).
In the Klein and Alony (1993) follow-up study, a verbal or gestural praise contributed
favorably to children's cognitive and social-emotional development if it was
accompanied by explanations that related the "success" to its causes or associated
(compared or contrasted) it with other experiences. With regard to rewarding or
encouraging young children, we have to be aware of the pendulum of psychological
"style" and its dangers. Young children depend on adults for mediation of
competence. Quality mediation requires a recognition of children's individual needs,
including those related to the amount and type of reward they may require.

It has been well established in psychoeducational literature that children from poor families generally score lower on a variety of cognitive measures related to intelligence and academic performance as compared to middle-class children. Mothers' intelligence or years of schooling was repeatedly pointed out as a powerful predictor of children's future cognitive performance. The following finding from the MISC intervention and follow-up study are of special interest in view of the above facts. The correlation between mother's years of schooling and their mediation to their infants and young children prior to the intervention was almost identical in the intervention and the comparison (control) group (for the intervention group $r = 0.43$, and for the control group, $r = 0.45$). Three years following the intervention, the correlation between mother's years of schooling and their mediation went down (to 0.21: df = 41; $p > 0.05$) in the intervention group, while remaining almost constant $r = 0.42$; df = 16, $p < 0.05$) for the control group. Furthermore, the correlation between mothers' years of schooling and children's Bayley Mental Scales for both groups prior to the intervention was 0.36 (df = 57; $p < 0.01$). Following the intervention, the correlation between mother's years of school and children's PPVT scores was 0.23 (df = 41; $p > 0.05$) for the intervention group and 0.41 (df = 16; $p > 0.05$) for the control group. These findings suggest that the quality of maternal mediation can be modified and once modified, the link between maternal schooling and mothers' behavior towards her child can be modified as well, resulting in a breakup of the commonly found linkage between mothers' education and children's cognitive achievements. Poor mothers can improve their mediation and contribute to their child's cognitive development as well as middle-class mothers.

1.3 Long-Term Intervention Effects on the Mothers

In a follow-up study carried out six years following the MISC intervention in Israel, it was found that 75% of the mothers in the intervention group (and only a few of the mothers in the control group) found jobs and were working out of home. Working out of home was coupled with higher satisfaction with one's self. This could be viewed, at least partially, as related to the empowerment effect of the intervention. Those mothers who initially viewed themselves as helpless and as having little potential to affect their children's development, as well as their own lives, gained an awareness of some basic elements of effective interaction with others (babies and children were the direct target, but the objective was to improve the process of adult–child interaction). Mothers clearly expressed in interviews or written reports that they began to use the criteria of mediation in their everyday lives in relation to other members of the family as well as friends and authority figures. For example, Jasmin, a 23-year-old mother of two babies, told about her own experience:

> "I used to get up in the morning and start with some chores. By the time it was noon and I had to feed the children, I realized I had not done anything. I would do part of one thing, then go to

another, then remember that I had to finish the first, I was disorganized. When I tried to improve my own mediated regulations of behavior to my son, I realized that I needed it myself. I needed to plan before doing to decide what to do first and what to do later. If I had to buy milk. I checked if there was anything else I needed at the grocery or bank, which is right next to it. This way I saved myself a lot of time and effort. I used to have problems with my neighbor, so I decided to use some mediation of competence. It worked wonders. Now I really see the good in her and she sees the good in me."

The distribution of parent's perception of what they wanted their children to become showed that more parents in the intervention group following the MISC program wanted wiser children, children who can learn better, whereas parents in the comparison group expressed wanting more disciplined children.

Parents who participated in the program expressed feeling more capable of affecting their children's development as compared to parents in the comparison group (Klein & Alony, 1993). Differences in attitudes and aspirations of parents in relation to boys (higher academic aspirations) as compared with girls were less marked in the group that participated in the program as compared to the comparison group. It seems that sex differences became a part of other characteristics of the children that need to be considered and responded to in the process of mediating to them.

It appears that mothers use concepts of mediation criteria and apply those to their benefit in understanding, criticizing or constructing interactions with others. In the three-year follow-up study described earlier, it was clearly demonstrated that significant differences in the quality of mediation occurred following the intervention and that those lasted at least three years following the intervention. Based on mothers' interviews six years following the MISC intervention, it appears that mothers felt more competent about their parenting, as well as their interaction with school authorities and with other adults in general.

1.4 Effects of the MISC on Mother–Infant Attachment

The link between mediational experiences as defined within the framework of the MISC approach and type of attachment as defined by Bowlby (1980) has been more recently established in research (Tal & Klein, 1994). The type of attachment between infants and their mothers at twelve or eighteen months was found to be related to children's subsequent cognitive and social emotional development. Children who were rated as securely attached to their mothers at one year of age were found to score higher on school achievement measures and displayed less adjustment problems in later life as compared to children who were not securely attached (displaying anxious and avoidant attachment). In recent years several intervention programs have been designed in an attempt to prevent attachment problems or reduce their effects (Lyons-Ruth et al., 1990; Lieberman, Weston & Pawl, 1991). These programs are based on a psychotherapeutic approach with some developmental guidance. The MISC approach, designed to enhance the quality of mediation provided to the child, with its special focus on the affective as well as the cognitive components of a mediational interaction, was hypothesized to affect the quality of attachment as well as cognitive development of infants and young children.

The study was conducted in Givat Olga, a small urban community in Israel, located near the city of Hedera. All families who had babies born between February 15, 1990 and February 28, 1991 were contacted and asked if they would be willing to participate in a study of child development that would involve videotaping their babies and discussing their development. Of all mothers contacted, 115 mothers, comprising 75% of the mothers contacted, agreed to participate. Throughout the study 14 of them left for various reasons (moving to another location, illness in the family, mothers going out to work, etc.). The mothers and infants were randomly divided into two groups. Fifty mother–infant pairs in the intervention group, and 51 in the control group. The final sample included 45 boys and 54 girls, equally distributed between the two groups. Of the infants in the study 36% were first-born children. The average number of children per family was three. All the participating infants had normal Bayley Mental Development Scale age scores.

The research design included a pre-assessment, intervention, and a post-assessment. The pre- and post-intervention assessments included a ten minute videotape session of mother–infant free play (analyzed using the Observing Mediational Intervention [OMI]; Klein & Alony, 1993), and an interview designed to obtain basic information about mothers' perception of their children themselves, their potential to affect their children's development, the child's day; and so on. The intervention program for the experimental group was based on the MISC and included eleven individual guidance meetings with the mothers and four videotaping sessions at the mother–infant local health centers.

The intervention proceeded as follows: One videotaping session was followed by three guidance meetings in which the videotape was analyzed in line with the mediation criteria observed. A similar procedure was carried out following the second and third videotaping sessions. Two meetings were scheduled after the fourth and last taping. The taping occurred once every two months and the meetings approximately once very two weeks. The control group had the same number of videotaping sessions as well as meetings, but the discussions about the videotaped sessions focused on general issues related to feeding, motor development, or other questions raised by the mothers. No information was given to the control group mothers regarding the criteria of mediation which are basic components of the MISC.

Following the intervention when the infants were about twelve- to thirteen-months-old, they were videotaped during another ten minutes free play session and in the sequence of short experiences comprising Ainsworth's "Strange Situation" paradigm. Children were assessed again using the Bayley Mental Development Scales. The assessments and rating of attachment were carried out "blindly" (by people unaware of whether children were in the control or experimental group). The findings confirmed the basic hypothesis that improving the quality of mother–infant mediational interaction in the experimental group will reduce the number of anxious attachments in this group. Nine out of 49 children in the experimental group, as compared with 19 out of 50 children in the control group, were found to be anxiously attached. In addition (as was found in the other studies on the effects of the MISC), the experimental group children scored an average of 132 (SD = 9.41) on the Bayley Mental Development Scales as compared to 122 (SD = 9.45) for the control subjects.

The most important factors in mothers' interaction with their infants in relation to attachment was the frequency of her responding to the infants initiatives, especially when the responses appeared together with behaviors which conveyed acceptance and mediated competence to the young children. This study confirmed the possibility of enhancing the learning potential of young children and ensuring a positive, healthy social-emotional adjustment through the application of an intervention designed to enhance the quality of mediation provided to infants during their first year of life.

Positive human emotions, such as feelings of love or elation, are often associated with or result from thoughts which are related in some form with variation of phrases such as: "This is good" or "This is bad".

Parents as well as professionals are more aware of educational goals related to teaching children new skills or ideas, and are less conscious of mediated feelings, directly as well as indirectly through mediation commonly associated with cognitive enhancement. By helping a child "know" or understand, one also helps them differentiate and develop feelings. In this context, parents as mediators have an effect on children's early development through implicitly constructing the experiential pool into which all future experiences will fall and be coded.

With the emergence of the child's language skills, parents rely more on words to effect emotional development through mediational behaviors of affecting and expanding (i.e. labeling, explaining, and associating).

1.5 The MISC with Very Low Birth Weight Infants and Young Children

Very Low Birth Weight (VLBW) infants are considered to be "at risk" for developmental difficulties and have been found to be highly susceptible to variations in the quality of the environment in which they live. The current section summarizes the results of a series of studies involving a population of VLBW Israeli children and their parents, and a follow up study with the same population three years following the MISC intervention.

1.1.1 Study 1

A study by Klein et al. (1987a) was designed to compare the performance of 42 VLBW three-year-olds with two control groups, one composed of their siblings (15 children), and another composed of 40 normal-birth-weight children, on a series of cognitive measures, including several subtests of the Wechsler Intelligence Scale for Children-Revised (WISC-R), the Illinois Test of Psycholinguistic Abilities (ITPA), and the Developmental Test of Visual Motor Integration. The study was also intended to assess the relationship between the quality of parental interaction and cognitive performance of children born weighing below 1.5 kg, which is considered the cutoff point for infants at special risk of nonsurvival and/or of a developmental lag.

Parents' quality of interaction with their children was assessed using the Observing Mediational Intervention (OMI) method (Klein, 1996).

VLBW children were found to perform as well as their siblings and the normal-birth-weight control group on most of the cognitive measures used, with the exception of auditory sequential memory (ASM) on the ITPA and understanding of word meaning, as measured by the Peabody Picture Vocabulary Test (PPVT).

The observational measure of the quality of parent–child interaction based on mediational criteria was found to correlate with cognitive performance of the VLBW subjects (Klein, 1988), whereas no significant correlations were found between birth weight and those same cognitive measures. In other words, the quality of parent–child interaction was a better predictor of these children's mental development than their birth weight. Study 1 was the first in which mediational observation was applied with VLBW subjects. Based on the findings of this study, the OMI was found to contribute to the prediction of cognitive performance of VLBW children.

1.1.2 Study 2

Correlations between the quality of mediation and test performance of the VLBW subjects found in Study 1 were deemed sufficient for drawing conclusions regarding a cause-and-effect relationship between these variables. In order to examine the latter relationship. VLBW subjects in Study 1 were randomly divided into an experimental and a control group. No significant differences were found between the intervention and control groups on all background variables. The average birth weight of the intervention group was 1.207 g (SD = 246) and of the control group, 1.231 g (SD = 170).

The MISC intervention was offered to all participating parents of VLBW subjects in the experimental group. The objective of this intervention was to improve the quality of parent–child interaction in the VLBW group and to assess the effects of this intervention on the children.

The intervention began with two observations of parent–child interactions at home. Each observation included a feeding, a bathing, and a play session with the child. Based on the observational data, a profile of results for the five primary mediational criteria was constructed for each mother–child dyad. A trained mediator described and clarified to the mother those criteria on which she had shown evidence of constructive interactions with her child. Only later were these criteria related to those that needed to be encouraged and reinforced. Mediators did not come into the subjects' homes with a set of preplanned exercises or toys. They related to what was available in the home and to the ongoing content of mother–child interaction at that time. Indicators of success of the intervention were (a) change in mothers' behavior toward the children as measured by an increase in the frequency of the occurrence of behaviors exemplifying the basic criteria of mediation, and (b) improvement in mothers' ability to verbalize basic aspects of a quality interaction. The intervention took place over a period of seven months, with most families receiving home visits every month to six weeks, depending upon the extent of mediation shown in the initial home profile. One year after the intervention, the quality of parent–child interaction was found to have improved significantly on all five of the primary criteria of quality interaction. Furthermore, test scores of the VLBW subjects in the experimental group were shown to be consistently higher than those of the control group, although none of these differences reached statistical significance. On two measures (ASM and PPVT), VLBW subjects in the experimental group scored as well as or better than their siblings or normal controls. In contrast, it should be noted that prior to the intervention, members of the VLBW group had scored significantly lower than the other groups on both of these measures. Following the intervention, parents of small for gestational age (SGA) children, who are typically viewed as most at risk, interacted with their children better than did parents of VLBW children who were born appropriate for gestational age (AGA).

1.1.3 Study 3

Three years after the intervention described in Study 2, when the children were six years old, the families were visited again by graduate students trained in observation and testing procedures, and who were unfamiliar with the family visited. Of the original 42 families of VLBW subjects in Study 1, 36 families were contacted, and 29 of them agreed to participate in the follow-up study. It should be noted that all the parents in the experimental group who could be reached agreed to participate; four families could not be located, and two parents in the control group refused to participate because their children "were in special education classes and were over-tested already".

The quality of mediation was assessed using the OMI at the homes of each family. Mothers were asked to play with their children with a puzzle task using an eighty-piece puzzle brought by the observer. In addition, the children were individually tested in their homes on the following measures: the Vocabulary and

Similarities Subtests of the WISC-R, PPVT, Draw a Person, the Developmental Test of Visual Motor Integration, and the Auditory Sequential Memory Test of the ITPA. Mothers were asked to evaluate their children's performance and to rate them on a five-point scale with regard to language development, gross and fine motor co-ordination, and sociability.

The effects of the intervention on the quality of mother–child interaction persisted three years after the intervention. Significant differences were found between the mothers in the intervention group and the control group on each of the five criteria of mediation. All differences were in favor of the intervention group.

The VLBW experimental group showed significantly more spontaneous sharing of information with their mothers than did the control group, and spontaneously pointed out more associations between things, than the control group.

No significant differences in performance of VLBW children in the intervention group as compared to the control group were found on most of the cognitive measures, with the exception of the PPVT. However, a consistent trend in favor of the experimental group was found on all the seven measures used in this study. Similarly, no differences were found between the SGA and AGA following the intervention.

Comparing the children's scores on the cognitive measures one and three years after the intervention in the experimental and control groups, and for the SGA and AGA groups, revealed that on the auditory sequential memory test the SGA children in the intervention group scored higher than those in the control group, and higher than the AGA subjects in both the experimental and control groups. In other words, the group of children that were expected to do worse achieved the highest scores following the intervention.

Mothers' evaluation of their children's performance with regard to language, gross- and fine-motor co-ordination, and sociability, revealed that more children in the control group, as compared to the intervention group, had difficulties in these areas. At Follow-up 1 (one year following the intervention), 5 children in the intervention group were rated by their parents as having language problems, as compared with 5 in the control group. At Follow-up 2 (three years following the intervention), 2 children in the intervention group and 5 in the control group were rated as having such problems. One child in the intervention group and 4 in the control group were rated as having gross-motor co-ordination difficulties on Follow-up 1, and none was rated as such in either group on Follow-up 2. As for the fine-motor co-ordination, none of the intervention group children and 4 of the controls were rated as having difficulties one year following the intervention, and none of the intervention children and 2 of the control group children were rated as having fine-motor problems three years following intervention. Regarding sociability ratings, 1 child in the intervention group and 2 of the control group were rated as having sociability difficulties on Follow-up 1. Three years following the intervention there was still 1 child in the intervention group and 4 in the control group who were rated as having sociability problems. Two of the children in the control group and one of the children in the intervention group were attending special education classes three years following the intervention. It should be noted that the children in special education classes were not tested because of parental refusals to participate in the follow-up.

1.6 Summary

The MISC intervention was designed (a) to enhance the quality of interaction between parents and their children who were born at VLBW consequently, (b) to improve the children's cognitive performance. Despite the fact that the intervention was not intensive (one home visit every four or six weeks), it was found to have a significant and long-lasting effect upon parents' behavior. Three years after the intervention, intervention group mothers showed more focusing, exciting, expanding, rewarding, and regulating behaviors as compared to control group mothers. The differences between parents in the intervention and control groups appeared to grow over the years with regard to the amount of mediated encouragement and expansion of ideas. Learning the criteria of mediation apparently sensitized parents in the intervention group to notice more opportunities for mediation of competence and transcendence as their children approached school age. Parental expanding and rewarding behaviors appeared to be predictive of young children's cognitive performance at a later age more than most of the other criteria of mediation (Klein et al., 1987b). Thus, it may be expected that the intervention group will continue to perform better than the control group on various cognitive tasks. It appears that for the population of parents of VLBW children, even a brief intervention enhancing parental awareness of the determinants of a quality interaction is sufficient to produce long-lasting changes in the quality of their interaction with their children. In other populations, such as low-SES families, the same objective required a more intensive intervention (Klein & Alony, 1993).

The effectiveness of the intervention described in the current study could also be related to the *how* of the intervention in addition to the *what*. In every home visit, the mediators used all the basic criteria of mediation in their own interactions with the parent. The meetings between the parent and the mediator consisted of quality interactions (i.e. focusing, exciting, expanding, rewarding, and regulatory behaviors). Parents were guided to do what they did naturally with their children, but with greater awareness of the potent factors within each interaction. Several of the mothers in the intervention group remarked that following the intervention they had gained more confidence in what they were doing with their children, had more patience, and enjoyed the children more than before. One of the mothers said:

> "I always wanted to do more for my child, I was told to stimulate, so I showed her things and spoke to her, but once I caught her attention I did not know what to do … I took another object and again tried to catch her attention. Now I know how to make things excite her. I show her what they mean, how to find other things like them, or how to connect one experience with others she has had in the past."

No differences were found between the groups following intervention with regard to the number of items listed in response to the question "What can be done to enhance a child's cognitive development?" It is interesting to note, however, that whereas control group parents listed what could be done *to the child*, parents who participated in the intervention repeatedly referred to the need to *match* what they want to do with the child's needs, capacities, and preferences.

Parents in the SGA group were found to provide their children with significantly more intentionality and reciprocity, more mediated feelings of competence, and more regulation of behavior than the parents of the AGA group. A possible explanation of these findings could be related to the fact that the VLBW children born SGA have been found to be more at risk than VLBW AGA infants. Parents of at-risk infants were reported to increase their mediational efforts in line with their perceptions of the urgency of their infants' position. Extra parental efforts to enhance the development of the smaller, apparently weaker babies were discussed previously by Field et al. (1982) in their report on the early development of preterm discordant twins. The finding regarding higher levels of parental mediation provided to SGA as compared to AGA children could at least be partially related to the fact that the SGA babies in the current study stayed in the hospital an average of 8.5 days longer than did the AGA babies. During this period and the follow-up visits, the parents were instructed to interact with the babies and to stimulate them, particularly in face-to-face interactions. The parents' sharpened awareness of the infants' need for interaction and the greater urgency of their condition could have increased the SGA mothers' behaviors directed toward focusing, rewarding, and regulating the children's attention. It is interesting to note that the SGA parents did not provide their children with more mediation of meaning, nor did they expand and explain more than the AGA parents. Parental concern to be active and enhance their children's development was not sufficient to produce differences with regard to expanding and exciting behaviors (transcendence and mediation of meaning). Apparently, a change in mediation regarding the latter criteria requires more than a natural concern or general instructions to stimulate the child (i.e. to do more for or with the child).

The population of VLBW children in the current study was originally found to perform as well as their siblings and normal controls on all measures of cognitive performance, with the exception of ASM and vocabulary. Following the intervention, no differences were found between the experimental group and the control group with regard to most of the measures, including ASM. All VLBW subjects appeared to function on norm on the ASM measure. The intervention group did, however, score higher than the control group on the vocabulary measure (PPVT). Considering the central role of language and verbal intelligence in cognitive performance of children, this finding is of extreme importance.

In a follow-up study (Klein & Alony, 1993) of normal birth weight, low-SES infants and their families who had received the same intervention as described in this study, it was found that an improvement in the quality of maternal mediating behavior not only affected children's performance on language and reasoning measures, but also increased children's spontaneous naming of things and the expressions of relationships or associations between various objects and behaviors. These children requested more information, showed more excitement, and spontaneously used more verbal rewards for other people's performance. In short, all these behaviors actually mirror the type of mediating behaviors used by their parents. It is possible that these behaviors of spontaneously sharing or mediating to others found in the experimental group children may affect the ease and quality of their social interactions with their parents, as well as with teachers and peers throughout their development. This possibly is especially important in light of the finding that VLBW subjects are rated as passive, withdrawn, or shy (Bjerre & Hansen, 1976; Wallace, 1984). If the current intervention affected the children in the direction of more spontaneous, meaningful verbal interchange, the outcome of the intervention may be more significant when the child will be found in more and more situations in which learning and social adjusting require enhanced active participation in social interaction.

Although the criteria of mediation may be regarded as criteria of maternal teaching behaviors and, as such, focus on cognitive aspects of development, achieving quality mediation implies creating a good match between the adult's intention to interact with the child and the child's needs and interests. This basic requirement, combined with the criterion of sharing excitement (mediating meaning) and encouraging the child (mediating competence), could be considered as important contributors to a supportive parent–child relationship with the potential to affect emotional as well as cognitive development.

In conclusion, the quality of parental mediation can be modified. The gains in mediation are sustained over time and are associated with lower frequencies of anxious mother–infant attachment and improved children's cognitive functioning. Higher frequencies of mediation, specifically of expansion and of request for meaning as well as of mediated competence, are related to better cognitive performance in young children from low SES families. Modification of mediational patterns provided to children born at very low birth weight resulted in improved mediation including a decrease in the amount of repeated ("unused") focusing behaviors and an increase in the frequency of more elaborate forms of mediation, building upon the initial focusing attempts. Verbal skills and sequential memory which were repeatedly reported as areas of difficulty for very low birth weight children were found to improve as a result of enhanced parental mediation. It may thus be concluded that a focus on parental mediation adds predictive power to early assessment and may provide important information for planning early interventions.

15

The Diversity of Instrumental Enrichment Applications

Alex Kozulin

1 Introduction

Instrumental Enrichment (IE) is a cognitive intervention program developed by Feuerstein et al. (1980) with the aim of correcting the deficient cognitive functions and enhancing the learning potential of adolescents and adults. This is a theory-based program derived from Feuerstein's (1990) theories of structural cognitive modifiability and mediated learning experience. IE materials include 14 booklets of paper-and-pencil tasks aimed at creating in students cognitive prerequisites of learning and developing their learning strategies. IE booklets cover such domains as analytic perception, orientation in space and time, principles of comparison and classification, and so on. Teaching IE presupposes special didactics based on the principles of mediated learning which emphasize intentionality of teacher/student interaction, transcendence of the principles discovered in the course of study, mediation of meaning, and a number of other parameters elaborated by Feuerstein (1990).

Even before the publication of the first edition of the *Instrumental Enrichment* book (Feuerstein et al. 1980), several researchers trained at the Hadassah-WIZO-Canada Research Institute in Jerusalem initiated studies aimed at validating the IE methodology and applying it in different settings and with different populations. At the present moment the bibliography of IE based research and implementation studies includes several hundreds items. It would be impossible and unnecessary to attempt a comprehensive review of all these studies in this chapter. My aim here is to present a selected sample of programs as an illustration of the directions in the development of IE based studies. The period covered here is from 1980. Programs in the following major areas of application are included:

- Learning disabled students;
- Children with special learning disabilities, such as reading problems;
- Normal low achieving students;
- Gifted students;
- Culturally different and minority students;
- Blind and deaf learners.

2 Learning-Disabled Students

The most obvious area of implementation of the IE programs is the remedial teaching of socially disadvantaged, special education students. In the US a large scale systematic attempt to evaluate the effect of the IE program on such a group was undertaken by Jensen and Singer (1987) in 1982–1987. The target group in this study included 13–17-year-old special education students from the inner city schools of two school districts in Connecticut. The average baseline IQ of the participating students was 74–76. Students were tested at the mid-point of the study about one year after it started, and post-tested at the end of the study which took two to three years to accomplish. Altogether 142 students participated in the mid-point testing, and 121 at the end of the study. Students from the control group received a regular special education curriculum.

The general hypothesis of the authors was that the IE program recipients would outperform controls when confronted with novel intellective tasks and school subject matter. The students' performance data were analyzed in terms of acquisition, near transfer, and far transfer. The task of acquisition included IE materials familiar to the student adapted to a test format. For the assessment of the near transfer of cognitive strategies learned through IE certain intellective tasks such as the subtests of Thurstone PMA, the French Kit and subsequent parts of IE material were used. For the assessment of the far transfer more advanced parts of IE material in the test form were used, as well as the French Kit and the tests of vocabulary and mathematics.

The mid-point examination revealed that those students who received one year or less of IE outperformed, on a statistically significant level, the control group in acquisition and near transfer, but not in far transfer. Those students who at the mid-point had more than one year of IE outperformed the control group in all three categories. This result not only substantiated the author's general hypothesis, but also confirmed earlier observations that the true benefits of the IE program for special education students should not be expected until the second year of the enrichment program.

For the analysis of the end-of-study data two groups of experimental subjects were identified: those who attended more than 70% of IE lessons and those who attended less than 70%. The first group was designated as a High-IE, and the second one as a Low-IE group. When the results of intellective tests were compared, the High-IE group was found significantly more advanced than the Low-IE group in all three categories: acquisition, near transfer and far transfer. This rather clear result was, however, complicated by the fact that in the far transfer No-IE controls scored better than the Low-IE group. Moreover, though High-IE did significantly better than the control group on the vocabulary test, the controls outperformed them in mathematics. These discrepancies in the far transfer results posed a more fundamental question of the relationship between cognitive modification associated with IE and performance in the academic content areas. On the one hand proficiency in solving the IE type problems is not a goal in itself, therefore success in the acquisition is not enough. After all, the ultimate goal of the

IE program is to increase students' cognitive modifiability in such a way that they benefit more from direct exposure to learning materials. At the same time, it would be naïve to expect dramatic changes in students' academic performance if the regular curriculum is not co-ordinated with the IE program. The authors suggested that the failure of the IE program to consistently influence the far transfer is associated with the absence of a coherent special education curriculum in the schools where the research project was carried out.

There is also an interesting "discrepancy" between the students' performance data, which is only mildly optimistic regarding the effect of IE, and teachers' questionnaires data. Teachers were asked to fill 30-item questionnaires rating students on items derived from cognitive functions IE was supposed to address (e.g. spontaneous comparative behavior, uses of past experience and projections into the future, etc.). Teachers' responses yielded four factors corresponding to Input, Elaboration, and Output phases, and the Cognitive Control factor which together accounted for 72.65% of variation. A statistically significant difference in the improvement of performance along these four factors was established between High-IE and Low-IE students. The authors claim that prolonged observation enables teachers to register data regarding their students which is difficult to collect from direct measurement of student performance. That is why there is reason to believe that the effect of IE is actually stronger than is shown in direct measures.

The authors conclude that, as scissors indeed have two blades, the effective functioning of the child will require both good cognitive skills and a knowledge base on which they can be applied (Jensen, 1990). We cannot but agree with this conclusion. One of the major problems in the application of IE with learning-disabled or/and socially disadvantaged populations lies in the fact that often content learning does not provide the necessary support for developing cognitive functions. When a student does not receive material to which the "bridging" from IE can be done, there is little hope for progress in content areas.

Another large scale study was conducted by Mulcahy and Associates (1994) on behalf of the Department of Education of Alberta, Canada. Altogether 900 fourth- and seventh-grade students participated in the study, among them approximately 200 learning-disabled students. A student was defined as learning-disabled if his or her verbal and non-verbal scores in the Canadian Cognitive Abilities test were within one standard deviation of the mean, while his or her achievement scores were one standard deviation or more below the mean on the reading sub-scale of the Canadian Achievement Test.

The project tested the effectiveness of two cognitive intervention Programs — IE and SPELT (The Strategies Program for Effective Learning/Thinking). The major difference between these programs is that while IE is a general strategies program that has its own learning material, SPELT is a content-based program. SPELT program teachers taught their students learning strategies, strategy transfer and strategy generation using content material of mathematics and language. Students in the IE and SPELT program classes received 120 minutes of cognitive intervention per week for a period of two school years. The time for IE lessons was usually taken from the pool of language hours. Students in the control classes received the regular program. Effectiveness of the programs was assessed through testing in the following areas: Cognitive abilities; Academic achievement in reading and mathematicsz; Affective perceptions including perceived competence, self-concept and locus of control; Cognitive strategies and metacognitive awareness.

The results demonstrated no influence of either one of the programs on cognitive ability as measured by the Canadian Cognitive Abilities Test that included verbal, non-verbal, and quantitative tasks. IE proved to be effective in improving the students' mathematics concepts, reading strategies in the 4th graders and mathematics-problem solving strategies in the 7th graders. There was also a shift toward internal locus of control in the 4th graders. At the same time SPELT was effective in improving mathematics concepts in the 4th graders, reading comprehension, reading strategies, comprehension monitoring, and mathematics problem-solving strategies. One should be cautious in interpreting these general results because in some of the areas (e.g. in mathematics concepts) improvement observed at the end of the program disappeared one year later.

One may conclude that both IE and SPELT were effective in promoting learning strategies in learning-disabled students. There was also some influence on academic achievement especially in mathematics. There is no surprise in the fact that the SPELT program seemed to be more effective in promoting reading strategies. Being a content-based program SPELT promoted, during the language lessons, those strategies that would be tested at the end of the program. At the same time IE lessons were given at the expense of language hours. The authors of the study consider their results warranting recommendation to include cognitive education lessons into the school curriculum as one of its integral parts.

One of the primary tasks of the IE program when applied to learning-disabled children is the remediation of deficient cognitive functions. Therefore, the researcher's task is not only to ascertain the effect of IE as manifested in the gross improvement in the intellective and motivational spheres, but also to identify changes in specific cognitive functions. This has been done by Beasley (1984; see also Shayer & Beasley, 1987). Deficient functions were identified with the help of the LPAD procedure before and after the 18 months of IE intervention. Altogether 14 cognitive functions belonging to the Input (3), Elaboration (6) and Output (5) phases were assessed. It was discovered that learning-disabled students who received IE indeed showed significant improvement in terms of cognitive functions. Particularly significant improvement was observed in the need for logical evidence.

Another important parameter discovered in the Shayer and Beasley (1987) study was the relative improvement in standard and mediated performance on the Raven test. Students who received IE (experimental group) and the control group were pre- and post-tested with the Raven test both under mediated learning assessment conditions and standard conditions. Pre- and post-tests were one year apart. The results of the Raven test were expressed in mental age units. The difference for the experimental group between standard pre-and post-test was 1.9 years, while for the control group it was 1.0 year. The difference for the experimental group between the mediated pre- and post-test was 1.7 years while for the control group it was 0.2

years. These data indicate that the experimental group not only improved its performance under standard conditions, but what is more important it significantly increased its ability to learn and benefit from assistance. This can be expressed in Vygotsky's (1986) terminology as a significant advancement of the upper limit of the Zone of Proximal Development. For the control group this upper limit changed insignificantly (0.2 years) while for the group that received IE it surged ahead for 1.7 years. This upward movement indicates that one of the major objectives of the IE program for learning-disabled children — the improvement of the ability to learn — has been achieved.

Apart from general cognitive enrichment of learning-disabled students some specific areas of deficiency, such as impulsivity, can be remediated. In a study of Niles (1989) 30 black adolescents with impulsivity problems from the residential treatment center in the state of New York received 20 weeks of IE lessons, two lessons per week. The author reports a statistically significant improvement from pre- to post-test in the control of impulsivity as measured by Kagan Matching Familiar Figures Test. Improvement occurred both in terms of latency of responses and the number of errors. There was also an improvement in the cognitive sphere as measured by the Raven Standard Matrices.

3 Dyslexia and Reading Problems

Since deficiency of the cognitive functions described by Feuerstein et al. (1980, Chapter Four) manifests itself in a variety of areas including those essential for proficient reading it was hypothesized that the IE program can be beneficial for children with reading problems. In a study conducted by Sanchez Pietro (1991) 47 eight-year-old students from a rural public school in Spain were selected based on their low scores on the test of language which measured spoken language, written language, vocabulary, and grammar skills. The experimental (25 students) and control (22 students) groups were matched on such parameters as age, IQ, and socio-economic status.

The experimental group was given three hours of IE per week for a period of three years. The following IE instruments were used: Organization of Dots, Orientation in Space I, Comparisons, Analytic Perception, Categorization, Temporal Relations, Instructions. In addition to these instruments, the author designed special materials facilitating the transfer of IE tasks to language.

At the end of the three-year period students were post-tested on the intelligence and language tests. There was a statistically significant difference in the improvement of the performance of the experimental group both in verbal and intellectual areas. The test of reading demonstrated differential improvement in all four language areas but particularly in vocabulary and grammar. Verbal IQ as measured by WISC was significantly higher in the experimental group in vocabulary, comprehension, and similarities.

Another study of IE intervention with children who have reading problems has been reported by Kaplan (1990). The comparison of this study with the previous one can be instructive for those who wish to apply the IE program with children who have reading problems. Kaplan (1990) selected 20 nine–ten-year-old students on the basis of their impulsivity reflected in the low reading scores on the Neale's (1973) Analysis of Reading Ability Scale. Ten students constituted an experimental group and ten students a control group. The experimental group received two IE sessions per week for a period of twelve weeks. Bridging to reading ability was undertaken with the help of Boning's (1982) "reading for the main idea" materials. The experimental group students received Organization of Dots and one page from Illustrations ("Stirring up a hornet's nest").

When the author used *t*-test she was unable to identify any significant differences between the performance of the control group and the experimental group after intervention. The result of the covariance analysis indicated, however, that the experimental group improved its reading performance in accuracy and comprehension. Children in this group also seemed to become less impulsive than those in the control group as measured by Porteus Mazes test. At the same time the control group improved its reading speed significantly more than the experimental one. The author suggests that fast readers are not necessarily good readers, and that the experimental group may actually read at a speed which is better for accuracy and comprehension. It is implied that the higher speed of reading of the control group may reflect their higher level of impulsivity. This suggestion is not very convincing because reading accuracy and comprehension in the control group also improved though not to the same degree as in the experimental group.

One may conclude that though short term IE intervention (12 weeks) may bring some improvement to reading performance, it is firmly advised to follow the standard IE intervention format — at least two years of intervention involving a wider range of IE instruments. Only then can one expect significant results.

4 Low Achieving Students

Another large group which may benefit from the IE program is the group of lower achieving normal students. It is believed that lower achievement, apart from other factors, is determined by inadequate development of cognitive skills.

In a study of Ruiz (1985; see also Savell, Twohig & Rachford, 1986) ten — fourteen-year-old students from higher and lower socio-economic status (SES) groups participated for 2 years in the IE program. They studied 5 hours per week, for a total of 275 hours. The effectiveness of the IE program was assessed with the help of pre- and post-tests of general intellectual abilities (Cattell-II), academic performance in mathematics and language, and in self-concept. The experimental IE group (318 students) was compared to the control group of equal size. The author reports statistically significant gains for the experimental group in all three spheres: general intellectual abilities, academic performance and the self-concept.

Before intervention the higher-SES group showed higher results in all three spheres. Some difference remained after intervention, but both groups improved their performance. As to intellectual abilities, both groups benefited equally, while in academic performance the higher-SES group benefited more. It is interesting that pre-test differences in self-concept disappeared after intervention. Since one of the major concerns of any cognitive education program is its long term effect, the follow-up studies are quite important. Ruiz (1985) undertook such a study 2 years later with a sample of 57 matched pairs of students from the experimental and control groups. In this case the pre- and post-test measure was a non-verbal intelligence test of Lorge-Thorndike. Both low and high-SES experimental groups continued to outperform the controls. Moreover, 80% of the experimental group students who were at the top of the group during the pre-test 2 years earlier continued to remain at the top, while only 44% of the students in the control group retained their top position. These data indicate that those students who gained most from IE continued to perform better after the IE program had ended.

Another large scale IE intervention program for low achieving students is reported by Alvarez et al. (1992). The authors selected a group of 246 low achieving students from 5, 6, and 7 grades in Puerto Rico's public schools eligible for enrichment programs. Half the students ($N = 23$) received the IE program for one, two or three years. The control group received an ordinary enrichment program. The experimental group that studied IE for three years finished all 14 instruments, the two-year program — 11 instruments, and the one-year program — 7 instruments. Experienced IE counselors visited each participating school at least eight times and evaluated the teacher's style and mediational input with the help of a special scale. Pre- and post-testing of experimental and control groups included Raven Standard Matrices and the Cattell's Intelligence Test (Form A and B).

The authors report a statistically significant difference between experimental and control groups in the intellectual performance measured both by Raven and Cattell post-tests. They also report differences in experimental group performance depending on the length of IE intervention. There is a significant gain in Raven's scores between first and second year, with less improvement during third year. Cattell-A scores demonstrated insignificant improvement from the first to second year and significant gains during the third. Cattell-B scores grew steadily from the first to second and third year almost in equal proportion.

Teachers' style and ability to mediate was assessed on the basis of reports filed by IE-counselors. Then the performance of groups that received IE with appropriate mediation were contrasted with those which received inappropriate mediations as judged by IE-counselors' reports. Statistically significant differences were found in the performance of these two groups, especially as measured by Cattell Tests. The authors also report preliminary data on better performance in mathematics tests by the experimental group that received three years of IE.

The above studies help to formulate certain guidelines for the successful use of the IE program with low achieving normal students: (a) The length of the intervention should be at least two years; (b) A wide range of IE instruments should be used; (c) The teacher's mediation style should be monitored by experienced IE counselors.

The last point, namely the mediational style of the teacher is of paramount importance. Though IE instruments are devised in such a way that mere exposure to them may have a positive effect on a student, still the essence of the IE program lies in the combination of instruments and mediation. In this respect some interesting observations on teachers' attitudes and their instructional style can be gleaned from Blagg's (1991) study in which he reports no improvement in low achievers' performance under the influence of IE. We will focus on the teacher's aspect, since other aspects of Blagg's study have already been critically reviewed by Haywood (1992).

Firstly, Blagg reports that teachers had difficulty getting students involved in conversation and discussion of IE materials because the instructional style in their school was not conducive to student discussion. This observation touches upon a serious problem. If the teacher who just started teaching IE, as was the case in Blagg's and other studies, continues to use non-mediational and authoritarian style in his/her teaching of other subjects this conveys an ambivalent message to students. IE appears unconnected to other subjects, not only in content, but also in its form of presentation. Instead of being a source of change in thinking IE, under such conditions, remains a "stranger" within the curriculum. This possibility is confirmed by another of Blagg's observations, namely that teachers had serious problems bridging IE material to everyday life. Students did not want to participate in bridging, instead they worked with IE materials as abstract puzzles. This observation indicates that teachers failed to convey to the students the meaning of the IE lesson. At the same time it also indicated that students, probably, resisted changing their learning attitudes because IE attitudes were not reinforced during content lessons taught by the same teachers. Finally, teachers complained that participation in the IE program requires too much preparation: "up to two hours homework". This remark reveals the general attitude of participating teachers who apparently do not consider serious lesson preparation as a natural part of their professional activity. Such an attitude implies that teachers rely primarily on the ready-made instructional materials or standard recitation. One can hardly expect an appropriate mediational style in a teacher with such an attitude toward instruction.

5 Culturally-Different Immigrant and Minority Students

It is important to remember that the initial stimulus for the development of the IE program came from the realization of the fact that immigrant and minority children have special learning needs (Feuerstein et al., 1980). Many of these children, though second generation immigrants, still experienced serious difficulties at school. Moreover, conventional remediation and enrichment programs which focused on content subject material often failed to produce any substantial change in the minority students' performance (Rand, Tannenbaum & Feuerstein, 1979).

The IE program offers an essentially different orientation placing emphasis on the acquisition of general learning strategies which are the core prerequisite for any formal learning. Such an emphasis is particularly important for culturally-different students whose native culture (or sub-culture) does not foster formal learning mechanisms. Another aspect of the IE program which has particular importance for culturally-different students is its saturation with various graphic-symbolic devices (schemas, tables, graphs, plans and maps). These graphic-symbolic devices provide the basis for psychological tools (Vygotsky, 1986) which under regular conditions are acquired by children in the course of their "natural" learning experiences, and which are often missing in culturally-different students.

There are three major populations of culturally-different students who received the IE program: new immigrant students; minority students; and adult immigrants in the job training programs. In the study of Debrey (1994) a group of adolescents the majority of whom were immigrants to France from Asia and Africa received the IE program for two years. Although the overall cognitive achievements of the IE group were only slightly better than in the control group, case studies of several new immigrant students demonstrated significant change in the attitude toward formal learning and the ability to benefit from it. The author claims that it was exactly through the participation in the IE lessons that immigrant adolescents became reintegrated into the school system. Somewhat similar results were obtained by Crotti (1993) in her work in Switzerland with educationally-deprived immigrant adolescents from Portugal, Spain and Kosovo (former Yugoslavia).

An Israeli study (Kozulin, 1995) of the influence of IE on the cognitive development of new immigrants from Ethiopia was conducted in a somewhat different context. Thousands of Ethiopian Jews arrived in Israel as a group first in the mid-1980s and more recently during the course of the dramatic airlift "Operation Solomon" in 1991. The integration of Ethiopian immigrant children in the Israeli educational system was planned on the national level, and included special intensive Hebrew training programs ("ulpanim") and supplementary lessons at school. It turned out, however, that the lack of previous educational experience continued to hamper the new immigrant students' progress even after they acquired basic Hebrew. LPAD group assessment confirmed that there is a serious gap between the new immigrant students' high learning potential and low performance level (Kaniel et al., 1991). In the study reported here (Kozulin, 1995) 15 adolescent girls started receiving the IE program three years after their arrival in Israel. At the time of IE intervention all of them were placed in a special "immigrants" class in one of Jerusalem's boarding schools. The IE program was taught for two academic years, four hours per week for a total of approximately 220 hours. IE teaching was augmented by "bridging" exercises which linked the principles acquired in the course of IE lessons to the tasks of content lessons and everyday life experiences.

During the course of intervention certain specific cognitive and learning characteristics of the participating students were identified. At the beginning of the program students demonstrated an insufficient knowledge base and poor under-standing of such superordinate concepts as size, form, origin, use, etc. The concepts like "degree of similarity" or "mistake" had to be taught through special learning activities. The students were also poorly prepared for the use of contemporary learning materials which employ a great variety of graphic-symbolic devices such as tables, graphs, charts, etc. These devices had to be specially explained to the students. During the learning process the students needed special help in the following areas: Defining the problem in the field of data; separating the problem domain from the domain of possible answers; working with several sources of information; and planning their own actions. In the field of language acquisition the students revealed significant disparity between relatively quick and successful acquisition of communicative speech and protracted problems with comprehension of abstract concepts. Observations made during IE lessons resulted in recommendation for content subject teachers. These recommendations focused on the necessity to identify cognitive elements of content material teaching and teaching these elements first using simpler content, and only then to introduce more difficult content. Apart from teachers' observations the occurrence and magnitude of cognitive change was assessed by the Raven Standard Progressive Matrices test at the beginning and at the end of intervention. The change from pre-test to post-test was statistically significant. Moreover, while the IE group reached at the post-test the normative level of Israeli students, the matching non-IE group stayed at the much lower level.

A number of studies conducted in South Africa should be considered as occupying an intermediate position between IE programs for immigrant and minority students. The peculiar situation in South Africa where the ethnic majority, black and "colored" students, actually had a minority or even immigrant status created very special educational conditions. These conditions were characterized by substandard education provided to these students, multi-lingualism which received no appropriate support, and general social disadvantage under conditions of racial separation system. Skuy et al. (1994) conducted a study with 200 seventh- to eleventh-grade students in the black suburb of Johannesburg. Students were randomly divided into three groups: one group received a combination of IE (4 hours/week) and conventional educational enrichment program; a second group received a combination of IE (2 hours/week), academic enrichment and a program specially designed for this project which focused on the development of creativity and a socioemotional sphere of students (CASE); a third, control group received only the academic enrichment. The experiment was conducted over two years on the 52 Saturdays from 9 a.m. to 3 p.m. Students in the IE groups also received special "bridging" from IE to academic subjects.

The results obtained demonstrated the trend toward post-intervention superiority of the IE, and IE/CASE groups over the control group in cognitive, creativity and socioemotional measures. In the cognitive sphere the authors reported a statistically significant advantage of IE/CASE and IE groups over the control group in Similarities sub-test of the WISC-R. This finding is important because it is exactly the sphere of verbal conceptualization that constitutes the major problem for the disadvantaged minority students. Significant results of IE and IE/CASE intervention were also obvious in the sphere of creative activity. It is noteworthy, that the quality of MLE interactions between teachers and students was specially assessed during this study, with IE and IE/CASE groups scored as having the higher level of MLE interaction than the control group. This indicates that the IE program was indeed taught according to the principles of MLE. The authors conclude, that the combination of IE with the program of socioemotional development may constitute the best combination for disadvantaged minority students who need not only cognitive enrichment but also an explicit strengthening of their personality and emotional sphere.

Another South African study (Skuy et al., 1995) explored the effects of the IE program on four different groups of primary school students in one and the same mining town: black, "colored", white-English and white-Afrikaans. The participating students studied in segregated classes. The IE program included three components: (1) Teaching the IE program for 30 min. every week for a duration of a school year; (2) A series of seminars for teachers on the theory and practice of mediated learning experience (MLE). Teachers received an "MLE work manual" and were trained to infuse content lessons with the MLE oriented interactions. In addition teachers were presented with particular cognitive operations covered during the IE teaching, and lesson materials aimed at the development of these operations; (3) Teachers received packages of lesson materials which helped them to "bridge" thinking skills developed during IE lessons into the academic curriculum. The effectiveness of the intervention was measured by cognitive, creativity, self-concept, and academic (English reading) measures.

At the pre-test the black group showed significantly lower results than the other groups. At the post-test all four groups of students demonstrated significant improvement in cognitive measures; black and "colored" students also demonstrated improvement in the area of creativity and English reading skills. It is significant that even a limited amount of direct IE teaching (20 hours) turned out to be effective, because it was complemented by the MLE-based training of content subject teachers.

IE intervention also proved to be beneficial for the adult learners belonging to immigrant or/and minority populations. Skuy and Mentis (1993) conducted a number of IE intervention programs for black and "colored" students in South African colleges. Though statistically significant results were achieved only in one out of five colleges, the trends in all of them were in a positive direction of providing students with higher levels of cognitive functioning, self-confidence, and creativity.

In a pilot study conducted at the Hebrew University in Israel (August-Rothman & Zinn, 1986) a group of new immigrants from Ethiopia received IE intervention as a part of their preparatory academic studies. IE principles were "bridged" to the mathematics curriculum. Two types of data were obtained: grades in mathematics and admittance to regular university study. During the first year of preparatory studies the IE group received higher grades in mathematics than the control group which received no IE. During the second year the latter group also started receiving IE; the second year mathematics grades of this group were better than the first year grades of the same group. The ultimate test of the students' advancement was their admittance to regular university study. If after the first year of preparatory studies only 1 out of 15 candidates was admitted, after the second year this number reached 7. University lecturers also reported significant change in the students' learning skills, attitudes and ability to master material.

In another Israeli study (Kozulin & Lurie, 1994) a group of new immigrant teachers from Ethiopia received intensive IE intervention as a part of their retraining course leading to certification as teachers in Israel. Cognitive performance of the participants was assessed with the help of the Block Design test and the Raven matrices test. The initial level of cognitive performance of the participants was much lower than could be expected taking into account their educational level. Apparently, the educational system which brought them up focused on narrow skills and failed to prepare them for coping with novel problem-solving tasks. One may say that tools and activities associated with formal schooling, though formally acquired, remained poorly mediated to these teachers. Intensive IE intervention which continued for 16 months for a total of 352 hours brought about a dramatic and statistically significant improvement in the participants' cognitive performance. It was also demonstrated that a sub-group of students who received an additional 130 hours of exposure to the IE program showed even better results than a matching sub-group of their peers.

Several groups of new immigrant students from Ethiopia studying in grades 8 through 10 of four Israeli boarding schools participated in a study of Kozulin, Kaufman and Lurie (1997). IE intervention included 4–5 hours of IE lessons per week for a period of one school year. The IE principles were then "bridged" to specially designed curriculum in reading and mathematics. Both cognitive performance and academic achievement of students were measured. The authors concluded that success of the program depended on the combination of several factors including initial cognitive and school skills level of the students, IE teachers' mediational ability, and the school commitment to implementation of the program. It was shown that the initial low level of students can be overcome and considerable progress achieved when the IE teacher is competent and the school supportive. At the same time even high learning potential demonstrated by students during the pre-program dynamic assessment does not guarantee success if the teacher and the school show poor commitment to the program.

6 Gifted Students

Apart and beyond its role as a developmental and rehabilitational program, IE can also serve as an enrichment program. That is why children with above-average potential constitute a legitimate group for IE intervention. A large scale study of IE undertaken by Mulcahy and Associates (1994) included a sub-sample of 200 gifted fourth- and seventh-grade students. (For a description of Mulcahy's study see Learning-Disabled section above.) A student was defined as gifted if he or she obtained scores one or more standard deviation above the mean on the verbal and the non-verbal sub-scales of Canadian Cognitive Abilities Test, was rated as being above average in reading and at grade or above grade level in mathematics on Canadian Achievement Test, and was rated as being above the mean on all three of the Renzulli and Hartman's Scales for the Rating of Behavioral Characteristics of Superior Students (motivation, learning, and creativity).

The results of the study indicate that in the cognitive abilities test the IE group scored higher than both the control and the SPELT group in the verbal area. In the non-verbal area the SPELT group was ahead. Some advantage of the IE group was also observed in mathematics concepts, but this advantage observable at the end of the intervention period disappeared one year later. IE students, however, were consistently better than control students in cognitive strategies both in reading and in mathematics.

7 Sensorially Impaired Students

7.1 Deaf Learners

The special needs of the deaf learners require particular efforts in the development of their cognitive strategies, metacognitive functions, and certain cognitive operations and functions which in hearing students are developing on the basis of verbal communication (Braden, 1994). Sign language as a preferred medium of communication of the deaf students continues to generate controversy as to the limits of its ability to render concepts in the same way as they are acquired and used by the hearing students (Martin, 1993). For these reasons IE had been tried as a program for the enhancement of cognitive skills in the deaf learners (Thickpenny, 1982; Keane, 1993).

In more recent studies summarized by Martin (1995) a number of benefits provided by IE intervention were discussed. One of them is a statistically significant improvement of the cognitive performance of the IE group students relative to non-IE controls. The cognitive performance was measured by Raven Matrices. The second improvement was observed in the area of domain specific functions such as reading comprehension, mathematics comprehension and mathematics concepts. In addition to objective tests the change in students' behavior and performance was evaluated with the help of teachers' ratings. It is important that teachers who provided these ratings did not participate in IE implementation, and as such had no vested interest in supporting this program. The teachers found the following trends in the IE group students: increased self-control and sense of responsibility, increased willingness to help other students and greater readiness to work in a group format, greater openness to alternative solutions, and decreased impulsivity. Somewhat similar results in the field of cognitive and domain specific performance were obtained for a group of deaf college students. The IE group outperformed controls in Raven Matrices, reading comprehension and mathematics tests.

What is still missing in the majority of IE for the deaf studies is a detailed analysis of the mediational strategies attuned to the special needs of this population. Apart from this important question about didactics of teaching IE to deaf learners, there are several other questions mentioned by Martin (1995): What kind of relationships exist between the preferred communicative system of the deaf learner (sign language, finger spelling, or/and oral communication) and his/her ability to benefit from the IE program? Is there any difference in the effectiveness of IE instruction provided by hearing vs. deaf teachers? How to "bridge" IE program to vocational training and career development of the deaf individuals?

7.2 Blind Learners

Unlike all other types of learners, blind students seemed to have an insurmountable difficulty in using IE materials for the simple reason that these materials are presented in a graphic modality inaccessible to this population. The first major problem facing the developers of the Braille version of IE instruments was to create input and response modalities suitable for the blind individuals who cannot use the graphic input of the regular IE instruments, and as a rule, cannot respond by drawing figures or signs. This problem has been resolved by the Italian team of Portulano and Patino (1993) and the ICELP team headed by Gouzman (1995) by using capsule Minolta paper. Braille text, drawings, and other graphic elements printed on this paper become perceptible in a tactile way after special thermal treatment. The French team of Sibaud (1993) suggested using plastic thermoform sheets on which drawings and Braille text can be embossed. One should be aware, however, that thermoform technology does not allow the same degree of precision in reproduction of graphic images as the capsule paper technique. The problem of response modality has been resolved by placing capsule paper sheets on magnetic boards and providing students with ferromagnetic response tokens (Gouzman, 1995). The page of capsule paper with the task printed on it is placed on the magnetic board; the student explores the task in a tactile way, selects an appropriate response token in the box and then places it in a proper position on the page.

The second major problem of the Braille IE program is how to redesign the IE instruments so that they respond to the special needs of the blind learners while retaining the essence of the regular IE instruments. This has been achieved by identifying the most essential elements of the pictorial material used in the regular IE instruments and retaining only these elements in the Braille IE version. Figure 1 demonstrates samples of Braille IE pages from the instruments: "Orientation in Space − 1", "Analytic Perception", and "Comparisons". In addition, special pre-IE learning materials on capsule paper were developed including images of geometric shapes, every-day objects and facial expressions (see Figure 2). The development and use of these pre-IE learning materials was necessitated by the fact that the majority of the blind learners completely lacked any experience with quasi-visual representations of objects and processes. As a result they were deprived of imaginative thinking, had episodic grasp and representation of reality, suffered from the narrowness of the psychological field, and insufficient development of some cognitive functions. All these deficiencies can be successfully remediated with the help of the Braille IE program.

To date the ICELP version of this program has been used with the following populations of blind students: primary and secondary school students integrated into regular schools, students at the special school for the blind, young adults at the

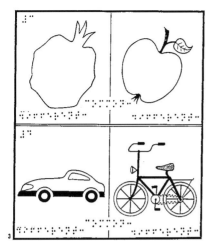

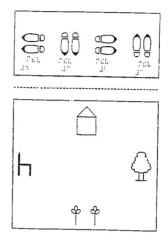

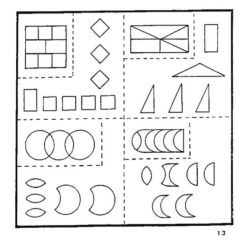

Figure 1: Samples of Braille IE tasks "Orientation in Space 1", "Comparisons", and "Analytic Perception" (©Feuerstein, HWCRI, 1995)

preparatory University course, elderly new immigrants in the intensive Hebrew program (Gouzman, 1997). The outcome of the program implementation included changes in the behavior, cognition and self-image of the blind learners. In the field of behavior students demonstrated greater alertness and involvement during the lessons. Some of them for the first time started actively interacting with their sighted peers. The self-image of the blind learners improved significantly, with students setting for themselves much higher educational and employment goals. Cognitively a very significant change has occurred with the blind learners acquiring "quasi-visual" representation of objects and processes, learning to use schematic

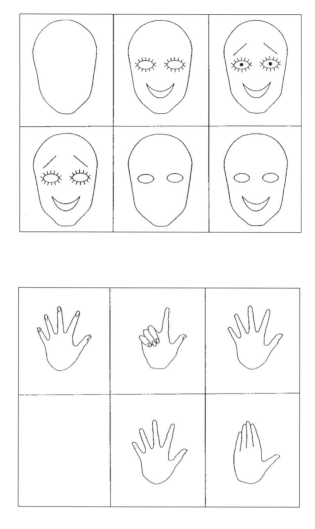

Figure 2: Samples of facial expressions and gestures serving as pre-IE tasks

representations and models, developing learning strategies and expanding the area of their cognitive functioning.

8 Conclusion

Originally developed as a remedial cognitive program for adolescents at risk the IE program proved to be rich and flexible enough to be applicable with different populations of learners. Such a diversity of applications brought to the fore some of the questions that were previously not considered as central. One of them is the correspondence between the didactics of IE teaching and the goals of IE application with a specific target group (e.g. new immigrant students, sensorially-impaired students, gifted students, and so on). Different goals may require appropriate didactical changes transmitted to IE teachers working with specific populations. The second question that reappears constantly in the IE research, is the relationships between cognitive changes induced by the IE program and the students' achievement in content learning expected by the educational system. Pure improvement of cognitive functioning of the students is rarely accepted by the educational system as a valuable outcome unless it is accompanied by tangible results in content areas. Thus, greater attention should apparently be paid to the style of content teaching that is supposed to be co-ordinated with IE intervention. Finally, the question remains of the optimal time and effort to be invested in the application of IE. Unlike the original IE studies reported by Feuerstein et al. (1980) more recent applications rarely include all 14 instruments, and usually allocate only 2 hours per week for IE teaching instead of 3–5 as recommended in the IE manual. Not surprisingly some of these applications produce no significant results. It remains to be seen, therefore, what amount of IE teaching is sufficient for producing the desirable results without overburdening the resources of the educational system.

16

Cognitive Education and Reading Disability

J. P. Das, Rauno K. Parilla, and Timothy C. Papadopoulos

1 Introduction

The age of innocence in remedial training is over. Whereas even twenty years ago the art of remediation was an eclectic conglomeration of commercial products and seat-of-the-pants clever thinking procedures, the scene has changed drastically ever since theoretical models and scientific research have impacted on the enterprise of providing programs for ameliorating cognitive difficulties of various kinds.

The change that brought in a loss of innocence to the field of remediation was heralded by at least three separate forces, as they appeared in the disciplines of psychology and education. One of the first was research and demonstration of the value of early stimulation. Taking their cue from animal research, where rats were cognitively stimulated by varied and exciting environments to become "maze-bright", Hunt and his students, among them Haywood, established the legitimacy of cognitive stimulation in early childhood (Tzuriel & Haywood, 1992). The whole movement of early intervention, especially for disadvantaged children, was initiated by what we learned from animal experiments. Another influential line of research stemmed from memory training for individuals with mental retardation. The pioneering experiments of Butterfield and Belmont, inspired by distinguished theorists and experimenters such as Ellis, Zeaman, House and Zigler, demonstrated the malleability of basic cognitive capacities, such as rote memory, through strategy training (Belmont & Butterfield, 1977). Thus, it was deemed possible that even the limited capacity of individuals with mental retardation cannot be regarded as limited. Lastly, the resurrection of interest in accelerating maturation through learning, so clearly advocated by Vygotsky (1934, 1962, 1978) helped bring a paradigm shift in the field of remedial training and simultaneously launched a new discipline, *cognitive education*.

It was in regard to these three seminal influences that Feuerstein's contribution can be evaluated. The time was ripe for Reuven Feuerstein to mediate, not unlike a midwife, the genesis of mediated learning that would facilitate the development of the learning potential of each and every individual, irrespective of level of intellectual functioning. Cognitive education, with its short history and long future, has now been competently discussed in a recent book by Ashman and Conway (1997). Its predecessor was the book *Dynamic Assessment*, edited by Lidz (1987). Between these two books, critical, as well as the sympathetic readers, in regard to Feuerstein, will find creditable accounts of the contributions that Feuerstein and his colleagues and followers have made mainly to two fields: (a) to the field of assessment of learning potential and (b) to techniques of remedial treatment that take individuals through their zones of proximal development.

Let us begin this chapter with a personal note relating to Reuven Feuerstein. Das and Feuerstein spent about two weeks together in Edmonton when the latter was invited as a distinguished visiting scholar to the University of Alberta. An interview was recorded and has since been published (Snart, 1985). We would like to provide a few excerpts from that interview. First of all, Das and Feuerstein discussed the "teaching of intelligence" as Nick Hobbs used the term in his foreword to Feuerstein's text *Instrumental Enrichment*. The interviewer asked if they believed in the teaching of intelligence, that is, that intelligence can be taught? Obviously, both Feuerstein and Das did.

Feuerstein remarked that what we refer to as intelligence can be meaningfully modified and changed and we do not have to consider observed behavior changes as simply peripheral, and not structural. He continued on the same theme, reacting to Das' probing arising from Jensen's famous paper *How much can we boost IQ?* Feuerstein said that Jensen's data is to be questioned for one particular reason: it is based on conventional test procedures or, at best, on coaching methods which certainly are not supposed to affect the capacity of the individual in a structural way. In Feuerstein's approach, if a child is working on the Raven's Progressive Matrices test, for example, "I am mediating to the child as we do it. The test or the task itself represents for me a very simple pretext for changing some structural processes" (Snart, 1985; p. 6).

To this Das remarked that what Feuerstein was doing was perhaps changing habits of thought in the child. To the question, "Should we teach content or habits of thought?" Feuerstein said that from his point of view, similar to what has been stressed by Das, teaching habits of thinking should not be done alone. It should be a parallel endeavor to the teaching of content. "We have to impose a great deal of integration between the 'non-content' and the 'academic' approaches such that there will be a mutual benefit from both" (Snart, 1985; p. 7). Das thought that Luria and Vygotsky, predecessors of the Feuerstein mode of thinking, had suggested that culture and cultural interventions, such as literacy, not only change the content of thinking but the structure of thought as well. It would not be too much to assume that it changed the structure of the higher cortical functions.

The last excerpt from their interview relates to Feuerstein's preferred model of the mind and, by inference, the neural structure underlying mental processes. Feuerstein said that he was firmly convinced there had to be more clarity as to how certain interactions are affected, or do affect, the brain. The interdependence within the brain in regard to its function has certainly come to be an exciting area of research. "I have a real inclination to the Pribram model — the holographic mind. In looking for ways by which one can affect certain parts of the brain by exercising others, one is being rather 'holographic'. The most remarkable feature of a holographic picture is that if you cut out a piece of the picture, it represents all the totality of what is represented in the total picture and this concept is very appealing to me." (Snart, 1985; pp. 13–14).

To the above Das replied, "Yes, and that's the message one gets when reading Pavlov and his work with dogs — that no function is placed uniquely within any one part of the brain, even in the dog." (Snart, 1985; p. 14). Thus, the ground work for structural modifiability is laid in the holographic picture of the mind or the brain, while allowing for distinct but interdependent functional organizations of cognitive activities. We would like to suggest that the four major functional organizations are Planning, Attention, Simultaneous processing, and Successive processing (PASS Theory of Intelligence; Das, Naglieri & Kirby, 1994).

In the remainder of this chapter, we will first lay the groundwork and present reading as a cognitive activity. Then we will provide a discussion of PASS and the PASS Reading Enhancement Program (PREP) that focuses on cognitive remediation of reading problems. This description is followed by a review of PREP studies. Finally, we will conclude this chapter by reporting results from an ongoing longitudinal study utilizing both PASS and PREP.

2 Reading as a Cognitive Activity

Reading remediation provides numerous examples of the gap between theory and practice in remedial training. When educational and cognitive psychologists were unraveling the cognitive basis of word reading skills, curriculum and remedial programs mainly ignored the research and sometimes were not based on any alternative body of research. To an outsider, the guiding assumption seemed to be that once children understand the significance of reading as a holistic activity, they will learn to read. Unfortunately, large numbers of children do not, and would certainly benefit from training in the basic cognitive skills underlying reading (see Adams, 1990, for a more detailed discussion of whole language vs. phonics arguments). In sum, reading remediation was rather theoretically neutral if not insular to advances in theories on cognitive functions underlying reading. It was not the natural outcome of theoretical understanding or empirical findings; instead, the cognitive basis of reading and reading failure were side-stepped. Changes in remediation techniques began to gain limited popularity, mainly because of a renewed interest in Vygotsky and the influence of Feuerstein's "learning potential" movement. We will present next an account, a brief one, of the cognitive basis of word reading as it has been developing in the research literature. This will lead us to discussing a reading remediation program based on the idea of reading as a cognitive activity.

2.1 More on Word Reading: Distal and Proximal Processes

When confronted with a word, a beginning reader can either recognize the word by sight (often referred to as 'sight reading') attempt to guess the word from context, or recode the string of letters in terms of their respective sounds or phonemes; this activity is usually referred to as phonological coding. Sight reading and guessing from context are strategies commonly associated with poor rather than fluent reading (see e.g. Share, 1995) whereas phonological coding is the most commonly used strategy of good readers. The reason is simple: the spoken lexicon is far bigger than the words that can be recognized by sight or reliably guessed from the context.

Thus, when a beginning reader is confronted with a previously unseen word, he or she is faced with at least five inter-related tasks which must be undertaken to reliably recognize the word. First, all (or at least most) of the letters have to be recognized and differentiated from their visually confusing neighbors (e.g. b-d, g-q-p; O-D, E-F, V-Y). Second, the sounds (phonemes) of the letters or letter combinations must be retrieved and differentiated from their phonetically confusing neighbors (e.g. /g/-/k/; /b/-/p/, /t/-/d/, /s/-/z/). Third, all phonemes must be stored in working memory in their exact order of presentation. Fourth, the entire set of phonemes in working memory has to be blended together to form a phonological representation of the whole word. Finally, this phonological representation of the word has to be used to gain access to the lexicon. If the word is in the child's (spoken) lexicon, he or she can move on to the next word.

To accomplish these five tasks, we will argue, a beginning reader will require the use of both proximal and distal cognitive processes as well as the necessary knowledge base without which the processes will be void of content. In the context of word reading, the necessary *knowledge base* can be defined as consisting of two components: (a) knowledge of letters/letter combinations and the sounds they make, and (b) a spoken lexicon that allows the recognition of words after they have been sounded out. The *proximal cognitive processes* are the mostly linguistic skills that are directly related to the five tasks mentioned above. The most frequently recognized proximal processes in word reading are phonological processes, defined commonly as cognitive processes that deal directly with the sound structure of the spoken language. Wagner and Torgesen (1987) suggested three sub-categories of phonological processes: (a) phonological awareness — awareness of the sound structure of language; (b) phonological recoding in lexical access — recoding written symbols into a sound-based representational system to get from the written word to its lexical referent; and (c) phonetic recoding in working memory — recoding written symbols into a sound-based representation system to maintain them efficiently in working memory. Wagner (1988) divided phonological awareness further into phonological analysis (the ability to break whole words into their constituent phonemes) and phonological synthesis (the ability to blend isolated phonemes together to form whole words). Thus, following this outline we have four categories of proximal processes or skills: phonological analysis, phonological synthesis, phonological recoding in lexical access, and phonological recoding in working memory.

It is easy to understand how each of these processes, combined with letter knowledge and the lexicon, play a role in accomplishing the last four of the five tasks outlined above. Accordingly, children with reading difficulties have been found to perform poorer than their normally reading peers in tasks as varied as deleting phonemes from three-letter words, repeating random word or digit series, naming letters and sounds rapidly, and repeating nonsensical sentences or series of words consecutively (Das, Mishra & Kirby, 1994; Das, Mok & Mishra, 1993; Kirby, Booth & Das, 1996; Papadopoulos et al., 1997; Shankweiler et al., 1995; Watson & Willows, 1995). A recent review by Share and Stanovich (1995, p. 9) concluded that "there is virtually unassailable evidence that poor readers, as a group, are impaired in a very wide range of basic cognitive tasks in the phonological domain". This seems to be true for both "garden variety" poor readers (Stanovich, 1988) and for the reading disabled population (Rack, Snowling & Olson, 1992; Siegel & Ryan, 1988; Snowling, Goulandris & Defty, 1996). In one of the most frequently cited articles in the field, Torgesen, Wagner and Rashotte (1994) took the argument a step further and suggested that phonological processing abilities are causally related to normal acquisition of reading skills. The strongest support for this claim can be found in longitudinal studies examining the relationship between pre-readers' phonological processing scores and their reading development one to three years later (e.g. Bradley & Bryant, 1985; Wagner et al., 1997).

The first task the beginning reader faces, recognizing and differentiating printed letters, requires orthographic coding rather than phonological processing. Orthographic coding is a difficult construct and both its definition and role in reading has not been agreed upon (see Vellutino, Scanlon & Tanzman, 1993). We will follow here Vellutino, Scanlon and Tanzman (1993) and define orthographic coding as the ability to represent the unique array of letters that defines a printed word. Moreover, Vellutino, Scanlon and Tanzman (1993, p. 322) suggest that orthographic coding ability is "a visual coding ability that depends on such facets of the visual system as visual feature analysis, attention to visual detail, and visual pattern analysis, as well as on such general abilities as the ability to detect, represent, and categorize invariance".

The problem with orthographic coding is that there seems to be a distinction between clinical studies of acquired dyslexia, which often report cases of "visual dyslexia" (e.g. Newcombe & Marshall, 1981) and large scale correlational studies on developmental dyslexia, which often report that orthographic skills do not account for any additional variance in reading after phonological skills were accounted for (however, see Barker, Torgesen & Wagner, 1992). It seems reasonable to assume that an activity such as word recognition is not possible without some sophistication in processing of the visual information contained in printed letters (Vellutino & Denckla, 1996). Therefore it seems likely that the experimental tasks purportedly assessing orthographic processing have not yet managed to isolate visual information processing, rather than that orthographic processing plays no role in word reading (see Vellutino, Scanlon & Tanzman, 1993, for a similar argument).

Distal cognitive processes are more general and modality unspecific underlying cognitive processes. These enable the development of proximal processes. Thus, the influence that distal cognitive processes have on reading is not necessarily direct but can be mediated by one or several proximal processes. More specifically, we will suggest that two types of cognitive processes are relevant for word reading: (a) those that contribute to the development of phonological and orthographic processing, and (b) those that allow the successful deployment of phonological and orthographic skills. The PASS (planning, attention, simultaneous and successive processing) theory of intelligence (Das, Naglieri & Kirby, 1994) includes both kinds of processes.

3 The Four Cognitive Functions and Reading: the PASS Theory in Brief

The Planning, Attention-Arousal, Simultaneous and Successive (PASS) cognitive processing model is described as a modern theory of ability within the information processing framework. It is based on Luria's analyses of brain structures (1966, 1973, 1980). Luria described human cognitive processes within the framework of three functional units. The function of the first unit is cortical arousal and attention; the second unit codes information using simultaneous and successive processes; and the third unit provides for planning, self-monitoring, and structuring of cognitive activities. Luria's work on the functional aspects of brain structures formed the basis of the PASS model and was used as a blueprint for defining the important components of human intellectual competence. Because thorough reviews of the PASS model and related research are presented elsewhere (Das, Kirby & Jarman, 1979; Das, Naglieri & Kirby, 1994; Naglieri, 1989; Naglieri & Das, 1990), only a brief summary is provided here.

The cognitive processes that occur within the three functional units are responsible for and involved in all cognitive activity (see Figure 1). The *first functional unit of Attention-Arousal* is located in the brain stem and reticular activating system (Luria, 1973). This unit provides the brain with the appropriate level of arousal or cortical tone and "directive and selective attention" (p. 273). Attentional processes are engaged when a multidimensional stimulus array is presented to the subject, in a task requiring selective attention to one dimension and the inhibition of responses to other, often more salient stimuli. Luria stated that only under optimal conditions of arousal can the more complex forms of attention involving "selective recognition of a particular stimulus and inhibition of responses to irrelevant stimuli" occur (Luria, 1973; p. 271). Moreover, only when sufficiently aroused and when attention is adequately focused can an individual utilize processes within the second and third functional units.

The *second functional unit is associated with simultaneous and successive processing of information*. Luria's description of the second functional unit follows the work of Sechenov. Luria described "two basic forms of integrative activity of the cerebral cortex" (Luria, 1966; p. 74). The processes of the second functional unit are responsible for "receiving, analyzing, and storing information" (Luria, 1973; p. 67) through the use of simultaneous and successive processing. *Simultaneous processing* is associated with the occipital-parietal areas of the brain (Luria, 1966). The essential aspect of simultaneous processing is surveyability, that is, each element is related to every other element. For example, in order to produce a diagram correctly when given the instruction "draw a triangle above a square that is to the left of a circle under a cross", the relationships among the shapes must be

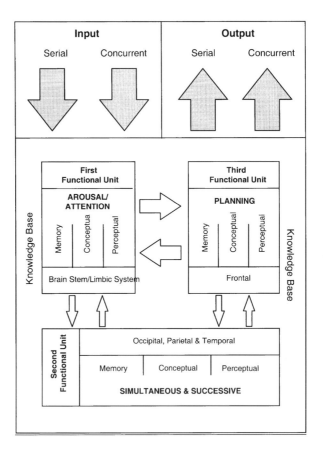

Figure 1: The PASS model of intelligence (adapted from Das, Naglieri & Kirby, 1994)

correctly comprehended. *Successive processing* is associated with the fronto-temporal areas of the brain and involves the integration of stimuli into a specific serial order where each component is related to the next. That is, in successive synthesis, "each link integrated into a series can evoke only a particular chain of successive links following each other in serial order" (Luria, 1966, p. 77). For example, in language processing, successive processes are involved with decoding and production of syntax and with speech articulation.

The *third functional unit is concerned with plans and decision-making*. It is located in the prefrontal divisions of the frontal lobes of the brain (Luria, 1980). Luria stated that "the frontal lobes synthesize the information about the outside world … and are the means whereby the behavior of the organism is regulated in conformity with the effect produced by its actions" (p. 263). Planning processes provide for the programming, regulation and verification of behavior, and are responsible for behavior such as asking questions, problem solving, and the capacity for self-monitoring (Luria, 1973). Other activities of the third functional unit include regulation of voluntary activity, impulse control, and various linguistic skills such as spontaneous conversation. The third functional unit provides for the most complex aspects of human behavior including personality and consciousness (Das, 1980; Das, Kar & Parrila, 1996).

The PASS theory provides a model to conceptualize human intellectual competence that is a blend of neuropsychological, cognitive and psychometric approaches. Operational definitions of the four processes and the rationale for test construction are derived from the theory which consequently led to the identification of valid and reliable measures of each PASS process, contained in a new battery of cognitive tests, the Das-Naglieri Cognitive Assessment System (Naglieri & Das, 1997).

The four cognitive processes contribute to performance but do not determine it completely. *Output*, or performance, is the response or behavior that can be influenced by at least three other major factors: knowledge base, motor planning of the output, and motivation. All cognitive processes operate within the context of the existing knowledge base. It includes information that we have accumulated by both formal (e.g. through instruction and reading) and informal (e.g. experience) means (Das, Naglieri & Kirby, 1994). This fund of accumulated knowledge can greatly enhance information processing by providing it with appropriate context but it can also hinder it by introducing irrelevant material or unproductive habits. Moreover, individuals sometimes show a gap between what they know and what they can do, that is, between knowledge and performance. Output, or performance, may have to be properly programmed before we can express what we know. Performance can thus be influenced by cognitive processing and knowledge base, as in Figure 1, but also by factors such as the ability to come up with an appropriate motor program, as well as motivational and personality factors. Reading a word aloud in a foreign language, for example, can have an output problem — assembling the right pronunciation and forming a motor program for articulation.

3.1 Word Reading and PASS Theory

Theoretically, successive and simultaneous processing are both important for word reading. Dual-route theories of word recognition, for example, suggest that a word is recognized either through direct visual access, or through phonological coding of its sounds. The first should relate to mainly simultaneous processing via orthographic processing, and the second primarily to successive processing via phonological processing. Thus, the two processes should show correlations with word reading. Figure 2 shows a simplified presentation of these relationships.

Due to the importance of phonological processing in word decoding, successive processes are naturally expected to be more important at this level. Similarly, Share (1994) suggested a "domain-general temporal processing dysfunction" in reading-

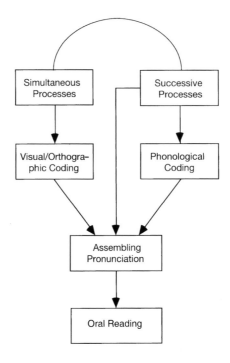

Figure 2: Processes underlying word recognition (adapted from Das, Naglieri & Kirby, 1994)

disabled children to account for inconsistencies in phonological processing literature.

After the very initial stages of letter and visual word identification, simultaneous processing may play a secondary role in word reading. It should, however, be more strongly related to reading comprehension (Kirby & Das, 1990; Kirby & Williams, 1991). In reading comprehension, simultaneous processing is needed in the relating of meaningful units and in their integration into higher level units (Kirby, Booth & Das, 1996). Planning and attention are necessary in all levels of reading, although common decoding tasks are not likely to be affected by minor differences in these executive processes. However, their importance should rise as a function of task complexity.

Several empirical studies have examined the relationships between PASS processes and reading. As would be expected from the above description, poor successive processing has surfaced as a primary characteristics of children with reading problems (e.g. Das, Mishra & Kirby, 1994; Kirby, Booth & Das, 1996; Kirby & Robinson, 1987; Leong, 1980; Snart, Das & Mensink, 1988). Intervention studies, reviewed in detail below, have shown improvements in reading as a result of training in successive processing. Moreover, successive processing problems experienced by poor readers have not been limited to verbal material and can persist even after the effect of short-term memory is controlled for (Eden et al., 1995).

Existing studies have also indicated that, in particular, simultaneous processing but also planning, are indeed important for reading comprehension (Das et al., 1979; Kirby & Das, 1977; Das, Mensink & Mishra, 1990; Das, Snart & Mulcahy, 1982; Kirby & Gordon, 1988; Little et al., 1993; Naglieri & Das, 1988). In sum, these studies demonstrate that simultaneous processing and planning measures with no reading component are good predictors of reading comprehension, whereas successive measures are better predictors of word reading performance. We should also note that none of the above mentioned studies have included young enough subjects to examine the role of simultaneous processing in letter recognition. The role of attention is less clear and several studies have found no differences between good and poor readers. However, if the attention task used involves phonological stimuli, then it can be associated with reading problems (Das, Mishra & Kirby, 1994).

4 Cognitive Remediation of Reading

The above characterization of reading as an interplay between knowledge base and proximal and distal cognitive processes suggests that deficient reading can result from problems with any of these components. The most profound problems would rise from deficient distal processes. However, when reading remediation programs have been based on research of reading as a cognitive activity, they have generally focused on proximal processes and/or knowledge base (letter and letter-sound knowledge) to the exclusion of distal processes that may underlie problems in proximal processes. Phonological processing training studies with young children have consistently reported positive effects on reading, particularly if they included explicit instruction in letter-sound associations (see e.g. Bradley & Bryant, 1985; Ball & Blachman, 1991; Byrne & Fielding-Barnsley, 1991). The problem is that the training studies have shown the largest effects in enhancing the reading skills of regular students, rather than remediating or preventing problems of at-risk students. The studies that have actually targeted at-risk students[1] have produced inconclusive evidence on the efficacy of phonologically based remediation programs: training in phoneme segmentation and blending skills produces positive effects on these skills, but these effects seldom transfer to word reading and decoding (see e.g. Barker & Torgesen, 1995; Hurford et al., 1994; Mantzicopoulos et al., 1992). The only study that we are aware of that produced unequivocally positive results was that of Blachman et al. (1994). They reported improvement of the treated at-risk children compared to control children after a year long intervention that consisted of first teaching phonological processing and letter-name and letter-sound knowledge, and then building on and expanding this

---

[1]By at-risk students, we are referring to a group of students who were identified using one or several screening instruments besides the teachers' perceptions and academic performance measures.

284 J. P. Das, Rauno K. Parilla, and Timothy C. Papadopoulos

knowledge by using a specific reading program. Their study raised the question of changing the reading curriculum altogether.

An alternative approach to reading remediation, one that we have utilized in our work, is to start from the distal processes and build upon them. We will now introduce PREP (PASS Reading Enhancement Program) which is an elaboration of that approach. This is followed by a review of studies that have examined the effectiveness of PREP with elementary school age children.

4.1 PREP: PASS Reading Enhancement Program

The PASS Reading Enhancement Program (PREP)[2] is based on well-accepted theories of child development and cognitive psychology. It aims at improving the information processing strategies that underlie reading — namely, simultaneous and successive processing — while at the same time avoiding the direct teaching of word reading skills. PREP is also founded on the premise that the transfer of principles can be facilitated through inductive rather than deductive inference (Carlson & Das, 1997; Das, Mishra & Pool, 1995). Accordingly, the program is structured so that tacitly acquired strategies are likely to be used in appropriate ways. Attention and planning are also aspects of each task. Specifically, attention is required and used in performing each task, and planning is augmented by encouraging the children to engage in discussions, both during and following their performance.

An integral part of the structure of each task is to develop strategies such as rehearsal, categorization, monitoring of performance, prediction, revision of prediction, sounding, and sound blending. Thus, children develop their ability to use these strategies through experience with the tasks. Rather than being explicitly taught strategies by the tutor, children are encouraged to become aware of their use of strategies through verbalization. Growth in the ability to use strategies and be aware of appropriate opportunities for their use is expected to develop over the course of remediation.

The program consists of ten tasks that vary considerably in content and the requirements of the student. Each task involves both a global training component and a curriculum-related bridging component. The global component includes structured, non-reading tasks that require the application of simultaneous or successive strategies. These tasks also provide children with the opportunity to internalize strategies in their own way, thus facilitating transfer (Das, Mishra & Pool, 1995). The bridging component involves the same cognitive demands as its matched global component and provides training in simultaneous and successive processing strategies, which have been closely linked to reading and spelling (Das, Naglieri & Kirby, 1994).

---

[2]Since PREP was recently described in detail by Das and Kendrick (1997), only a brief overview of the program is offered below. Those interested in the program are encouraged to examine the D.A.S and Kendrick article for further detail.

The global tasks begin with content that is familiar and non-threatening so that strategy acquisition occurs in small stages (Das, Mishra & Kirby, 1994). Complexity is introduced gradually. Through verbal mediation (occurring through specific discussions of strategies used) the global and bridging components of PREP encourage children to apply their strategies to academic tasks such as word decoding. The global and bridging components are further divided into three levels of difficulty. This allows the child to progress in strategy development and, for those who already have some successful processing strategies in place, to begin at an appropriate level.

A system of prompts is also integrated into each global and bridging component. The series of prompts creates a scaffolding network that supports and guides the child to ensure that tasks are completed with a minimal amount of assistance and a maximal amount of success. A record of these prompts provides a monitoring system for teachers to determine when material is too difficult for a child or when a child is able to successfully progress to a more difficult level. A criterion of 80% correct responses is required before a child can proceed to the next level of difficulty. If this criterion is not met, an alternate set of tasks, at the same difficulty level, is used to provide the additional training required.

To summarize briefly, PREP is a reading enhancement program that aims at improving the information processing strategies that underlie reading, while at the same time avoiding the direct teaching of word reading skills.

4.2 Review of PREP studies

Early studies using experimental versions of PREP produced positive results in both cognitive processing tasks and reading performance. That poor reading may coexist with cognitive processing deficits that go beyond phonological processing (Das, 1995a) became apparent with the first intervention study. Krywaniuk and Das' (1976) sample consisted of Grade 3 Canadian Native children attending a reservation school. All of the children were poor in both English reading and in several successive processing tests such as serial and free recall of words, short-term memory for visually presented digits, and a cross-modal coding task. An 18-hour intervention program that focused on successive processing (and to a lesser extent simultaneous processing in which the children had no problems) was given to 20 children whereas the remaining 15 children received only 3 hours of intervention and returned to their classes.

The results indicated that longer intervention improved serial and free recall, visual digit memory, and word recognition, but not WISC scores or any of the other cognitive test scores. In sum, intervention was successful in raising both successive processing and reading scores, which were targeted, but did not effect the non-targeted cognitive processes.

Brailsford, Snart and Das (1984) provided 15 hours of remedial training in simultaneous and successive processes to a group of learning-disabled children, aged 9 to 12, enrolled in reading resource room programs. The matched control group received the same amount of remedial reading instruction. The results showed significant group by time interaction in one simultaneous task, in all successive processing tasks, and in the Standard Reading Inventory scores (McCracken, 1966), all in favor of the remediated group. Similar gains were not evident in the Gates–MacGinitie reading comprehension subtest. This result could be interpreted to suggest that simultaneous and successive processing strategies emphasized in training generalized to a reading task requiring active organizational strategies but not to the more structured multiple choice format reading task.

The training tasks used in both of these early studies could be best described as global in terms of their relation to reading, that is, they did not include training in reading related proximal processes. Therefore, the positive results are even more surprising and offer strong support for cognitive remediation. Later studies have replicated the positive results with a combination of global and bridging tasks, whereas training in either component alone has not necessarily been successful. Das, Mishra and Pool (1995) used PREP with a group of Grade 3 and 4 students with reading disabilities who exhibited delays of at least 12 months on either the Word Identification or Word Attack sub-test of the WRMT-R. Participants were first divided into two groups, PREP remediation and a no-intervention control group. The PREP group received 15 sessions of training involving groups of two students, over a period of $2\frac{1}{2}$ months. Children in the control group participated in regular classroom activities. After the intervention, both groups were tested again using the Word Identification and Word Attack sub-tests. The results indicated that while both groups gained during the intervention period, the PREP group gained significantly more on both Word Identification and Word Attack, as evidenced by a significant Group × Time interaction. In the second part of this study, children from the control group received either the global or the bridging component of PREP for the same length of time. Neither of these groups benefited from the program to the same extent as the original PREP group that received both components.

Similarly, Molina, Garrido and Das (1997) found that when a Spanish version of full PREP (20 hours of remediation) was given to a group of 9- and 10-year-old Spanish children with reading difficulties, they did significantly better than a matched control group in reading, planning, simultaneous processing, and successive processing tasks. Similar gains were not evident in the group that received only the bridging component of the PREP (10 hours of training). The lack of positive results in this case, however, could have resulted also from the shorter intervention that the bridging group received.

Carlson and Das (1997) report on two studies using a small-group version of the PREP for underachieving Grade 4 students in Chapter 1 programs. In the first study, the experimental group received 15 hours of "add-on" training with PREP over an eight-week period. Both the PREP and control groups (22 and 15 students, respectively) continued to participate in the regular Chapter 1 program. Word Attack and Word Identification tests were administered at the beginning and at the end of the intervention. The results showed significant improvement following training in PREP, as well as significant Group × Time interaction effects. The second study replicated these results with a larger sample of Grade 4 students. Since these original studies, several other replication studies completed in the same school district have essentially reproduced the original results with children from Grades 3, 4, 5, and 6, and with both bilingual (Spanish–English) and monolingual (English) children (Carlson, 1996). Moreover, these results have been robust even when the remedial sessions have included up to 10 participants. We should also note that in one of these studies, positive results were found both on reading and on successive processing tasks, thus providing a replication of the earlier findings by Krywaniuk and Das (1976) and Brailsford, Snart and Das (1984).

Finally, the effectiveness of a modified PREP (for an older group of children) was studied by Boden and Kirby (1995). A group of fifth- and sixth-grade students who were identified a year earlier as poor readers were randomly assigned to either a control or an experimental group. The control group received regular classroom instruction and the experimental group received PREP, in groups of four students, for approximately 14 hours. As in previous studies, the results showed differences between the control and PREP groups on the Word Identification and Word Attack tests after treatment. In relation to the previous year's reading scores, the PREP group performed significantly better than the control group.

Taken together, these studies make a clear case for the effectiveness of PREP in remediating deficient reading skills during the elementary school years. Moreover, most of the studies included participants experiencing rather severe difficulties in learning to read and thus qualifying as "reading disabled" rather than just poor readers. We believe that these are precisely the children who are most in need of cognitive remediation.

5 Longitudinal Study with Young Children "At-Risk"

The studies reviewed above have not addressed the effectiveness of the PREP program in preventing rather than remediating reading problems. This is the main focus of the study presented here. Moreover, most studies did not employ a stringent control condition, a plausible competing program. Thus, we will now report preliminary results that extend research on PREP with three important changes: (1) the control condition is a competing program given to a carefully matched group of children; (2) the participants are beginning readers in Grade 1 and therefore younger than the Grade 3 to Grade 6 participants in the previous studies; and (3) the training is shorter in duration than in most of the previous PREP studies.

5.1 Participants and Procedure

The initial group of participants consisted of 101 kindergarten children identified by their teachers as being at-risk for experiencing early reading difficulties (excluding ESL and mentally challenged students) who were subsequently given an assessment battery consisting of 9 cognitive tasks (2 planning tasks, 2 attention tasks, 2 simultaneous processing tasks, and 3 successive processing tasks taken from the standardized version of the Das-Naglieri Cognitive Assessment System; Naglieri & Das, 1997) and 3 phonological processing tasks (rhyming, sound isolation, phoneme elision) during the Spring of their kindergarten year.

Ninety of these children were given the same assessment tests together with Word Attack and Word Identification tests again in Grade 1. Sixty-one of them (22 of which were female) scored below the 26th percentile on both Word Attack and Word Identification (WRMT-R) and were included in the remediation. In this group, there was an attrition of 3 participants during the intervention. The mean age for this group was 76.6 months (SD = 3.8). After identifying the final sample, two matched remediation groups were formed. Matching was performed by clustering participants on the basis of 14 standardized criterion variables, which included 9 cognitive processing tasks, 3 phonological processing tasks, and 2 reading tasks (Word Attack and Word Identification). Although matching took place simultaneously in a 14-dimensional space, the subsequent t tests on raw scores showed no significant differences between the groups on any of the 15 variables (all $ps > 0.3$).

Remediation took place over two months during the Spring of Grade 1 and consisted of 18 twenty-minute sessions which were administered during school hours by trained experimenters. Students were worked with individually or in groups of two or three, depending on the number of students receiving particular remediation in their schools. The variation in the groupings was similar across both programs in the beginning of the remediation.

The PREP group received eight of the ten tasks in the original program which were adapted for the Grade 1 level. The following eight tasks were presented to the children in the order listed: Window Sequencing, Connecting Letters, Joining Shapes, Matrices, Related Memory Set, Transportation Matrices, Tracking, and Shape Design. For a detailed description of the tasks and procedures, see Das and Kendrick (1997).

The second remediation group received a meaning-based program that emphasized the philosophy of the whole-language approach to teaching reading. The meaning-based program in the present study was designed as follows. In order to provide opportunities for learning to read in a natural way, children were read stories that they selected from the instructor's collection of quality children's literature. The stories, which were rich in language, covered a wide range of topics. No direct, systematic reading instruction was provided. Instead, the children participated in discussions about events and pictures in the stories as they related to their own personal experience. The overall objective of the meaning-based program was to encourage children to derive meaning from print by reconstructing the author's message, based on their own experiences.

Post-testing included only the Word Identification and Word Attack tests and took place after each child had completed the remediation. The Word Attack test was used to measure participants' ability to apply phonic and structural analysis skills to pronouncing nonsense or low frequency words that are not recognizable by sight. This ability is often called spelling-to-sound correspondence and is one of the most commonly used predictors of early reading skills. Stimulus words in this test consisted of simple consonant-vowel combinations (e.g. "dee", "apt", "ift"). The Word Identification test requires the participant to read isolated (and, at this level, also high frequency) words (e.g. "is", "you", "and").

5.2   Results and Discussion

Table 1 presents the means and standard deviations for the pre- and post-test Word Attack and Word Identification raw scores for both remediation groups.

Separate independent samples *t* tests showed that the pre-test scores did not differ significantly for either measure, whereas the post-test scores for Word Attack were significantly different. Testing Time (2) × Remediation Group (2) repeated measures ANOVAs were computed separately for Word Attack and Word Identification. The main effect of Testing Time was significant in both analyses, indicating that over the three-month period the participants had advanced in their basic reading skills. For Word Attack, the Remediation Group × Testing Time interaction was also significant. This result indicates that the PREP group improved significantly more than the meaning-based group in pseudoword reading. No significant interaction was obtained for Word Identification although the PREP group seemed to benefit slightly more from the remediation.

Perhaps the most rigorous test of an intervention program's success is whether or not it produces relative gains in terms of standardized norms. Accordingly, both the pre-test and post-test percentile scores were calculated and compared to the monthly age norms provided in the Woodcock manual. Table 2 presents the means and standard deviations for the pre- and post-test Word Attack and Word Identification percentile scores.

Table 2 shows that on the Word Attack task, children in the PREP group gained 13.66 percentile points in standing relative to the norm sample whereas the meaning-based group gained approximately half as much, that is, 6.71 percentile points. For Word Identification, the gains were more limited for both groups: the

Table 1: Word attack and word identification scores as a function of remediation and testing time.

	Word attack		Word identification	
	Pre-test **Mean (SD)**	**Post-test** **Mean (SD)**	**Pre-test** **Mean (SD)**	**Post-test** **Mean (SD)**
PREP (*n* = 29)	0.31 (0.66)	4.03 (4.30)	4.00 (3.81)	13.24 (8.30)
Meaning (*n* = 29)	0.14 (0.35)	1.93 (2.46)	3.52 (3.50)	11.31 (8.82)

Table 2: Word attack and word identification percentile scores as a function of remediation and testing time.

	Word attack		Word identification	
	Pre-test Mean (SD)	**Post-test Mean (SD)**	**Pre-test Mean (SD)**	**Post-test Mean (SD)**
PREP ($n = 29$)	3.85 (0.77)	17.55 (3.05)	8.22 (1.66)	12.91 (2.58)
Meaning ($n = 29$)	2.69 (0.36)	9.41 (1.86)	7.10 (1.46)	10.84 (2.26)

PREP group gained 4.69 percentile points and the meaning-based group gained 3.74 percentile points.

A detailed examination of individual performances indicated that 14 children from the PREP group gained 15 percentile points or more during the remediation, exhibiting significant gains relative to the norm sample. Eight children scored at the 30th percentile or higher on the Word Attack post-test. In the meaning-based group, 7 participants gained 15 percentile points or more, and 2 participants scored at the 30th percentile or higher during post-testing. On Word Identification, similar gains were made by 4 participants from the PREP group and by 2 participants from the meaning-based group. Taken together, these results show that 9 participants who were included in the PREP remediation group would not have qualified as having a significant early reading problem if they had been tested after the remediation. In contrast, only 3 participants from the meaning-based remediation group displayed similar progress.

In sum, these results indicate that while both programs were effective in producing small gains on a word recognition task, PREP produced significantly larger gains on the pseudoword reading task. Given the unproportionally high number of exception (irregular spelling) words in the Word Identification test, it may not be surprising that the positive effect of PREP did not generalize into this task — after all, the main purpose of PREP is to enhance the cognitive processes on which phonological decoding is based. While Word Attack measures directly phonological decoding, Word Identification requires familiarity with the exception words included in the test, and this required reading practice as well as skill.

A major empirical concern of this chapter was understanding and remediation of reading difficulties. The findings from older studies as well as the preliminary results from the study presented here point to the need for a theoretically derived remediation program with training in relevant cognitive processes. The PASS theory allows us to go beyond phonological training and use PREP. In terms of PASS, successive processing is suggested to be the locus of reading difficulties, not merely a correlate of them. If this is correct, then improving successive processing is necessary for some designated children improving the basic word-level skills. The studies reviewed above certainly give support for this interpretation. Cognitive remediation can help students' reading skills.

6 A Final Word

In conclusion, this chapter presents a recent review, a stock taking, as it were, of the level of sophisticated research in the field of cognitive education. We hope to convince the reader that the eclectic non-theoretical approach to remedial training belongs to the past. The theoretical underpinnings of remediation that we have illustrated include the Vygotskian notion of expanding children's zones of proximal development, a notion that is clearly manifested in the mediated learning and instrumental enrichment research of Feuerstein. Together with Vygotsky, we believe that children with intellectual handicap of one kind or another actually face dual handicaps — that of intellectual deficiency, that prevents them from learning, and that of negative reaction from society to their handicapping condition (Das, 1995b). Feuerstein has battled against both of these handicaps. The message from the front is that he is winning!

Note: J. P. Das, JP Das Developmental Disabilities Centre, University of Alberta, Edmonton, Canada; Rauno K. Parilla, Faculty of Education, Queen's University, Kingston, Canada; Timothy C. Papadopoulos, University of Cyprus.
Acknowledgements: This research was funded by a grant from the Social Sciences and Humanities Research Council of Canada (SSHRC) to John Kirby and J. P. Das. The authors wish to thank the Edmonton Public School Board, and especially the students, teachers, and principals for their participation and co-operation. We would also like to thank Richard Wagner for providing the Phoneme Elision and Sound Isolation tasks.

Correspondence concerning this article should be addressed to J. P. Das, JP Das Developmental Disabilities Centre, 6–123G Education North, University of Alberta, Edmonton, AB, T6G 2G5, Canada. Electronic mail can be sent to j.p.das@ualberta.ca.

17

Cognitive-Developmental Therapy: Overview

H. Carl Haywood

Cognitive-developmental psychotherapy is an approach to individual and group psychotherapy that incorporates cognitive education (learning about thinking, thinking about learning) into a formal structured psychotherapy paradigm. Its development has been stimulated by four clinical observations.

The first observation is that some number of the interpersonal and intrapsychic problems that people encounter may be due more to failure to have developed effective thinking modes than to classical psychopathology. That is to say, people fairly often get into psychological and social difficulty because they have not learned to think effectively: they lack some essential cognitive structures, or they lack experience at identifying the cognitive structures they have, selecting appropriate ones to match their situations, applying these thinking modes to the solution of real-world problems, and then evaluating their effectiveness.

The second observation is that, even when people get instruction in the formal modes of logical thought, they often need help in making the applications of these thinking modes to the solution of problems in their everyday lives. That is to say, application does not occur automatically: people have to learn to apply effective thinking strategies, just as they have to learn to generate them in the first place.

The third observation is that people are quite often unwilling to expose their own thought processes to scrutiny, even their own scrutiny, until they are in an affectively safe and supportive relationship. Thus, one of the classical dynamics of psychotherapy, the "trusting relationship", becomes a prerequisite to cognitive change as well as to affective change. My students and I had observed that some adolescents in particular seemed unable to make significant progress in classroom-oriented cognitive education without the added component of individual psychotherapy, and that these same clients made encouraging progress toward independent problem solving when the two components were combined into a single treatment scheme.

The fourth observation is that cognition is not the whole problem, nor is it the whole solution (see, for example, Goleman, 1995). People think, but they also feel, and they also will. Traditional psychology had consciousness divided into the three components of *cognition* (thinking), *conation* (feeling), and *volition* (willing — the

[1]Professor of Psychology, emeritus, Vanderbilt University, Nashville, TN, and Dean of the Graduate School of Education and Psychology, Touro College, New York, NY. This chapter was written while the author was an active faculty member of Vanderbilt, and put in final form at Touro.

motivational component). Although it is unproductive to conceive of these as separate or even separable parts or processes, it is also unproductive to deny or ignore any of these aspects of human functioning (Haywood, 1992). According to this point of view, then, it might very well be true that problems could have their origin in failure to acquire effective modes of logical thought, but the solutions would have to involve a broad spectrum of personal functioning. Thus, a combination of cognitive education and more traditional psychotherapy seemed optimal.

This approach is distinguished from other therapies that share the title "cognitive" by three principal characteristics. The first is reliance on a formal, structured program of cognitive education rather than merely a "cognitive" orientation during psychotherapy. The second is the deliberate and planful merging of the educational and psychodynamic components into a composite strategy and unified program of treatment. The third is the essentially *metacognitive* nature of the method. This last distinction means that the emphasis is on encouraging clients to focus attention on their own processes of thinking, perceiving, learning, and problem solving, and to generate their own strategies, learn how to select appropriate strategies, learn to apply them appropriately to the understanding and solution of psychological and social problems, and learn to evaluate their effectiveness. This is quite different from other cognitive therapies in which the emphasis is on helping clients to learn and to apply predetermined (therapist-determined) modes and strategies of thinking. In other words, in this metacognitive approach a major goal is to have clients become capable of generating, selecting, applying, and evaluating their own cognitive strategies rather than merely learning somebody else's strategies.

1 Goals

The major goal of cognitive-developmental psychotherapy is to enhance the personal and social functioning effectiveness of clients by making them more proficient in thinking rationally and applying systematic thought to the conceptualization and solution of their personal and social conflicts. Specifically, the goals are:

1. To enhance development and integration of cognitive, social, and affective systems.
2. To enhance mental health (rather than merely to relieve psychopathology or distress), defined as effective and satisfying functioning in important life domains.
3. To enhance development of cognitive structures and strategies that are basic to the general functions of organized perception, thought, learning, and problem solving.
4. To define, locate, and specify the relation of "in-trouble" behavior, unproductive social relationships, and personal pain to ineffective cognitive processes/structures.

5. To establish connections between generalizable principles of logical thought and their applications in everyday life.

Cognitive-developmental therapy (CDPsy) is *cognitive* in that its primary emphasis is on acquisition and systematic application of formal processes of logical thought.

CDPsy is *developmental* in that its overall goal is to help clients to reach developmental levels, in both cognitive and social realms, that they have not reached before, rather than merely to restore them to a previously enjoyed state of health. Further, there is the assumption that the problems themselves are products of inadequate processes in development; thus, one intervenes in development itself and attempts to set clients on a higher psychological developmental trajectory than they have enjoyed in the past.

1.1 Sequence and Objectives

Sequence is particularly important in this approach, guided by sequential objectives. The first objective is to *establish an affective climate* that is non-threatening and in which clients will be willing to expose their own thinking processes to their and the therapist's scrutiny. Unless this is done, work toward the ensuing objectives will be difficult to accomplish.

The second objective is to *diagnose clients' specific cognitive deficiencies*. This is done through dynamic assessment of learning potential (see, e.g. Feuerstein, Rand & Hoffman, 1979; Haywood & Tzuriel, 1992; Lidz, 1987), and is combined with assessment of affective and motivational dimensions of the clients' personalities.

The third objective is to *help the clients to acquire the most important and generalizable cognitive processes* related to their cognitive deficiencies and their specific problems (e.g. learning, social interaction, self concept).

The fourth objective is to *stimulate and enhance the development of task-intrinsic motivation*; i.e. to help clients to reach a state wherein they seek satisfaction, and find it, in engaging in tasks, particularly mental work, and in doing so for the sake of doing so, without reliance on task-extrinsic incentives or rewards and without reliance on external confirmation of the validity of their own activities, efforts, plans, and strategies. The corollary objective, of course, is to reduce simultaneously the clients' task-extrinsic motivational orientation; i.e. to reduce the extent to which they attempt to avoid dissatisfaction by concentrating their attention on the non-task aspects of the environment, such as ease, comfort, safety, security, avoidance of effort, practicality, and material gain. For a more extensive discussion of task-intrinsic motivation, see Haywood and Switzky (1986).

The fifth objective is to *establish logical and habitual connections* between the principles and strategies of logical thought that have been learned in the cognitive education phase of this treatment to the applications of such principles and strategies in defining, understanding, and ultimately solving the problems of the clients' everyday lives.

The sixth objective is to *bring about a state of "functional autonomy" in application of cognitive processes* to personal problem solving. This means to turn "ability" to think systematically into "disposition" to do so, and it includes identifying appropriate applications and carrying them out systematically.

The ultimate goal (culmination of the foregoing objectives) is to enhance the development of persons who think of themselves as cognitively competent (because they are), who look to themselves, particularly their systematic thinking processes, for solutions to problems, who derive some satisfaction from applying rational thought to personal problem solving, who recognize personal, learning, and social problems as analyzable and solvable, and who spontaneously use systematic thought in everyday contexts.

2 Procedures

2.1 Establishing the Affective Climate

One's own cognitive processes are a highly personal matter. It is not a trivial thing to invite or even to tolerate someone else's inspection of those processes. "How I think" is my business. This is an especially sensitive area if one suspects that one's thinking processes might be found to be inadequate, which is quite frequently the state of mind with persons who have had difficulty with school learning, with self concept, with interpersonal and even intrafamilial relations, or who have experienced any of a wide variety of psychological conflicts and problems. At the same time, it is important to recognize that little real work can be done toward improving overall cognitive functioning until teacher-therapists are allowed to examine at close range their clients' actual, personal thinking styles, processes, and strategies. It is apparent, then, that some preliminary work must be done first. That first step in CDPsy is referred to as "establishing the affective climate". It is, in many ways, similar to the necessary first phase in any good approach to psychotherapy: build an atmosphere of mutual trust and respect, confidence in the therapist's caring, trustworthiness, and competence, and habits of non-judgmental disclosure and examination. The following principles help to guide this important first phase.

Showing sincere interest in the clients and their problems is essential. Phony interest will be detected and destructive. Therapists who cannot manifest sincere interest in helping clients to achieve the goals of CDPsy should not adopt this approach. Showing interest incorporates several forms of specific behavior. First, therapists listen. During this phase they do not react evaluatively, do not give advice, and they try to maintain the classical "affective neutrality" in a limited sense. That limited sense is simply that CDPsy therapists must show an active interest in clients, including liking them if that is possible, and certainly actively seeking their further development, while being non-judgmental in their reactions to clients' disclosures, behavior, or histories. The therapists are thus not affectively neutral so much as they are non-judgmental; they are clearly on the clients' side.

This is in many ways a data-gathering stage. This does not mean that therapists must be totally inactive or even non-directive. Questions may be asked for the purposes of clarifying (for the therapists and for the clients) information and its interpretations, focusing attention on important aspects of what is being discussed, and communicating therapists' interest in what the clients say, as well as focusing on the relation between incidents and the accompanying feelings and thoughts. Comments may be offered that suggest understanding, general affective support (e.g. "I know that must have been a very hard time for you."), and interest in the joint client-therapist quest for solutions and for cognitive change (e.g. "That makes me wonder how you thought about this problem at the time it was happening, and how your thoughts changed over the next few days."). Care is indicated in using these latter techniques. While it is useful to establish immediately that the general approach will be a cognitive and metacognitive one, meaning that attention will be focused upon the clients' thinking processes, too much and too sudden metacognitive focus may threaten some clients and drive them into panic and away from therapy. Too little such emphasis may lead to non-cognitive habits of interaction in the therapy sessions; i.e. to the expectation that the therapist will be passive, not very helpful, and not too interested, as well as the expectation that the therapist will be non-demanding of the client. Some of these considerations can be dealt with, in part, in the general introduction to CDPsy, i.e. in what the therapist and client understand in the first session.

What to tell the client is, then, an important consideration for session #1. There is, of course, no precise script, since each therapist must express these events in his/her own natural way, using his/her own personality as the most important instrument of psychotherapy, just as in other approaches. In general, using words and repetitions appropriate to each client's and each therapist's functioning level and personality, a CDPsy therapist will make the following points:

1. The purpose of these meetings is to help you become better able to use your intelligence (thinking, brain) to think your way through problems that confront both you and many others.
2. There is some relationship between these meetings and the classes you are having about thinking and problem solving. In those classes, you are learning some rules about thinking. In our meetings, we will discuss how you can use those rules in your everyday life.
3. I am here to help you to make that "bridge". Your job is to talk to me about your life, partly so I can get to know you better, and partly so I can understand any problems that you might be having. [NOTE: In the case of non-self-referred clients, such as prisoners or hospital patients, it may be necessary for the therapist to be more specific; e.g. "... such as why you are here, or why you keep getting into trouble, or why you just do not seem to do well in school".] My job is to ask you questions, answer your questions when you ask them — and when I can, and help you to understand how you can think your way through problems in your life. You see, each of us has his own job. They are not the same, but both jobs are related to the same goal: we both want you to be more

successful [in staying out of jail, in school work, in getting along with others, etc.] If we both do our job, and work together, I think we can make a lot of progress.

4. There are also some things that we do not have to do. Can you think of some? Yes, you do not have to say anything you do not want to say, or answer any questions you do not want to answer. You do not have to continue to come to these meetings if you do not want to (if that is true). In the same way, it is not my job to do things for you, such as find out when you can go home or try to get some privileges for you. My only job is to help you think your way through problems. Doing it is your job.

5. You might feel a little uncomfortable at first. I might, too. We really do not know each other very well, and we might even have a hard time at first knowing what to talk about. Here are some suggestions: I would like to know your background, your history. Not in a lot of detail, but enough to help me to feel that I know you. You might tell me about your family, about school, about your special likes and dislikes. I would also like to know what things bother you, how you got here, and what you think about those things. Then, when we know each other a little better, I hope that we can discuss in greater detail the things that really bother you, that get you in trouble, or that you feel stand in your way. As we do that, I will often be asking you how you think about problems, how you could look at something differently, and how you could apply good thinking rules to the solution of everyday problems. As we do those things, I think you might be surprised to learn that you are capable of doing some pretty complicated thinking. Also, when you do that, applying the rules of thinking that you will be discussing in the other part of this work, you may be surprised to see how well you can work out some problems just by thinking about them.

6. Now is a good time for both of us to understand what we are supposed to do in these meetings. Do you have any questions about it? Maybe you could tell me your understanding of what our jobs are.

After the introductory session, anxiety in both therapist and client will be less than at first, if only because the first session outlined in the foregoing paragraphs will have reduced the social ambiguity that is common early in therapeutic relationships. This period of "establishing an affective climate" will be quite useful in extending the period of assessment, i.e. in continuing diagnostic study. While in general clients may talk about whatever they wish to talk about, therapists have a responsibility to guide clients' conversation toward matters of real concern to the clients rather than letting them fritter the time away by talking about inconsequential things. The problem, of course, is that therapists cannot always make that distinction reliably. One should both listen and look. Listening has two foci: content, and process. Listening for content is easy, and it is seductive. One can easily get so "sucked in" to the content of clients' verbal productions that one loses sight of the flow, the long-range intent, and the affective display of the content production. It is, of course, necessary to pay attention to the content, because it is important for its own sake and because one does not wish to be caught napping, revealing ignorance of what the client has been saying, and thus suggesting lack of interest. At the same time, it is at least equally important to try to understand such matters as:

(a) *what* the client is attempting to accomplish over time; e.g. what impression the client is trying to create in the therapist's mind or what material the client is trying to avoid discussing;

(b) *how* the client is expressing his/her thoughts; i.e. what qualities of logical organization, association, or apparent randomness appear in the client's productions;

(c) *the feelings* that are expressed by the client. Looking is important because the client's movements, facial expressions, body orientation, eye contact, enthusiasm, and general affect (e.g. as expressed by "blushing") may be quite important clues to the value the client places on the content being discussed.

The principal ideas and feelings that the therapist wishes to develop in the client during this initial phase are: (a) trust and confidence in the therapist; (b) a sense of shared participation in the enterprise of enhancing the client's development; (c) willingness to disclose personal information; (d) optimism about the possibility of improving the client's life by achieving more effective functioning, i.e. by dealing more effectively with day-to-day circumstances as well as large problems; (e) at least the beginning of the notion that solutions to life's problems are possible, and that they will come from the client.

One should not be in a great rush to get through this phase, because the success of subsequent phases depends upon establishing the attitudes and feelings discussed in the preceding paragraph. For some clients success in this domain can be achieved in two or three meetings. For others, the process may require several more. Therapists can know when to begin to move (not precipitately) to the next phase by the following criteria:

1. There is a visible relaxation in the client's defensive and resistant attitudes.
2. Embarrassing silences are fewer or absent.
3. The client begins to discuss matters that are clearly of greater consequence to him/her.
4. The client begins to take a more active role in thinking about his/her problems, i.e. to examine possible solutions as well as to present problems.

2.2 The Cognitive Education Phase

In a general sense, cognitive education is taking place throughout cognitive developmental psychotherapy, in all its phases and in all its techniques. Even so, one of the unique characteristics of this approach is the *definition* of the cognitive education aspect as a clearly identifiable part of the enterprise. It is important to emphasize the *separable* cognitive education phase, as well as to identify the cognitive aspects of the individual psychotherapy.

Any formal, organized, structured program that is centered on the teaching and learning of *metacognitive* processes may be used. The one that I prefer, and use consistently, is *Instrumental Enrichment* ("IE"; Feuerstein et al., 1980). IE is especially appropriate for CDPsy because it has the following characteristics:

1. It is *structured*; i.e. the cognitive and metacognitive processes on which it is focused are pre-selected, the sequence of lessons is prescribed, and the teaching methods are prescribed.
2. It is *basic* and *metacognitive*; i.e. the cognitive and metacognitive processes that are emphasized in this program are those that are thought to be fundamental and generalizable to a wide variety of thinking tasks, perceptual and learning strategies, and content applications, and its primary goal is to make clients able to structure their own thinking, and to generate and apply their own cognitive strategies. This is vastly different from programs (cognitive, rather than metacognitive) in which specific thinking and problem solving strategies are taught, the mastery of which constitutes the goal of the programs.
3. It is *teacher directed*; i.e. the teachers lead the quest for cognitive change in the clients, prescribe exercises, and serve as partners and resource persons in that quest.
4. It is *developmental*; i.e. it is sequenced from less to more cognitively complex activity and process, and its goals are developmental ones (to bring about *structural* cognitive change so that the clients' cognitive processes reach levels never before attained).

In the ideal situation, the teaching should be done by someone other than the psychotherapist. The primary reason for this is that the teaching and therapeutic roles are different in important ways, and it is difficult to keep these roles separated if the same person is doing both. Nevertheless, the therapist must maintain a close relation to the education phase, and must know what is being taught, what difficulties are being encountered, and how the clients respond to different forms of educational intervention.

Cognitive education should be offered for a minimum of three hours per week. The total number of hours of cognitive education will depend upon the developmental levels and particular deficiencies of the clients, and their response to teaching. On the average, a minimum of 60–75 hours will be needed to produce clearly measurable, generalizable, and durable cognitive changes (see, e.g. Haywood et al., 1982; Haywood et al., 1984).

Similarly, the starting place (choice of initial instruments) must depend upon the clients' developmental levels and diagnosed deficiencies (preferably by use of dynamic assessment of learning potential). With retarded adolescent clients, it is usual to begin with instrument number 1, *Organization of Dots*, and to proceed with *Orientation in Space I* and *Analytic Perception*. In some cases, one will want to abbreviate these instruments, especially if the clients are doing quite well or are showing signs of boredom and disengagement. *Family Relations* is a particularly useful instrument with slow-learning adolescents and young adults, perhaps because its content is almost universally familiar and relevant. With intellectually-advanced clients, one can either skip or go quickly over these basic instruments and concentrate on more advanced ones such as *Cartoons* and *Syllogisms*. The program consists of 15 such instruments, each with many pages of paper-and-pencil exercises and a teacher guide. The typical teaching procedure is to begin a "class" with an introduction of the necessary concepts and related vocabulary, followed by a discussion of the concepts and their applications in everyday life, followed then by distribution of the paper-and-pencil exercises, which can be done as a demonstration of the clients' understanding of the concepts.

The teaching is done according to a "mediational teaching style" that is markedly different from more traditional approaches to teaching (Haywood, 1987, 1993). It is based upon the concept of *mediated learning experience* (Feuerstein et al., 1980; Feuerstein & Rand, 1974), which is the process by which adults help children to understand the *generalized meaning* of events they encounter in their environments. Every interaction between a client and a teacher has the potential to be a mediated learning experience. In order to qualify, an interaction should have at least the first three, and usually has all six, of the following criteria (from Feuerstein et al., 1979, 1980):

Intentionality. The teacher intends to use the interaction to produce change in the student. Often, this becomes bidirectional; i.e. the client seeks cognitive change through interactions with the teacher.

Transcendence. The changes that the teacher (and often the client) intends to produce must transcend the immediate experience that forms the basis of the interaction. This means that giving information, for example, cannot constitute the end of a MLE, but the mediator must go on to use that interaction to help the client understand some generic aspect of living, thinking, learning, or understanding.

Communication of meaning and purpose. There are no cognitive secrets. Teachers help clients to understand the reasons for the activities that are being done, or the explanations that are being given, in relation to their cognitive developmental goals. Further, all events have at least two levels of meaning: a "content" meaning and a "cognitive" meaning. Both levels of meaning are dealt with in mediated interactions.

Mediation of a feeling of competence. Correct responses/processes are acknowledged, as are incorrect ones, and rewarded with praise. This constitutes the first half of this criterion. The second half is to make certain that the client understands exactly what he/she has done that merits reward, and what can be done again in order to reproduce the same warm glow of triumph and satisfaction.

Regulation of behavior. Often, mistakes are made simply because one did not take sufficient time, and did not reflect sufficiently, to understand the nature of the task before responding. This impulsive responding can be reduced to the great benefit of the client. On the other hand, many clients, especially children, block the expression of responses that are clearly available to them. In order to unblock responding, teachers must create an affectively safe environment, assure success, and enter into a collaborative conspiracy with clients.

Sharing. This is the most difficult. It is essential that the teacher–learner relationship be one of shared enterprise. The enterprise is the quest for cognitive change in the learner. The sharing reflects both the learner's need/wish for cognitive change and the teacher's commitment to facilitating that change. Sharing does not imply equality of roles; indeed, differentiation of roles facilitates the development of sharing. The attitude must be "we are in this together and will see it through together". There must also be role definition: you can count on me for these things, I shall expect these other things from you.

Mediational teachers do not tell learners what concepts they are to understand and learn; rather, they *elicit* understanding, and the expression of that understanding, from the learners. It is quite important that the learners verbalize themselves the cognitive concepts, rules, generalizations, and strategies that they are learning. Mediational teachers arrange environments in such ways as to make it quite likely that the learners will be able to express relevant rules and concepts. They do that primarily by *questioning*, by *questioning processes* specifically, by *asking for examples*, by *challenging* both correct and incorrect responses, and by *bridging* from abstract concepts, rules, and strategies to their applications in the clients' everyday lives (see Haywood, 1985).

More can be found about mediational teaching in several papers on that subject by Feuerstein, Haywood, and others.

2.3 The Middle Phase of Therapy

After the initial phase of establishing a therapeutic affective climate, and once the cognitive education phase has begun, the two major components, cognitive education and individual psychotherapy, proceed simultaneously and in concert. When a facilitating affective relationship has been established, the roles of the therapist become the following: (a) to *receive and accept* the problems, enthusiasm, and accounts of the client; (b) to *mediate* those experiences in cognitive ways; (c) to *bridge* between the abstract cognitive processes acquired in the cognitive education phase and their potential applications in everyday life; (d) to continue to *serve as an affective and intellective resource* for the client.

Clients are encouraged to discuss problems that they encounter in their everyday lives. Therapists help them to sort out these problems, generally into "stacks" labelled major and minor, mine and theirs, general and situation-specific. Priorities can be established by discussing the relative importance of the problems, i.e. the clients' concern with them.

Therapists meet these problem-oriented discussions with acceptance, then with a metacognitive direction; i.e. by asking clients to think about their own thinking and problem solving processes, asking such questions as the following:

> *What* do you usually do in that situation?
> *Why* do you do it?
> *How* do you go about defining, examining, solving that kind of problem?

> *How else* could you possibly do it?
> *How* do some other people solve this same kind of problem?
> *When* and *how* could you apply *which* strategies and principles/rules that you have learned in cognitive education to the solution of these problems?

Clients' suggested solutions are invariably accepted — not necessarily validated! That is to say, one accepts their attempts, even pointing out the validity of the *parts* that are in fact valid, and then suggests that it is possible that alternative solutions might be even better ("Yes, the first part is right. You could begin that way. What could you do next, instead of —— ?"). In doing so, it is important to mediate the feeling of competence while encouraging a *metacognitive attitude,* i.e. a habit of examining one's own cognitive processes and strategies.

Certain cognitive exercises have particular relevance and importance to clients who have psychological distress, either of an intrapsychic nature or of an interpersonal nature. Such exercises should have a prominent place in cognitive developmental psychotherapy. These include: *planning, identifying choice situations, making choices* (including identifying goals, identifying alternative courses of action, relating actions to goals, comparing possible solutions on several dimensions, first serially and then simultaneously), *examining the logical validity* of analyses and interpretations of events, *considering alternative interpretations* and the evidence that would support them, *classifying* one's events, problems, situations, and activities, and *evaluating* the effectiveness and appropriateness of solutions and plans. These should not be constructed and assigned in a mechanical or universal fashion, but therapists need to be able to use them as the clients' needs dictate.

Homework is an extremely useful mechanism. It should not be given in the nature of an imposed assignment, but rather by way of negotiation and mutual agreement. An example: A client is determined to believe that his life is totally controlled by others, including parents, teachers, bosses, even siblings and peers. The client and the therapist have been discussing choice making, but the client says that he never has any choices to make. They might agree that between sessions the client will keep a list, usually some specified number, of occasions when choices were presented to him, and list by each his own response to the choice situation. The list is to be brought in for discussion at the next session. When it is brought in, the therapist must avoid the temptation to say, "See, I told you that you really had choices!" Instead, the therapist must reward the work of collecting the list, and then discuss with the client such aspects as the variety of circumstances in which different choices occurred and the client's different (or consistent) modes of response to them. Often, the therapist will ask the client to add to the list by thinking of other situations in which he would like to have choices and how he might behave in order to obtain choices, and to nominate alternative modes of response to the previously listed choice situations (e.g. instead of sullen rejection, polite thanks), and to consider the potential consequences of each mode of response.

Throughout all of this cognitive work, it is essential to remember that there is an affective life, and that it is going on. It is also important to remember that the affective life is not separate from the cognitive one. People have thoughts about their feelings, and feelings about their thoughts. People also have feelings that they cannot readily relate to thoughts, for which they often cannot even identify the sources. In fact, it is when people cannot readily identify, label, or trace the sources of their feelings that "bizarre" behavior may occur. Common examples are laughing at funerals and crying at weddings. Both are examples of such strong emotion that the feelings overflow the usual pathways and lead to behavior that is difficult to match with the situation. Persons faced with occasions of great joy often cry, for example, when children first see their parents (and vice-versa!) on the children's return from summer camp. In extreme psychopathology, as in the major psychiatric disorders, feelings become so threatening that persons develop ways to avoid them and appear to be "numb". In less severe cases, they develop what classical psychoanalysts referred to as "defenses against affect".

Cognitive developmental psychotherapists must always consider the affective aspects of their clients' psychological lives, and be prepared to deal with those aspects on affective as well as cognitive bases. Therefore, discussing clients' feelings is important and should not be neglected. Dealing with those feelings, especially when they are strong (rather than casual) and psychodynamically important, can take many traditional (i.e. not essentially cognitive) forms. Adherence to cognitive developmental principles does not require abandoning other, less cognitive, explanations or ignoring affective, even intrapsychic, sources of psychological conflict. Practitioners of cognitive developmental psychotherapy, then, use what they know of psychodynamics and the affective domain. Techniques include support, reflection, interpretation, reassurance (especially reassurance on an evaluative, personal dimension and reassurance of cognitive competence). Because the approach does benefit from some internal consistency and integrity, these techniques should be interlaced with invitations to think, to employ cognitive principles, rules, and strategies that have been learned, and to generate and apply one's own solutions — and then to defend those solutions both cognitively and affectively!

Cognitive developmental psychotherapy comes to a close when: (a) clients are systematically generating and applying cognitive strategies for solving their personal and interpersonal problems; (b) clients are experiencing significantly less personal distress; (c) there is confirmation from others that social interactions have improved; (d) clients are realistically optimistic about the future — not merely in a naïve optimism, but about their own ability to *think* their way out of problems.

Evidence of the success of cognitive developmental psychotherapy should include: (a) demonstration of improved cognitive competence in basic domains of thinking; (b) improved learning of content; (c) lessened personal distress; (d) demonstration of generalization of cognitive rules, principles, and strategies, i.e. of their use in novel situations; (e) when appropriate and possible, reduction of "in trouble" and disturbing behavior.

2.4 Special Applicability to Adolescents

Cognitive developmental psychotherapy is especially useful, and especially difficult, with disturbed, low functioning, and/or delinquent adolescents. One reason for this special application is that adolescence is a developmental period that is not generally characterized by reflective, logic-supported action, but rather by affectively controlled, often impulsive, strongly peer-influenced behavior. Further, adolescence is a time when expectations change; i.e. people are expected to behave in ways that reflect maturity that they may not have attained. Habits of childhood have to be abandoned; e.g. children are expected (some of the time) to behave selfishly and to be governed by their feelings and wants, but adolescents, while still expected to behave in such childish ways some of the time, are expected at other times to behave in more reflective, mature ways. Because they are larger than children, indeed, often as large as adults, they are expected implicitly to know much more than any one might actually know or even have had opportunity to learn. Finally, it appears to be true that relatively many of the problems for which adolescents seek or are put into psychotherapy are less the products of classical psychopathology than of failure to have acquired effective modes of logical thought, i.e. are less *pathological* than *developmental*. Thus, adolescents are often distressed by poor interpersonal relations, but more often because they do not know how to behave in socially gratifying ways than because they have pathological fears, anxieties, or compulsions. They often make poor decisions, or simply fail to make good ones, not so much out of incapacity or neurotic/psychotic motives but because of the lack of effective decision-making cognitive processes. They often get into trouble in situations in which others are inclined to think that they have made bad choices, when in fact they have not made any choices at all but instead behaved like mollusks — not seeking, but accepting or being at the mercy of whatever floats past. Because adolescence is characterized by poor temporal perspective, brief delays of gratification become intolerable.

In addition, very many of the problems that adolescents encounter are reality problems, not necessarily neurotic ones. The chief developmental task of childhood is education, and that task continues into adolescence, but at adolescence it has to compete with many other demanding developmental tasks. For example, another developmental task of childhood is to internalize one's parents' values and standards, which is a relatively low-energy task, but the analogous task for adolescents is to establish one's personal independence, which is a far more energy-consuming task. Further, this latter developmental task is very likely to produce interpersonal and intrafamilial conflict.

By the time one has gone to school for 10 years, one is expected to know many things, but to the extent that education has been inadequate, those expectations may be unrealistic. Education can be inadequate for a variety of reasons: poor teaching, absence of teaching, absence of the children, low aptitude in the children, psychological distress in the children and/or the parents, family problems, or failure to have developed the cognitive tools for effective content learning. When it has been inadequate, *real* distress follows: school failure, parental pressure, low self concept, difficulty in getting jobs, invidious comparisons with peers, future-oriented existential anxiety (who am I, why am I dumb, what will become of me?).

For all these reasons, and many more, a cognitive developmental approach to the treatment of distressed, low-functioning, or delinquent adolescents seems especially appropriate. That is why there are certain approaches and techniques that are an integral part of cognitive developmental psychotherapy that seem (and are) especially relevant to the adolescent and young adult periods.

The first such principle is *peer separation*. Adolescents are very strongly influenced by their perceptions of what their age peers expect of them. Usually, peers expect older, rather than younger, behavior; i.e. adolescents are expected by their age peers to behave in ways that are characteristic of their (often unrealistic) picture of adult behavior, and are specifically expected not to behave in ways that are interpreted as child-like. Childhood is to be abandoned, scorned, surpassed. In very many social situations, the peer group simply will not permit the kind of therapeutic participation, at both cognitive and affective levels, that must take place if real cognitive change is to occur.

The principal reason why peer separation is essential is the requirement of *induced regression*. To the extent that adolescents have problems because they have not acquired some of the culture-characteristic modes of systematic thought (logic structures, in Piagetian terms), their therapy requires that they acquire those modes of thought. Doing so requires them to accept tasks and engage in psychological behavior that is often interpreted as, and indeed is, characteristic of an earlier developmental period. For example, it is necessary to learn to control impulsivity, to build habits of spontaneous comparison, to classify, to seek logical evidence to support one's actions, to be precise and accurate both in data gathering and in expression, to consider multiple sources of information simultaneously. Some of the most efficient and effective ways to learn those cognitive operations involve exercises that appear to be child-like. In the case of the cognitive education program recommended as part of cognitive developmental psychotherapy, i.e. *Instrumental Enrichment*, these exercises require such activities as connecting dots to form geometric figures, locating embedded figures, orienting oneself in space in relation to both stable and relative referents. Getting clients to accept these activities is vital to their progress but counter to an adolescent peer culture. One must, then, encourage the dropping of the adolescent herd defenses. In order to accomplish that, it is essential that the clients achieve quick success and see relevance to their everyday lives. In a more general sense, extending the period of childhood is itself therapeutic, because it permits disturbed adolescents, with the therapist's sanction, to relax, to stop working so hard to be what they cannot yet become, and to bask for a last time in the blissful nonchalance of childhood. This is greatly to be encouraged! [NB: The essential ideas of "peer separation" and "induced regression" were derived from work reported by Feuerstein and Krasilowsky (1967, 1971). The present author thanks them, and accepts responsibility for the elaborations in this chapter.]

2.5 Applicability to Retarded and Slow Learning Persons

One of the unique aspects of CDPsy is the fact that it specifically includes, rather than excluding as do many psychotherapeutic approaches, clients who are intellectually low functioning. Young adults, adolescents, and children with IQs as low as 45 have been treated with this method, with, as usual, varying degrees of success — but usually *some* success (Haywood, 1986, 1987, 1988, 1989; Haywood & Menal, 1992; Wingenfeld, Vaught & Haywood, 1991). One major reason for the applicability of CDPsy to persons in this group is that it is specifically addressed to the *development* of the very tools of perception, thinking, learning, and problem solving that are most often deficient — and perhaps at the root of many of the difficulties — in mildly and moderately mentally retarded persons and persons of low-normal intelligence. Cognitive incompetence leads to motivational deficits (Haywood & Switzky, 1986) and to further performance deficiencies, which may lead in turn to lowered self esteem and eventually to difficulty in social interaction as well as to "intrapsychic" problems and conflicts (Haywood, 1988, 1989).

Classical psychodynamic therapies are extremely difficult with persons of low intelligence, essentially because they rest upon rich verbal interchange and logical analysis of psychological events and phenomena that are quite abstract in their nature. CDPsy has as a major goal the development of the very abilities whose deficient development makes it difficult for low-IQ persons to derive benefit from psychodynamic therapies. The talking is about events that are highly familiar to the clients: their own thoughts, their own performance, their own behavior. Further, the cognitive education phase relies upon a set of materials that can be extended to the developmental level of the clients, allowing one to apply the principle of "starting where they are". A strong principle in this phase is to continue working on specific cognitive processes until they are integrated into the client's repertoire; thus, failure is not a part of this experience, because one does not proceed to the next step until success is achieved in the present one. As clients become more cognitively competent (and they always do!) in the cognitive education phase, and more trusting of the therapist, the psychotherapeutic work can gain pace. Adjustments that may be made include: a longer period of therapy, emphasizing a longer period of cognitive education; use of developmentally earlier levels of cognitive education materials, and thus emphasis on developmentally earlier cognitive processes (e.g. those that define operatory thought; if necessary, use of a cognitive education program, such as *Bright Start: Cognitive Curriculum for Young Children* [Haywood, Brooks, & Burns, 1992] as a prelude to *Instrumental Enrichment*); eliciting a greater number of "bridges" of cognitive principles and strategies to a wider variety of real-life situations; "time out" to teach the content (information, facts, vocabulary) necessary to understand the concepts of both cognition and further content learning, as well as social interaction. This last part can be accomplished with great benefit by establishing and maintaining alliances with others in the social ecology of retarded persons: their teachers, counselors, parents.

2.6 "Targets" of CDPsy

My students and I have done this form of psychological treatment with a variety of clients. The first client was a 25-year-old man who was in trouble with the law. He had above-average intelligence, but engaged in "stupid" behavior that got him into trouble. By using dynamic assessment of learning potential, we located some specific deficiencies in his cognitive development, as well as some areas of significant strength that could be used in approaching remediation of the deficient cognitive functions. We then gave him 3 hours per week of cognitive education and 1 hour every 2 weeks of individual psychotherapy, with close coordination between the "teacher" and the "therapist". These efforts were crowned with success, which lead us to try the method with others.

The second individual case (Haywood & Menal, 1992) was with a 15-year-old mildly retarded girl who was already the mother of a 2-year-old child, was in the custody of the Department of Correction, and was headed for a repetitious cycle of in-trouble behavior. Moderate success (again using dual therapists) lead to further generalization of the method.

Next, we used the method with a group of adolescents who resided in a state-operated residential school for "neglected and dependent" children (Haywood, 1986–1988). These clients were not necessarily retarded, or delinquent, or emotionally disturbed, but were more likely to be any or all of these than if they had been drawn randomly from the population. They tended to be low school achievers, hostile toward authority, and to have multiple unresolved psychological conflicts centering around personal worth, family belongingness, and personal goals (actually, absence of them!).

The next clients were mildly mentally retarded and intellectually low functioning adolescents who were adjudicated delinquents and were in the custody of the Department of Correction, residing in a youth correctional facility.

The next clients were quite similar to the low functioning delinquent adolescents, but were residing in a community-based group home while still in the legal custody of the Department of Correction (Wingenfeld, Vaught & Haywood, 1991). They either had been in a residential correctional center or had been sent to the group home as an alternative to such commitment.

In these situations, acceptance of and co-operation with the program by staff members has been essential. Ultimately, our plan has been to train staff members of these facilities, at least to do the cognitive education part and, we hope, to do both parts of this treatment. We are still working on that! Systematic quantitative evaluation is in progress.

In general, preliminary data suggest that: (a) significant deficiencies in cognitive functioning are present in the clients that we have seen, and can be related to their personal and interpersonal difficulties; (b) beginning is difficult — clients do not easily confront their own thinking processes, often do not see the reasons for doing so, and especially when they are not self-referred they tend to be initially unco-operative; (c) a minimal commitment of at least 3 hours per week of cognitive education — more if possible — is essential to the success of such a program; (d) the cognitive education sessions tend to be viewed as classes, but the individual therapy hours are cherished, even though further cognitive work is done in those sessions; (e) gains are recorded in cognitive functioning; (f) some (inconsistent) gains have been seen in self concept; (g) some gains are seen in individual planning behavior; (h) there are (inconsistent) reductions in in-trouble behavior; (i) we have seen occasional quite strong therapeutic relationships develop; (j) clients appear to be more ready to anticipate consequences of their behavior, to recognize when they have choices to make, to know how to make those choices by considering various alternatives, and to relate their own behavior to their goals and outcomes.

18

Mediated Learning Experience and the Counseling Process

Louis H. Falik

In this chapter the contribution of Reuven Feuerstein's theory of structural cognitive modifiability (SCM) and conceptualization of mediated learning experience (MLE) is applied to the processes of counseling and psychotherapy. The theory and practical applications developed from it are viewed as significantly generative and heuristic, contributing both to a more holistic and integrative approach to processes, and generating specific interventions.

Counseling and psychotherapy are complex processes. Counseling at its core is an interpersonal relationship, essentially similar to all other forms of interpersonal interactions, but different in its focused, purposive, goal-oriented intentionality. Fully functioning human experience encompasses these qualities, at different times and for different purposes — as interactions occur between parents and their children, teachers and their students, husband and wife, or any other intimate and meaningful human interaction. When the relationship is that of counseling, elevating its purpose beyond the social or incidental, its focus requires attention to dimensions of interpersonal interviewing skills, assessing the present concerns of the client, understanding the dynamics of behavior and change, and the acquisition and use of a repertoire of techniques and appropriate interventions. To be effective these skills must be employed in an organized, systematic and intentional way. Once mastering the skills of interpersonal interviewing, the counselor must then conceptualize the dynamics of the client's experience and develop responses and interventions that are clearly related both to the process of counseling and to helping the client to achieve behavioral change objectives that move the client's process forward toward relevant and desired outcomes. The parameters of MLE both create the conditions for this to occur, but also guide toward the development of specific interventions which become integrative, purposeful, restorative.

The process of counseling can be viewed as having several distinct domains. The beginning counselor or therapist often sees them as such, and finds it difficult to envision their integration. Without integration there will be no sense of cohesion, for the client or counselor. As one acquires more experience the process potentially becomes integrated, with the responses of the counselor becoming seamless, spontaneous, and intuitive. For many, however, finding that integration, and using it in the service of effectiveness is difficult, requiring an understanding of the components, identifying and practicing them, and elaborating them in a meaningful and far-sighted manner. MLE is posed as serving to make this integration and development possible, as a dynamic organizer for the larger process and functional dimensions.

In this sense, Feuerstein's development of the MLE concepts, in theory and application, creates the bridge from the acquisition of interviewing skills to the clinical processes necessary for intervention, providing a kind of connective tissue. There are many aspects to the achieving of this dynamic connection, and others have written eloquently about it (see Kottler, 1986).

1 The Process of Counseling

Before proceeding further, perhaps it is necessary to set the context. What is the process of counseling? The counselor listens to the client's story, works to understand its details and sequences, and shares with the client in the process of the telling. There is an engagement with the client in a mutual experience, reciprocally meaningful to the client and the counselor. At the outset of a counseling relationship, the content of the client's experience is of relatively more importance … in the details of the story and specifics of their experience. This is what is most comfortably contained in the first mutual aspects of the relationship. The process is what is important to the counselor … what it is like to mutually interact with the client, in the building of the comfortable, trusting, accepting, and satisfying relationship. Thus at the outset, the client and counselor have different need states: the client's content drives the session, and the counselor uses the content to move the focus toward the process, where the significant work will occur. At later stages the balance shifts, with content driving the client and counselor ever deeper into the process, which is used for therapeutic gain. To do this, there needs to be a "laying of a foundation" upon which this progression will be based. Early activities in the counselor's skill repertoire are directed to creating this foundation, of building what has been called the working alliance.

The counselor keeps in focus the responsibility to help the client, and the need to listen to the client in order to understand the client's experience in such a way that will enable the identification of the elements which have the potential to facilitate change. The client is drawn out, encouraged to elaborate and clarify. The counselor becomes involved in the intimate details of the client's experience, and assists in sorting out and accessing the client's experience. At some point the counselor begins to act to bring to the client's attention some of the elements of change potential, what has been heard, and what is missing, confusing, or thematically significant (that is, what is heard over and over or in slightly different forms). Having done this, the client is assisted in understanding more clearly what is the issue of concern (framing), and what are the deeper, more meaningful, and more important issues to address in the therapeutic process (reframing). Here is where some of the bridges are.

A word about the use of the term "therapeutic". It is useful to differentiate the generic from the specific. Early in the development of counselors or therapists, it is useful to consider the process in its most general sense, as its dictionary definition suggests: pertaining to treating or curing. Later, as more experience and wisdom is accumulated, specific and particular formats of treatment are conceptualized, linked to articulated theoretical constructs, and associated with formal or prescribed interventions. As useful as this may be, it is here that some danger lies. Consider the therapeutic process in this way: the creation of conditions which make possible the client's change, in spite of resistances, fears, pessimism, past experiences, self-imposed or other-determined limitations. What the counselor says or does, or does not do or say, and how it is done, contributes to the creation of a therapeutic condition, the nurturance and facilitation of a change potential. It starts long before any interventions are undertaken, and in fact must be present and well founded for interventions to be meaningful and effective. It is here that the mediational potential of the relationship, as conceptualized in Feuerstein's MLE formulations has its initial and generative effects. Simply put, *what* does the counselor do or say, *when* is it said or done, and *how* is it said or done? These questions are essential to the nature of the decision-making that is available to the counselor as the interactional process is underway. These and other bridging issues come together in a theoretical conception and a model which can be constructed based on the theory and practice of MLE.

2 The Theory of Structural Cognitive Modifiability

The underlying theory that is the basis MLE, and which brings together the complex phenomena of the counseling process in a meaningful and useful way is that of Feuerstein's structural cognitive modifiability (SCM). Although cognitive in its structure, SCM can be viewed as a generic, organizing theory which applies to a wide range of cognitive and social development. Considered broadly, it can be seen as having the potential to deepen the understanding of general social development, and thus be applied to a wide range of psychotherapeutic theories and approaches. And as any good theory should, it lends itself to model building, so as to guide the practitioner toward operational concepts and activities which are consistent with the theory and helpful in determining practice.

Feuerstein's theory of SCM is influenced by the work of Jean Piaget (1955, 1968) and Lev Vygotsky (Kozulin, 1990). From Piaget he draws on the importance of observing the developmental phases of learning and thinking as they influence behavior, and from Vygotsky the importance of social interaction in enhancing and developing the individual's potential. The former contributed to the identifying and defining of cognitive functions, the latter to the formulation of the concept of mediated learning experience. Applications of SCM require the use of both of these constructive applications in our understanding of the deeper dynamics of behavioral development and the potential for behavior change. It has been proposed elsewhere (Falik & Feuerstein, 1990) that the theory of SCM can be applied to the counseling and psychotherapeutic process, conceptualizing the dynamics of counseling and developing responses and interventions which clearly can be related to behavioral change objectives. The development of a model which incorporates these concepts, and integrates them with basic interpersonal interviewing processes assists the counselor to approach counseling or psychotherapy in a planful, systematic, and organized manner.

The theory of structural cognitive modifiability (SCM) rests on three central tenets: that in considering the human organism there is a strong relationship between the parts and the whole of the person; that the human being is naturally drawn to becoming involved in the process of change, or transformation; and that human development is self-perpetuating, self-regulating, and actively seeking to be involved in the process of change. In the context of counseling and psychotherapy, clients come with apparent impediments in this supposedly natural progression. What is it, one must ask, that causes this blockage or denial of what is posed as the natural tendencies of the person?

Feuerstein (1980) believes that the answer lies at the heart of the process of SCM. The human organism is an open system, with naturally occurring needs which render him or her receptive to change and modification. Development is not fixed or immutable, rather it is open to continuous change in response to the demands of the environment. When the conditions of human existence are favorable, the individual develops adaptational mechanisms and uses them to respond in ways which further development, elaborate new or modified adaptations, and experience growth and change, in formal, objective, and measurable terms and in the sense of inner, subjective, existential formations. Feuerstein writes of modifiability not simply in terms of "the acquisition of bits and pieces of knowledge or the mastery of specific academic or vocational skills, but with, in the broadest sense, the ultimate destiny of the retarded performer" (Feuerstein, 1980, p. 3). And in his phrase "the broadest sense" one can easily relate to any individual who, for a variety of reasons, has not experienced success in functioning — using own resources, drawing inferences, making decisions, planning ahead to anticipate future consequences — some of the wide range of cognitive and social behaviors which are required to successfully adapt and be adaptive.

An essential part of the SCM theory is that it is not directed simply at changing specific behaviors, but at changes of an inner structural nature which have the power to alter the course of development, at both behavioral and inner process/experience levels. When Feuerstein uses the term "cognitive modifiability" he means the creation of structural changes, changes within the organism that are "brought about by a deliberate program of intervention that will facilitate the generation of continuous growth by rendering the organism receptive and sensitive to internal and external sources of stimulation" (Feuerstein, 1980, p. 9). Piaget described "cognitive schemata" which are essentially configurations of structural qualities that the individual has incorporated as a consequence of learned experience, and which serve to organize current thinking and future behavioral responses. We know structural change has occurred when we can observe the following parameters (for further discussion of these concepts, the reader is referred to Feuerstein, 1995):

Retention/Permanence: When the individual is able to maintain changes under conditions which are essentially similar as those under which the change was initially achieved. The experience of stability over time and the sense of continuity and inner integrity are indicators that the change has been structurally integrated. The lack of retention/permanence shows itself in the client who appears to have acquired an insight or skill, but it doesn't stay, and needs to be repeatedly re-learned or re-experienced. A teacher once described a child as a "disappearing learning type", in that the student needed to be taught the same thing repeatedly, and never did appear — in the teacher's view — to acquire that which was being taught. The child being described had not internalized the learning as an aspect of structural change and thus did not experience permanence. As with all these parameters, they are both felt from within (the client "knows" and feels it) and observed from without.

Resistance: The reader must be careful to differentiate this parameter from the more commonly used psychodynamic meaning of the term. Here we refer to the individual's holding on to that which has been learned or experienced in the face of demands from situations or tasks which are *different* from that in which the initial learning or change occurred. Can the individual resist or withstand the pressure of differing situational, affective, or task conditions? For example, will a client who has gained control over impulsivity under conditions of stress and increased vigilance continue with this control when conditions permit more relaxed functioning? Changes that have been structurally incorporated, into the "cognitive schemas" of the individual, will be resistant to situational and affective changes in the context confronted by the individual.

Flexibility/Adaptability: The "other side of the coin" of resistance, this parameter considers the application of achieved changes to situations that differ from the original. Feuerstein has described this as the "plasticity of change," once the individual is "exposed to tasks and conditions which no longer permit or require the application of the learned behavior with the same frequency, purpose, or manifest goal. In other words, a structurally modified behavior will be flexibly and adaptively applied to situations which present altered conditions" (Feuerstein, 1995, p. 29.9). An illustration of this quality, related to the example offered above, is the individual who vigilantly controls impulsivity in situations where such control is no longer necessary, and may in fact be adaptively impaired — the overly controlled, timid or fearful individual who cannot generate appropriate or acceptable responses.

Generalizability/Transformability: This is perhaps the most "human" of the parameters of structural cognitive change. It refers to the capacity to abstract and represent experience, beyond the immediate or concrete, into the farther reaches of experience — what Feuerstein refers to as the phenomenon of distance in cognitive processing (Feuerstein, Feuerstein & Schur, 1997). The client's ability to see beyond the immediate situation, the specific insight or task acquired, to the larger issues of life, is to *transcend* and be *transformed* by experience. It is in this sense that the self-perpetuating and self-regulating aspect of SCM is realized, and is consistent with the basic nature of the human condition. We are at our most human, and most connected both with our inner experience and intimate relationships with others when we are in touch with and able to utilize this quality. The importance of this parameter as a dimension of structural cognitive change cannot be over-emphasized. When it occurs and is shared in the context of a counseling or psychotherapeutic relationship, *both* counselor and client may view it as a kind of epiphany (which will be remembered by both of them forever, and which is testament to meaningful change for them both).

These qualities of structural cognitive change require a specific and focused interpersonal intervention, which Feuerstein has labeled and described as "mediational." Mediated learning experience (MLE) closes the "loop", integrating the tasks to be learned or responded to (selected and structured stimuli), the nature of the respondents' skills, attributes and functions (the cognitive and socially developed responses), with a carefully designed and implemented interpersonal interaction (manifested as teaching, parenting, or therapeutic interventions).

3 Mediated Learning Experience

According to Feuerstein's theory there are two kinds of learning experience necessary for human development. Direct learning, which is most simply characterized by behavioral psychologists as S–R (stimulus and response), which exposes the individual to stimuli which produce changes in behavior and consequent learning. Piaget imposed a more cognitive focus on the process of direct learning by adding an "O" to the schema, representing the organism upon which the stimuli acts and from whom responses are generated (S–O–R). In direct learning, as in touching a hot stove or spilling a glass of water, the stimuli impose themselves directly on the organism and the organism reacts. Even though such experience is initially not systematic and may even be random, the power of a direct learning experience is such that it can affect pervasive and lasting structural change in the individual. Feuerstein and others (see for example, Skuy, Mentis & Mentis, 1991) have described this kind of experience as "incidental" learning. It makes it no less important in the whole experience of the individual, but does not permit the full potential of human development, and may contain some dangerous consequences (if, for example, direct learning is harmful, inconsistent, unavailable, etc.).

A second kind of learning that is necessary for fully human development is that of mediated learning experience (MLE). Feuerstein describes MLE as a natural and necessary aspect of human existence, without which the full expression of what it is to be human cannot be fulfilled. Its universality is such that it is hard to conceive an effective parent/child, teacher/student, or counselor/client interaction that does not contain elements of MLE. However, all interactions are not mediational:

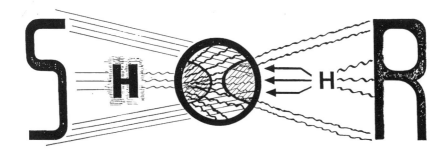

Figure 1. Mediated learning experiences model (MLE) (Feuerstein & Feuerstein 1991).

> An interpersonal interaction is mediational to the extent that it contains a dynamic process between an active and involved human (an "organism" who in the counseling/psychotherapy paradigm is the client) and another human who is experienced, intentioned, and who interposes him or herself between the client and the external sources of stimulation and responding. The interposition is not passive — the intervening person acts to mediate to and for the client by *framing*, *selecting*, *focusing*, and *feeding back* environmental experiences in such away as to produce ... appropriate learning set and habits (Feuerstein, 1979, p. 71, italics added).

Feuerstein (1980) further describes how the experience of the organism, and the environment in which the interaction takes place is transformed by the mediator:

> This mediating agent, guided by his intentions, culture, and emotional investment, selects and organizes the world of stimuli for the (client). The mediator selects stimuli that are most appropriate and then frames, filters, and schedules them; he determines the appearance or disappearance of certain stimuli and ignores others. Through this process of mediation, the cognitive structure of the (client) is affected ... The (client) acquires behavior patterns and learning sets, which in turn become important ingredients of his capacity to become modified through direct exposure to stimuli (p. 16).

In the context of counseling, the client is defined as having some kind of need, and the counselor effectively acts in an intentional, experienced, focused, and interested manner directed toward helping the client meet those needs. The "H" that Feuerstein has added to Piaget's conception of the cognitive learning process is thus an active and involved "therapeutic" agent. Additionally, however, the activity must be planful, systematic, organized, and directional. To achieve this, the criterial components of MLE are introjected into the interaction (see Figure 2), and become an integral part of the outcome process. It is this differentiation and focus

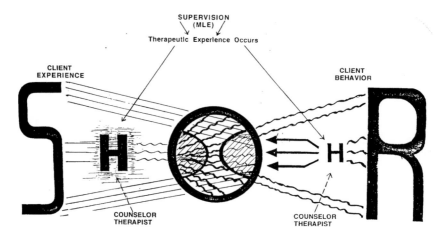

Figure 2. Mediated learning experience model in clinical supervision. Adapted from Feuerstein & Feuerstein (1991). L. H. Falik, Mediational Counseling. All Rights Reserved (1996).

upon the criterial elements that MLE (as a process and set of operational guidelines) that serves to orient the counseling relationship to achieve desired goals (Falik & Feuerstein, 1990; Feuerstein & Feuerstein, 1991).

MLE occurs when intentional, planned, and carefully organized mediational interventions are part of the interaction between mediator and mediatee. While not all interpersonal interactions are mediational, all interactions have the potential to be. Meaningful behavioral or emotional change occurs and is integrated into the cognitive schemata of a client when the interactions of the mediator, either as a consequence of framing the stimuli or filtering responses stimulates inner, lasting, flexible and adaptive changes. Changes can be and are actually both internal and external, although not necessarily experienced by the client simultaneously or sequentially. MLE, used in a systematic and planful way, enables the counselor (mediator) to organize responses and consider the interaction from a number of perspectives, both developmental and clinical.

To elaborate what was discussed above, and place it into the context of SCM theory, it can now be pointed out how modifiability (e.g. the propensity for change in the individual) is effectively experienced when the interactions of the counselor, acting as mediator, either as a consequence of intervening between the stimulus (the experience of the client) or the response (the client's behavior), serve to stimulate inner, lasting, meaningful changes in the client (the organism).

4 Social/Behavioral Parameters of Mediated Learning Experience

Twelve criterial elements of mediated learning experience have been identified and described (see Feuerstein & Feuerstein, 1991; Falik, 1996; Skuy, Mentis & Mentis,

1996). The first three, (1) intentionality/reciprocity, (2) transcendence, and (3) meaning, can be considered *universal*, in that they must be present to some degree in all interpersonal encounters for mediation to occur. They create the conditions for modifiability. The next group, the mediation of (4) feelings of competence, (5) regulation and control of behavior, (6) sharing behavior, (7) individuation and psychological differentiation, (8) goal seeking/setting/achieving, and the (9) mediation of challenge, novelty and complexity are *situational*, in that not all encounters have the capacity to offer mediational opportunities or that situations can be created to present these specific mediational opportunities. The last group, (10) mediation of an awareness of the human being as a changing entity, (11) the search for an optimistic alternative, and (12) the feeling of belonging relate to the belief system of the individual, contributing to modifiability once universal and situational mediation has been experienced.

The mediational interactions associated with each parameter, with specific reference to the counseling and psychotherapeutic process can be described as follows:

Intentionality/Reciprocity: conveys a purposeful and directed interaction, with attention and activity focused on the purpose of the encounter, and containing empathetic listening, clear communication, and opportunities for retrospection and collaboration.

Transcendence: bridges the immediate encounter to broader issues of experience and future meaning, identifying generalizations and recurring themes, directing the immediate "here and now" to anticipated future experience.

Meaning: infuses the encounter with the importance and relevance of feelings and activities, identifying and confirming values, acceptance of feelings and validating the reasons for the interaction.

Competence: confirming (at a feeling level) abilities and skills, creating an optimistic belief in success, empowering confidence, task accomplishment, self-reflections on abilities and achievements.

Self-Regulation and Control of Behavior: experiencing and modifying environments to provide opportunities for self-monitoring, making adjustments in responses or perspectives, developing skills through active structuring, developing insight into needs, skills, and both past and future experiences.

Sharing Behavior: involving another individual in activities of co-operation and empathy, using listening, interpersonal sensitivity, openness and acceptance, and the acceptance of commonality of experience.

Individuation and Psychological Differentiation: emphasizing the uniqueness and difference of the individual, valuing the independence and diversity of human experience, and identifying, valuing, and accepting individual behavioral and cognitive styles as they manifest themselves in behavior.

Goal Seeking, Planning, Achieving Behavior: seeking realistic goals, setting meaningful and achievable goals, planning their achievement, and monitoring the extent to which they were achieved.

Challenge, Novelty and Complexity: confronting novel, complex, difficult experiences with an optimistic approach to the real and/or perceived difficulty, structuring encounters for positive outcomes by developing skills and supportive attitudes.

Self-Change: encourages the perspective of the human being as needing and able to change, with expectations of potential for growth and the acceptance of changes already or to be experienced.

Optimistic Alternatives: facilitates an awareness of the positive potential for change and the available opportunities in the range of experiences available, encouraging the scanning of immediate experience and the reframing of past experiences into growth and change potentials.

Feeling of Belonging: confirming the relevance of social and emotional connections, at the level of interpersonal and situational contact, validating the importance and meaningfulness of relating to others, outside of the boundaries of self and more limited experience.

This list is neither exclusive or exhaustive, does not represent the totality of mediational potential, and does not offer specifics on what will or should occur. Rather, the MLE criteria serve as parameters to direct the structuring of the mediational experience, and as such relate to the questions addressed earlier in regarding "What to say or do", "When to say or do it", and "How to say or do it". In further training experiences, the counselor learns to consider and adapt reactions and interventions in the light of these criterial dimensions. A variety of specifics emerge, linked and integrated into a perspective encompassing the operational criteria (e.g. being planful, systematic, consistent, and directional), adding dimensions of focus and organization leading to effective counseling responses and interventions.

5 The Development of an Integrative Model

The potential of MLE to affect the quality of the counseling process can be enhanced if it is viewed in the context of the multiple dimensions of that process. This can be achieved by constructing a model that integrates the criterial elements of MLE with counseling process parameters so that they can be used in a planful and systematic manner. Model building has three structural components and two functional foci.

At the structural level, the model has:

(1) *A theoretical component*: reflecting concepts and constructs that orient the process toward an organized and systematic perspective,
(2) *An operational component*: creating dimensions or elements that reflect relevant phenomena and processes, and that are consistent with the theoretical constructs, and
(3) *A methodological component*: adaptive implications for knowledge and skill acquisition.

At the functional level the model offers a *molar* and a *molecular* perspective. It is molar as it organizes traditional and known concepts into meaningful and useful patterns, which can then be applied more efficiently. It is molecular as it identifies process elements that can be utilized to take knowledge to deeper levels and broaden its effect.

There are a number of previously identified and well agreed upon process dimensions into which the MLE criteria can be integrated (see Carkhuff, 1969; Cormier & Cormier, 1991; Egan, 1986; Ivey, 1994). The microskills movement in counseling research and training has focused on various phases, aspects, and elements generic to the counseling process. Adding MLE to this structural conception strengthens the connections and bridges processes, for the reasons described above. Given an understanding of the role of MLE in the development of both general human learning experiences, and the identification of specific functional criteria which characterize interpersonal encounters, the building of a model which bridges the phase and process elements of counseling with the mediational parameters holds the promise of significantly enhancing our understanding of the acquisition and development of effective counseling skills and process interventions.

The model thus developed is described as *integrated*. It represents a "structural view" of the counseling and psychotherapeutic process. The practitioner must ask, when using any model, whether the view incorporated is consistent with his or her sense of what the integral process is all about. No less is demanded here. For the model here proposed, a structure is created that differentiates between the process of counseling, which is defined as the "how" of counseling, and the content of counseling, defined as the "what". Using language which has been used in other contexts, it may be useful to view the skills, techniques, and specifics of functions (the "how") as the *tactical* level of interaction, and the planned interventions and responses that are generated as a consequence of the process (the "what") as the *strategic* level. Using the terms tactical and strategic may help to orient thinking about the difference between the necessary tools and the goal-directed, purposiveness necessary. Both levels must be attended to and reflected in the development of the counseling process to achieve the ultimate measure of effectiveness, some kind of behavioral or intra-personal change.

6 Integrating MLE into a Counseling Process Model

The intention of the model is to integrate the parameters of MLE with process dimensions of the counseling relationship. There is a large and growing literature in the field relating to counseling process dimensions, reflective of many theoretical approaches and conceptions of human nature and behavior. A general consensus has developed regarding the essential common or generic elements. This is largely due to the development of what has come to be called the "microskills" movement, stimulated first by the work of Carkhuff and his associates (see Carkhuff & Berenson, 1976). A less widely known, but equally significant contribution was the work of Norman Kagan (1980), whose IPR approach framed a more general identification of process elements, consistent with the microskills approaches (see also Cormier & Cormier, 1991; Egan, 1986; Ivey, 1991). Thus, while various writers use different emphases, sequences, and nomenclature, the counseling skills training literature gives us a holistic and generic view of the interviewing and therapeutic process which can be synthesized and summarized into a model which is both heuristic and applicational.

Given the above described general agreement and differential labeling, it is clearly possible for the model to identify general process elements present in a counseling interaction, to reflect the client and counselor's experience, and relate to the pacing, choice of initial responses, and issues of framing and reframing which are part of the establishment and implementation of an effective relationship. The function of the model is to guide the counselor toward clarifying his or her conceptualization of what is occurring, what needs to occur, and the formulation of effective responses and interventions that are meaningfully employed at appropriate places in the process. Additionally, the model can retrospectively enable the counselor to review what has occurred and make decisions regarding modification or focus for future interventions.

The integrated model is composed of four inter-related and dynamic elements — two *major dimensions*:

(1) Developmental **phases** or stages of the counseling process which represent temporal and experiential aspects of a counseling relationship. Within the model, the phases are attending, listening, responding, and intervening.
(2) The functional **components of MLE** as criterial parameters that guide the general and specific therapeutic objectives of the encounter (see descriptions above);

and *two response modalities*, that are present in all interpersonal interactions and which enter into the specific formulation of counseling responses:

(3) The **focus of the interaction** on content or process, and
(4) the formulation of the **quality of the response** in an overt/explicit or a covert/implicit manner.

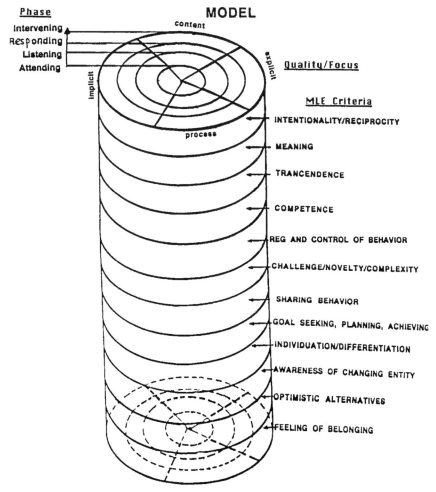

Figure 3. Counseling process: an integrative model.

These elements, as reflected in the model, provide a descriptive picture of the relevant interactive dynamics of the counseling process. The model is designed to structurally convey the dynamic interaction among the elements as the counseling process unfolds (see Figures 3 and 4): that is, any given response can be analyzed according to the extent to which it reflects the dimensions and modalities of the model. These elements, as reflected in the model, provide a descriptive picture of the relevant interactive dynamics of the counseling process, enhanced by the inclusion of the MLE criteria. The more explicit elaboration of the qualities and interactional nature of the phases and foci of the process is beyond the scope of this chapter, and is in process of being explicated in the form of a teaching text (Falik, under the working title *Mediational Counseling*, in preparation.)

Figure 4. A model for integrating mediated learning experience criteria into the counseling process.

7 In Summary

Feuerstein's theory of structural cognitive modifiability (SCM) and his mediated learning experience (MLE) constructs appear to have a highly significant applicability to the process of counseling and psychotherapy. The development of an integrated model for the counseling process, and the author's experience using the resulting concepts and structures in a variety of training and consultation activities attests to their value. There are other cornerstone concepts of Feuerstein (notably his delineation of the cognitive functions, which can be meaningfully reframed into social/behavioral contexts) which can be added to this development. While this author's direct experience with this work is at an early and admittedly limited stage, there is great promise for the future. The whole movement of cognitive psychology, the cognitive therapies, and their integration and extension into what might be called the humanistic/existential framework appears to rest well within the context provided by the MLE perspective and structures.

Selected Bibliography of Reuven Feuerstein

Books

Richelle, M. & Feuerstein, R. (1957). *Enfants Juifs Nord-Africans*. Jerusalem: Youth Aliyah.

Feuerstein, R. & Richelle, M. (in collaboration with A. Ray) (1963). *Children of the Mellah: Socio-Cultural Deprivation and its Educational Significance*. Jerusalem: Szold Foundation (in Hebrew).

Feuerstein, R., Rand, Y. & Hoffman, M. (1979). *The Dynamic Assessment of Retarded Performers: The Learning Potential Assessment Device (LPAD)*. Baltimore, MD: University Park Press.

Feuerstein, R., Rand, Y., Hoffman, M. & Miller, R. (1980). *Instrumental Enrichment: An Intervention Program for Cognitive Modifiability*. Baltimore, MD: University Park Press.

Feuerstein, R., Rand, Y. & Rynders, J. (1988). *Don't Accept Me as I Am: Helping "Retarded" People to Excel*. N.Y.: Plenum Press (Second revised edition published by Skylight in 1997; Hebrew translation published by Freund in 1998; Dutch translation: *Laat me niet zoals ik bem*. Rotterdam: Leminscaat, 1993; Italian translation: *Non accettarmi como sono*. Milan: R.C.S. Libri).

Feuerstein, R., Klein, P. & Tannenbaum, A. (Eds.) (1991). *Mediated Learning Experience: Theoretical, Psychosocial, and Learning Implications*. Tel Aviv and London: Freund.

Feuerstein, R. (1998) *The Theory of Mediated Learning Experience: About Human as a Modifiable Being*. Jerusalem: Ministry of Defense Publications (In Hebrew).

Chapters and articles

Feuerstein, R. & Richelle, M. (1958). Perception and drawing of the North African Jewish and child. *Megamot, 9*, 156–162 (in Hebrew).

Feuerstein, R. & Krasilowsky, D. (1967). The treatment group technique. *Israeli Annals of Psychiatry and Related Disciplines, 5*, 61–90.

Feuerstein, R. & Shalom, H. (1967). Methods of assessing the educational level of socially and culturally disadvanged children. *Megamot*, No. 2–3: 177–187 (in Hebrew).

Feuerstein, R. & Shalom, H. (1968). The Learning Potential Assessment Device. In B.W. Richards (Ed.). *Proceedings of the First Congress of the International Association for the Scientific Study of Mental Deficiency*. Reigate, UK: Michael Jackson.

Feuerstein, R. (1970). Less differences de fonctionnement cognitif dans des groupes socio-ethniques differents. Ph.D. thesis. Sorbonne, Paris.

Feuerstein, R. (1970). A dynamic approach to causation, prevention, and alleviation of retarded performance. In C. Haywood (Ed.). *Social-Cultural Aspects of Mental Retardation*. N.Y.: Appleton, Century, Crofts.

Feuerstein, R., Hanegby, R. & Krasilovsky, D. (1970). The corrective object relations: Theory and treatment group technique. *Psychological Processes, 1, 2*.

Feuerstein, R. (1971). Low functioning children in residential and day settings for the deprived. In M. Wolins & M. Gottesman (Eds.). *Group Care: An Israeli Approach*. N.Y.: Gordon and Breach.

Feuerstein, R. (1971). The redevelopment of the socio-culturally disadvantaged adolescent in group care. In M. Wolins & M. Gottesman (Eds.). *Group Care: An Israeli Approach*. N.Y.: Gordon and Breach.

Feuerstein, R. (1972). Alleviation of retarded performance. In H.P. David (Ed.). *Child Mental Health in International Perspective*. New York: Harper and Row.

Feuerstein, R. (1972). Cognitive assessment of the socio-culturally deprived child and adolescent. In L.J. Cronbach and P. Drenth (Eds.). *Mental Tests and Cultural Adaptation*. The Hague: Mouton.

Feuerstein, R. & Krasilowsky, D. (1972). Intervention strategies for the significant modification of cognitive functioning in the disadvantaged adolescent. *The Journal of the American Academy of Child Psychiatry, 11*, 572–582.

Feuerstein, R., Krasilowsky, D. & Rand, Y. (1974). The evolvement of innovative educational strategies for the integration of high risk adolescents in Israel. *Phi Delta Kappan, 35*, 556–581.

Feuerstein, R. & Rand, Y. (1974). Mediated Learning Experience: An outline of proximal etiology for differential development of cognitive functions. *Journal of International Council of Psychology, 9–10*, 7–37.

Feuerstein, R. (1976). Dynamic assessment of cognitive modifiability in retarded performers: The Learning Potential Assessment Device. In B.B. Wolman (Ed.). *International Encyclopedia of Neurology, Psychiatry, Psychoanalysis and Psychology*, Section XII. New York.

Feuerstein, R., Hoffman, M., Krasilowsky, D., Rand, Y. & Tannenbaum, A. (1976). The effects of group care on the psychosocial habitation of immigrant adolescents in Israel, with special reference to high-risk children. *International Review of Applied Psychology, 25*, 189–201.

Feuerstein, R. (1977). Mediated Learning Experience (MLE): A theoretical basis for cognitive modifiability during adolescence. In P. Mittner (Ed.). *Research to Practice in Mental Retardation: Education and Training*, vol. 2. Baltimore, MD: University Park Press.

Rand, Y., Feuerstein, R., Tannenbaum, A., Jensen, M. & Hoffman, M. (1977). An analysis of the effects of Instrumental Enrichment on disadvantaged adolescents. In P. Mittner (Ed.). *Research to Practice in Mental Retardation: Education and Training*, vol. 2. Baltimore, MD: University Park Press.

Feuerstein, R., Krasilowsky, D. & Rand, Y. (1978). Modifiability during adolescence. In J. Anthony (Ed.). *Yearbook of the International Association for Chile Psychiatry and Allied Professions*. London: Wiley.

Feuerstein, R. (1979). Ontogeny of learning. In M.T. Brazier (Ed.). *Brain Mechanisms in Memory and Learning*. New York: Raven Press.

Rand, Y., Feuerstein, R., Hoffman, M. & Jensen, M. (1979). Cognitive modifiability in retarded adolescents. *American Journal of Mental Deficiency, 83*, 539–550.

Rand, Y., Tannenbaum, A. & Feuerstein, R. (1979). Effects of Instrumental Enrichment on the psycho-educational development of low-functioning adolescents. *Journal of Educational Psychology, 71*, 751–763.

Feuerstein, R. & Jensen, M. (1980). Instrumental Enrichment: Theoretical basis, goals, and instruments. *The Educational Forum, 44*, 401–423.

Feuerstein, R. (1981). Mediated learning experience in the acquisition of kinesics. In R.

Saint-Claire & B. Hoffer (Eds.). *Developmental Kinesics: The Emerging Paradigm.* Baltimore, MD: University Park Press.

Feuerstein, R., Miller, R., Rand, Y. & Jensen, M. (1981). Can evolving techniques better measure cognitive change? *The Journal of Special Education, 15,* 201–219.

Feuerstein, R. & Hoffman, M. (1982). Intergenerational conflict of rights: Cultural imposition and self-realization. *Viewpoints in Teaching and Learning, 58,* 44–63.

Feuerstein, R. (1984). On the desirability of preserving family and communal traditions. In *The Integration of Immigrant Adolescent: A Selection of Articles of Youth Aliyah.* Jerusalem: Jewish Agency.

Feuerstein, R., Jensen, M., Rand, Y. & Hoffman, M. (1984). Instrumental Enrichment: An intervention program for structural cognitive modifiability. In J. Segal, S. Chipman, & R. Glaser (Eds.). *Thinking and Learning Skills,* vol. 1, Hillsdale, N.J.: Erlbaum.

Feuerstein, R. & Klein, P. (1985). Environmental variables and cognitive development. In S. Harel & N.J. Anastasiow (Eds.). *The At-Risk Infant: Psycho-Socio-Medical Aspects.* Baltimore, MD: Paul Brookes.

Feuerstein, R., Rand, Y., Jensen, M., Kaniel, S., Tzuriel, D., Ben Schachar, N. & Mintzker, Y. (1985/86). Learning potential assessment. *Special Services in the Schools, 2,* 85–106.

Feuerstein, R. (1986). The foster home group experiment. In Y. Kashti & M. Arieli (Eds.). *Residential Settings and the Community.* Tel. Aviv: Freund.

Feuerstein, R., Hoffman, M., Rand, Y., Jensen, M., Tzuriel, D. & Hoffman, D. (1986). Learning to learn: Mediated learning experience and Instrumental Enrichment. *Special Services in the Schools, 3,* 49–82.

Feuerstein, R., Rand, Y., Jensen, M., Kaniel, S. & Tzuriel, D. (1987). Prerequisites for assessment of learning potential: The LPAD model. In C. Lidz (Ed.). *The Dynamic Assessment.* N.Y.: Guilford Press.

Arieli, M. & Feuerstein, R. (1987). The two-fold care organization: On the combination of group and foster situations. *Child and Youth Care Quarterly, 16,* 168–184.

Jensen, M. & Feuerstein, R. (1987). The LPAD: from philosophy to practice. In C. Lidz (Ed.). *The Dynamic Assessment.* N.Y.: Guilford Press.

Feuerstein, R., Jensen, M., Rand, Y., Kaniel, S. & Tzuriel, D. (1988). Cultural difference and cultural deprivation: A theoretical framework for differential intervention. In R.M. Gupta & P. Coxhead (Eds.). *Cultural Diversity and Learning Efficiency.* London: Macmillan.

Strauss, R., Mintzker, Y., Feuerstein, R., Wexler, M-R. & Rand, Y. (1988). Social perception of the effects of Down Syndrome facial surgery: A school-based study of ratings by normal adolescents. *Plastic and Reconstructive Surgery, 81,* 841–846.

Tzuriel, D. and Samuels, M. & Feuerstein, R. (1988). Non-intellective factors in dynamic assessment. In R.M. Gupta and P. Coxhead (Eds.). *Cultural Diversity and Learning Efficiency.* London: Macmillan.

Kaniel, S. & Feuerstein, R. (1989). Special needs of children with learning difficulties. *Oxford Review of Education, 15,* 165–179.

Feuerstein, R. (1990). The cognitive modifiability of persons with Down Syndrome. In E. Chigier (Ed.). *Looking Up at Down Syndrome.* Tel Aviv & London: Freund.

Feuerstein, R. (1990). Mediating cognitive processes to the retarded performer. In M. Schwebel, C. Maher & N. Fagley (Eds.). *Promoting Cognitive Growth over the Life-span.* Hillsdale, NJ: Erlbaum.

Feuerstein, R. (1990). The theory of structural cognitive modifiability. In B. Presseisen (Ed.) *Learning and Thinking Styles: Classroom Interaction.* Washington, DC: National Education Association.

Beker, J. & Feuerstein, R. (1990). Conceptual foundations of the modifying environment in group care and treatment settings for children and youth. *Journal of Child and Youth Care, 5*, 23–33.

Falik, L. & Feuerstein, R. (1990). Structural cognitive modifiability: A new cognitive perspective for counseling and psychotherapy. *International Journal of Cognitive Education and Mediated Learning, 1*, 143–150.

Feuerstein, R. (1991). Cultural difference and cultural deprivation. Differential patterns of adaptability. In N. Bleichrodt & P. Drenth (Eds.). *Contemporary Issues in Cross-Cultural Psychology*. Amsterdam: Swets & Zeitlinger.

Feuerstein, R. & Feuerstein, S. (1991). Mediated learning experience: A theoretical review. In R. Feuerstein, P. Klein & A. Tannenbaum (Eds.). *Mediated Learning Experience: Theoretical, Psychosocial, and Learning Implications*. Tel Aviv and London: Freund.

Feuerstein, R., Rand, Y., Hoffman, M., Egozi, M. & Ben-Schachar, N. (1991). Intervention programs for retarded performers: Goals, means, and expected outcomes. In L. Idol and B. Jones (Eds.). *Educational Values and Cognitive Instruction*. Vol. 2. Hillsdale, NJ: Erlbaum. (Reprinted in M. Ben-Hur (Ed.). *On Feuerstein's Instrumental Enrichment*. Palatine, IL: IRI/Skylight, 1994).

Feuerstein, R. & Tannenbaum, A. (1991). Mediating the learning experience of gifted underachievers. In B. Wallace & H. Adams (Eds.). *Worldwide Perspectives on the Gifted Underachievers*. Bicester, UK: AB Academic Publishers.

Beker, J. & Feuerstein, R. (1991). Toward a common denominator in effective group care programming. *Journal of Child and Youth Care, 7*, 20–34.

Beker, J. & Feuerstein, R. (1991). The modifying environment and other environmental perspectives in group care. *Residential Treatment of Children and Youth, 8*, 21–37.

Kaniel, S., Tzuriel, D., Feuerstein, R., Ben-Schachar, N. & Eitan, T. (1991). Dynamic assessment: Learning and transfer abilities of Ethiopian immigrants to Israel. In Feuerstein, R., Klein, P. & Tannenbaum, A. (Eds.). *Mediated Learning Experience: Theoretical, Psychosocial, and Learning Implications*. Tel Aviv and London: Freund.

Tzuriel, D. & Feuerstein, R. (1992). Dynamic assessment for prescriptive teaching. In C. Haywood & D. Tzuriel (Eds.). *Interactive Assessment*. New York: Springer.

Feuerstein, R. & Kozulin, A. (1995). The Bell Curve: Getting the facts straight. *Educational Leadership, 52*(7), 71–74.

Durkin, R., Beker, J. & Feuerstein, R. (1995). Can environments modify and enhance the development of personality and behavior? *Residential Treatment for Children and Youth, 12*, 1–14.

Feuerstein, R. (1996). The mediated learning experience: Langeveld memorial lecture. University of Utrecht.

Feuerstein, R., Feuerstein, Ra. & Schur, Y. (1997). Process as content in education of exceptional children. In A. Costa & R. Liebman (Eds.). *Supporting the Spirit of Learning: When Process is Content*. Thousand Oaks, CA: Corwin Press. (Reprinted in A. Kozulin (Ed.). *The Ontogeny of Cognitive Modifiability*. Jerusalem: ICELP, 1997).

Feuerstein, R., Feuerstein, Ra. & Gross, S. (1997). The learning potential assessment device. In D. Flanagan, J. Genshaft & P. Harrison (Eds.). *Contemporary Intellectual Assessment*. New York: Guilford Press.

Feuerstein, R., Falik, L. & Feuerstein, Ra. (1998). Feuerstein's LPAD. In R. Samuda (Ed.). *Advances in Cross-Cultural Assessment*. Thousand Oaks, CA: Sage.

Feuerstein, R., Jackson, Y. & Lewis, J. (1998). Feuerstein's IE and structural cognitive modifiability. In R. Samuda (Ed.). *Advances in Cross-Cultural Assessment*. Thousand Oaks, CA: Sage.

References

Chapter 1

Denzin, N.K. & Lincoln, Y.S. (1994). *Handbook of Qualitative Research*. Thousand Oaks, CA: Sage.

Feuerstein, R., Rand, Y. & Hoffman, M. (1979) *The Dynamic Assessment of Retarded Performers*. Glenview, Illinois: Scott, Foresman and Company.

Feuerstein, R., Rand, Y. Hoffman, M. & Miller, R. (1980). *Instrumental Enrichment*. Glenview, Illinois: Scott, Foresman and Company.

Feuerstein, R., Rand, Y. & Rynders, J. (1988). *Don't Accept Me as I Am*. New York: Plenum Press.

Feuerstein, R., Klein, P. & Tannenbaum, A. (Eds.) (1991). *Mediated Learning Experience: Theoretical, Psychosocial and Learning Implications*. London: Freund.

Feuerstein and associates (1997).

Gall, M., Borg, W. & Gall, J. (1996). *Educational Research*. White Plains, N.Y.: Longman.

Kozulin, A. (Ed.) (1986). *Lev Vygotsky, Thought and Language*. Cambridge, MA: MIT Press.

Presseisen, B. & Kozulin, A. (1994). Mediated Learning: The Contribution of Vygotsky and Feuerstein in Theory and Practice. In M. Ben-Hur (Ed.) *On Feuerstein's Instrumental Enrichment: A Collection*. Palatine, IL: IRI/Skylight.

Chapter 2

Avanzini, G. (1985). "Les méthodes". In Arnaud, P. & Broyer, G. *Psychopédagogie des activites physiques et sportives*. Toulouse: Privat.

Buchel, F. (1990). "Analyse cognitive et métacognitive de l'éducation de la capacité d'apprentissage". In Paravy, G. (Ed.). *Pédagogies de la mediation*. Lyon: La Chronique Sociale.

Feuerstein, R. (1990). Le PEI. In G. Paravy, op. cit.

Feuerstein, R. (1996). Entretien avec Claudine Longhi. In Paravy, G. (Ed.). *Médiation éducative et éducabilite cognitive*. Lyon: La Chronique Sociale.

Hadji, Ch. (1992). *Penser et agir l'education*. Paris, ESF éditeur.

Hadji, Ch. (1994). "Evaluation et affectivité". *Cahiers Binet-Simon*, 639–40 (2–3), 183–195.

Hadji, Ch. (1996). "Comment le PEI pourrait-il bénéficier de l'évaluation qu'il mérite?" In Paravy, G. (Ed.) op. cit.

Hadji, Ch. (1998) "Qual rapport au vrai l'acte éducatif engage-t'il?" In Hadji, Ch. & Baillér, J. *Recherche et éducation*. Bruzelles: De Boeck Université.

Vygotsky, L. (1935). "Le problème de enseignement et du developpement mental à l'âge scolaire". In Schneuwly, B. & Bronckart, J. P. *Vygotsky aujourd'hui*. Neuchatel. Paris: Delachaux et Niestlé.

Chapter 3

Block, P. (1987). *The Empowered Manager*. San Francisco, CA: Jossey-Bass.
Caine, R.N. & Caine, G. (1997). *Education on the Edge of Possibility*. Alexandria, VA: Association for Supervision and Curriculum Development.
Costa, A. & Garmston, R. (1994). *Cognitive Coaching: A Foundation for the Renaissance School*. Norwood, MA: Christopher Gordon.
Costa, A. & Kallick, B (1995). *Assessment in the Learning Organization: Shifting the Paradigm*. Alexandria, VA: Association for Supervision and Curriculum Development.
Costa, A. & Liebmann, R. (1997). *Process as Content: Envisioning a Renaissance Curriculum*. Thousand Oaks, CA: Corwin Press.
Costa, A. & O'Leary, P.W. (1992). Co-cognition: The co-operative development of the intellect. In N. Davidson & T. Worsham (Eds.). *Enhancing Thinking through Co-operative Learning*. New York: Teachers College Press.
Evered, R. & Selman, J. (1989). Coaching and the art of management. *Organizational Dynamics* (Autumn, 1989): Vol. *18*, pp. 16–32 (1987).
Feuerstein, R., Feuerstein, R.S. & Schur, Y. (1997). Process As Content In Education Particularly For Retarded Performers. In Costa, A. & Liebmann, R. (Eds.). *Supporting the Spirit of Learning: When Process is Content*. Thousand Oaks, CA: Corwin Press.
Frymier, J. (1987). Bureaucracy and the Neutering of Teachers. *Phi Delta Kappan*, (September), p. 10.
Fullan, M. (1992). *Change Forces*. New York, NY: Falmer.
Goerner, S.J. (1995). Chaos and deep ecology. In *Chaos Theory in Psychology*. F.D. Abraham & A.R. Gilgen (Eds.). Westport, Conn: Praeger.
Glickman, C. (1985). *Supervision of Instruction: A Developmental Approach*. Newton, MA: Allen & Bacon, p. 18.
Goodlad, J.I. (1984). *A Place Called School: Prospects for the Future*. New York: McGraw Hill.
Harvey, O.J. (1966). System structure, flexibility and creativity. In *Experience, Structure, and Adaptability*. O.J. Harvey (Ed.). New York: Springer.
Hateley, B. & Schnidt, W. (1995). *A Peacock in the Land of Penguins*. San Francisco, CA: Berrett-Koehler.
Hunt, D.C. (1978). Conceptual level theory and research as guides to educational practice. *Interchange*, (1977–1978): Vol. *8*, pp. 78–80.
Jackson, P. (1968). *Life in Classrooms*. New York, N.Y.: Holt Rinehart Winston.
Joyce, B. & Showers, B. (1988). Student Achievement through Staff Development. New York, N.Y.: Longmans, Inc.
Land, G. & Jarman, B. (1992). *Breakpoint and Beyond: Mastering the Future Today*. New York: Harper.
Leonard, G. (1978). *The Silent Pulse: A Search for the Perfect Rhythm that Exists in Each of Us*. New York: Bantam Books Inc.
MacLean, P. (1978). A mind of three minds. Educating the Triune brain. In *Education and the Brain*. Chall, J.E. & Mursky, (Eds.). Chicago: University of Chicago Press.

McNerney, R.F. & Carrier, C.A. (1981). *Teacher Development*. New York: MacMillan Publishing Company.

Oja, S.N. (1980). "Developmental Theories and the Professional Development of Teachers," presentation at the annual meeting of the American Educational Research Association, Boston, MA, April.

Rosenholtz, S. (1989). *Teacher's Workplace: The Social Organization of Schools*. New York, N.Y.: Longman, Inc.

Saphier, J. & King, M. (1985). Good seeds grow in strong cultures. *Educational Leadership*, March, 67–74.

Sarason, S. (1991). *The Predictable Failure of Educational Reform*. San Francisco, CA: Jossey-Bass.

Shavelson, R. (1976). Teacher decision making. *The Psychology of Teaching Methods. 1976 Yearbook of the National Society for the Study of Education. Part I*. Chicago, IL: University of Chicago Press.

Senge, P. (1990). *The Fifth Discipline*: New York, N.Y.: Doubleday.

Sprinthall & Theis-Sprinthall. (1983). "The teacher as an adult learner: a cognitive developmental view", *Staff Development: 82nd Yearbook of the National Society for the Study of Education Part II*. Chicago, IL: University of Chicago Press.

Wheatley, M. (1992). *Leadership and the New Science*. San Francisco, CA: Berrett-Koehler.

Vygotsky, L (1978). *Mind in Society*. Cambridge, MA: Harvard University Press.

Witherall, C.S. & Erickson, L. (1978). "Teacher Education and Adult Development." *Theory Into Practice*. (June, p. 12).

Chapter 4

Ames, C. (1992). Achievement goals and the classroom motivational climate. In D.H. Schmuck & I.L. Meece (Eds.). *Student Perceptions in the Classroom*. Hillsdale, NJ: Erlbaum.

Anderson, M.L. (1994). The many and varied social constructions of intelligence. In T.R. Sarbin & J. Kitsuse (Eds.). *Constructing the Social*. London: Sage.

Bardon, J. (1983). Psychology applied to education: a speciality in search of an identity. *American Psychologist*, *38*, 185–196.

Bardon, J. (1986). The school psychologist as an applied educational psychologist. In S. Elliott and J. Witt (Eds.). *The Delivery of Psychological Services in Schools: Concepts, Processes and Issues*. Hillsdale, N.J.: Erlbaum.

Ben-Hur, M. (1994). *On Feuerstein's Instrumental Enrichment: a Collection*. Palatine, Illinois: IRI/Skylight.

Blagg, N. (1991). *Can We Teach Intelligence?* Hillsdale, NJ: Erlbaum.

Burden, R.L. (1987). Feuerstein's instrumental enrichment programme: important issues in research and evaluation. *European Journal of Psychology of Education*, *11*(1), 3–16.

Burden, R.L. (1994). Trends and developments in educational psychology: an international perspective. *School Psychology International*, *15*(4), 293–347.

Burden, R.L. (1997a). Translating values into rights: respecting the voice of the child. In G. Lindsay & D. Thompson (Eds.). *Values into Practice in Special Education*. London: David Fulton.

Burden, R.L. (1997b). Research in the real world: an evaluation model for use by applied educational psychologists. *Educational Psychology in Practice*, *13*(1), 13–20.

Burden, R.L. & Williams, M. (Eds.) (1998). *Thinking Through the Curriculum*. London: Routledge.

Burden, R.L. & Nicholls, S.L. (2000). Evaluating the process of introducing a thinking skills programme into the secondary school curriculum. *Research Papers in Education (in press)*.

Cline, T. (Ed.) (1992). *The Assessment of Special Educational Needs*. London: Routledge.

Crookes, G. & Gass, S.M. (Eds.) (1993). *Tasks in a Pedagogical Context*. Clevedon: Multilingual Matters.

Csikszentmihalyi, M. & Csikszentmihalyi, I.S. (Eds.) (1988). *Optional Experience*. Cambridge: Cambridge University Press.

de Charms, R. (1984). Motivation enhancement in educational settings. In C. Ames and R.E. Ames (Eds.). *Research on Motivation in Education (Vol. 1)*. New York: Academic Press.

Dweck, C.S. (1985). Intrinsic motivation, perceived self-control and self-evaluation maintenance: an achievement goal analysis. In C. Ames & R. Ames (Eds.). *Research on Motivation in Education Vol. 2*. London: Academic Press.

Dweck, C.S. & Leggett (1988). A social-cognitive approach to motivation and personality. *Psychological Review*, 95, 256–273.

Feuerstein, R., Rand, Y. & Hoffman, M. (1979). *The Dynamic Assessment of Retarded Performers*. Glenview, Illinois: Scott Foresman.

Feuerstein, R., Rand, Y., Hoffman, M. & Miller, R. (1980). *Instrumental Enrichment*. Glenview, Illinois: Scott Foresman.

Fox, D. & Prilleltensky, I. (1997). *Critical Psychology*. London: Sage.

Freire, P. (1970). *Pedagogy of the Oppressed*. New York: Continuum.

Freire, P. (1973). *Education for a Critical Consciousness*. New York: Continuum.

Freire, P. & Faundex, A. (1989). *Learning to Question*. New York: Continuum.

Fullan, M. (1993). *Change Forces*. London: Falmer.

Gupta, R.M. & Coxhead, P. (Eds.) (1988). *Cultural Diversity and Learning Efficiency*. London; Macmillan.

John, M. (1994). The UN convention on the rights of the child: development and implications. *Education and Child Psychology*, 11(4), 7–17.

Kamin, L. (1974). *The Science and Politics of IQ*. New York: Erlbaum.

Kozulin, A. (Ed.) (1997). *The Ontogeny of Cognitive Modifiability: Applied Aspects of Mediated Learning Experience and Instrumental Enrichment*. Jerusalem: ICELP.

Lauchlan, F. & Elliott, J. (1998). Using dynamic assessment materials as a tool for providing cognitive intervention to children with complex learning difficulties. *Educational and Child Psychology*, 14(4), 137–148.

Lidz, C. (Ed.) (1987). *Dynamic Assessment*. New York: Guildford Press.

Male, D. (1992). An investigation into the learning and memory processes of children with moderate learning difficulties. Unpublished PhD thesis, University of London.

Nicholls, J.G. (1979). Quality and equality in intellectual development: the role of motivation in education. *American Psychologist*, 34, 1071–1084.

Nunan, D. (1989). *Designing Tasks for the Communicative Classroom*. Cambridge: Cambridge University Press.

Prabhu, N.S. (1987). *Second Language Pedagogy*. Oxford: Oxford University Press.

Savell, J.M., Twohig, P.T. & Rachford, D.L. (1986). Empirical status of Feuerstein's Instrumental Enrichment techniques as a method of teaching thinking skills. *Review of Educational Research*, 56(4), 382–409.

Tomlinson, P., Edwards, A., Finn, G., Smith, L. & Wilkinson, E. (1992). *Psychological Aspects of Beginning Teacher Competence*. Leicester: British Psychological Society.

Wang, M. (1983). Development and consequences of students' sense of personal control. In J.M. Levine & M. Wang (Eds.). *Teacher and Student Perceptions: Implications of Learning.* Hillsdale, NJ: LEA.

Williams, M. & Burden, R.L. (1997). *Psychology for Language Teachers.* Cambridge: Cambridge University Press.

Chapter 5

Adams, M.J. (Ed.) (1986). *Odyssey: A Curriculum for Thinking. (Vols. 1–6).* Watertown, MA: Charlesbridge.

Bandura, A. (1977). Self-efficacy: Toward a unifying theory of behavioral change. *Psychological Review, 84,* 181–215.

Baron, J.B. & Sternberg, R.J. (Eds.). (1987). *Teaching Thinking Skills: Theory and Practice.* New York: Freeman.

Bouchard, T.J., Jr. & McGue, M. (1981). Familial studies of intelligence: A review. *Science, 212,* 1055–1059.

Bradley, R.H. & Caldwell, B.M. (1984). 174 Children: A study of the relationship between home environment and cognitive development during the first 5 years. In A.W. Gottfried (Ed.). *Home Environment and Early Cognitive Development: Longitudinal Research.* San Diego, CA: Academic Press.

Brown, A.L., Campione, J.C., Bray, N.W. & Wilcox, B.L. (1973). Keeping track of changing variables: Effects of rehearsal training and rehearsal prevention in normal and retarded adolescents. *Journal of Experimental Psychology, 101,* 123–131.

Butterfield, E.C., Wambold, C. & Belmont, J.M. (1973). On the theory and practice of improving short-term memory. *American Journal of Mental Deficiency, 77,* 654–669.

Campione, J.C., Brown, A.L. & Ferrara, R. (1982). Mental retardation and intelligence. In R.J. Sternberg (Ed.). *Handbook of Human Intelligence* (pp. 392–490). New York: Cambridge University Press.

Csikszentmihalyi, M. & Robinson, R.E. (1986). Culture, time, and the development of talent. In R.J. Sternberg & J.E. Davidson (Eds.). *Conceptions of Giftedness* (pp. 264–284). New York: Cambridge University Press.

Davidson, J.E. & Sternberg, R.J. (1984). The role of insight in intellectual giftedness. *Gifted Child Quarterly, 28,* 58–64.

Dennis, W. (1973). Children of the Creche. New York: Appleton-Century-Crofts.

Detterman, D.K. & Sternberg, R.J. (Eds.). (1982). *How and How Much can Intelligence be Increased.* Norwood, NJ: Ablex.

Edgerton, R. (1967). *The Cloak of Competence.* Berkeley: University of California Press.

Feldhusen, J.F. (1986). A conception of giftedness. In R.J. Sternberg & J.E. Davidson (Eds.). *Conceptions of Giftedness* (pp. 112–127). New York: Cambridge University Press.

Feuerstein, R. (1979). *The Dynamic Assessment of Retarded Performers: The Learning Potential Assessment Device, Theory, Instrument, and Techniques.* Baltimore, MD: University Park.

Feuerstein, R. (1980). *Instrumental Enrichment: An Intervention Program for Cognitive Modifiability.* Baltimore, MD: University Park Press.

Feuerstein, R., Rand, Y. & Rynders, J.E. (1988). *Don't Accept Me as I Am: Helping "Retarded" People to Excel.* New York: Plenum.

Flynn, J.R. (1984). The mean IQ of Americans: Massive gains 1932 to 1978. *Psychological Bulletin, 95,* 29–51.

Flynn, J.R. (1987). Massive IQ gains in 14 nations: What IQ tests really measure. *Psychological Bulletin, 101*, 171–191.

Gardner, H., Krechevsky, M., Sternberg, R.J. & Okagaki, L. (1994). Intelligence in context: Enhancing students' practical intelligence for school. In K. McGilly (Ed.). *Classroom Lessons: Integrating Cognitive Theory and Classroom Practice* (pp. 105–127). Cambridge, MA: Bradford Books.

Herrnstein, R.J, (1973). *IQ in the Meritocracy*. Boston: Atlantic Monthly Press.

Herrnstein, R.J., Nickerson, R.S. de Sanchez, M. & Swets, J.A. (1986). Teaching thinking skills. *American Psychologist, 41*, 1279–1289.

Herrnstein, R.J. & Murray, C. (1994). *The Bell Curve*. New York: Free Press.

Jensen, A.R. (1980). *Bias in Mental Testing*. New York: Free Press.

Juel-Nielsen, N. (1965). Individual and environment: A psychiatric-psychological investigation of monozygous twins reared apart. *Acta Psychiatrica et Neurologica Scandinavia* (Monograph Supplement, 183).

Lazar, I. & Darlington, R. (1982). Lasting effects of early education: A report from the consortium for longitudinal studies. *Monographs of the Society for Research in Child Development, 47* (2–3, Serial No. 195).

Merton, R.K. (1968). The Matthew effect in science. *Science, 159*, 56–63.

Messick, S. & Jungeblut, A. (1981). Time and method in coaching for the SAT. *Psychological Bulletin, 89*, 191–216.

Newman, H.H., Freeman, F.N. & Holzinger, K.J. (1937). *Twins: A Study of Heredity and Environment*. Chicago: University of Chicago Press.

Nisbett, R. (1995). Race, IQ, and scientism. In S. Fraser (Ed.), *The Bell Curve Wars: Race, Intelligence and the Future of America* (pp. 36–57). New York: Basic Books.

Ramey, C. (1994). Abecedarian project. In R.J. Sternberg (Ed.), *Encyclopedia of Human Intelligence*. (Vol. 1, pp. 1–3). New York: Macmillan.

Reis, S.M. & Renzulli J.S. (1992). Using curriculum compacting to challenge the above-average. *Educational Leadership, 50*(3), 51–57.

Renzulli, J.S. (1986). The three-ring conception of giftedness: a developmental model for creative productivity. In R.J. Sternberg & J.E. Davidson (Eds.). *Conceptions of Giftedness* (pp. 53–92). New York: Cambridge University Press.

Scarr, S. & McCartney, K. (1983). How people make their own environment: A theory of genotype-environmental effects. *Child Development, 54*, 424–435.

Scarr, S. & Weinberg, R.A. (1976). IQ test performance of black children adopted by white families. *American Psychologist, 31*, 726–739.

Schooler, C. (1987). Psychological effects of complex environments during the life span: A review and theory. In C. Schooler & K. Warner Schaie (Eds.). *Cognitive Functioning and Social Structure Over the Life Course* (pp. 24–49). Norwood, NJ: Ablex.

Shields, J. (1962). *Monozygotic Twins Brought up Apart and Brought up Together*. London: Oxford University Press.

Sternberg, R.J. (1985). *Beyond IQ: A Triarchic Theory of Human Intelligence*. New York: Cambridge University Press.

Sternberg, R.J. (1987). Most vocabulary is learned from context. In M.G. McKeown & M.E. Curtis (Eds.). *The Nature of Vocabulary Acquisition* (pp. 89–105). Hillsdale, NJ: Lawrence Erlbaum.

Sternberg, R.J. (1994). Diversifying instruction and assessment. *The Educational Forum, 59*(1), 47–53.

Sternberg, R.J. (1995). *In Search of the Human Mind*. Orlando: Harcourt Brace College Publishers.

Sternberg, R.J. (1997). What does it mean to be smart?. *Educational Leadership*, *54*(6), 20–24.

Sternberg, R.J. & Clinkenbeard, P. (1995). A triarchic view of identifying, teaching, and assessing gifted children. *Roeper Review*, *17*(4), 255–260.

Sternberg, R.J. & Davidson, J.E. (1982, June). The mind of the puzzler. *Psychology Today*, *16*, 37–44.

Sternberg, R.J., Ferrari, M., Clinkenbeard, P. & Grigorenko, E.L. (1996). Identification, instruction, and assessment of gifted children: A construct validation of a triarchic model. *Gifted Child Quarterly*, *40*, 129–137.

Sternberg, R.J. & Grigorenko, E.L. (Eds.). (1997). *Intelligence: Heredity and Environment*. New York: Cambridge University Press.

Sternberg, R.J., Okagaki, L. & Jackson, A. (1990). Practical intelligence for success in school. *Educational Leadership*, *48*, 35–39.

Sternberg, R.J. & Spear-Swerling, L. (1996). *Teaching for Thinking*. Washington, DC: American Psychological Association.

Sternberg, R.J. & Williams, W.M. (1996). *How to Develop Student Creativity*. Alexandria, VA: Association for Supervision and Curriculum Development.

Stevenson, H.W. & Stigler, J.W. (1992). *The Learning Gap*. New York: Summit.

Subotnik, R., Kassan, L., Summers, E. & Wasser, A. (1993). *Genius Revisited*. Norwood, NJ: Ablex.

Terman, L.M. (1925). *Genetic Studies of Genius: Mental and Physical Traits of a Thousand Gifted Children* (Vol. 1). Stanford, CA: Stanford University Press.

Terman, L.M. & Oden, M.H. (1959). *Genetic Studies of Genius: Vol. 5. The Gifted Group at Mid-Life*. Stanford: Stanford University Press.

Williams, W.M., Blythe, T., White, N., Li, J., Sternberg, R.J. & Gardner, H.I. (1996). *Practical Intelligence for School: A Handbook for Teachers of Grades 5–8*. New York: Harper Collins.

Zigler, E. (1971). The retarded child as a whole person. In H.E. Adams & W.K. Boardman, III (Eds.), *Advances in Experimental Clinical Psychology* (*Vol. 1*) (pp. 47–121). New York: Pergamon Press.

Zigler, E. & Berman, W. (1983). Discerning the future of early childhood intervention. *American Psychologist*, *38*, 894–906.

Chapter 6

Abelson, R.P. (1986). Beliefs are like possessions. *Journal for the Theory of Social Behavior*, *16*(3), 223–250.

Abelson, R.P. & Prentice, D.A. (1989). Beliefs as possessions: a functional perspective. In A.R. Pratkanis, S.J. Breckler & A.G. Greenwald (Eds.). *Attitude, Structure and Function*, Hillsdale, NJ: Erlbaum, 361–381.

Adler, A. (1930). *Individual Psychology*. In C. Murchison (Ed.). *Psychologies of 1930*, Clark University Press.

Allport, G.W. (1937). *Personality: A Psychological Interpretation*. New York: Holt.

Allport, G.W., Vernon, P.E. & Lindzey, G. (1960). *Study of Values*. Cambridge, MA: Riverside Press.

Ansbacher, H.C. & Ansbacher, R.R. (Eds.), (1956). *The Individual Psychology of Alfred Adler*. New York: Basic Books.

Beck, A.L. (1942). *The Story of Oriental Philosophy*. New York: The New Home Library.

Cantor, N. (1990). From thought to behavior: "having" and "doing" in the study of personality and cognition. *American Psychologist, 45*(6), 735–750.

Combe, G.A. (1864). *System of Phrenology.* Boston (MAS): Marsh, Carper & Lyon.

Cornin, J.H. (1952). Confucius. In *Encyclopedia Americana,* pp. 497–499.

Diamond, S. (1957). *Personality and Temperament.* New York: Harper.

Dittmar, H. (1992). The Social Psychology of Material Possessions: To Have is to Be. Harvester Wheatsheaf (UK), St Martin's Press.

Feuerstein, R., Rand, Y., Hoffman, M. & Miller, R. (1980). *Instrumental Enrichment.* Baltimore, MD: University Park Press.

Feuerstein, R., Klein, P. & Tannenbaum, A. (Eds.) (1991). *Mediated Learning Experience.* Tel-Aviv and London: Freund.

Fischer, K. (1909). *Spinosas Leben, Werke und Lehre.*

Flavel, J.H. (1978). Cognitive Monitoring, Paper presented at the Conference on Children's Oral Skills, University of Wisconsin.

Frankel, V. (1970). *Man's Search for Meaning: an Introduction to Logotherapy.* Tel-Aviv (Hebrew trans.).

Freud, S. (1923). *The Ego and the Id.* London: Hogarth Press.

Freud, S. (1926). *Inhibitions, Symptoms and Anxiety.* London: Hogarth Press.

Freud, S. (1940). *An Outline of Psychanalysis.* London: Hogarth Press.

Freud, S. (1954). *The Origins of Psychoanalysis: Letters to Wilhelm Fliess.* New York: Basic Books.

Fromm, E. (1976). *To Have or to Be?* New York: Harper & Row.

Gall, F.J. (1818). *Anatomy and Physiology of the Nervous System in General and the Brain in Particular.*

Gall, F.J. & Spurzheim, J.G. (1809). *Recherches sur le Système Nerveux.* Paris: Schoel.

Gardner, H. (1983). *Frames of Mind.* New York: Basic Books.

Gardner, H. (1998). Are there additional intelligences? The case for natural, spiritual and existential intelligences. In J. Kane (Ed.), *Education, Information, and Transformation,* Engelwood Cliffs (NJ): Prentice Hall.

Guilford, J.P. & Zimmermann, W.S. (1956). Fourteen dimensions of temperament. *Psychological Monographs, 70*(10), (No. 417).

Hackmann, H.F. (1910). *Buddhism as a Religion.* London.

Joachim, H.H. (1964). *A Study of the Ethics of Spinosa.*

Jung, C.G. (1933). *Psychological Types.* New York: Harcourt & Brace.

Krech, D., Crutchfield, R.S. & Ballachey, E.L. (1962). *Individual in Society.* New York: McGraw-Hill.

Kretschmer, E. (1925). *Physique and Character.* New York: Harcourt.

Kook, A.I.H., Lights (Oroth), (1985a). Jerusalem: Mossad Harav Kook (Hebrew).

Kook, A.I.H., Holy Lights (Oroth Hakodesh), (1985b). Jerusalem: Mossad Harav Kook (Hebrew).

Kyokai, B.D. (1980). *The Teaching of Buddha.* Tokyo: Kosaido Printing Co.

Lillie, A. (1900). *Buddha and Buddhism.* Edinburgh: T. & T. Clark.

MacKinon, D.W. (1963). Identifying and developing creativity. *Journal of Secondary Education, 38,* 166–174.

Marcel, G. (1965). *Being and Having: An Existentialist Diary.* New York: Harper & Row.

Murray, H.A. (1938). *Explorations in Personality.* New York: Oxford University Press.

Prentice, D.A. (1987). Psychological correspondence of possession, attitudes and values. *Journal of Personality and Social Psychology, 53*(6), 993–1003.

Rand, Y. (1993). Modes of Existence (MoE): To Be, To Have, To Do — Cognitive and

Motivational Aspects. Paper presented at the International Conference of the Association for Cognitive Education, Nof Genossar, Israel.

Rank, O. (1932). *Art and Artist* (trans. By C.F. Atkinson), New York: A.A. Knopf.

Reichenberg, R. (1995). Student-Cooperating Teacher Interaction within the Framework of Practical Teacher Experience and its Interaction with Modes of Existence, Attitudes towards Education and Reflective Thinking, Ph.D. Dissertation, Bar-Ilan University, Israel (Hebrew).

Sartre, J.P. (1957). *L'être et le Néant*. Paris: Gallimard.

Sheldon, W.H. & Stevens, S.S. (1942). *The Varieties of Temperament*. New York: Harper.

Sheldon, W.H., Stevens, S.S. & Tucker, W.B. (1940). *The Varieties of Human Physique: an Introduction to Constitutional Psychology*. New York: Harper.

Sheldon, W.H. (1944) Constitutional factors in personality. In J. McV. Hunt (Ed.). *Personality and the Behavioral Disorders*, New York: Ronald Press.

Sheldon, W.H., Dupertuis, C.W. & McDermott, (1954). *Atlas of Men: A Guide for Somatotyping the Adult Male at all Ages*. New York: Harper.

Soloveitchik, J.B. (1975). *Lessons in Jewish Thought*. Jerusalem: Zionist Organization, Department for Thora Education in the Diaspora. (Hebrew).

Soloveitchik, J.B. (1981). *Philosophical Considerations and Evaluation*. Jerusalem: Zionist Organization, Department for Thora Education in the Diaspora. (Hebrew).

Spiro, M.E. (1975). *Children of the Kibbutz*. Cambridge: Harvard University Press.

Spurzheim, J.K. (1815) *The Physiognomical System of Drs. Gall and Spurzheim*.

Staehelin, B. (1969). *Haben and Sein* (Having and Being). Zurich: Editio Academica.

Stagner, R. (1961). *Psychology of Personality*. New York: McGraw-Hill.

Sternberg, R.J. (1985). *Beyond IQ, A Triarchic Theory of Human Intelligence*. New York: Cambridge University Press.

Sternberg, R.J. (1988). *The Triarchic Mind: A new Theory of Intelligence*. New York: Viking Penguin.

Sternberg, R.J. (1997a). A triarchic view of giftedness. In N. Colangelo & G.A. Davis (Eds.). *Handbook of Gifted Education* (second edition), pp. 43–53. Boston: Allyn & Bacon.

Sternberg, R.J. (1997b). Intelligence and lifelong learning: what's new and how can we use it? *American Psychologist, 52*, 1134–1138.

Thorndike, R.L. (1966). *Dimensions of Temperament*. New York: The Psychological Corporation.

Tillich, P. (1952). *The Courage to Be*. New Haven: Yale University Press.

Trotter, W. (1920). *Instincts of the Herd in Peace and War*. London: Unwin.

Vernon, P.E. & Allport, G.W. (1931). *A Study of Values*. Boston: Houghton-Mifflin Co.

Welker, W.I. (1956). The determinants of play and exploration in chimpanzees. *Journal of Physiological Psychology, 49*, 84–89.

Winthrop, H. (1957). The consistency of attitude patterns as a function of body type. *Journal of Personality, 25*, 372–382.

Zirkel, S. & Cantor, N. (1990). Personal construal of a life task: those who struggle for independence. *Journal of Personality and Social Psychology, 58*, 172–185.

Chapter 7

Allport, G.W. (1937). *Personality: a Psychological Interpretation*. New York: Holt.

Belk, B.W. (1991). The ineluctable mysteries of possessions. In: F.W. Rusin (Ed.). *To Have*

Possessions: A Handbook of Ownership and Property — Special Issue of Journal of Social Behavior and Personality, 6(6), 17–55.

Dewey (1933). *How we Think: A Restatement of the Relation of Reflective Thinking to the Educative Process*. Chicago (IL): DC Heath; Boston (MA); Heath & Co.

Dittmar, H. (1992). *The Social Psychology of Material Possessions: To Have is To Be.* Harvester Wheatsheaf, UK: St. Martin's Press.

Enz, J.B. & Cook, J.S. (1990). *Student Teachers' and Cooperating Teachers' Perspectives of Mentoring Functions: Harmony or Dissonance.* Arizona State University Press.

Feiman-Nemser, S. (1990). *Conceptual Orientation in Teacher Education.* Issue paper, East Lansing (MI): NCRTE, Michigan State University.

Feuerstein, R. & Rand, Y. (1974). Mediated learning experiences: an outline of the proximal etiology for differential development of cognitive functions. In Leah Gold-Fein (Ed.) *International Understanding: Cultural Differences in the Development of Cognitive Processes*, pp. 7–37.

Feuerstein, R., Rand, Y. & Hoffman, M.B. (1979). *The Dynamic Assessment of Retarded Performers: The Learning Potential Assessment Device, Theory, Instruments and Techniques*: Baltimore: University Park Press.

Fromm, E. (1976). *To Have or to Be.* London (UK): Abacus Edition, Cox and Wyman Ltd.

Habermas, J. (1971). *Knowledge and Human Interests*, Boston (MA): Beacon Press.

Hersh, R.H., Hull, R. & Leighton, M.S. (1982). Student teaching. In H. Mitzel (Ed.). *The Encyclopedia of Education Research* (fifth Edition), New York: The Free Press, pp. 1812–1822.

Kagan, M.D. (1993). Context for the use of classroom cases. *American Educational Research Journal*, *30*,(4), 703–723.

Kemis, S. & McTaggard, R. (1982). *The Action Research Planner* (third edition). Greelong: Deakin University Press.

Kremer, L. (1978). Teachers' attitudes toward educational goals, as reflected in classroom behavior. *Journal of Educational Psychology*, *70*(6), 993–997.

Kremer, L. (1982). Teachers' attitudes toward educational goals and their reflection in teaching. *Trends*, *26*(2), 193–203.

Kremer, L. & Moore, M. (1979). Belief system and positions among teaching students. *Educational Studies*, *24*, 141–146.

Louden, W. (1992). Understanding reflection through collaborative research. In A. Hargraves & M.G. Fullan (Eds.). *Understanding Teacher Development*. New York: Teacher College Press, Columbia University, pp. 178–215.

MacPherson, C.B. (1962). *The Political Theory of Possessive Individualism.* Oxford (UK): Oxford University Press.

McCraken, G. (1990). *Culture and Consumption.* Indianapolis (IN): Indiana University Press.

Odell, S. (1990). Experienced teachers guiding novice teachers. In T. Stoddart (Ed.). *Perspectives on Guided Practice*, pp. 33–43. East Lansing (MI): NCRTE, Michigan State University Press.

Rand, Y. (1993). Modes of Existence (MoE): To Be, To Have, To Do — Cognitive and Emotional Aspects. Paper presented at the International Association for Cognitive Education, Nof Genosar (Israel).

Rand, Y. & Tannenbaum, A.J. (1995). To Be, To Have, To Do, (BHD), An Integration and Expansion of Existing Concepts (Accepted).

Reichenberg, R. (1995). Student — Co-operating Teacher Interaction within the Framework of Practical Teaching Experience and its Interaction to Modes of Existence, Attitudes toward Education and Reflective Teaching, Ramat-Gan (Israel), Doctoral Dissertation.

Ross, D.D. (1987). Reflective Teaching, Meaning and Implications for Pre-service Teacher Educators, Paper presented at the Reflective Inquiry Conference, Huston (TX).

Ross, D.D. (1990). In search of examples of guided practice. In T. Stoddart (Ed.). *Perspectives on Guided Practice.* East Lansing (MI): NCRTE, Michigan State University Press, pp. 43–51.

Ross, D.D., Bondy, E. & Kyle, D.W. (1993). *Reflective Teaching for Student Empowerment.* New York: Macmillan Publishing Company.

Schon, D.A. (1983). *The Reflective Practitioner: How Professionals Think in Action*, New York: Basic Books.

Schon, D.A. (1987). *Educating the Reflective Practitioner: Toward a New Design in Teaching and Learning in the Professions.* San Francisco (CA): Jossey-Bass Inc. Publishers.

Schwebel, A.L., Schwebel, B.L., Schwebel, C.R. & Schwebel M. (1992). *The Student Teacher's Handbook* (second edition), pp. 33–63. London: Lawrence Erlbaum Associates Publishers.

Stoddart, T. (Ed.) (1980). *Perspectives on Guided Practice, Technical Series*, pp. 1–90. East Lansing (MI): NCRTE, Michigan State University.

Zeichner, K.M. (1980). Myths and realities: field-based experiences, in pre-service teacher education. *Journal of Teacher Education, 31*(6), 45–55.

Zeichner, K.M. (1983). Alternative paradigms of teacher education. *Journal of Teacher Education, 34*(3), 3–9.

Zeichner, K.M. (1988). Learning from experience in graduate teacher preparation. In K.A. Woolflok (Ed.). *Research Perspective on the Graduate Preparation of Teachers.* Englewood Cliffs (NJ): Prentice Hall, pp. 12–29.

Zeichner, K.M. (1990). When you have said reflection, you haven't said it all. In T. Stoddart (Ed.). *Perspectives on Guided Practices*, pp. 59–69. East Lansing (MI): NCRTE, Michigan State University.

Zilberstein, M. (1994a). Qualifying teachers for lesson planning under two conceptual approaches: curricular and instructional, Tel Aviv. *Ways of Teaching, 2*, 105–150 (Hebrew).

Zilberstein, M. (1994b). *Analysis of Teaching Situations — Portrait of a Professional Teacher,* Tel Aviv, Mofet. Ministry of Education and Culture (Hebrew).

Zilberstein, M. (1995). *Case Literature – An Alternative Method of Training and Refreshing Teachers*, pp. 121–133. Tel-Aviv, Mofet Inst. Ministry of Education and Culture, (Hebrew).

Ziv, S. (1990). Practical experience in teacher education, problems and attitudes, Tel Aviv, Mofet Inst., Ministry of Education and Culture, pp. 25–43 (Hebrew).

Ziv, S. (1991). The cooperating teacher in teacher training, problems and coping modes. *Pages, 10.* CR&D Inst. (Mofet), Ministry of Education and Culture, pp. 24–35 (Hebrew).

Ziv, S., Katz, P., Zilberstein, M. & Tamir, P. (1995). *Work Characteristics of Pedagogic Mentors in the Teacher Training System in Israel.* Research Report. Tel Aviv: CR&D Inst. (Mofet) (Hebrew).

Chapter 8

Babylonian Talmud, Tractate Taanit 7a, Artscroll, Mesorah Publications Ltd, NY, 1995.

Babylonian Talmud, Tractate Kiddushin 30/1, Artscroll, Mesorah Publications Ltd, NY, 1995.

Clarke, H. (1977). Inferences in comprehension. In D. La Berge and S. Samuel (Eds.) *Basic Processes in Reading. Perception and Comprehension*. Hillsdale, NJ: Lawrence Erlbaum.

Feuerstein, R. & Feuerstein, S. (1991), Mediated learning experience: A theoretical review. In R. Feuerstein, P.S. Klein & A.J. Tannenbaum (Eds.). *Mediated Learning Experience (M.L.E.). Theoretical, Psychosocial and Learning Implications*, pp. 3–52. London: Freund

Kraut, R. & Tory Higgins, E. (1984). Communication and social cognition. In *Handbook of Social Cognition*, pp. 3–52. Lawrence Erlbaum: Hillsdale, NJ, 1984.

Leibowitz, N. (1941–1970). Works published by the World Zionist Organization, Jerusalem.

Lives, G.J. (1960). Socrates an ironic holy man. *MOLAD*, *5*, 113–119 (Hebrew).

Maimonides. *Hilchot Talmud Torah Tractate*. (Hilchot Talmud Torah, IV, par. 4–8).

Neusner, Jacob (1984). *The Talmudic Argument: A study in Talmudic Reasoning and Methodology*. Cambridge: Cambridge University Press.

Rabbi Eliezer (1965). *Pirkei of Rabbi Eliezer* (tr. by Gerald Friedlander). New York: Hermon Press.

Psalms 127/5. In Harold Risch (Ed.) *The Holy Scriptures*. Jerusalem: Koren Publishers Ltd, 1989.

Resnick, L. (1987). *Education and Learning to Think*. Washington, D.C.: National Academy Press.

Simon, E. (1949). *The Educational Meaning of Socratic Irony*. Tel Aviv: Dinaburg Book. (Hebrew).

Steinsaltz, A. (1989). *The Talmud, The Steinsaltz Edition: A Reference Guide*. New York: Random House.

Tomasello, M., Kruger, A.C. & Ratner, H.H. (1993). Cultural learning. *Behavioral and Brain Sciences*, *16*, 495–552.

Chapter 9

Blatt, Shaya et al.

Feuerstein, Ra.S. (1997). The coherence of the theory of modifiability. In A. Kozulin (Ed.). *The Ontogeny of Cognitive Modifiability*. Jerusalem: ICELP.

Feuerstein, Ra.S. (1999). Deficient cognitive functions as the teacher's tool. In D. Tzuriel (Ed.). *Mediated Learning Experience*. Kiriat Bialik: Ach Publishers (in Hebrew).

Feuerstein, R. (1968). *Instrumental Enrichment: Intervention Program for Cognitive Modifiability*. Jerusalem: Hadassah WIZO Canada Institute.

Feuerstein, R. (1991). The theory of structural cognitive modifiability. In B. Presseisen (Ed.). *Thinking and Learning Styles: Classroom Interactions*. Washington, DC: National Educational Association.

Feuerstein, R., Feuerstein, R.S. & Gross, S. (1997) The Learning Potential Assessment Device. In D.P. Flanagan, J.J. Genshaft & P.L. Harrison (Eds). *Contemporary Intellectual Assessment*. pp. 297–313. New York and London: Guilford Press.

Feuerstein, R. & Feuerstein, S. (1991). Mediated Learning Experience: a theoretical review. In R. Feuerstein, P.S. Klein & A.J. Tannenbaum (Eds.). *Mediated Learning Experience* (MLE), pp. 3–52. London and Tel Aviv: Freund.

Feuerstein, R. & Hoffman, M.B. (1990). Theory of structural cognitive modifiability. In B. Presseisen (Ed.), *Learning and Thinking Styles: Classroom Interaction.* National Education Association and Research for Better Schools. Washington D.C., pp. 68–134. SCM.

Feuerstein, R., Hoffman, M., Krasilowsky, D., Rand, Y. & Tannenbaum, A. (1976). The effects of group care on the psychosocial habilitation of immigrant adolescents in Israel with special reference to high-risk children. *International Review of Applied Psychology, 25,* 189–201.

Feuerstein, R. & Krasilowsky, D. (1971). The treatment group technique. In M. Wollins & M. Gottesman (Eds.). *Group Care: An Israeli Experience.* New York: Gordon and Breach.

Feuerstein, R. Krasilowsky, D. & Rand, Y. (1979). Ontogeny of learning. In M.T. Brazier (Ed.). *Brain Mechanisms in Memory and Learning.* Proceedings of the International Brain Research Organization Symposium, Royal Society. London, UK 1977. New York: Raven Press. SCM.

Feuerstein, R., Rand, Y. & Hoffman, M. (1979). *The Dynamic Assessment of Retarded Performer: The Learning Potential Assessment Device.* Baltimore, MD: University Park Press.

Feuerstein, R., Rand, Y., Hoffman, M. & Miller, R. (1980). *Instrumental Enrichment.* Baltimore, MD: University Park Press.

Feuerstein, R., Feuerstein, R. & Schur, Y., (1977). Process as content in education of expectional children. In A. Lozulin (Ed.). *The Ontogeny of Cognitive Modifiability.*

Feuerstein, R. & Richelle, M. (1963). *Children of the Melah. Socio-Cultural Deprivation and Its Educational Significance.* The North African Jewish Child (Research Report). Jerusalem. the Szold Foundation for Child and Youth Welfare (Hebrew). SCM.

Feuerstein, R. Feuerstein, R.S. & Schur, Y. (1997). Process as content in regular education and in particular education of the low functioning retarded performer. In A.L. Costa & R.M. Liebmann (Eds.). If Process were Content: Sustaining the Spirit of Learning. Thousand Oaks, CA: Corwin.

Feuerstein, R., Feuerstein, R.S. & Schur, Y. (1999). "IE, Developmental stages in the program and its application". In Elad Peled (Ed.). *Fifty Years of Israeli Education* (Hebrew). Ministry of Defence, Jerusalem, Israel.

Hebb, D.O. (1949). *The Organization of Behavior.* N.Y.: Wiley.

Hunt, Mc.V. (1961). *Intelligence and Experience.* N.Y.: Ronald Press.

Lidz, C. (Ed.) (1987). *Dynamic Assessment.* New York: Guilford Press.

Rand, Y., Mintzker, Y., Miller, R., Hoffman, M.B. & Friedlender, Y. (1981). The Instrumental Enrichment program: Immediate and long-term effects. In P. Mittler (Ed.). *Frontiers of Knowledge in Mental Retardation: Social, Educational, and Behavioral Aspects.* Baltimore, MD: University Park Press.

Rand, Y., Tannenbaum, A. & Feuerstein, R. (1979). Effects of Instrumental Enrichment on the psycho-educational development of low-functioning adolescents. *Journal of Educational Psychology, 71,* 751–763.

Richelle, M. & Feuerstein, R. (1957). Enfants Juifs Nord-Africans. Jerusalem: Youth Aliyah.

Schaie, K.W. (1973). Problems in descriptive development research of adulthood and aging. In J. Nesselroade & I. Reese (Eds.). *Life Span Developmental Psychology: Methodological Issues.* New York: Academic Press.

Vygotsky, L (1978). *Mind in Society.* Cambridge, MA: Harvard University Press.
Vygotsky, L. (1986). *Thought and Language* (rev. ed.). Cambridge, MA: MIT Press.

Chapter 10

Alvarez-Ortiz, L.A. (1996). *Relationship Between Home and School Mediation, Parental Perception, and the School Functioning of Pre-school mainland Puerto Rican Children.* Unpublished doctoral dissertation, Temple University, Philadelphia, PA.

Feuerstein, R., Klein, P.S. & Tannenbaum, A.J. (1991). *Mediated Learning Experience (MLE): Theoretical, Psychosocial, and Learning Implications.* London: Freund Publishing House, Ltd.

Glasier-Robinson, B.A. (1986). *The Relationship Between Mediated Learning and Academic Achievement.* Unpublished master's thesis, Bryn Mawr College, Bryn Mawr, PA.

Glasier-Robinson, B.A. (1990). *Improving the Ability of Low SES Mothers to Provide Mediated Learning Experiences for their Four-year-old Children.* Unpublished doctoral dissertation, Bryn Mawr College, Bryn Mawr, PA.

Green, B.L. (1996) *The Impact of Training on the Mediational Interactions of Mothers of Pre-school Children with Disabilities.* Unpublished doctoral dissertation, Temple University, Philadelphia, PA.

Jepsen, R.H. & Lidz, C.S. (accepted). Group dynamic assessment: Reliability and validity of a cognitive dynamic assessment procedure with adolescents with developmental disabilities.

Jitendra, A.K. & Rohena-Diaz, E. (1996). Language assessment of students who are linguistically diverse: Why a discrete approach is not the answer. *School Psychology Review, 25,* 40–56.

Lidz, C.S. (1991). *Practitioner's Guide to Dynamic Assessment.* New York: Guilford Press.

Lidz, C.S. (1992). Extent of incorporation of dynamic assessment in cognitive assessment courses: A national survey of school psychology trainers. *Journal of Special Education, 26,* 325–331.

Lidz, C.S., Bond, L.A. & Dissinger, L.G. (1991). Consistency of mother-child interaction, using the Mediated Learning Experience Rating Scale. *Special Services in the Schools, 6,* 145–165.

Lidz, C.S. & Greenberg, K.H. (1997). Criterion validity of a group dynamic assessment procedure with rural first grade regular education students. *Journal of Cognitive Education, 6,* 89–99.

Lidz, C.S., Jepsen, R.H. & Miller, M.B. (in press). Relationships between cognitive processes and academic achievement: Application of a group dynamic assessment procedure with multiply handicapped adolescents. *Education and Child Psychology, 14,* 56–67.

Lidz, C.S. & Thomas, C. (1987). The Pre-school Learning Assessment Device: Extension of a Static Approach. In C.S. Lidz (Ed.). *Dynamic Assessment: An Interactional Approach to Evaluating Learning Potential* (pp. 288–326). New York: Guilford Press.

Reinhart, B.M. (1989). *Cognitive Modifiability in Developmentally-Delayed Children.* Unpublished doctoral dissertation, Yeshiva University, New York, NY.

Thomas, C.M (1986). *The Effects of Mediation on the Performance of Disadvantaged Pre-school Children on Two Cognitive Tasks.* Unpublished doctoral dissertation, Bryn Mawr College, Bryn Mawr, PA.

van der Aalsvoort, G.M. (1997). The quality of social interaction between pre-school teachers and pre-schoolers with little interest in cognitive games. *Journal of Cognitive Education, 5,* 255–262.

Weinblatt, A.S. (1993). *Maternal Style and Mediational Practices under Varying Mother-Child Interactive Conditions.* Unpublished doctoral dissertation, Yeshiva University, New York, NY.

Zambrana-Ortiz, N. & Lidz, C.S. (1995). The relationship between Puerto Rican mothers' and fathers' Mediated Learning Experiences and the competence of their preschool children. *Journal of Cognitive Education, 4,* 17–32.

Chapter 11

Beckmann, J.F. (1994). *Lernen und Komplexes Problemlösen. Ein Beitrag zur Konstruktvalidierung von Lerntests* [Learning and complex problem solving. A contribution to validating learning potential tests]. Bonn: Holos.

Beckmann, J.F. & Guthke, J. (1995). Complex problem solving, intelligence, and learning ability. In P. A. Frensch & J. Funke (Eds.). *Complex Problem Solving: The European Perspective,* (pp. 177–200). Hillsdale, NJ: Lawrence Erlbaum Associates.

Beckmann, J.F. & Guthke, J. (1999). *Diagnostik schlußfolgernden Denkens [Assessing reasoning ability].* Göttingen: Hogrefe.

Beckmann, J.F., Guthke, J. & Vahle, H. (1997). Analysen zum Zeitverhalten bei computergestützten adaptiven Intelligenz-Lerntests [Analysis of item response latencies in computer-aided adaptive intelligence tests]. Diagnostica, 43, 40–62.

Bourmenskaya, G.V. (1990). *Wygotskis Idee von der "Zone der nächsten Entwicklung" in der Sowjetischen Entwicklungspsychologie* [Vygotsky's notion of the "zone of proximal development" in Soviet developmental psychology]. Unpublished manuscript, University of Moscow, Institute of Psychology.

Büchel, F.P. & Scharnhorst, U. (1993). The learning potential assessment device (LPAD): Discussion of theoretical and methodological problems. In J.H.M. Hamers, K. Sijtsma & A.J.M.M. Ruijssenaars (Eds.). *Learning Potential Assessment,* (pp. 83–111). Amsterdam: Swets & Zeitlinger.

Budoff, M. (1967). Learning potential among young adult retardates. *American Journal of Mental Deficiency, 72,* 404–411.

Budoff, M., Meskin, J. & Harrison, R.H. (1971). Educational test of the learning potential hypothesis. *American Journal of Mental Deficiency, 76,* 159–169.

Buffart, H. & Leeuwenberg, E.L.J. (1983). Structural information theory. In H.G. Geißler, H. Buffart, E.L.J. Leeuwenberg & V. Sarris (Eds.). *Modern Issues in Perception,* (pp. 48–72). Amsterdam: North-Holland Publishing Company.

Campione, J.C. & Brown, A.L. (1987). Linking dynamic assessment with school achievement. In C. Lidz (Ed.). *Dynamic Assessment,* (pp. 82–115). New York: Guilford Press.

Carlson, J.S. & Wiedl, K.H. (1980). Applications of a dynamic testing approach in intelligence assessment: Empirical results and theoretical formulations. *Zeitschrift für Differentielle und Diagnostische Psychologie, 4,* 303–318.

Cole, M. (1991). Conclusions. In L.B. Resnick, J.B. Levine & S.D. Tesley (Eds.). *Perspectives on Social Shared Cognition,* (pp. 398–417). Washington, DC: American Psychological Association.

de Weerdt, E.H. (1927). A study of the improvability of fifth grade school children in certain mental functions. *Journal of Educational Psychology, 18,* 547–557.

Epstein, S. & O'Brian, E. (1985). The person–situation debate in historical and current perspective. *Psychological Bulletin, 98,* 513–537.

Ewert, O.M. (1992). Instruktionspsychologie — ein neues Selbstverständnis der Pädagogischen Psychologie [Instructional psychology — a new self-definition of educational psychology]. *Bildung und Erziehung, 45,* 265–276.

Feuerstein, R., Rand, Y. & Hoffman, M.B. (1979). *The Dynamic Assessment of Retarded Performers: The Learning Assessment Potential Device, Theory, Instruments and Techniques.* Baltimore: University Park Press.

Frensch, P.A. & Funke, J. (Eds.). (1995). *Complex Problem Solving. The European Perspective.* Hillsdale, NJ: Lawrence Erlbaum Associates.

Glutting, J. & McDermott, P.A. (1990). Principles and problems in learning potential. In C.R. Reynolds & R.W. Kamphaus (Eds.). *Handbook of Psychological and Educational Assessment of Children,* (pp. 296–347). New York: Guilford Press.

Greeno, J.G. (1992). *The Situation in Cognitive Theory: Some Methodological Implications of Situativity.* Paper presented at the American Psychological Society, San Diego.

Grigorenko, E.L. & Sternberg, R. (1998). Dynamic testing. *Psychological Bulletin, 124,* 75–111.

Guthke, J. (1972). *Zur Diagnostik der intellektuellen Lernfähigkeit* [Diagnosing intellectual learning ability]. Berlin: Deutscher Verlag der Wissenschaften.

Guthke, J. & Gitter, K. (1991). Prognose der Schulleistungsentwicklung mittels Status- und Lerntests in der Vorschulzeit [Predicting school achievement by means of static and learning tests applied to preschoolers]. In H. Teichmann, B. Meyer-Probst & D. Roether (Eds.). *Risikobewältigung in der lebenslangen Psychischen Entwicklung,* (pp. 141–147). Berlin: Verlag Gesundheit.

Guthke, J. & Wiedl, K.-H. (1996). *Dynamisches Testen. Zur Psychodiagnostik der intraindividuellen Variabilität* [Dynamic Assessment. On Psychodiagnosis of intraindividual variability]. Göttingen: Hogrefe.

Guthke, J. & Wingenfeld, S. (1992). The learning test concept: Origins, state of the art, and trends. In H.C. Haywood & D. Tzuriel (Eds.). *Interactive Assessment,* (pp. 64–94). New York: Springer.

Guthke, J., Beckmann, J.F., Stein, H., Vahle, H. & Rittner, S. (1995). *Adaptive Computergestützte Intelligenz-Lerntestbatterie (ACIL)* [The Adaptive, Computer-Assisted Intelligence Learning Test Battery]. Mödlingen: Schuhfried GmbH.

Hamers, J.H.M., Sijtsma, K. & Ruijssenaars, A.J.J.M. (Eds.). (1993). *Learning Potential Assessment.* Amsterdam: Swets & Zeitlinger.

Haywood, H.C. & Tzuriel, D. (Eds.). (1992). *Interactive Assessment.* New York: Springer.

Hegarty, S. & Lucas, D. (1978). *Able to Learn? The Pursuit of Culture-Fair Assessment.* London: N.F.E.R. Publishing Company.

Hessels, M.G.P. (1995). How valid are learning potential scores? A comparison of the validities of learning potential test scores and traditional IQ scores. *European Journal of Psychological Assessment, 11*(Suppl. 1), 82.

Ivanova, A.J. (1973). *Das Lernexperiment als Methode der Diagnostik der geistigen Entwicklung der Kinder* [The learning experiment as a method of assessing children's mental development]. Moscow: Pedagogika.

Kern, B. (1930). *Wirkungsformen der Übung* [Effects of practice]. Münster: Helios.

Klein, S. (1970). *Kiserlet egy uj tipusu Intelligencia Teszt Kialakitazara* [An experiment to develop a new type of intelligence test]. Budapest: Akademiai Kiado.

Kornmann, R., Meister, H. & Schlee, J. (Eds.). (1983). *Förderdiagnostik. Konzept und*

Realisierungsmöglichkeiten [Treatment-oriented assessment — the concept and how it can be realised]. Heidelberg: Schindele.

Kozulin, A. & Falik, L. (1995). Dynamic cognitive assessment of the child. *Current Directions in Psychological Science, 4*, 192–196.

Krypsin-Exner, J. (1987). *Ergopsychometrie und Hirnleistungsdiagnostik in der klinischen Psychologie und Psychiatrie* [Ergopsychometry and assessment of brain performance in psychology]. Regensburg: Roderer.

Leutner, D. (1992). *Adaptive Lehrsysteme* [Adaptive teaching systems]. Weinheim: Psychologie Verlags Union.

Leutner, D. & Schrettenbrunner, H. (1989). Entdeckendes Lernen in komplexen Realitätsbereichen: Evaluation des Computer-Simulationsspiels "Hunger in Nordafrika" [Learning by discovery in complex situations: Evaluation of the computer simulation "Famine in the Sahel"]. *Unterrichtswissenschaft, 17*, 327–341.

Lidz, C.S. (1991). *Practitioner's Guide to Dynamic Assessment*. New York: Guilford Press.

Lompscher, J. (Ed.). (1972). *Theoretische und Empirische Untersuchungen zur Entwicklung geistiger Fähigkeiten* [Theoretical and empirical research on the development of mental abilities]. Berlin: Volk und Wissen.

Meumann, E. (1922). *Vorlesungen zur Einführung in die Experimentelle Pädagogik und ihre Psychologischen Grundlagen (1)* [Lectures introducing experimental education and its psychological foundations]. (2nd ed.). Leipzig: Engelmann.

Probst, H. (1979). *Kritische Behindertenpädagogik in Theorie und Praxis* [Critical education theory of the handicapped: In theory and practice]. Solms-Oberbiel: Jarick.

Resnick, L.B. (1991). Shared cognition. In L.B. Resnick, J.B. Levine & S.D. Teasley (Eds.). *Perspectives on Social Shared Cognition*, (pp. 1–19). Washington, DC: American Psychological Association.

Schlee, J. (1985). Förderdiagnostik — Eine bessere Konzeption? [Treatment-oriented assessment — a better scheme?] In R.S. Jäger, R. Horn & K. Ingenkamp (Eds.). *Tests und Trends (Jahrbuch der Pädagogik)*, (pp. 82–208). Weinheim: Beltz.

Schmitt, M. (1990). *Konsistenz als Persönlichkeitseigenschaft?* [Consistency as a personality trait?] Berlin: Springer.

Snow, R.E. (1990). Progress and propaganda in learning assessment. *Contemporary Psychology, 35*, 1134–1136.

Steyer, R. & Schmitt, M. (1992). Basic components of Latent State-Trait-Theory. In R. Steyer, H. Gräser & K.F. Widaman (Eds.). *Consistency and Specificity: Latent State-Trait-Models in Differential Psychology*, (pp. 1–19). New York: Springer.

van der Heijden, M. K. (1993). *Consistency in Approach: A Diagnostic Investigation of Eight Aspects of Arithmetic Behavior*. Unpublished doctoral dissertation, University of Leiden, Netherlands, Leiden.

Vygotsky, L.S. (1964). *Denken und Sprechen* [Thinking and speech]. Berlin: Akademie-Verlag. (Original work published 1934)

Vygotsky, L.S. (1987). *Ausgewählte Schriften. In deutscher Sprache herausgegeben von J. Lompscher* [Selected writings. Issued in German by J. Lompscher]. Berlin: Volk und Wissen.

Wallasch, R. & Möbus, C. (1977). Validierung und Kreuzvalidierung des Göttinger Formreproduktionstests von Schlange et al. (1972) und der Background Interference Procedure von Canter (1970) zur Erfassung von Hirnschädigungen bei Kindern zusammen mit zwei anderen Auswertungssystemen für den Bender Gestalt Test [Identifying children with brain lesions]. *Diagnostica, 23*, 156–172.

Wiedemann, M. (1993). *Lernfähigkeit im Rahmen des BIS* [Learning ability within the framework of BIS]. Unpublished doctoral dissertation, FU Berlin, Berlin, Germany.

Wiedl, K.H. & Herrig, D. (1978). Ökologische Validität und Schulerfolgsprognose im Lern- und Intelligenztest: Eine exemplarische Studie [Ecological validity and prediction of success in school on the basis of learning tests and traditional intelligence tests]. *Diagnostica, 24,* 175–186.

Wiedl, K.H., Guthke, J. & Wingenfeld, S. (1995). Dynamic assessment in Europe: Historical perspectives. In J.S. Carlson (Ed.). *Advances in Cognition and Educational Practice. European Contributions to Dynamic Assessment,* (Vol. 3, pp. 33–82). Greenwich: JAI Press Inc.

Wieland, W. (1991). *Zur Bewährung von Lerntests im Hilfsschul-Aufnahmeverfahren* [Validation of learning tests in the selection procedure for special schools]. Unpublished diploma theses, University of Leipzig, Leipzig.

Zubin, J. (1950). Symposium on statistics for the clinician. *Journal of Clinical Psychology, 6,* 1–6.

Chapter 12

Anderson, J.R. (1983). *The Architecture of Cognition.* Cambridge, MA: Harvard University Press.

Baddeley, A.D. (1992). Working memory. *Science, 255,* 556–559.

Baillargeon, R.H. (1993). *The Development of Mental Capacity: A Latent Trait Investigation of a Neo-Piagetian Model.* Unpublished doctoral dissertation, York University, Toronto.

Baillargeon, R., Pascual-Leone, J. & Roncadin, C. (1998) *Mental Attentional Capacity: Does Cognitive Style Make a Difference? Journal of Experimental Child Psychology, 70,* 143–166..

Baskind, S. (1997). *Mental Capacity Assessment of Deaf Children.* Unpublished Master's thesis, York University, Toronto.

Bebko, J. (1984). Memory and rehearsal characteristics of profoundly deaf children. *Journal of Experimental Child Psychology, 38,* 415–428.

Carpenter, P. & Just, M. (1992). A capacity theory of comprehension: Individual differences in working memory. *Psychological Review, 99,* 122–149.

Case, R. (1992). The role of the frontal lobes in the regulation of cognitive development. *Brain and Cognition, 20,* 51–73.

Case, R., Okamoto, Y., Henderson, B. & McKeough, A. (1993). Individual variability and consistency in cognitive development: New evidence for the existence of central conceptual structures. In R. Case & W. Edelstein (Eds.). *The New Structuralism in Cognitive Development* (pp. 71–100). Basel: Karger.

Colangelo, N. & Davis, G. (1991). *Handbook of Gifted Education.* Needham Heights, MA: Allyn & Bacon.

Demetriou, A. (Ed.) (1988). *Neo-Piagetian Theories of Cognitive Development: An Integration.* Amsterdam: North-Holland Press.

Dempster, F. (1992). The rise and fall of the inhibitory mechanism: Toward a unified theory of cognitive development and aging. *Developmental Review, 12,* 45–75.

Dworsky, S. (1996). *Problems of Mental Capacity Assessment: The Role of Component Skills in Deaf and Hearing Children.* Unpublished Master's thesis, York University, Toronto.

Emmorey, K., Kosslyn, S. & Bellugi, U. (1993). Visual imagery and visual-spatial language: Enhanced imagery abilities in deaf and hearing ASL signers. *Cognition, 46*, 139–181.

Engle, R. & Cantor, J. (1993). Working-memory capacity as long-term memory: An individual differences approach. *Journal of Experimental Psychology: Learning, Memory & Cognition, 19*, 1101–1114.

Feuerstein, R., Rand, Y. & Hoffman, M.B. (1979). *The Dynamic Assessment of Retarded Performers*. Baltimore: University Park Press.

Feuerstein, R., Rand, Y., Hoffman, M.B. & Miller, R. (1980). *Instrumental Enrichment*. Baltimore: University Park Press.

Globerson, T. (1983). Mental capacity and cognitive functioning: Developmental and social class differences. *Developmental Psychology, 19*, 225–230.

Houde, O. (1992). *Catégorisation et développement Cognitif* [Categorization and cognitive development]. Paris: Presses Universitaires de France.

Houde, O. (1994). La reference logico-matematique en psychologie: Entre methode universelle et rationalite arrogante [The logico-mathematic issue in psychology: Between universal method and arrogant rationality]. In O. Houde & D. Mieville (Eds.). *Pensee logica-matematique: Nouveaux objects interdisciplinaires* (pp. 47–119). Paris: Presses Universitaires de France.

James, W. (1961). *Psychology: The Briefer Course* (G. Allport, Trans.). New York: Harper Torchbooks.

Johnson, J., Fabian, V. & Pascual-Leone, J. (1989). Quantitative hardware-stages that constrain language development. *Human Development, 32*, 245–271.

Johnstone, A. & El-Banna, H. (1986). Capacities demands and processes: A predictive model for science education. *Education in Chemistry, 64*, 80–85.

Kozulin, A. (1990). *Vygotsky's Psychology: A Biography of Ideas*. Cambridge, MA: Harvard University Press.

Langer, E.J. (1989). *Mindfulness*. Reading, MA: Addison-Wesley.

Lidz, C.S. (Ed.) (1987). *Dynamic Assessment: An Interactional Approach to Evaluating Learning Potential*. New York : Guilford Press.

Luria, A.R. (1973). *The Working Brain: An Introduction to Neuropsychology*. New York: Basic Books.

Marschark, M. (1993). *Psychological Development of Deaf Children*. New York: Oxford University Press.

McFarland, R. (1972). *Information Processing in Reflective and Impulsive Children: A Test of a Quantitative Developmental Model*. Unpublished Master's thesis, York University, Toronto.

Miller, R., Pascual-Leone, J., Campbell, C. & Juckes, T. (1989). Cross-cultural similarities and differences on two neo-Piagetian tasks. *International Journal of Psychology, 24*, 293–313.

Molenaar, P.C.M. & van der Maas, H.L.J. (1994). Commentary. *Human Development, 37*, 177–180.

Niaz, M. & Caraucan, E. (1996). "*Learning to learn*" ability: A neo-Piagetian Interpretation of the Potential for Learning. *Perceptual Motor Skills, 86*, 1291–1298.

Niaz, M. & Lawson, A. (1985). Balancing chemical equations: The role of developmental level and mental capacity. *Journal of Research in Science Teaching, 22*, 41–51.

Oltman, P.K., Raskin, E. & Witkin, H.A. (1971). *Group Embedded Figures Test*. Palo Alto, CA: Consulting Psychologists Press.

Parnasis, I., Samar, V., Bettger, J. & Sathe, K. (1996). Does deafness lead to enhancement of visual spatial cognition in children? Negative evidence from nonsigners. *Journal of Deaf Studies and Deaf Education, 1*, 145–152.

Pascual-Leone, J. (1970). A mathematical model for the transition rule in Piaget's developmental stages. *Acta Psychologica, 32*, 301–345.

Pascual-Leone, J. (1978). Compounds, confounds and models in developmental information processing: A reply to Trabasso and Foellinger. *Journal of Experimental Child Psychology, 26*, 18–40.

Pascual-Leone, J. (1980). Constructive problems for constructive theories: The current relevance of Piaget's work and a critique of information-processing simulation psychology. In R. Kluwe and H. Spada (Eds.). *Developmental Models of Thinking* (pp. 263–296). New York: Academic Press.

Pascual-Leone, J. (1983). Growing into human maturity: Toward a metasubjective theory of adulthood stages. In P.B. Baltes & O.G. Brim (Eds.). *Life-Span Development and Behavior (Vol. 5)* (pp. 117–156). New York: Academic Press.

Pascual-Leone, J. (1984). Attention, dialectic and mental effort: Towards an organismic theory of life stages. In M.L. Commons, F.A. Richards & G. Armon (Eds.). *Beyond Formal Operations: Late Adolescence and Adult Cognitive Development* (pp. 182–215). New York: Praeger.

Pascual-Leone, J. (1987). Organismic processes for neo-Piagetian theories: A dialectical causal account of cognitive development. *International Journal of Psychology, 22*, 531–570.

Pascual-Leone, J. (1989). An organismic process model of Witkin's field-dependence-independence. In T. Globerson & T. Zelniker (Eds.). *Cognitive Style and Cognitive Development* (pp. 36–70). Norwood, NJ: Ablex.

Pascual-Leone, J. (1990a). An essay on wisdom: Toward organismic processes that make it possible. In R.J. Sternberg (Ed.). *Wisdom: Its Nature, Origins, and Development* (pp. 244–278). New York: Cambridge University Press.

Pascual-Leone, J. (1990b). Reflections on life-span intelligence, consciousness and ego development. In C. Alexander & E. Langer (Eds.). *Higher Stages of Human Development: Perspectives on Adult Growth* (pp. 258–285). New York: Oxford University Press.

Pascual-Leone, J. (1995). Learning and development as dialectical factors in cognitive growth. *Human Development, 38*, 338–348.

Pascual-Leone, J. (1996). Vygotsky, Piaget, and the problems of Plato. *Swiss Journal of Psychology, 55*, 84–92.

Pascual-Leone, J. (1997a). Divergent validity and the measurement of processing capacity (Commentary on Pulos). *International Journal of Behavioral Development, 20*, 735–738.

Pascual-Leone, J. (1997b). Metasubjective processes: The missing "lingua franca" of cognitive science. In D. Johnson & C. Erneling (Eds.). *The Future of the Cognitive Revolution* (pp. 75–101). New York: Oxford University Press.

Pascual-Leone, J. & Baillargeon, R. (1994). Developmental measurement of mental attention. *International Journal of Behavioral Development, 17*, 161–200.

Pascual-Leone, J. & Goodman, D. (1979). Intelligence and experience: A Neo-Piagetian approach. *Instructional Science, 8*, 301–367.

Pascual-Leone, J. & Ijaz, H. (1989). Mental capacity testing as a form of intellectual-developmental assessment. In R. Samuda, S. Kong, J. Cummins, J. Pascual-Leone & J. Lewis. *Assessment and Placement of Minority Students* (pp. 143–171). Toronto: Hogrefe International.

Pascual-Leone, J. & Irwin, R. (1994). Noncognitive factors in high-road/low-road learning: I. Modes of abstraction in adulthood. *Journal of Adult Development, 1*, 73–89.

Pascual-Leone, J. & Johnson, J. (1991). The psychological unit and its role in task analysis: A reinterpretation of object permanence (pp. 153–187). In M. Chandler & M. Chapman

(Eds.). *Criteria for Competence: Controversies in the Assessment of Children's Abilities.* Hillsdale, NJ: Erlbaum.

Pascual-Leone, J. & Johnson, J. (1999). A dialectical constructivist view of representation: Role of mental attention, executives, and symbols. In I.E. Sigel (Ed.). *The Development of Representational Thought: Theoretical Perspectives.* Hillsdale, NJ: Erlbaum.

Pascual-Leone, J., Johnson, J., Baskind, S. & Dworsky, S. (1997). *Individual Differences on Measures of Mental-Attentional Capacity.* Paper presented at the meeting of the Society for Research in Child Development, Washington, DC.

Pascual-Leone, J. & Morra, S. (1991). Horizontality of water level: A neoPiagetian developmental review. *Advances in Child Development and Behavior, 23,* 231–276.

Pascual-Leone, J. & Sparkman, E. (1980). The dialectics of empiricism and rationalism: A last methodological reply to Trabasso. *Journal of Experimental Child Psychology, 29,* 88–101.

Peressini, M. (1996). *A Neo-Piagetian Investigation of Giftedness.* Unpublished Master's thesis, York University, Toronto.

Piaget, J. (1969). *The Mechanisms of Perception* (G. N. Seagram. Trans.). London: Routledge & Kegan Paul.

Piaget, J. (1970). *Structuralism.* New York: Basic Books.

Porath, M. (1992). Stage and structure in the development of children with various types of giftedness. In R. Case (Ed.). *The Mind's Staircase* (pp. 303–317). Hillsdale, NJ: Erlbaum.

Proctor, R. & Reeve, T. (1990). *Stimulus–Response Compatibility.* Amsterdam: North Holland.

Rappaport, D. (1960). *The Structure of Psychoanalytical Theory: A Systematizing Attempt.* New York: International Universities Press.

Rey, A. (1963). *Connaissance de l'Individu par les Tests.* Bruxelles: Charles Dessart.

de Ribaupierre, A. (1975). *Cognitive Space and Formal Operations.* Unpublished doctoral dissertation, University of Toronto, Toronto.

de Ribaupierre, A. & Bailleux, C. (1994). Developmental change in a spatial task of attentional capacity: An essay toward an integration of two working memory models. *International Journal of Behavioral Development, 17,* 5–35.

Roncadin, C. (1996). *A Neo-Piagetian Analysis of Cognitive Development in Intellectual Giftedness.* Unpublished Master's thesis, York University, Toronto.

Runco, M. (1986). Maximal performance on divergent thinking tests using total ideational output and a creativity index. *Educational and Psychological Measurement, 52,* 213–221.

Salomon, G. (February, 1992). *Rocky Roads to Transfer.* Final Report, University of Arizona.

Salomon, G., & Globerson, T. (1987). Skill may not be enough: The role of mindfulness in learning and transfer. *International Journal of Educational Research, 11,* 623–637.

Salomon, G. & Perkins, D.N. (1989). Rocky roads to transfer: Rethinking mechanisms of a neglected phenomenon. *Educational Psychologist, 24,* 113–142.

Samuda, R., Kong, S., Cummins, J., Pascual-Leone, J. & Lewis, J. (Eds.) (1989). *Assessment and Placement of Minority Students.* Toronto: Hogrefe International.

Sedighdeilami, F. (1996). *The Performance of "Gifted" and "Mainstream" Children in a Mental Attention Informative-Processing Task.* Unpublished Master's thesis, York University, Toronto.

Segalowitz, S., Unsal, A. & Dywan, F. (1992). Cleverness and wisdom in 12-year-olds: Electrophysiological evidence for late maturation of the frontal lobe. *Developmental Neuropsychology, 8,* 279–298.

Severtson, E. (1994). *Development of Multiplicative Reasoning*. Unpublished Master's thesis, York University, Toronto.

Severtson, E., Johnson, J. & Pascual-Leone, J. (1995). *(Mis)conceptions of Area in Children and Field Dependent Adults*. Paper presented at the meeting of the Society for Research in Child Development, Indianapolis, IN.

Shallice, T. (1982). Specific impairments of planning. In D.E. Broadbent & L. Weickrantz (Eds.). *The Neurobiology of Cognitive Functions* (pp. 199–209). London: The Royal Society.

Shultz, T., Schmidt, W., Buckingham, D. & Mareschal, D. (1995). Modeling cognitive development with a generative connectionist algorithm. In T. Somon & G. Halford (Eds.). *Developing Cognitive Competence: New Approaches to Process Modeling* (pp. 205–261). Hillsdale, NJ: Erlbaum.

Smolensky, P. (1988). On the proper treatment of connectionism. *Behavioral and Brain Sciences, 11*, 1–74.

Stankov, L. (1988). Aging, attention, and intelligence. *Psychology and Aging, 3*, 59–74.

Stewart, L. & Pascual-Leone, J. (1992). Mental capacity constraints and the development of moral reasoning. *Journal of Experimental Child Psychology, 54*, 251–287.

Stuss, D. (1992). Biological and psychological development of executive functions. *Brain and Cognition, 20*, 8–23.

Thelen, E. & Smith, L.B. (1994). *A Dynamic Systems Approach to the Development of Cognition and Action*. Cambridge, MA: MIT Press.

Todman, J. & Cowdy, N. (1993). Processing of visual-action codes by deaf and hearing children: Coding orientation of M-capacity? *Intelligence, 17*, 237–250.

Todman, J. & Seedhouse, E. (1994). Visual-action code processing by deaf and hearing children. *Language and Cognitive Processes, 9,* 129–141.

Tzuriel, D. & Haywood, H. (1992). The development of interactive-dynamic approaches for assessment of learning potential. In H. Haywood & D. Tzuriel (Eds.). *Interactive Assessment* (pp. 3–37). New York: Springer-Verlag.

van der Maas, H. & Molenaar, P. (1992). Stagewise cognitive development: An application of catastrophe theory. *Psychological Review, 99*, 395–417.

van der Veer, R. & Valsiner, J. (1991). *Understanding Vygotsky: A Quest for Synthesis*. Cambridge, MA: Blackwell.

Vygotsky, L. (1978). *Mind in Society: The Development of Higher Psychological Processes*. M. Cole, V. John-Steiner, S. Scribner & E. Souberman (Eds.). Cambridge, MA: Harvard University Press.

Wertheimer, M. (1959). *Productive Thinking* (M. Wertheimer, Ed.). New York: Harper.

Wechsler, D. (1991). *Wechsler Intelligence Scale for Children* (3rd Ed.). San Antonio, TX: The Psychological Corporation.

Witkin, H. & Goodenough, D. (1981). *Cognitive Styles, Essence and Origins: Field Dependence and Field Independence*. New York: International Universities Press.

Chapter 13

Beery, K.E. (1982). *Revised Administration, Scoring and Teaching Manual for the Developmental Test of Visual–Motor Integration*. Cleveland: Modern Curriculum Press.

Bornstein, M. & Tamis-LeMonda, C. (1990). Activities and interactions of mothers and their first born infants in the first six months of life. *Child Development, 61*, 1206–1217.

Bradley, R.H. & Caldwell, B.M. (1984). *Home Observation for Measurement of the Environment*, (HOME) (rev. ed.). Little Rock, AK: University of Arkansas.

Bronfenbrenner, U. (1979). *The Ecology of Human Development*. Cambridge, MA: Harvard University Press.

Campione, J.C. (1989). Assisted assessment: taxonomy of approaches and an outline of strengths and weaknesses. *Journal of Learning Disabilities, 22*, 151–165.

Carew, J.V. (1980). Experience and the development of intelligence in young children at home and in day care. *Monographs of the Society for Research in Child Development, 45* (67, Serial No. 187).

Clarke-Stewart, K.A. (1973). Interactions between mothers and their young children: Characteristics and consequences. *Monographs of the Society for Research in Child Development, 38* (6–7, Serial No. 153).

Embretson, S.E. (1992). Measuring and validating cognitive modifiability as ability: A study in the spatial domain. *Journal of Educational Measurement, 29*, 25–50.

Feuerstein, R., Rand, Y. & Hoffman, M.B. (1979). *The Dynamic Assessment of Retarded Performers: The Learning Potential Assessment Device: Theory, Instruments, and Techniques*. Baltimore: University Park Press.

Feuerstein, R., Rand, Y., Haywood, H.C., Kyram, L. & Hoffman, M. (1995). *Learning Propensity Assessment Device (LPAD)-Manual*. Jerusalem: The International Center for Enhancement of Learning Potential.

Feuerstein, R., Rank, Y., Hoffman, M. & Miller, R. (1980). *Instrumental Enrichment*. Baltimore: University Park Press.

Feuerstein, R., Rand, Y. & Rynders, J.E. (1988). *Don't Accept Me as I Am*. New York: Plenum.

van Geert, P. (1994). Vygotskian dynamics of development, *Human Development, 37*, 346–365.

Goodenough, F.L. (1926). *Measurement of intelligence by drawings*. New York: Harcourt Brace.

Grigorenko, E.L. & Sternberg, R.J. (1998). Dynamic testing. *Psychological Bulletin, 124*, 75–111.

Guthke, J. & Stein, H. (1996). Are learning tests the better version of intelligence tests? *European Journal of Psychological Assessment, 12*, 1–13.

Hamers, J.H.M., Sijtsma, K. & Ruijssenaars, J.J.M. (Ed.) (1993). *Learning Potential Assessment*, (pp. 83–111). Amsterdam: Swets & Zeitlinger

Haywood, H.C. & Tzuriel, D. (Eds.) (1992). *Interactive Assessment*. New York: Springer-Verlag.

Joreskog, K.G. & Sorbom, D. (1986). *LISREL VII: Analysis of Linear Structural Relationships by the Method of Likelihood*. Chicago: National Educational Resources.

Klein, P.S. (1988). Stability and change in interaction of Israeli mothers and infants. *Infant Behavior and Development, 11*, 55–70.

Klein, P.S. (1996). *Early Intervention: Cross-Cultural Experiences With a Mediational Approach*. New York: Garland

Kozulin, A. & Presseisen, B.Z. (1995). Mediated learning tools and psychological tools: Vygotsky's and Feuerstein's perspectives in study of student learning. *Educational Psychologist, 30*, 67–75.

Lidz, C.S. (1987) (Ed.). *Dynamic Assessment*. New York: Guilford.

Lidz, C.S. (1991). *Practitioner's Guide to Dynamic Assessment*. New York: Guilford.

Lidz, C.S. (1997). Dynamic assessment: Psychoeducational assessment with cultural sensitivity, *Journal of Social Distress and the Homeless, 6*, 95–111.

Missiuna, C. & Samuels, M. (1989). Dynamic assessment of preschool children in special education with special needs: Comparison of mediation and instruction. *Remedial and*

Special Education, 5, 1–22.

Raven, J.C. (1956). *Guide to Using the Colored Progressive Matrices, Sets A, Ab, and B*. London: H.K. Lewis.

Rey, A. (1956). *Test de Copie et de Réproduction de Mémoire de Figues Géométriques Complexes* [Test of copying and memory reproduction of geometric figures]. Paris: Centre de Psychologie Appliquée.

Rohner, R.P. (1978). *The Warmth Dimension: Foundation of Parental Acceptance-Rejection Theory*. Newbury Park, CA: Sage.

Samuels, M.T., Tzuriel, J. & Klein, P. (1998a). The Children's Analogical Thinking Modifiability Test, Ramat-Gan, Israel, Bar-Ilan University. *Journal of Psychoeducational Assessment, 16*, 270–274.

Samuels, M.T. & Tzuriel, D. (1998b). The Children's Inferential Thinking Modifiability Test, Ramat-Gan, Isreal: Bar-Ilan University. *Journal of Psychoeducational Assessment, 16*, 275–279.

Samuels, M.T., Killip, S.M., MacKenzie, H. & Fagan, J. (1992). Evaluating pre-school programs: The role of dynamic assessment. In H.C. Haywood & D. Tzuriel (Eds.). *Interactive Assessment* (pp. 251–271), New-York: Springer-Verlag.

Santostefano, S. (1978). *A Biodevelopmental Approach to Clinical Child Psychology*. New York: Wiley

Snijders & Snijders-Oomer (1970).

Sroufe, L.A. (1983). Infant-caregiver attachment and patterns of adaptation in preschool: The roots of maladaptation and competence. In M. Perlmutter (Ed.). *Minnesota Symposia in Child Psychology* (Vol. 16). Hillsdale, NJ: Erlbaum.

Sroufe, L.A. & Waters, E. (1997) Attachment as an organizational construct. *Child Development, 48*, 1184–1199.

Super, C. & Harkness, S. (1986). The developmental niche: A conceptualization at the interface of society and the individual. *International Journal of Behavioral Development, 9*, 545–570.

Tzuriel, D. (1989). Inferential cognitive modifiability in young socially disadvantaged and advantaged children. *International Journal of Dynamic Assessment and Instruction, 1*, 65–80.

Tzuriel, D. (1991a). Cognitive modifiability mediated learning experience and affective-motivational processes: A transactional approach. In R. Feuerstein, P.S. Klein, & A. Tannenbaum (Eds.). *Mediated Learning Experience* (MLE) (pp. 95–120), London: Freund.

Tzuriel, D. (1991b). *The Children's Inferential Thinking Modifiability (CITM) Test — Manual*. School of Education, Bar Ilan University.

Tzuriel, D. (1992a). The dynamic assessment approach: A reply to Frisby and Braden. *Journal of Special Education, 26*, 302–324.

Tzuriel, D. (1992b). *The Children's Inferential Cognitive Modifiability (CITM) Test–Manual*. School of Education, Bar-Ilan University, Ramat-Gan, Israel.

Tzuriel, D. (1996). Mediated learning experience in free-play versus structured situations among preschool low- medium- and high-SES. *Child Development and Care, 126*, 57-82.

Tzuriel, D. (1997a) Dynamic interactive assessment of young children: Basic principles and measures. In J.M. Martinez-Beltran, J. Lebeer & R. Garbo (Eds.). *Is Intelligence Modifiable?*. Madrid: Bruno.

Tzuriel, D. (1997b). The relation between parent–child mediated learning interactions and children's cognitive modifiability. In A. Kozulin (Ed.). *Applied Aspects of Mediated Learning Experience and Instrumental Enrichment*. Jerusalem: The International Center for Enhancement of Learning Potential.

Tzuriel, D. (1997c). A novel dynamic assessment approach for young children: Major dimensions and current research. *Educational and Child Psychology, 14*, 81–103.

Tzuriel, D. (1998). *Cognitive Modifiability: Dynamic Assessment of Learning Potential* (in Hebrew). Tel Aviv: Sifriat Poalim.

Tzuriel, D. (in press-a). *Dynamic Assessment of Young Children*. New York: Plenum Press.

Tzuriel, D. (1999a). Parent–child mediated learning transactions as determinants of cognitive modifiability: Recent research and future directions. *Genetic, Social, and General Psychology Monographs, 125*, 109–156

Tzuriel, D. (1999b). Dynamic assessment of preschool children: Principles and measures. In D. Tzuriel (Ed.) *Mediated Learning Experience: Theory, research, and applications* (pp. 182–212). Haifa: Ach Press, Oranim College, and the International Center for Enhancement of Learning Potential. (In Hebrew).

Tzuriel, D. (in press-b). The Cognitive Modifiability Battery (CMB) — assessment and intervention: Development of a dynamic assessment instrument. In C.S. Lidz and J. Elliot (Eds.). *Dynamic Assessment: Prevailing Models and Applications*. New York: Lawrence Erlbaum.

Tzuriel, D. (in press-c). Dynamic assessment of young children: educational and intervention perspectives. *Educational Psychology Review*.

Tzuriel, D. (in press-d). The Cognitive Modifiability Battery: Assessment and intervention. In C.S. Lidz and J. Elliott (Eds.). *Dynamic assessment: Prevailing models and applications*, Greenwich, CT: JAI Press.

Tzuriel, D. & Alfassi, M. (1994). Cognitive and motivational modifiability as a function of Instrumental Enrichment (IE) program. *Special Services in the Schools, 8*, 91–128.

Tzuriel, D. & Caspi, N. (1992). Dynamic assessment of cognitive modifiability in deaf and hearing pre-school children. *Journal of Special Education, 26*, 235–252.

Tzuriel, D. & Eiboshitz, Y. (1992). A structured program for visual motor integration (SP-VMI) for pre-school children. *Learning and Individual Differences, 4*, 104–123.

Tzuriel, D. & Eran, Z. (1990). Inferential cognitive modifiability as a function of mother–child Mediated Learning Experience (MLE) interactions among Kibbutz young children. *International Journal of Cognitive Education and Mediated Learning, 1*, 103–117.

Tzuriel, D. & Ernst, H. (1990). Mediated learning experience and structural cognitive modifiability: Testing of distal and proximal factors by structural equation model. *International Journal of Cognitive Education and Mediated Learning, 1*, 119–135.

Tzuriel, D. & Gerafy, O. (1997). Changes in teachers' attitudes and mediational teaching as a function of dynamic assessment training. Unpublished manuscript, School of Education, Bar-Ilan University, Israel.

Tzuriel, D. & Hatzir, A. (June 1999). The effects of mediational strategies of fathers and mothers and amount of time they spent with their young children on children's cognitive modifiability. Paper presented at the 7th International Conference of the International Association for Cognitive Education (IACE), Calgary, Alberta Canada.

Tzuriel, D. & Haywood, H.C. (1992). The development of interactive–dynamic approaches for assessment of learning potential. In H.C. Haywood & D. Tzuriel (Eds.). *Interactive Assessment* (pp. 3–37). New York: Springer-Verlag.

Tzuriel, D. & Kaufman, R. (1999). Mediated learning and cognitive modifiability: Dynamic assessment of young Ethiopian immigrants in Israel. *Journal of Cross-Cultural Psychology, 30*, 359–380.

Tzuriel, D., Kaniel, S., Kanner, A. & Haywood, H.C. (1999). The effectiveness of Bright Start program in kindergarten on transfer abilities and academic achievements. *Early Childhood Research Quarterly*.

Tzuriel, D., Kaniel, S., Zeliger, M., Friedman, A. & Haywood, H.C. (1998). Effects of the Bright Start program in kindergarten on use of mediated learning strategies and children's cognitive modifiability. *Child Development and Care, 143*, 1–20.

Tzuriel, D. & Klein, P.S. (1985). Analogical thinking modifiability in disadvantaged, regular, special education, and mentally retarded children. *Journal of Abnormal Child Psychology, 13*, 539–552.

Tzuriel, D. & Klein, P.S. (1987). Assessing the young child: Children's analogical thinking modifiability. In C.S. Lidz, (Ed.). *Dynamic Assessment* (pp. 268–282). New-York: Guilford.

Tzuriel, D. & Klein, P.S. (1991). *The Children's Analogical Thinking Modifiability — Manual.* School of Education, Bar Ilan University.

Tzuriel, D. & Schanck, T. (July, 1994). Assessment of learning potential and reflectivity-impulsivity dimension. Paper presented at the 23rd International congress of Applied Psychology, Madrid, Spain.

Tzuriel, D. & Weiss, S. (1998a). Cognitive modifiability as a function of mother–child mediated learning interactions, mother's acceptance-rejection, and child's personality. *Early Development and Parenting, 7*, 79–99.

Tzuriel, D. & Weiss, S. (1998b). Prediction of children's cognitive modifiability by specific mediated learning strategies in mother–child interactions. Unpublished manuscript. School of Education, Bar-Ilan University.

Tzuriel, D. & Weitz, A. (1998). Mother–child Mediated Learning Experience (MLE) strategies and children's cognitive modifiability among Very Low Birth Weight (VLBW) and Normally Born Weight (NBW) children. Unpublished manuscript, School of Education, Bar Ilan University.

Valsiner, J. (1984). Construction of the zone of proximal development in adult-child joint interaction: The socialization of meals. In B. Rogoff & J.V. Wertsch (Eds.). *Children's Learning in the "Zone of Proximal Development": New Directions in Child Development.* (Vol. 23, pp. 65–76). San Francisco: Jossey Bass.

Vygotsky, L.S. (1978). *Mind in Society.* Cambridge, MA: Harvard University Press.

Wachs, T.D. (1992). *The Nature of Nurture.* Newbury Park, CA: Sage.

Wertsch, J.V. (1984). The zone of proximal development: Some conceptual issues. In B. Rogoff & J.V. Wertsch (Eds.), *Children's learning in the 'zone of proximal development': New directions in child development.* (Vol. 23, pp. 7–18). San Francisci: Jossey Bass.

Chapter 14

Bjerre, L. & Hansen, E. (1976). Psychomotor development and school adjustment of 7-year-old children with low-birth-weight. *Acta Paediatrica Scandinavia, 65*, 25–30.

Bowlby, J. (1980). *Attachment and Loss. Vol. 1. Attachment.* New York: Basic Books.

Collins, W.A. (1984). Commentary: Family interaction and child development. In M. Perlmutter (Ed.). *Parent–Child Interaction and Parent–Child Relations in Child Development* (pp. 241–258). The Minnesota Symposia on Child Psychology, Vol. 17, Hillsdale. NJ: Erlbaum.

Feuerstein, R. (1979). *The Dynamic Assessment of Retarded Performers.* New York: University Park Press.

Feuerstein, R. (1980). *Instrumental Enrichment: Redevelopment of Cognitive Functions of Retarded Performers.* New York: University Park Press.

Field, T.M., Walden, T., Widmayer, S. & Greenberg, R. (1982). The early development of preterm discordant twin pairs: Bigger is not always better. In L.P. Lipsett & T.M. Field (Eds.). *Infant Behavior and Development: Prenatal Risk and Newborn Behavior* (pp. 153–163). Norwood, NJ: Ablex.

Klein, P.S. (1988). Stability and change in interaction of Israeli mothers and infants. *Infant Behavior and Development, 11*, 55–70.

Klein, P.S. (1991). Improving the quality of parental interaction with very low birth weight children: A longitudinal study using a mediated learning experience model. *Infant Mental Health Journal, 12*(4), 321–337.

Klein, P.S. (1996). *Early Interventions: A Cross Cultural Application of a Mediational Approach.* NY: Garland Pub.

Klein, P.S. & Alony, S. (1993). Immediate and sustained effects of maternal mediation behaviors in infancy. *Journal of Early Intervention, 71*(2), 177–193.

Klein, P.S., Raziel, P., Brish, M. & Birenbaum, E. (1987a). Cognitive performance of 3-year-old born at very low birth weight. *Journal of Psychosomatic Obstetrics and Gynecology, 7*, 117–129.

Klein, P.S., Weider, S. & Greenspan, S.L. (1987b). A theoretical overview and empirical study of mediated learning experience: Prediction of preschool performance from mother–infant interaction patterns. *Infant Mental Health Journal, 8*(2), 110–129.

Lazar, I., Darlington, R., Murray, H., Royce, J. & Snipper, A. (1982). The lasting effects of early education: A report from the Consortium for Longitudinal Studies. *Monographs of the Society for Research in Child Development, 47*(2), Serial No. 195.

Lepper, M.R. (1981). Intrinsic and extrinsic motivation in children: Detrimental effects of superfluous social controls. Aspects of development of competence. *Minnesota Symposia on Child Psychology, 14*, 155–214.

LeVine, R.A. (1980). Anthropology and child development. *New Directions for Child Development, 8*, 71–86.

Lieberman, A., Weston, D. & Pawl, J. (1991). Preventive intervention and outcome with anxiously attached dyads. *Child Development, 62*, 199–210.

Lyons-Ruth, K., Connell, D., Grunebaum, H. & Botein, S. (1990). Infants at social risk: Maternal depression and family support services as mediators of infant development and security of attachment. *Child Development, 61*, 85–99.

Tal, C. & Klein, P.S. (1994). *Effects of the MISC on Mother–Infant Attachment.* Paper presented at the 4th Conference of the International Association of Cognitive Education. Ginosar. Israel.

Wallace, J. (1984). Indicators of cognitive functioning in school-aged low-birth-weight children. Paper presented at the International Conference on Infancy Studies, New York, NY.

Chapter 15

Alvarez, V., Santos, J., Santiago, S. & Lebron, F. (1992). *Effecto del programma de Enriqueimiento Instrumental de Feuerstein en las habilidades cognoscitivas de una muestra de estudiantes puertoriquenos.* Instituto de Investigacion Cientifica, Centro Caribeno de Estudios Postgraduados, San Juan, Puerto Rico.

August-Rothman, P. & Zinn, B. (1986). *Application of IE Principles to a Mathematics Course for Young Ethiopian Adults.* Student Counseling Services. Jerusalem: Hebrew University.

Beasley, F. (1984). *An Evaluation of Feuerstein's Model for the Remediation of Adolescents' Cognitive Deficiencies.* Ph.D. thesis. University of London.

Blagg, N. (1991). *Can We Teach Intelligence?* Hillsdale, NJ: Erlbaum.

Boning, R.A. (1982). *Teacher's Manual Specific Skills Series.* New York: Barnell Loft.

Braden, J.P. (1994). *Deafness, Deprivation, and IQ.* New York: Plenum.

Crotti, S. (1993). Application du programme d'enrichisement instrumental (PEI) de Feuerstein. In M.Rey-von Allmen (Ed.). *Psychologie Clinique et Interrogations Culturelles,* pp. 311–329. Paris: CIEMI.

Debrey, R. (1994). Reviving thought processes in pre-adolescents. In M. Ben-Hur (Ed.). *On Feuerstein's Instrumental Enrichment,* pp. 145–160. Palatine, IL: IRI/Skylight.

Feuerstein, R. (1990). The theory of structural cognitive modifiability. In B. Presseisen (Ed.). *Teaching and Learning Styles,* pp. 68–134. Washington, DC: National Education Association.

Feuerstein, R., Rand, Y., Hoffman, M. & Miller, R. (1980). *Instrumental Enrichment.* Baltimore, MD: University Park Press.

Gouzman, R. (1995, December). Instrumental Enrichment program for the blind learners. Paper presented at the 2nd Conference of the European Association of Mediated Learning and Cognitive Modifiability (EAMC). Madrid, Spain.

Gouzman, R. (1997). Major problems of blind learners using tactile graphic materials and how to overcome them with the help of IE Braille program. In A.Kozulin (Ed.). *The Onthogeny of Cognitive Modifiability,* pp. 261–272. Jerusalem: ICELP.

Haywood, C. (1992). Evaluation of IE in England. *Contemporary Psychology, 37,* 206–207.

Jensen, M. & Singer, J. (1987). *Structural Cognitive Modifiability in Low Functioning Adolescents: An Evaluation of Instrumental Enrichment.* Report submitted to the State of Connecticut Department of Education. New Haven: Yale University.

Jensen, M. (1990). Change models and some evidence for phases and their plasticity in cognitive structures. *International Journal of Cognitive Education and Mediated Learning, 1*(1), 5–16.

Kaniel, S, Tzuriel, D., Feuerstein, R., Ben-Schachar, N. & Eitan, T. (1991). Dynamic assessment: Learning and transfer abilities of Ethiopian immigrants to Israel. In R. Feuerstein, P. Klein & A. Tannenbaum (Eds.). *Mediated Learning Experience,* 179–209. London: Freund.

Kaplan, M. (1990). *Improving Reading Performance in Inattentive Children Through Mediated Learning Experience.* Ph.D. thesis. University of Pretoria.

Keane, K. (1993). *Application of Mediated Learning Theory to a Deaf Population.* Unpublished doctoral dissertation. Teachers College, Columbia University, New York.

Kozulin, A. (1995, December). Inducing cognitive change in adolescent immigrants from Ethiopia. Paper presented at the 2nd Conference of the European Association of Mediated Learning and Cognitive Modifiability. Madrid, Spain.

Kozulin, A. & Lurie, L. (1994, July). Psychological tools and mediated learning: Cross-cultural aspects. Paper presented at the 12th Congress of Cross-Cultural Psychology. Pamplona, Spain.

Kozulin, A., Kaufman, R. & Lurie, L. (1997). Evaluation of the cognitive intervention with immigrant students from Ethiopia. In A. Kozulin (Ed.). *The Onthogeny of Cognitive Modifiability,* pp. 89–130. Jerusalem: ICELP.

Martin, D. (1993). Reasoning skills: A key to literacy for deaf learners. *American Annals of the Deaf, 138*(2), 82–86.

Martin, D. (1995, July). Mediated learning experience and deaf learners. Paper presented at the International Congress on Education of the Deaf. Tel-Aviv.

Mulcahy, R. and Associates (1994). Cognitive education project. In M. Ben-Hur (Ed.). *On Feuerstein's Instrumental Enrichment,* pp. 129–144. Palatine, IL: IRI/Skylight.

Neale, M.D. (1973). *Neale Analysis of Reading Ability Manual*. London: Macmillan Educational.

Niles, R. (1989). *Effects of Adult Modeling and Adult Direction on Impulsive Behavior of Learning Disabled Adolescents*. Ph.D. thesis. New York: Fordham University.

Portulano M.C. & Patino, F. (1993). Instrumental Enrichment: A tool for integrating blind and visually-impaired children into mainstream education. Paper presented at the 1st Conference of the European Association of Mediated Learning and Cognitive Modifiability (EAMC). Antwerpen, Belgium.

Rand, Y., Tannenbaum, A. & Feuerstein, R. (1979). Effects of Instrumental Enrichment on the psychoeducational development of low-functioning adolescents. *Journal of Educational Psychology*, *71*(6), 751–763.

Ruiz, C.J. (1985). *Cognitive Modifiability and Irreversibility*. Publication No. 4. University of Guayana, Venezuela.

Sanchez Pietro, M.D. (1991). A study of IE as a tool for improving language proficiency. *Teaching Thinking and Problem Solving*, *13*(3), 9–16.

Savell, J.M., Twohig, P.T. & Rachford, D.L. (1986). Empirical status of Feuerstein's "Instrumental Enrichment" technique as a method of teaching thinking skills. *Review of Educational Research*, *56*, 381–409.

Sibaud, E. (1993). Application and reflections on IE aparted for the visually handicapped. Paper presented at the 1st Conference of the European Association of Mediated Learning and Cognitive Modifiability (EAMC). Antwerpen, Belgium.

Skuy, M. & Mentis, M. (1993). Application and adaptation of Feuerstein's Instrumental Enrichment programme in South Africa. Report to the Centre for Science Development, Human Sciences Research Council. University of Witwatersrand, Johannesburg.

Skuy, M., Mentis, M., Nkwe, I. & Arnott, A. (1994) Combining Instrumental Enrichment and creativity/socioemotional development for disadvantaged gifted adolescents in Soweto. In M. Ben-Hur (Ed.). *On Feuerstein's Instrumental Enrichment*, pp. 161–190. Palatine, IL: IRI/Skylight.

Skuy, M., Mentis, M., Durbach, F., Cockcroft, K., Fridjhon, P. & Mentis, M. (1995). Crosscultural comparison of effects of IE on children in South African mining town. *School Psychology International*, *16*(3), 265–282.

Shayer, M. & Beasley, F. (1987), Does instrumental enrichment work? *British Educational Research Journal*, *13*, 101–119.

Thickpenny, J.P. (1982). *Teaching Thinking Skills to Deaf Adolescents: The Implementation and Evaluation of Feuerstein's Instrumental Enrichment*. Unpublished M.A. thesis. University of Auckland.

Vygotsky, L. (1986). *Thought and Language*. (Rev. ed). Cambridge, MA: MIT Press.

Chapter 16

Adams, M.J. (1990). *Beginning to Read*. Cambridge, MA: The MIT Press.

Ashman, A. & Conway, R.F. (1997). *An Introduction to Cognitive Education. Theory and Applications*. New York, NY: Routledge.

Ball, E.W. & Blachman, B.A. (1991). Does phoneme awareness training in kindergarten make a difference in early word recognition and developmental spelling. *Reading Research Quarterly*, *26*, 49–66.

Barker, T.A. & Torgesen, J.K. (1995). An evaluation of computer-assisted instruction in phonological awareness with below average readers. *Journal of Educational Computing Research*, *13*, 89–103.

Barker, T.A., Torgesen, J.K. & Wagner, R.K. (1992). The role of orthographic processing skills on five different reading tasks. *Reading Research Quarterly, 27,* 334–345.

Belmont, J. & Butterfield, E. (1977). The instructional approach to developmental cognitive research. In R. Kail & J. Hagen (Eds.). *Perspectives on the Development of Memory and Cognition.* Hillsdale, NJ: Erlbaum.

Blachman, B.A., Ball, E.W., Black, R.S. & Tangel, D.M. (1994). Kindergarten teachers develop phoneme awareness in low-income, inner-city classrooms: Does it make a difference? *Reading & Writing: An Interdisciplinary Journal, 6,* 1–18.

Boden, C. & Kirby, J.R. (1995). Successive processing, phonological coding, and the remediation of reading. *Journal of Cognitive Education, 4,* 19–31.

Bradley, L. & Bryant, P. (1985). *Rhyme and Reason in Reading and Spelling.* Ann Arbor, MI: The University of Michigan Press.

Brailsford, A., Snart, F. & Das, J.P. (1984). Strategy training and reading comprehension. *Journal of Learning Disabilities, 17,* 287–290.

Byrne, B. & Fielding-Barnsley, R. (1991). Evaluation of a program to teach phonemic awareness to young children. *Journal of Educational Psychology, 83,* 451–455.

Carlson, J. (1996). *Improving Reading Among Underachieving Children in Chapter One Programs.* Paper presented at the International Congress of Psychology, August, Montreal, Canada.

Carlson, J. & Das, J.P. (1997). A process approach to remediating word-decoding deficiencies in chapter 1 children. *Learning Disability Quarterly, 20,* 93–102.

Das, J.P. (1980). Planning: Theoretical considerations and empirical evidence. *Psychological Report, 41,* 141–151.

Das, J.P. (1995a). Is there life after phonological coding? *Issues in Education, 1,* 87–90.

Das, J.P. (1995b). Some thoughts on two aspects of Vygotsky's work. *Educational Psychologist, 30*(2), 93–97.

Das, J.P., Cummins, J., Kirby, J.R. & Jarman, R.F. (1979). Simultaneous and successive processes, language and mental abilities. *Canadian Psychological Review, 20,* 1–11.

Das, J.P., Kar, B.C. & Parrila, R.K. (1996). *Cognitive Planning: The Psychological Basis of Intelligent Behavior.* New Delhi: Sage.

Das, J.P. & Kendrick, M. (1997). PASS Reading Enhancement Program: A short manual for teachers. *Journal of Cognitive Education, 5*(3), 193–208.

Das, J.P., Kirby, J.R. & Jarman, R.F. (1979). *Simultaneous and Successive Cognitive Processes.* New York: Academic Press.

Das, J.P., Mensink, D. & Mishra, R.K. (1990). Cognitive processes separating good and poor readers when IQ is covaried. *Learning and Individual Differences, 2,* 423–436.

Das, J.P. & Mishra, R.K. (1994). Assessment of cognitive decline associated with aging: A comparison of individuals with Down Syndrome and other etiologies. *Research in Developmental Disabilities, 16*(1), 11–25.

Das, J.P., Mishra, R.K. & Kirby, J.R. (1994). Cognitive patterns of children with dyslexia: A comparison between groups with high and average nonverbal intelligence. *Journal of Learning Disabilities, 27,* 235–242, 253.

Das, J.P., Mishra, R.K. & Pool, J.E. (1995). An experiment on cognitive remediation of word-reading difficulty. *Journal of Learning Disabilities, 28,* 66–79.

Das, J.P., Mok, M. & Mishra, R.K. (1993). The role of speech processes and memory in reading disability. *The Journal of General Psychology, 12*(2), 131–146.

Das, J.P., Naglieri, J.A. & Kirby, J.R. (1994). *Assessment of Cognitive Processes.* Needham Heights, MA: Allyn and Bacon.

Das, J.P., Snart, F. & Mulcahy, R.F. (1982). Reading disability and its relation to information integration. In J.P. Das, R.F. Mulcahy & A.E. Wall (Eds.). *Theory and Research in Learning Disabilities* (pp. 85–110). New York: Plenum.

Eden, G.F., Stein, J.F., Wood, M.H. & Wood, F.B. (1995). Verbal and visual problems in reading disability. *Journal of Learning Disabilities, 28,* 272–290.

Hurford, D.P., Johnston, M., Nepote, P., Hampton, S., Moore, S., Neal, J., Mueller, A., McGeorge, K., Huff, L., Awad, A., Tatro, C., Juliano, C. & Huffman, D. (1994). Early identification and remediation of phonological-processing deficits in first-grade children at risk for reading disabilities. *Journal of Learning Disabilities, 27,* 647–659.

Kirby, J.R., Booth, C.A. & Das, J.P. (1996). Cognitive processes and IQ in reading disability. *The Journal of Special Education, 29,* 442–456.

Kirby, J.R. & Das, J.P. (1977). Reading achievement, IQ, and simultaneous-successive processing. *Journal of Educational Psychology, 69,* 564–570.

Kirby, J.R. & Das, J.P. (1990). A cognitive approach to intelligence: Attention, coding and planning. *Canadian Psychology, 31,* 320–331.

Kirby, J.R. & Gordon, C.J. (1988). Text segmenting and comprehension: Effects of reading and information processing abilities. *British Journal of Educational Psychology, 58,* 287–300.

Kirby, J.R. & Robinson, G.L. (1987). Simultaneous and successive processing in reading disabled children. *Journal of Learning Disabilities, 20,* 243–252.

Kirby, J.R. & Williams, N.H. (1991). *Learning Problems: A Cognitive Approach.* Toronto: Kagan and Woo.

Krywaniuk, L.W. & Das, J.P. (1976). Cognitive strategies in native children: Analysis and intervention. *Alberta Journal of Educational Research, 22,* 271–280.

Leong, C.K. (1980). Cognitive patterns of "retarded" and below average readers. *Contemporary Educational Psychology, 5,* 101–117.

Lidz, C.S. (1987). *Foundations of Dynamic Assessment.* New York: Oxford University Press.

Little, T., Das, J.P., Carlson, J. & Yachimowicz, D. (1993). The role of hierarchical skills in cognitive ability as moderators in deficits in academic performance. *Learning and Individual Differences, 5,* 219–240.

Luria, A.R. (1966). *Human Brain and Psychological Processes.* New York: Harper and Row.

Luria, A.R. (1973). *The Working Brain.* New York: Basic Books.

Luria, A.R. (1980). *Higher Cortical Functions in Man.* (2nd ed.). New York: Basic Books.

Mantzicopoulos, P., Morrison, D., Stone, E. & Setrakian, W. (1992). Use of SEARCH/TEACH tutoring approach with middle-class students at-risk for reading failure. *The Elementary School Journal, 92,* 573–586.

McCracken, R.A. (1966). *The Standard Reading Inventory Manual.* Klamath Falls, OR: Klamath Printing Company.

Molina, S., Garrido, M.A. & Das, J.P. (1997). Process-based enhancement of reading: An empirical study. *Developmental Disabilities Bulletin, 25,* 68–76.

Naglieri, J.A. (1989). A cognitive processing theory for the measurement of intelligence. *Educational Psychologist, 24,* 185–206.

Naglieri, J.A. & Das, J.P. (1988). Planning-Arousal-Simultaneous-Successive (PASS): A model of assessment. *Journal of School Psychology, 26,* 35–48.

Naglieri, J.A. & Das, J.P. (1990). Planning, attention, simultaneous and successive (PASS) cognitive processes as a model for intelligence. *Journal of Psychoeducational Assessment, 8,* 303–337.

Naglieri, J.A. & Das, J.P. (1997). *Das-Naglieri Cognitive Assessment System.* Itasca, IL: Riverside Publishing Co.

Newcombe, F. & Marshall, J. (1981). On psycholinguistic classifications of the acquired dyslexias. *Bulletin of the Orton Society*, *31*, 29–46.

Papadopoulos, T.C., Parrila, R.K., Das, J.P., & Kirby, J.R. (1997). A cognitive approach to diagnosis of early reading problems. In A. Richardson (Ed.). *Canadian Childhood in 1997*. Edmonton, Alberta: Kanata Learning Company.

Rack, J.P., Snowling, M.J. & Olson, R.K. (1992). The non-word reading deficit in developmental dyslexia: A review. *Reading Research Quarterly*, *27*, 28–53.

Shankweiler, D., Crain, S., Katz, L., Fowler, A. E., Liberman, A.M., Brady, S.A., Thornton, R., Lundquist, E., Dreyer, L., Fletcher, J.M., Stuebing, K.K., Shaywitz, S.E. & Shaywitz, B.A. (1995). Cognitive profiles of reading-disabled children: Comparison of language skills in phonology, morphology, and syntax. *Psychological Science*, *6*(3), 149–156.

Share, D.L. (1994). Deficient phonological processing in disabled readers implicates processing deficits beyond the phonological module. In K.P. van den Bos, L.S. Siegel, D.J. Bakker & D.L. Share, *Current Directions in Dyslexia Research*, (pp. 149–167). Lisse, Netherlands: Swets & Zeitlinger.

Share, D.L. (1995). Phonological recoding and self-teaching: sine qua non of reading acquisition. *Cognition*, *55*, 151–218.

Share, D.L. & Stanovich, K.E. (1995). Cognitive processes in early reading development: Accommodating individual differences into a model of acquisition. *Issues in Education*, *1*, 1–57.

Siegel, L.S. & Ryan, E.B. (1988). Development of grammatical sensitivity, phonological, and short-term memory in normally achieving and learning disabled readers. *Developmental Psychology*, *24*, 28–37.

Snart, F. (1985). Cognitive-processing approaches to the assessment and remediation of learning problems: An interview with J.P. Das and Reuven Feuerstein. *Journal of Psychoeducational Assessment*, *3*, 1–14.

Snart, F., Das, J.P. & Mensink, D. (1988). Reading disabled children with above-average IQ: A comparative examination of cognitive processing. *Journal of Special Education*, *22*(3), 344–357.

Snowling, M.J., Goulandris, N. & Defty, N. (1996). A longitudinal study of reading development in dyslexic children. *Journal of Educational Psychology*, *88*, 653–669.

Stanovich, K.E. (1988). Explaining the differences between dyslexic and the garden-variety poor reader: The phonological-core variable-difference model. *Journal of Learning Disabilities*, *21*, 590–604, 612.

Torgesen, J.K., Wagner, R.K. & Rashotte, C.A. (1994). Longitudinal studies of phonological processing and reading. *Journal of Learning Disabilities*, *27*, 276–286.

Tzuriel D. & Haywood, C.H. (1992). The development of interactive-dynamic approaches to assessment of learning potential. In C.H. Haywood & D. Tzuriel (Eds.). *Interactive Assessment* (pp. 3–37). New York: Springer-Verlag Inc.

Vellutino, F.R. & Denckla, M.B. (1996). Cognitive and neuropsychological foundations of word identification in poor and normally developing readers. In R. Barr, M.L. Kamil, P.B. Mosenthal & P.D. Pearson (Eds.). *Handbook of Reading Research: Volume II* (pp. 571–608). Mahwah, NJ: Lawrence Erlbaum Associates, Publishers.

Vellutino, F.R., Scanlon, D.M. & Tanzman, M. S. (1993). Components of reading ability: Issues and problems in operationalizing word identification, phonological coding, and orthographic coding. In G. Reid Lyon, *Frames of Reference for the Assessment of Learning Disabilities*, (pp. 279–329). Baltimore, MD: Paul H. Brookes.

Vygotsky, L. (1934). *Thought and Speech*. Moscow: Sotsekgiz.

Vygotsky, L. (1962). *Thought and Language*. Cambridge, MA: M.I.T. Press.

Vygotsky, L. (1978). *Mind in Society: The Development of Higher Psychological Processes.* Cambridge, MA: Harvard University Press.

Wagner, R.K. (1988). Causal relations between the development of phonological processing abilities and the acquisition of reading skills: A meta-analysis. *Merrill-Palmer Quarterly, 34,* 261–279.

Wagner, R.K. & Torgesen, J.K. (1987). The nature of phonological processing and its causal role in the acquisition of reading skills. *Psychological Bulletin, 101,* 192–212.

Wagner, R.K., Torgesen, J.K., Rashotte, C.A., Hecht, S.A., Barker, T.A., Burgess, S.R., Donahue, J. & Garon, T. (1997). Changing relations between phonological processing abilities and word-level reading as children develop from beginning to skilled readers: A 5-year longitudinal study. *Developmental Psychology, 33,* 468–479.

Watson, C. & Willows, D.M. (1995). Information-processing patterns in specific reading disability. *Journal of Learning Disabilities, 28*(4), 216–231.

Chapter 17

Feuerstein, R. & Krasilowsky, D. (1967). Treatment group technique. *Israeli Annals of Psychiatry and Related Disciplines, 5*(1), 69–90.

Feuerstein, R. & Krasilowsky, D. (1971). The treatment group technique. In M. Wollins & M. Gottesman (Eds.). *Group Care: An Israeli Approach.* New York: Gordon & Breach.

Feuerstein, R. & Rand, Y. (1974). Mediated learning experience: An outline of the proximal etiology for differential development of cognitive functions. *International Understanding,* 9–10, 7–37.

Feuerstein, R., Rand, Y. & Hoffman, M.B. (1979). *The Dynamic Assessment of Retarded Performers: The Learning Potential Assessment Device, Theory, Instruments, and Techniques.* Baltimore: University Park Press.

Feuerstein, R., Rand, Y., Hoffman, M.B. & Miller, R. (1980). *Instrumental Enrichment.* Baltimore: University Park Press.

Goleman, D. (1995). *Emotional Intelligence.* New York: Bantam Books.

Haywood, H.C. (1985). Teachers as mediators. *The Thinking Teacher, 2*(5), 7–8. [Available from Cognitive Education Project, Box 9 Peabody Station, Vanderbilt University, Nashville, TN 37203.]

Haywood, H.C. (1986, 1987, 1988). *Cognitive Developmental Therapy With Mildly Retarded Adolescent Delinquents: Annual Report.* Technical report submitted to the Tennessee Department of Mental Health and Mental Retardation. [Substantive parts available from the author.]

Haywood, H.C. (1987). A mediational teaching style. *The Thinking Teacher, 4*(1), 1–6.

Haywood, H.C. (1988). Treatment of mild and moderate mental retardation. In W.-T. Wu (Ed.). Looking toward special education in the 21st century: Proceedings of the 1988 International Symposium on Special Education, pp. 212–223 (Mandarin), 224–244 (English). Taipei: Special Education Association of the Republic of China.

Haywood, H.C. (1989). Cognitive-developmental psychotherapy. Paper presented at the Second International Conference on Mediated Learning, Knoxville, Tennessee, August.

Haywood, H.C. (1992). The strange and wonderful symbiosis of motivation and cognition. *International Journal of Cognitive Education and Mediated Learning, 2*(3), 186–197.

Haywood, H.C. (1993). A mediational teaching style. *International Journal of Cognitive Education and Mediated Learning,* (1), 27–38.

Haywood, H.C., Arbitman-Smith, R., Bransford, J. D., Delclos, V.R., Towery, J.R., Hannel, I.L. & Hannel, M.V. (1982). Cognitive education with adolescents: Evaluation of *Instrumental Enrichment*. Paper presented in A.M. Clarke & A.D.B. Clarke (Chm.), *Psychosocial Intervention: Possibilities and Constraints* (pp. 1–61). Symposium, 6th Congress of the International Association for the Scientific Study of Mental Deficiency (IASSMD), Toronto. [Available from first author.]

Haywood, H.C., Brooks, P.H. & Burns, S. (1992). *Bright Start: Cognitive Curriculum for Youhng Children*. Watertown, MA: Charlesbridge Publishing.

Haywood, H.C., Burns, S., Arbitman-Smith, R. & Delclos, V.R. (1984). Forward to fundamentals: Learning and the 4th R. *Peabody Journal of Education, 61*(3), 16–35.

Haywood, H.C. & Menal, C. (1992). Cognitive-Developmental Psychotherapy: An individual case study. *International Journal of Cognitive Education and Mediated Learning, 2*(1), 43–54. [French language version, same volume, pp. 43–54.]

Hayward, Brooks & Burns (1992).

Haywood, H.C. & Switzky, H.N. (1986). Intrinsic motivation and behavior effectiveness in retarded persons. In N.R. Ellis & N.W. Bray (Eds.). *International Review of Research in Mental Retardation*, Vol. 14, pp. 1–46. New York: Academic Press.

Haywood, H.C. & Tzuriel, D. (Eds.) (1992). *Interactive Assessment*. New York/Hamburg: Springer Verlag.

Lidz, C.S. (Ed.) (1987). *Dynamic Assessment*. New York: Guilford Press.

Wingenfeld, S., Vaught, S. & Haywood, H.C. (1991). Cognitive-Developmental Therapy with mildly mentally retarded juvenile offenders: Preliminary assessment. *The Thinking Teacher, 6*(1), 9–13.

Chapter 18

Carkhuff, R. (1969). *Helping and Human Relations* (Vols I and II). New York: Holt, Rinehart and Winston.

Carkhuff, R. & Berenson, B.G. (1976). *Teaching as Treatment*. Amherst, MA: Human Resource Development Press.

Cormier, W.H. & Cormier, L.S. (1991). *Interviewing Strategies For Helpers* (3rd ed.). Pacific Grove, CA: Brooks-Cole.

Egan, G. (1986). *The Skilled Helper* (3rd ed.). Monterey, CA: Brooks-Cole.

Falik, L.H. (1996). Mediated learning experience and the counseling process: an integrative model. *College of Education Review* (San Francisco State University), 8, 76–84.

Falik, L.H. & Feuerstein, R. (1990). Structural cognitive modifiability: A new perspective for counseling and psychotherapy. *International Journal of Cognitive Education and Mediated Learning, 1*(2), 143–150.

Feuerstein, R. (1979). *The Dynamic Assessment of Retarded Performers*. Baltimore, MD: University Park Press.

Feuerstein, R. (1980). *Instrumental Enrichment*. Baltimore, MD: University Park Press.

Feuerstein, R. (1995). *Revised LPAD Examiner's Manual*. International Center for the Enhancement of Learning Potential: Jerusalem, Israel.

Feuerstein, R. & Feuerstein, S. (1991). Mediated learning theory: A theoretical review. In R. Feuerstein, P.S. Klein, and A.J. Tannenbaum (Eds.). *Mediated Learning Experience: Theoretical, Psychosocial, and Learning Implications*. London: Freund.

Feuerstein, R., Feuerstein, R.S. & Schur, Y. (1997) Process as content in regular education and in particular in education of the low functioning retarded performer. In A.L. Costa and R.M. Liebmann (Eds.). *If Process Were Content; Sustaining the Spirit of Learning.* Thousand Oaks, CA; Corwin.

Ivey, A. (1994). *Intentional Interviewing* (4th ed.). Pacific Grove, CA: Brooks-Cole.

Kagan, N. (1980). Influencing human interaction: eighteen years with IPR. In A.K. Hess (Ed.), *Psychotherapy Supervision: Theory, Research, and Practice.* New York: John Wiley and Sons.

Kottler, J. (1986). *On Becoming a Therapist.* San Francisco, CA: Jossey-Bass.

Kozulin, A. (1990). *Vygotsky's Psychology: A Bibliography of Ideas.* Cambridge, MA: Harvard University press.

Piaget, J. (1955). *The Language and Thought of the Child.* London: Kegan Paul.

Piaget, J. (1968). *Judgment and Reasoning in the Child.* Totowa, NJ: Littlefield, Adams.

Skuy, M., Mentis, M. and Mentis, M. (1996). *Mediated Learning In and Out of the Classroom.* Arlington Heights, IL: Skylight.

Index